The Politics of Islamic Finance

The Politics of Islamic Finance

Edited by
CLEMENT M. HENRY
and RODNEY WILSON

EDINBURGH UNIVERSITY PRESS

© Editorial matter and organisation
Clement M. Henry and Rodney Wilson, 2004
© Copyright in the individual contributions
is retained by the authors

Edinburgh University Press Ltd
22 George Square, Edinburgh

Typeset in Baskerville
by Koinonia, Bury, and
printed and bound in Great Britain by
Antony Rowe Ltd, Chippenham, Wilts

A CIP record for this book is available
from the British Library

ISBN 0 7486 1836 8 (hardback)
       0 7486 1837 6 (paperback)

Contents

Introduction   1
Clement M. Henry and Rodney Wilson

Part I – Thematic Essays

1   Islamic Banks: The Rise of a New Power Alliance of Wealth and
    Shari'a Scholarship   17
    Monzer Kahf

2   Global Politics, Islamic Finance and Islamist Politics Before and
    After 11 September 2001   37
    Ibrahim Warde

3   The *Murabaha* Syndrome in Islamic Finance: Laws, Institutions
    and Politics   63
    Tarik M. Yousef

4   Marketing Commodities Does Not Happen on Commodity Markets:
    The Egyptian Bursat Al-'Uqud and Oil Futures Markets   81
    Ellis Goldberg

5   Financial Performances of Islamic *versus* Conventional Banks   104
    Clement M. Henry

6   Capital Flight through Islamic Managed Funds   129
    Rodney Wilson

Part II – Case Studies

7   Interest Politics: Islamic Finance in the Sudan, 1977–2001   155
    Endre Stiansen

8   The Kuwait Finance House and the Islamization of Public Life
    in Kuwait   168
    Kristin Smith

9   Jordan: A Case Study of the Relationship between Islamic Finance
    and Islamist Politics   191
    Mohammed Malley

10 The Political Economy of Islamic Finance in Turkey: The Role of
    Fethullah Gülen and Asya Finans   216
    Filiz Baskan

11 *Aiyyu Bank Islami?* The Marginalization of Tunisia's BEST Bank   240
    Robert P. Parks

12 The Rise and Decline of the Islamic Banking Model in Egypt   265
    Samer Soliman

Conclusion   286
Clement M. Henry and Rodney Wilson

Notes on the Contributors   296
Index   297

Introduction

Clement M. Henry and Rodney Wilson

In the wake of the 11 September 2001 terrorist attacks on the United States, the UN Security Council passed a resolution targeting transnational sources of terrorist funds. At least one offshore Islamic bank was shut down, and American officials, ignorant about Islamic finance, viewed any 'Islamic' bank with heightened suspicion. The Bush Administration targeted Al-Baraka in particular, confusing a Somalian funds-transfer agency with the transnational Islamic banking group that has the same name, a generic Arabic term for 'blessings'. Most Islamic capital-formation derives from legitimate business activity, however, and many governments in the Middle East and North Africa (MENA) tolerate and encourage the development of distinctively Islamic financial practices. As the United States and multinational institutions such as the IMF encourage the governments of the Middle East to adopt policies of economic liberalization, a new type of capitalism may be emerging, not based on a Western Protestant ethic, but rather on Islamic values and beliefs. It is important to distinguish the financial phenomena associated with this development from money laundering and terrorist funding.

This book focuses on the emerging connections between 'Islamic capital', broadly defined but with a focus on Islamic finance, and Islamist political movements in Middle Eastern and North African countries. Most of these opposition movements are at least as opposed to transnational terrorist networks as to the incumbent regimes. The 'Islamic' commerce that is expanding in much of the region also deserves the close attention in its own right of political analysts and policy-makers as well as economists. Islamic entrepreneurs and capitalists are largely self-defined, but operate through Islamic financial institutions or express their interests through other self-consciously Islamic forms of association. They accumulate or channel at least a salient part of their 'Islamic' capital through these distinctively 'Islamic' financial institutions, even if they also use conventional banks and stock exchanges. The Islamic banks are markers that serve to identify 'Islamic' capital and to distinguish it from other capital that is allocated through conventional banks. In this book we also cast our net more widely, by including not only the funds deployed by distinctively Islamic financial institutions but also the assets of Muslim entrepreneurs who, as in Turkey, are affiliated with Islamically oriented business associations, or who, as in Egypt, were black market money-changers advertising themselves as 'Islamic' despite their failure to be recognized by the formal Islamic financial sector.

By narrow as well as broad definitions, Islamic capital is growing. If taken to mean the funds invested through the religiously (*shari'a*) acceptable instruments of Islamic banks and other financial institutions, this capital grew in the late 1990s at an annual 10 to 15 per cent and according to some estimates may be valued at over $200 billion.[1] It seems to be driven primarily by investors, notably in the Gulf Cooperation Council (GCC) countries, who prefer gaining modest returns from Islamic banks to leaving their funds in the non-interest-bearing accounts (or non-'commission'-bearing ones, as the Saudis call them) of conventional banks.

The Islamic finance movement may also be party to a broader Islamist agenda. By 'Islamist' here is meant a determination to transform the present state of the world or at least some aspects of it to accord more closely with the principles of Islam. Financial practices may be a very limited aspect – and rather less provocative for some MENA and Western audiences than beards or veils. Dress codes attract attention and, rightly or wrongly, are taken to express more radical, totalistic aspirations for social change than arcane financial practices. As Vogel and Hayes observe, however, 'the surge in Islamic banking and finance is part of the much larger phenomenon of Islamic reassertion'.[2] If Islamic finance can be demonstrated to meet the requirements of modern commerce, then Islam may regulate other aspects of modern life. The task of this book is to explore the political implications of the slow but steady accumulation of Islamic capital.

The world of Islamic finance appears to be far removed from politics, but its apparent marginality also protects it from political repression. In a number of illiberal states the financial field still enjoys a degree of autonomy that is not accorded to political parties, formal NGOs and other bodies associated with official decision-making. Most, though not all, of the MENA states are illiberal, but they tend to be less closed financially than they are politically. Some of them tolerate Islamic banks as part of a strategy to legitimate themselves in the eyes of their religious publics.

THE ISLAMIC FINANCE MOVEMENT

Islamic bankers and economists would perhaps hesitate to call themselves a social movement but they appear to share a financial world view in which *riba* – interest or usury – is abolished while the time value of money as understood in contemporary financial theory is respected. Unconvinced Muslims, as well as other critical outsiders, observe that Islamic banks in reality keep interest but just call it by another name, such as commissions or profits (*ribha*). And indeed a principal form of credit extended by an Islamic bank, the *murabaha*, involves a simple mark-up on a sales price. The bank buys you a car for $30,000 and you owe the bank $33,000 a year from now, for example. This arrangement is perfectly acceptable from the standpoint of Islamic financial theory but looks to the outsider like a simple loan at 10 per cent interest. Repaying by five yearly installments of $7,913.92 would be equally acceptable and also implies an interest rate of 10 per cent. Islamic bankers use financial calculators just like other bankers to compute present and future values of investments. Financial transactions modelled on the *murabaha* constitute well over half of the assets of Islamic banks. Contracts engaging clients to return fixed payments to Islamic banks apparently constitute from 80 to 95 per cent of the latter's credit facilities, or 'investments'.[3] Since any fixed return can be understood as implied interest, there seems little to differentiate Islamic from conventional banks. Indeed, as Ibrahim Warde observes, no definition of an Islamic bank is entirely satisfactory.[4] He proposes a bank to be Islamic if run by Islamic principles and, one might add (at least in most cases), a *shari'a* board of religious supervisors to vet the bank's policies.

The movement is hardly monolithic. From its origins in the mid-1970s there were philosophic disagreements between one of its pioneers, an Egyptian, the late Dr Ahmed al Najjar, who sought wider financial participation among the poorer classes, and his Saudi sponsor, who was deploying substantial amounts of capital to compete with other commercial banks. Commercial forces may have eased out the idealists, although some still question the Islamic legitimacy of the *murabaha*. The 'purists', who tend to be Islamic economists rather than the jurists who actually decide what is legally permissible, insist on replacing *murabaha* with the distinctively Islamic financial instruments of *mudaraba* and *musharaka*, both of which require profit-sharing. *Mudaraba* is a contract whereby the bank provides funds to an entrepreneur in return for a share of the profits, or all of the losses, whereas *musharaka* – participation – is more akin to venture capital financing.[5] An Islamic bank can also be conceived as a *mudaraba* whereby the depositors invest in the bank – or entrepreneur *mudarrib* – that in turn funnels investments into other *mudaraba* or other Islamically acceptable placements. Profit-sharing with variable returns and risk-taking are the distinctive characteristics of the Islamic financier. The purists criticize existing Islamic financial institutions for deviating from an Islamic ideal of venture capitalism. They note that Islamic banks currently allocate less than 10 per cent of their credit facilities or investments to these distinctively Islamic profit-sharing instruments. Some argue that any contract offering a fixed return is just like a loan at a fixed interest rate and hence is not religiously acceptable.

The jurists, on the other hand, tend to think less theoretically and deductively than the economists. They reason case by case, on the basis of precedents and prior rulings in their respective juridical schools. The consensus is that *murabaha* is just as permissible as *mudaraba* or *musharaka*, as long the contract meets certain conditions. The critical one, in the above example of a *murabaha*, is that the bank actually has to own the car and sell it to the client, rather than merely advancing him or her funds to pay the car dealer. The *Fiqh* Academy in Jeddah went on record in 1988 against an 'artificial' *murabaha* whereby the bank never really owns the car.[6] Islamic banks are hence caught in a dilemma. Commercial banks in many countries, especially under those historically influenced by British or American banking practices, are supposed to restrict themselves to the financial business of taking deposits, lending them out and trading only in financial instruments. Yet the Islamic jurists insist that they be involved in the trading of the range of goods financed by their portfolios of *murabaha*. Otherwise they would be engaging in the 'ruse' of artificial *murabaha* that is now forbidden. At least one Islamic bank apparently takes these injunctions quite seriously. The Jordan Islamic Bank for Finance and Investment inaugurated a bonded warehouse in 1999, just as it was celebrating its twentieth anniversary.[7] Almost half (45.7 per cent, p. 56) of its financing and investments then consisted of *murabaha* (while *mudaraba* and *musharaka* amounted to less than 3 per cent).

Evidently the Islamic financial movement is attempting to adapt Islamic instruments originally designed for pre-industrial trade and handicrafts to a post-industrial global economy. Commercial banking already became a specialized industry in the nineteenth century, and European banking systems penetrated the MENA world as well. Driven by new technology and favourable deregulation by the United States and other industrialized countries, banking and finance became ever more specialized and relatively autonomous. In the latter half of the twentieth century the growth in international financial assets far outstripped that of any underlying investment and trade in goods and services. In this highly specialized world of international finance, with its dizzying rates of product innovation, conventional banks could not afford to build warehouses as well, even if commercial banking legislation permitted them to.

The movement may be at a serious competitive disadvantage with commercial banks, then, not least because of its lack of consensus on *murabaha* and many other matters. Each of the 186 or so Islamic banks (as indicated by the Directory of the International Institute of Islamic Banks) has an advisory committee of Islamic jurists, and they issue rulings that are not always mutually consistent. Conventional banks like Citibank or HSBC that have opened Islamic subsidiaries also have their religious advisory committees. Standardization is a major problem. For the movement to survive in the competitive financial world of the twenty-first century, the banks must be able to develop new instruments for both short-term liquid placements and long-term investments. Innovators need to know what is legally acceptable, yet any innovation faces a wide spectrum of legal opinion. If options (a discretionary contract to buy a good at a future time and price) were to prove acceptable, for instance, then Islamic financial engineering could mimic virtually any instrument that a conventional financial institution can devise. Highly restrictive rulings, by contrast, could conceivably outlaw much of the bread and butter *murabaha* trade financing in which the banks presently engage and preclude any significant innovation.

This book cannot enter into the details of what might or might not be legal to various *shari'a* boards. Indeed, as Warde suggests, 'legalistic concerns are only one aspect, and probably not the most crucial one, of the real world of Islamic finance'.[8] Eventually the financiers and their religious boards will make compromises with financial markets because these banks enjoy one major underlying competitive advantage: popular demand among pious Muslims for an alternative to interest-based savings accounts. Whether or not they build warehouses, the Islamic banks will no doubt muddle through despite inconsistent rulings and other obstacles to financial innovation. While few of them have become big enough 'not to fail', the host governments will not let them. Accounting practices vary widely but the Accounting and Auditing Organization for Islamic Financial Institutions (AAOIFI), established in Algiers in 1990 and now based in Bahrain, finally issued its first set of standards in June 1998. In addition to the *Fiqh* Academy in Jeddah, various other institutions are articulating a broad agenda for Islamic banking and finance, notably the Islamic Financial Services Board established in Kuala Lumpur in 2002.

At the core of the movement are two transnational groups that conduct their own dialogues: the Al-Baraka Group and the group of banks affiliated to Dar al-Maal al-Islami, a holding company controlled by Prince Mohammad Al-Faisal, son of the late King Faisal. The Faisal Group is also heavily represented in deliberations of the International Association of Islamic Banks, founded in 1977 under the auspices of the Islamic Development Bank owned by the member states of the organization of the Islamic Conference. Outside the umbrella organization, al Baraka has held annual meetings since the mid-1980s to develop common understandings of proper banking practices among its affiliates. In addition, many research institutions, in Europe and the United States as well as in the Muslim World, promote an academic discourse about Islamic financial institutions. In the United States the Harvard Islamic Finance Information Program, launched in 1995, has sponsored impressive publications and developed an important database. It also convenes annual conferences that contribute to the ongoing dialogues between academics and practitioners, including jurists, economists, bankers and other notables.

The most significant guarantee of Islamic finance's future may be the large Western multinationals that have opened Islamic windows for receiving deposits from their wealthy Gulf clients and for financing a variety of projects in the MENA world. One of our contributors has suggested that the distinctive set of

Islamic financial templates would survive and prosper in global financial markets even if existing Islamic banks stagnated or failed.[9] The French, led by the Banque Nationale de Paris, and the Swiss through UBS have lately joined the many American and British presences headed by Citibank and HSBC. The World Bank's International Financial Corporation has encouraged co-financing infrastructure projects with the Islamic Development Bank. Prominent multi-nationals, including oil and construction companies, have employed Islamic financial instruments in some project finance in the GCC states. Islamic finance, in short, is becoming respectable in international business circles, although, as noted earlier, the news seems not yet to have reached their corresponding political circles.

THE GROWTH OF ISLAMIC MARKET SEGMENTS

The Islamic banking movement includes both publicly- and privately-owned commercial banks. The Islamic Development Bank, founded in 1973 and owned by a consortium that by 1998 included fifty-two Muslim states, eventually assimilated some of the novel Islamic financial practices devised by the private sector. The first modern privately-owned Islamic bank opened in Dubai in 1975. The Dubai Islamic Bank practised interest-free banking but did not establish a religious supervisory council until 1998, when a manager embezzled funds and the bank needed a government rescue package.[10] After 1979 Iran, Pakistan, and Sudan all 'Islamized' their banking systems from above, but these bureau-cratically induced changes are less interesting than the evolution of privately-owned banks, including those in the Sudan that were 'Islamic' before the official Islamization of the 1980s. In MENA countries where privately-owned Islamic commercial banks compete with conventional publicly- and privately-owned ones, it is possible to compare their respective shares of commercial bank deposits.

Table I.1 pieces together the progress of these privately-owned banks in the MENA region, including Turkey, with the available data. For comparative pur-poses Malaysia is also included because its experience is often cited as exemplary in Islamic banking circles. The country's first exclusively Islamic bank, Bank Islam Malaysia Berhad (BIMB), has mobilized almost 2 per cent of Malaysian sight and savings account deposits (measured by lines 24 and 25 of the IMF's *International Financial Statistics*) and presumably a much larger share of the Muslim population's deposits. Officially founded in 1983, the bank developed out of a fund originally established to finance the pilgrimage of Muslims to Mecca. In 1999, following the reorganization of the Malaysian banking system in the aftermath of the 1997 Asia crisis, the operations of two conventional banks, Bank Bumiputra and the Bank of Commerce, were merged. The new institution,

Table I.1: Evolution of Islamic banks' share of commercial bank deposits by country, 1980–2001

	Year first established	share (%)						
		1986	1996	1997	1998	1999	2000	2001
Algeria	1991		0.4	0.5	0.8		1.0	
Bahrain	1979	6.7	9.8					
Egypt	1977	9.7	5.1				5.7	
including Banque Misr's Islamic branches' deposits			8.1				n.d.	
Iran		100	100	100	100			
Jordan (JIB)	1978	7.0	8.4	8.2	8.0	7.5	6.9	7.1
including Arab Islamic Bank					8.9	9.2	9.4	10.3
Kuwait	1977	18.0	16.2	16.3	15.5			
Lebanon	1991		0.1	0.0	0.1			
Qatar	1982	10.4	17.8	18.1				
Saudi Arabia	1988		11.3	11.1	11.5	12.3	13.9	
Sudan		17.0			27.9			
Tunisia	1983	0.2	0.6		0.6	0.7	0.8	
Turkey	1985	0.8		3.6	3.6	3.7	3.5	1.8
UAE	1975	3.2	7.9					
Yemen	1996			4				
Malaysia	1983		1.6	1.6				
including Islamic windows of conventional banks (rough estimate)			2	2				

Sources: IMF *International Financial Statistics*, Harvard Islamic Finance Information Program, various *Annual Reports* of banks, editors' data sets.

Bank Muamalet, was given the remit of operating as Malaysia's second exclusively Islamic bank. The Central Bank of Malaysia hopes to see Islamic deposits account for 10 per cent of all bank deposits in the country by 2010.

A number of observations are in order. In theory all banks in the Sudan operate according to *shari'a* principles, but those that were consciously self-styled Islamic banks before the system was Islamized are specified in the table. They seem to have increased their market share at the expense of the newer converts. In Saudi Arabia, the spiritual centre of the Islamic World, a single

Islamic bank, Al Rajhi Banking and Investment Corporation (ARABIC), has captured well over 10 per cent of the market, but Table I.1 does not include growing proportions of funds invested in the Islamic windows of other Saudi banks. In some of the smaller GCC states the Islamic sector is approaching 20 per cent. The GCC seems to be the principal area of growth, possibly to be joined by Jordan, where Arab Bank has opened a new totally-owned Islamic subsidiary, the Arab Islamic Bank. Until this recent development – the bank opened for business in 1998 – the movement in Jordan appeared to have flattened out at less than 10 per cent of the market.

Egypt has apparently experienced a slight decline since Islamic banking reached its peak in 1986. Table I.1 does not include the so-called Islamic investment management companies that used Islam as a marketing technique for money-changers who expanded their businesses to manage their clients' remittances. These companies were, with one or two exceptions (Sherif and possibly Saad),[11] fly-by-night 'investment' companies that simply funnelled Egyptian workers' remittances from the Gulf countries to hard currency accounts outside Egypt. They doubly harmed the officially recognized Islamic banks. They competed for deposits and slowed the growth of the official Islamic sector in the mid-1980s. Subsequently they discredited the entire idea of Islamic finance (even though they did little to practise it other than pay publicity fees to a few Islamic scholars) by going bust after 1987, when an agreement with the IMF to liberalize Egyptian foreign exchange rates destroyed their real competitive advantage. Meanwhile, however, the Egyptian government encouraged conventional banks, led by state-owned Bank Misr, to open Islamic finance windows to mobilize deposits from interest-averse Muslims. Table I.1 includes only Bank Misr and possibly understates the total Islamic share of deposits by a percentage point or two. In the rest of the Arab World, however, Islamic finance remains marginal.

Islamic banks are altogether absent from Iraq, Libya, Morocco, Oman and Syria, and they eke out a very marginal presence in Algeria, Lebanon and Tunisia. Conventional or Islamic, private-sector banks no longer existed in Iran after 1980, but the situation is changing. Some Iranian factions favour development of the private sector, and legislation authorizing the incorporation of private-sector banks was passed in the spring of 2000. Subsequently two private Islamic banks started operations in Iran in 2001, and in 2002 the Dubai Islamic Bank became the first Arab Islamic bank to open an office in Tehran, reflecting the increasingly buoyant trade across the Gulf.

The most dynamic private Islamic banks outside the Arab world are found in Turkey. Three of the five private Turkish 'special financial houses' are partly owned, respectively, by the Al-Baraka Group, the Faisal Group and the Kuwait Finance House. A sixth bank, opened by the İhlas Financial House in 1995,

Figure I.1: Islamic share of commercial bank deposits by per capita GDP, circa 1998

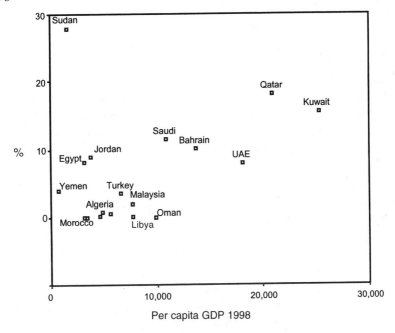

Notes: Syria clusters beside Morocco, having no Islamic banking. Lebanon and slightly wealthier Tunisia lie just under Algeria and have minuscule market shares.

failed in 2001 with the bankruptcy of the holding company, explaining the sharp decline in the market share of this sector. In fifteen years these banks had not collectively achieved even 4 per cent of the market, but the remnants after the collapse of İhlas Financial House in 2001 remain growth-oriented. They are methodically extending their branches networks into the provinces as well as in Istanbul and Ankara, and they have officially been integrated into Turkey's commercial banking system.

Islamic banking has apparently developed the most, apart from the Sudan, in the wealthiest petroleum-producing states. Indeed, it originated during that brief moment of apparently limitless prosperity when oil prices quintupled between 1973 and 1974, as an ingenious way of recycling some extra petro-dollars into pious activities. In the MENA, per capita income appears to be a fair predictor of the penetration of these banks into commercial markets. Figure I.1 graphs the Islamic shares of commercial bank deposits presented in Table I.1 against per capita GDP in 1998. With the exception of the Sudan, the richest GCC states of Kuwait and Qatar lead the rest of the pack. Excluding the GCC, however, the relationship could run the other way, with the poor of Sudan,

Yemen, Egypt and Jordan outdoing wealthier states such as Tunisia, Turkey, Libya and Malaysia. Obviously wealth is not the only factor that may be associated with Islamic finance.

POLITICAL OPPORTUNITIES AND CONSTRAINTS

We focus in this book upon the politics conditioning and sometimes enveloping these Islamic financial institutions. Islamic banking may be better off in liberalized, less restricted commercial banking environments than in heavily state-controlled ones. Further analysis will also suggest that Islamic banking is in greater need than conventional commercial banks of the liberalized climate advocated by international financial institutions – the so-called Washington Consensus. For, in order to generate better earnings, the Islamic banks need to engage in more equity-like financing that requires clear standards of accountability and transparency. Since they will need to engage in more equity-like financing than conventional banks, they stand to benefit more from financial structural adjustment programmes.

In some states, however, we see that Islamic banks carry a political handicap. Governments that declare war against political Islamists, such as Algeria and Tunisia, do not have thriving Islamic financial establishments. In most MENA countries the principal opposition to the incumbent regime is Islamist – even in Saudi Arabia, where the dynasty poses as a purified Islamic regime. To the extent, then, that Islamic banks are confounded in the public eye with political Islamism, they may be better off in a more liberal political climate like Kuwait or Jordan. Most Islamic financial institutions in fact deny any political associations and try, just like conventional bankers, to appear to be above 'politics'. But, just as the bankers of state-owned systems manage patronage machines for those in power, so Islamic bankers may find it difficult to avoid various political associations. In Kuwait the Kuwait Finance House enjoys close ties with certain government ministries and Islamist deputies in parliament. Our case studies will shed further light on the complex relationships between bankers and politicians.

*　　*　　*

This volume is divided into two parts. In Part I a set of thematic essays lays the groundwork for the country-specific political analyses of Part II. Monzer Kahf interprets the rise of Islamic banks since the 1970s as an alliance between private Muslim financiers and religious scholars. The *ulama* were generally preferred over more politicized Islamists because of the moral authority that the former exercised over potential banking clienteles. From the start, in other words, 'Islamic' capital kept at a certain distance from political Islam. As Ibrahim Warde points out in his essay, however, the international and particularly the American authorities responsible for tracking down terrorist money have occasionally missed such fine distinctions.

The political implications of Islamic capital accumulation will obviously be conditioned by the progress of America's war against terrorism and the impact of various wars upon the political stability of the region. But economic factors also matter. A principal disadvantage of most Islamic banks is that they cannot raise as much revenue from lucrative medium- and long-term financing or treasury operations as conventional banks. Greater use of their equity-like instruments (*mudaraba* and *musharaka*) would generate more revenue, but they presuppose the sorts of structural reform that international financial institutions have been trying, generally with only limited success, to promote in the MENA. Analytic findings may have important political implications, such as Islamic finance's greater need than conventional banks for economic liberalization. In this vein Tarik M. Yousef explains the prevalence of short-term financing instruments used by Islamic banks.

Ellis Goldberg carries the discussion further by exploring futures options in other Muslim contexts. He analyzes past Egyptian experiences with cotton futures and current experiences of oil-producing countries with their international markets. Were the 'call' and 'put' options of futures markets to become acceptable financial instruments, they could fill a crucial gap in the repertoire of Islamic finance. As matters stand, however, long-term Islamic finance largely depends on equity-like instruments. Clement M. Henry compares the financial performances of selected Islamic banks with comparable conventional ones to show why the Islamic banks may indeed be in greater need than conventional banks of structural adjustment and economic reform in the countries where they operate. Rodney Wilson completes our analytic section with the logical conclusion that, pending the necessary reforms, Islamic banks engage just as much, if not more than conventional banks, as conduits for Muslim capital to invest overseas. He studies the 'Islamic' mutual funds and other means of attracting mobile capital into Islamic financial institutions.

The steady accumulation of 'Islamic' capital may nevertheless have significant political repercussions at home, just as local political environments also affect financial performances. If a political regime tolerates the existence of an Islamist political opposition, such a constituency can also offer the Islamic financiers a loyal and lucrative clientele. Conversely, Islamic financial interests may conceivably moderate Islamist political confrontations with incumbent regimes. Part II of this volume offers case studies of Islamic banking experiences in countries that serve to illustrate possible scenarios relating incumbent regimes to their respective Islamist oppositions and to Islamic financial institutions. Unfortunately Saudi Arabia could not be included because its internal politics have not been sufficiently studied. The scenarios to be explored are:

Integration

Islamic capital channelled through private-sector Islamic banks builds up strong national business communities. The equity-like financing of Islamic banks is extended with the help of political monitors from Islamist parties who insist on probity and transparency in business operations. Greater proportions of equity financing make the Islamic banks more profitable with less risk than conventional banks. The business community, with much to lose in the event of conflict, moderates the oppositional activities of the political Islamists while giving them the necessary material support for autonomous political activity. Synergies between political Islamists and Islamic capitalists help the combined movements to achieve gradual acceptance in the political system, reinforcing trends toward greater political pluralism.

Separation

Islamic capital, like all capital, is 'coward' and avoids any association with political Islam. Indeed, that is its strength: Islamic financial institutions enjoy relative operational autonomy because the political regime considers them politically harmless yet, ever in need of legitimacy, does not wish to appear opposed to experimentations with *shari'a* practices in financial matters as long as the banks stay out of politics. Separated and blocked from any natural constituency of Islamically-minded entrepreneurs, however, the Islamic banks are heavily dependent on state subsidies to survive the competition from conventional banks. The state represses the political Islamists and any potential Islamically-minded business allies while demonstrating its support for Islam by subsidizing the banks and possibly even creating new ones under direct state control.

Uneasy coexistence

Elements of the state that favour structural adjustment ally with their counterparts in the Islamic financial institutions. These are permitted access to Islamically-minded entrepreneurs, and the state encourages a relatively autonomous Islamist business community while repressing Islamist political parties. Neither integration nor separation but rather an uneasy coexistence characterizes the respective relationships of the political Islamists with the Islamic business community, on the one hand, and with the state on the other.

Endre Stiansen leads off our case studies with the Sudan, the one country in which Islamic banks financed an Islamist political movement and helped it to seize power at least for a time – until the military leadership ousted Hassan Turabi from power in 1999. Kristin Smith follows with her study of Kuwait, another illustration of extremely close relations between an Islamic bank and an Islamist political movement. Whereas Sudan illustrates a pattern of mutual destruction, Kuwait highlights possible synergies between financiers and political clienteles.

Mohammed Malley and Filiz Baskan then respectively deal with Jordan and Turkey, two more complex cases of indirect connections and interactions between Islamic financial institutions and Islamist political factions and parties. Finally, Robert P. Parks and Samer Soliman discuss Tunisia and Egypt, respectively. Each country's regime represses its political Islamists, but the Egyptians treat Islamic banking with greater political sophistication than the Tunisians.

These case studies in turn enable Clement Henry and Rodney Wilson to draw further conclusions about the complex interrelationships between politics and finance within the Islamist movements of the MENA. We meanwhile gratefully acknowledge a number of prior meetings that facilitated our task. The co-editors of this volume first met 'virtually' by collaborating in a special issue (July–October 1999) of the *Thunderbird Review of International Business* devoted to Islamic finance. Subsequently Henry hosted a colloquium, sponsored by the Government Department and the Center for Middle Eastern Studies at the University of Texas, that included Moncer Kahf, Tarik Yousef and Mohammed Malley. Kristin Smith subsequently joined Kahf and Malley in a panel chaired by Henry at the Middle East Studies Association in November 2001. Finally, most of the contributors to the present volume convened in Florence at the Robert Schuman Center for Advanced Studies of the European University Institute on 20–24 March 2002 in a workshop co-chaired by the present co-editors. We wish to thank the organizers of the Third Mediterranean Social and Political Research Meeting for affording us the opportunity to meet and exchange views as we prepared this book. We also thank the Government Department and Center for Middle Eastern Studies at the University of Texas for their early support of this project. We are especially grateful to the Institute for Middle Eastern and Islamic Studies of the University of Durham for its indispensable support in bringing the project to fruition.

NOTES

1. Sheikh Saleh Kamel, Chairman, Saudi Dallah al-Baraka Group, *Al-Hayat*, 5 December 1999; cf. Ibrahim Warde, *Islamic Finance in the Global Economy* (Edinburgh: Edinburgh University Press, 2000), p. 6.
2. Frank E. Vogel and Samuel L. Hayes III, *Islamic Law and Finance: Religion, risk, and return* (The Hague: Kluwer Law International, 1998), p. 21.
3. Ibrahim Warde, *Islamic Finance*, p. 133.
4. Ibid. p. 5.
5. Mervyn K. Lewis and Latifa M. Algaoud, *Islamic Banking* (Cheltenham: Edward Elgar, 2001), pp. 49–51.
6. Vogel and Hayes, *Islamic Law*, p. 143.

7. Jordan Islamic Bank for Finance and Investment, 21st Annual Report, p. 14.
8. Ibrahim Warde, *Islamic Finance*, p. 11.
9. Monzer Kahf, 'Islamic Banks at the Threshold of the Third Millennium', *Thunderbird Review of International Business*, Special Issue: Islamic Banking, edited by Clement M. Henry, 41:4–5 (July–October 1999), pp. 445–60.
10. Simon Archer and Rifaat Abdel Karim (eds), *Islamic Finance: Innovation and Growth* (London: Euromoney Publications, 2002), p. 31.
11. Michel Galloux, 'The State's Responses to Private Islamic Finance Experiments in Egypt', *Thunderbird Review of International Business*, Special Issue: Islamic Banking, edited by Clement M. Henry, 41:4–5 (July–October 1999), pp. 481–500.

PART I

Thematic Essays

1

Islamic Banks: The Rise of a New Power Alliance of Wealth and *Shari'a* Scholarship

Monzer Kahf

Islamic banking in the Arab world created a new political alliance that unexpectedly emerged out of working relationships between the rich and wealthy on the one hand and many *shari'a* scholars on the other hand. These relationships continue to invigorate the *shari'a* scholars, who influence substantial segments of public opinion in most Muslim countries. One consequence is that the scholars encourage their followers and the wider Muslim public to use Islamic banks.

This chapter discusses the history of this new alliance, the factors contributing to the need of each of the two sides for this alliance for the help and support of the other, the transformation of the lifestyle and intellectual outlooks of allied *shari'a* scholars that has become redirected toward business, and their shaping of public opinion, in turn, resulting in new clienteles for Islamic banks. It will be concluded that the alliance serves to de-politicize or at least to remove the political stigma from several layers of the Islamic movement in most Muslim countries. The alliance opens up new spaces for cooperation as well as competition between governments and Islamist oppositions.

In summary the main points covered include:

- The history of this new alliance and how it came into existence;
- The factors contributing to the need of each of the two sides of this alliance for the help and support of the other;
- The transformation of the lifestyle of allied *shari'a* scholars;
- The effect of the *shari'a* scholars on expanding the business of bankers through the creation of a new class of clientele and the resulting change that is taking shape in the structure of economic power in several Muslim societies as represented in the emergence of new wealth that results from transforming energetic intelligentsia into businessmen;
- The effect of the new socio-economic coherence on de-politicizing or rather reducing the political stigma of several layers of the 'Islamic movement', and the resulting bridging of the gap between some Muslim governments and substantial segments of the Islamic opposition movement. In other words what is involved, as will be seen in the discussion later in the paper, is the creation of a new space for the interaction between the Islamists and the governments in the countries that have Islamic banks.

BACKGROUND

Islamic activists, *shari'a* scholars and religious leaders have always talked about the prohibition of *riba*. The majority of them have repeatedly expressed discontent with the Western-style banks that entered Muslim countries from the middle of the nineteenth century onwards. Several *fatwas* were issued to the effect that the interest-based activities of these banks were not compatible with the Islamic *shari'a*. Although there were a few faint voices that distinguished between *riba* and interest, especially from the ranks of government-appointed 'official' *muftis* and government 'polished' *ulama*, the overwhelming majority of *shari'a* scholars and the Muslim public viewed the operations of these foreign banks as being based on a prohibited activity.[1]

In the two decades from the early 1950s to the late 1960s, several writings by Muslim economists, bankers, *shari'a* scholars and political Islamists focused on the possibility of running financing institutions without interest, and on finding a *shari'a* compatible alternative formulation of the *riba*-based activities of conventional banks.[2] While these writings prepared the Muslim public to see the merits of Islamic banks and later to celebrate their founders as religious heroes, the actual establishment of Islamic banks unexpectedly came in two areas of the Muslim world far away from each other. Islamic Banks were concurrently established in the countryside of Lower Egypt and in metropolitan Kuala Lumpur in Malaysia.[3]

The Malaysian experience involved a distinctive form of relations with the government. While the political arena in Malaysia was being prepared for independence in the early 1950s, the newly emerging self-rule government supported the idea of establishing an investment institution that catered for the needs of the Malays, who comprised the overwhelmingly Muslim and poor majority of Malaysian society. The idea of financing *hajj* was very attractive to the Malay population, as they were mainly rural peasants living on coconuts and padi, yet they were having an increasing portion of the political power.

A few years after Malaysia's independence in 1956, the Pilgrims' Administration and Fund (Tabung Hajji) took its final shape as a government-sponsored and -supervised financial institution that collects savings for *hajj* and invests them in accordance with *shari'a*. The Fund was enhanced by legislative support that requires all Malays to process their *hajj* papers, including passports, through the Tabung Hajji; and since everybody has to go through this fund anyway, why not save with it as well? The Fund had an autonomous decision-making authority, with a government-appointed management and a nominal honorary subordination to the prime minister's office. It was able to increase its share in the real estate, industrial and agricultural sectors to a substantial amount. It had invented ideas and procedures of Islamic financing, on its own, without any interaction with what was going on in the Middle East to the extent that Middle Eastern Islamic economists and bankers only found out about Tabung Hajji in 1981 when it was presented to the Islamic Development Bank through the negotiations to establish the Islamic Bank of Malaysia.[4]

The Egyptian experiment in Islamic banking started in 1963. The late Ahmed al Najjar established a series of saving/investment houses in a few small towns in rural northern Egypt. This venture was known as the experiment of 'Mit Ghamr' after the name of the small town where the first of these houses was established. The Egyptian experiment emerged at a time when the government and the ruling class were ultra-sensitive against any Islamic political activity. Ahmed al Najjar and people close to him were in fact at a considerable distance from the Muslim Brotherhood. He himself was very far from being of any political affiliation or aspiration.[5] His religious background, and perhaps his economic interests too, go back to his uncle on his mother's side, the late Mohammad Abdullah al Arabi, who was a renowned professor of economics in Egypt and the first Arab economist to write on the Islamic economic system. His ideas for an Islamic economy were written in notes that were distributed to the students in his economics classes, both at the Cairo University and at the Institute of Higher Arab Studies of the Arab League in Cairo.

The experiment of the saving/investment houses did not last long. All the houses were closed and liquidated in 1967, probably because Islamic revivalists and former Muslim Brotherhood members infiltrated them as clients, depositors and probably employees.[6] Although al Najjar extensively wrote about this experiment in Lower Egypt, he never published any numerical data about the size and number of saving accounts nor the types and distribution of investment. He used to always emphasize the process of generating savings through local decision-making and the visible benefits of developmental use of these savings and the new energy these houses were able to create among poor peasants and small farmers.[7]

The success of the Mit Ghamr experiment was in its ability to spread from one small town to another, to induce more savings among the lowest income strata of Egyptian society and to create and encourage small-scale entrepreneurs. This may have brought pressure on the government to fill the vacuum created when the houses were closed. Hence, in 1971 the government of Egypt created the first Islamic bank, the Nasser Social Bank (NSB).[8] This bank was financed and owned by the government. In its establishment, the Egyptian government invoked Islamic principles such as interest-free financing and distribution of *zakat*. The founding act of the NSB requires public sector companies to donate 2.5 per cent (a rate selected because of its compatibility with the level of *zakat*) of their profit to this bank in order to build and accumulate its capital and reserves. The bank was also charged with the responsibilities of accepting *zakat* from those who volunteered to pay and to distribute it to deserving categories as stipulated in *shari'a*. The NSB plays an important role in financing small entrepreneurs and in serving low-income, usually religious, families with both its *riba*-free financing as well as the activity of its huge *zakat* department.

It is important to notice that these two experiments, in South East Asia and in the most populous Arab country, did not establish any relationships either with the Islamic movements and parties or with the Muslim religious scholars. They simply took the principle of the prohibition of *riba* for granted and innovated formulas of financing and of rewarding savers without indulging in interest. None of these two experiments had a *shari'a* board or a committee of religious experts to supervise the compliance of their contracts, procedures and policies with the rules of *shari'a*.

On the other hand, the concept of Islamic banking in these two experiments was essentially developmental. It involved collecting small savings from a large number of people and investing them, either on the basis of direct investment via the establishment of industrial, agricultural and large-scale construction projects *à la* Tabung Hajji, or via the distribution of small investments to craftsmen and small local entrepreneurs as with the Mit Ghamr banks. The emphasis on commercial banking and short-term placement did not occur to the founders of these early Islamic banks. The fact is that these two experiments did not have current accounts or cheque facilities. Current-account facilities were only introduced in Tabung Hajji in the mid-1980s. Hence, both experiments did not satisfy the normal daily financing needs of regular businesses, especially import, export and domestic trade and credit.[9]

Around the mid-1970s, two new experiences came into being, each of them involving large-scale banking: the Dubai Islamic Bank and the Islamic Development Bank. With the rise of national earnings of the oil-exporting Middle Eastern countries as a result of the huge increase in oil prices after the October 1973 war and the Arab oil embargo that ensued, the idea of establishing an international developmental bank for the Islamic World was suggested for two main reasons: 1) to enhance the Organization of the Islamic Conference as a potential power base for some of the newly enriched countries, especially Saudi Arabia and Algeria; and 2) to serve as a buffer institution for distributing financial aid from the Muslim oil-exporting countries, especially the Gulf states, to their brethren in Africa and Asia.[10]

The call for the establishment of the Islamic Development Bank came from the heads of state of Saudi Arabia, Algeria and Somalia. When the articles of agreement of the IDB were put on paper in 1974 the signatories supported a text that requires it to conduct its activities in accordance with the Islamic *shari'a*. This perhaps serves as a demonstration of the theory of Ijaz Kelani, of the Qaid-e-Azam University in Islamabad, that Muslim governments tend to be a lot more Islamic outside their own borders than within, especially as, except for Malaysia and Egypt, none of the twenty-five Muslim countries that signed the agreement establishing the IDB had at the time any Islamic bank and the three countries that called for its establishment did not allow any Islamic bank to operate on their territories until the mid-1980s!

Because of its underlying political structure, the IDB has not been able, at any point in time, to take major initiatives to facilitate the expansion of Islamic banking internationally. However, in several instances, it had supported national initiatives by subscribing to the capital, to a minor extent, of a few Islamic commercial banks in several of its member countries.[11]

In Dubai, a pious, innovative and well-known businessman who was on the one hand respected for his successful entrepreneurship and benevolent activities, and on the other hand was a close associate of the ruling family of Dubai, came forward in 1974 to establish and finance the Dubai Islamic Bank as the first commercial Islamic bank. His background and socio-political connections gave him a free hand to experiment the way he pleased, and he conducted the activities of his Islamic bank in accordance with his own understanding and style of both management and Islamic *shari'a*.

Both banks were established without *shari'a* boards or any form of systemic *shari'a* counseling. They were left to invent on their own how the principle of the prohibition of *riba* could be implemented in banking. It should be noted, though, that the IDB had initially been intended as a bank for the Islamic *umma*, rather than an Islamic bank. At the time when the bank's articles of agreement were drafted in 1973 and 1974, it was not yet known in any clear way how an Islamic bank would function and there were no precedents nor procedures or manuals for *shari'a*-compatible large-scale banking activities. The idea was simply that there was a need for an international banking institution to concentrate on financing government projects in the Muslim countries. It happened that this banking institution had a clause in its founding agreement to the effect that it must abide by the rules of *shari'a*.[12] This happened at a time when most government officials in the Muslim countries, including those who signed the articles of agreement of the IDB, had very little understanding of what Islamic banking implied and how banks could operate without interest. The IDB was created with no precedents as to how to draw its procedures and manuals, how to conduct its affairs in compatibility with the Islamic *shari'a*, or even what are the Islamic modes of financing that can be used in place of interest-based lending. In fact, the IDB had to wait until 1976 to make its first *murabaha* transaction, which was with the government of Algeria.[13]

The IDB and the Dubai Islamic Bank, acting separately, started establishing relationships with several *shari'a* scholars by inviting them for consultation on their activities and transactions, as well as seeking *fatwas* on specific questions and transactions. Yet, until 2003, the IDB did not have a formal *shari'a* supervisory board or committee, or an appointed *shari'a* council. As for the Dubai Islamic Bank, it did not have a *shari'a* committee until after a major change in management that took place in the aftermath of a financial scandal in 1997, which called for a restructuring of the bank. The new bank management established, for the first time, a *shari'a* consultative committee in 1999.

In general, the activities of the banks did not diverge much from the Islamic *shari'a*, although in 1985, when the OIC *Fiqh* Academy responded to a list of questions submitted two years earlier, the IDB had to revise some of its standing policies to make them *shari'a*-compatible.[14]

THE BIRTH OF AN ALLIANCE

The beginning of the new alliance between *shari'a* scholars and bankers had to wait until 1976 when the Faisal Islamic Bank of Egypt was established. The bank was the first to have a formal *shari'a* board consisting of selected *ulama* from Egypt. This tradition continued with the establishment of the Jordan Islamic Bank (1978), the Faisal Islamic Bank of Sudan (1978), the Kuwait Finance House (1979), and it went on with other Islamic banks throughout the Arab countries, Turkey, Bangladesh, and more recently, the private sector's Islamic banks in Pakistan.

Islamic banks in most Arab countries, West Africa, Malaysia, Indonesia, Turkey and Bangladesh were established as a result of private initiatives in which the driving force was provided by a few visionary personalities such as Prince Mohammad Al-Faisal (son of the late Saudi king Faisal bin Abd al Aziz), Sheikh Saleh Kamel of Saudi Arabia, Ahmed al Yasin of Kuwait, Sa'id Lutah of the UAE, Sami Hamoud of Jordan and Abd al Halim Isma'il of Malaysia. At the beginning, these private initiatives were influenced by intellectuals of the calibre of Ahmed al Najjar and Issa Abdu Ibrahim, both from Egypt, but the new Islamic capitalists (if the term can loosely be used) found their true allies in the *shari'a* scholars who were willing to work with them on the *shari'a* boards in each of the Islamic banks. For two years after the IDB began its operations, the Islamic banking movement did not see any institutional progress. When Prince Mohammad Al-Faisal adopted the idea, he was able to give it a momentum that carried his stamp for the last quarter of the twentieth century, through scores of new Islamic banks spreading from Pakistan to Guinea. The Prince knew from the beginning, however, that his alliance with al Najjar did not win him the confidence of prospective clients that he needed for the Faisal Islamic Bank of Egypt. He could not associate himself with the Muslim Brotherhood because of many factors, including the fact that its elitist style precludes it from offering him contacts with businesses in Egypt and other Arab countries. And he found

in the former Grand *Mufti* of Egypt a perfect ally who could grant him acceptance and legitimacy without any negative effect on his relations with the government. This was important, as Prince Mohammad Al-Faisal needed President
Sadat's support for a special law in order to allow the establishment and
operation of the first Islamic bank in Egypt.

Except for Sudan and Turkey, this policy of having special laws applies to all
Muslim states, especially the Arab countries. Sudan had at that time rising businesses owned and run by associates of the Islamic movement, notably supporters
of Turabi, to the extent that there formed a new middle class of businessmen
who posed a real threat to the traditional business class associated with the
traditionally political heavyweights: the Ansar movement of Sadiqh al-Mahdi
and al Khatmiyyah of Sayyid Ali al-Mirghani. Both the latter were in disgrace
because of their opposition to the regime of Nimairi. Led by Hassan al-Turabi,
the Islamists were collaborating with the government of Nimairi. Furthermore,
the Islamists of Sudan always kept close working relations with most of the
ulama and engaged with them. Prince Mohammad Al-Faisal did not have any
trouble working with both the Islamists and the *ulama* in establishing the first
Islamic bank in Sudan that also required a new special law.

When the Faisal Bank in Turkey was established in the late 1980s it benefited from a lull in hostility between the Kemalists and the Islamists during the
Özal presidency. The Faisal Finance House of Turkey gained the support of the
MÜSİAD (Independent Association of Industrialists and Businessmen) as well
as the Nursi-type *ulama* together; they all enjoyed a certain degree of freedom
before the election of 1998 that brought Erbakan to power and polarized Turkish politics in a way that led to the fall of Erbakan and the subsequent threat to
the special finance houses. At the same time that Prince Mohammad Al-Faisal
was working on his Egyptian Islamic bank, discussions for the establishment of
the Islamic Bank of Jordan were underway between Sami Hamoud, who needed
both Islamic legitimacy and venture capital support, and government officials.
The legitimacy was sought in the ranks of the Ministry of *Awqâf* and the
General Office of *Fatwa*. And once more a former Grand *Mufti* of Jordan was
recruited. Sheikh Saleh Kamel, a young business rival of the Prince, provided
the capital, with financial backing from the Saudi Arabian royal family. A new
alliance started to emerge between *ulama* and financiers-turned-bankers. This
alliance continued to prosper for the coming quarter of a century.

An examination of the motivation of Islamic bankers for their efforts to seek
the help of traditional *ulama* reveals that, unlike other Muslim intellectuals, the
shari'a scholars have close contacts with businessmen with small- and medium-
sized firms, and middle-income earners, from whom the clientele of Islamic
banks is to be derived. Most *shari'a* scholars have more daily contacts with the
Muslim populous than both the Islamic economic and finance intelligentsia and

Islamic movement activists.[15] Hence, the *shari'a* scholars were able to pave the way for the acceptance of these newly established banks as Islamic, they gave them the credibility and legitimacy they direly needed in exchange of a declared commitment, on the part of bankers, to abide by the rules of *shari'a* not only regarding the prohibition of interest – practically the only issue around which Muslim professional intelligentsia agreed – but also the detailed *fiqh* of financial transactions related to sale, *ijara* or leasing, money exchange, debt contracts and other rules and principles that determined the *shari'a*-compatibility of a given transaction. Noticeably, these details are usually known and decreed by the *shari'a* scholars (*fuqaha*) while Islamic economic and finance professionals usually have little acquaintance with them.

From that moment until the time of writing, the expansion and development of Islamic banking have always been associated with the involvement of well-known names in *fiqh* and in the circles of professional *shari'a* scholars. A number of *shari'a* experts have gained international status as they serve on the *shari'a* boards of several Islamic banks. These include, among others, Shaikhs Muhammad Taqi Usmani of Pakistan, Abd al Sattar Abu Ghuddah of Syria, Hussain Hamed Hassan and Yusuf al Qaradawi of Egypt, Muhammad ali al Qaradaghi of Qatar, Nizam Yaqubi of Bahrain, Muhammad al Siddiq al Darir of Sudan and Abdullah Bin Mani' of Saudi Arabia. There are many other *ulama* who serve on national level only in each Islamic bank.

When the new types of international Islamic investment funds emerged in the mid-1990s, their managers were also eager to get *shari'a* scholars on board in order to gain the acceptance and legitimacy that are indispensable in winning the support of potential clients. These Islamic investment funds were created to cater for the needs of Muslim investors while being administered and managed by reputable Western banks and fund managers.

Islamic bankers, professional economists and *shari'a* scholars have held many seminars, meetings, conferences and symposia on Islamic finance around the world that have further enhanced this new alliance. These meetings provide an opportunity to develop better working relationships between all these groups. For instance, there is the OIC *Fiqh* Academy that, since its inception in 1983, has been bringing together intellectuals, practitioners and *shari'a* scholars to discuss issues related to Islamic banking and finance. The Al-Baraka Group, headed by Sheikh Saleh Kamel, sponsors an annual seminar at which scores of economists and bankers meet with *shari'a* scholars to discuss different aspects of financing contracts used in the Islamic banks.

INTERACTION BETWEEN *SHARI'A* SCHOLARS AND THE NEW MUSLIM 'BOURGEOIS': FACTORS AND EFFECTS

The alliance between the *shari'a ulama* and the Islamic 'bourgeois' creates a new power structure in the socio-political arena in most Muslim countries that affects both the short-run struggle for economic and political influence and the long-run direction of the Islamic movement politics.

There are several factors that contributed to bringing a segment of the wealthy class and many *ulama* to this new alliance. On the part of financiers and bankers, their alliance with the *ulama* benefits them in several ways. First, it is a major tool for convincing the religious-minded public, especially potential depositors, to come forward to transact with these new banks. This is especially significant bearing in mind the long history of suspicion and apprehension that many Muslims maintain towards the entire banking sector, including central banking authorities and even their own governments that authorize such banks.

Second, the new alliance serves as a leverage for reaching new groups of clientele, those people who did not use the facilities of the banking system in the past because it relied on interest. The alliance is also used in competing with conventional banks and attempting to attract a substantial proportion of their depositors and finance-users. A study conducted in the mid-1990s by the Department of Islamic Financing Services in the National Commercial Bank of Saudi Arabia indicates that more than one-third of the clients of a conventional branch would be willing to shift to Islamic financial services once they are convinced they are truly Islamic.[16]

Third, the alliance with the *ulama* is used as a tool for improving the public relations of the new bankers, something they need very much, especially in asserting their new policies and in supporting their lobbying of governments, the media and the central banks. It helps create an image for the Islamic banks that relates them to the interests and concerns of the general public in their respective countries.[17]

Fourth, the alliance creates a kind of buffer that can be used in support of the main shareholders and professional managers of Islamic banks, who are usually drawn from conventional banks, in their dialogue with depositors, dormant shareholders and users of finance. Further, the owners of Islamic banks can also rely on the *shari'a* boards in influencing their managers. *Shari'a* boards may also be used to bail out the management in their relations with depositors and dormant shareholders, as can be seen from the *shari'a* board report of 1998 of Bank al Taqwa.[18]

From the point of view of the *shari'a* scholars, the new alliance brings them back to the forefront of the political scene at a time when they greatly need this boost, especially as the rising Islamic movement sidelined most of them.[19] This new alliance gives them a sense of achievement. With this new role they are actually working to fulfil the implications of the Islamic *fiqh* they've been learning and teaching all their lives. It improves their image among the Muslim public. It is, in a sense, a fulfilment of their life-long preaching that one should abide by the Islamic teachings in business transactions, of which the prohibition of interest is a cornerstone.

This alliance also gives the *ulama* a new source of income that by far exceeds what they were used to earning. It gives them an opening to a new lifestyle that includes air travel, sometimes in private jets, staying in five-star hotels, being under the focus of media attention and providing their opinions to people of high social and economic ranks, who are anxious to listen. In addition, they are frequently commissioned to undertake paid-for *fiqh* research and to find new solutions to problems that the new breed of bankers face. This new alliance also gives the *ulama* greater respectability in the social hierarchy, usually more than they were used to. In some Islamic banks, *shari'a* scholars reach positions such as vice president; in one case there is a *shari'a* scholar who serves as a deputy governor of a central bank in a Muslim country.[20]

Bringing the *ulama* back into the mainstream of Muslim society was itself a great achievement for them and a great fulfilment of their aspirations. They, in fact, have become real celebrities in their respective countries, and internationally.

The effect of the new alliance

This new alliance has several effects. First: it enhances Islamic *shari'a* research in several areas of finance and economics. According to the late Sheikh Mustafa al Zarka, the *fiqh* research preceded other areas of Islamic studies in its revival since the beginning of the twentieth century. Perhaps one can say that in the last three decades of the century there was more *fiqh* research in the financial and economic areas than in any other area. Although there are no statistical data as to subject-categorization of MA and PhD dissertations in the Arab and Islamic countries' universities and departments of *shari'a*, nor of the research papers submitted to different seminars and conferences, there is sufficient evidence to support this assertion. Those who are acquainted with this field of study realize that the number of publications on financial and economic *fiqh* exceeds by far publications on other *fiqh* areas, and the number of seminars and conferences related to this area also by far exceeds the number on other *fiqh* areas. For instance, the OIC *Fiqh* Academy for the first thirteen years of its activities from 1985 to 1997 made 97 resolutions, 51 of them relating to financial and economic issues, compared to 20 resolutions relating to medical matters and 11 on administrative guidance. This distribution is representative of most *fiqh* research in the last quarter of the twentieth century, especially if account is taken of the many specialized seminars and workshops held every year sponsored by Islamic banks.

Second: this new alliance helps modernize the *fiqh* opinions and rulings. It helps in addressing contemporary transactions from a *shari'a* point of view. As *riba* mingles with other contracts and avoidance of interest-based lending alone is insufficient to make a bank Islamic, there is a need to put everything on the table and without continuous *ulama* scrutinization and advice many *shari'a* violations may go unnoticed by Islamic bankers. Additionally, the bankers will find it difficult to devise modes of operation and of financing that are compatible with *shari'a*. This requires that *fuqaha* sit with economists, bankers and financiers and learn the details of every single transaction and get acquainted with new terminology, procedures and methods. All this is for the sake of developing *fiqhi* opinions on these issues that are new for *fuqaha*. Modernization of research in *fiqh* has taken on a long journey from letters of credit and letters of acceptance to foreign exchange hedging, syndicated financing, time-sharing and management of investment funds, with an ever-expanding list of new issues that are daily put on the desks of *shari'a* boards and subjected to *shari'a* scrutiny in seminars, workshops and conferences.

Third: this new alliance also brings together, on the common ground of Islamic banking and finance, some of the important segments of the wealthy strata in the Muslim societies (bankers and big businesses), middle-class people (lawyers, economists, depositors, bureaucrats and small entrepreneurs who use a lot of Islamic bank financing) and even the poor and the economically disadvantaged,[21] who benefit from the activity of many Islamic banks in the distribution of *zakat*.[22] The social and political effects of this new rapprochement are yet to be studied, but it has become normal for many poor and middle-class people to defend and befriend Islamic bankers and their activities, even in very poor countries like Yemen.

Fourth: this alliance also causes a real change in the lifestyle of many allied *ulama*. Bestowing a new income and new associations, it exposes them to experiences that were hard to even imagine in the past. The *ulama* that in the 1950s had weather-affected, dried-skin hands and humble clothing, sitting in the cold, teaching on the ground of mosques in Cairo, Damascus, Aleppo and Baghdad, are now replaced with soft-living *ulama* who are used to luxurious garments and services of five-star hotels and expensive restaurants. This new lifestyle of the Islamic banks' *ulama* has resulted in certain changes in viewpoint as well. Many of them are now accused of being bankers' window-dressers and of overstretching the rules of *shari'a* to provide easy *fatwas* for the new breed of bankers.

These allegations have caused negative reactions from *ulama* who are either not recruited by Islamic bankers or could not find opportunities to benefit from the expanding research agenda in the well-paid *fiqh* of finance. Hence, there is a new grouping and de-grouping in the socio-political stratification of the Muslim societies that have Islamic banks. Usually, except in the special cases that are discussed later, most Islamic movement activists take the side of non-allied *ulama*. This may provide some explanation of the attacks on Islamic banks that surface occasionally in meetings and workshops sponsored by purely academic institutions.[23]

Fifth: the new alliance also contributes to increasing social and economic coherence in the Muslim societies, through schemes that end with the finance-users becoming owners of their productive assets, including housing, as well as through micro-financing programmes which are always encouraged and supported by the *ulama*. In Sudan, for instance, the Islamic Bank of Sudan-West established a successful programme for small farmers and craftsmen. A similar programme to finance micro-industries by the Sudanese Faisal Islamic Bank followed.[24] The Jordan Islamic Bank was involved in a successful scheme to help taxi drivers become owners on a declining *musharaka* mode of finance. In addition, the Arafah Islamic Bank and the Islamic Bank of Bangladesh each has its own micro-financing programme.[25]

Despite the numerous studies of Islamic banking and finance, there is no statistical analysis of the distribution of Islamic banks' financing on the basis of the amount provided and the business size of recipients, yet such a study would be very useful. It is clear from repeated visits to many Islamic banks, reading their reports and discussions with their officers that most of the Islamic banks' financing is channelled to middle- and small-size entrepreneurs. This is consistent with data on the size and distribution of the credit markets and the share of Islamic banks in the respective markets in countries like Turkey, Bangladesh, Sudan, Jordan, Tunisia and Algeria. It is evident from personal contacts and observation that in five of the six Islamic banks established in Sudan before the 'Salvation Coup' of 1989, financing has been instrumental in creating a new and rising class of non-traditional businessmen.

Finally, it is interesting to look into the relationships or rather the effect of this new alliance on the relation between the Islamic revivalist movement and governments in the Arab countries. First of all, bearing in mind that capital is always risk-averse and does not like to enter into confrontations with governments, especially in the non-democratic systems that prevail in almost all Muslim countries, the bankers have always been very sensitive in selecting the type of *ulama* who are acceptable to both governments and the general public at the same time. Hence, they are very particular in avoiding extremists on both sides. They do not ally themselves with the so-called government-sponsored *ulama*, because that would make them lose credibility with most of their potential clients. Yet, at the same time, they avoid those *ulama* who are known as spokesmen of, or deeply allied with. the Islamic political movement in order to avoid creating any conflict with often dictatorial and unpredictable governments.

Ever since the establishment of the first Islamic bank in Dubai, Islamic bankers have relied on some kind of working relationship with their governments, as they have learned well the lesson of the Mit Ghamr experience. All other Islamic banks followed suit in either entering into some kind of partnership with their respective governments or keeping a close contact with the authorities while avoiding any relations that may annoy the ruling class on an employment as well as on business level. Depending on the type of government of the host country, the Islamic banks' policies of selecting board members and main officers varies from keeping strict association with professional technocrats to presenting persons of known commitment to Islamic teaching and behaviour.[26]

At the same time, Islamic bankers have not shied away from utilizing the services of 'moderate' Islamists, as long as it does not disturb the banks' relations with governments. Hence, many moderate Islamists have found peaceful havens in the Islamic banks, especially in Egypt and Jordan.

The Islamic banks and bankers have actually helped, among several other factors, in the emergence of favourable relationships between the moderate segment of the Islamic movement, mainly professional technocrats and open-minded *ulama* on the one hand and their respective governments on the other. This was of special importance, as it came at a time when many elements within the Arab Islamic movements were calling for revising the movements' positions on relations with governments and on strategies of political change – those reconciliatory reformists who abandoned the decades-raised banner of Sayyid Qutb ('Take Islam all together or leave it') for a step-by-step implementation of *shari'a*, or gradual Islamization, without attaching much of value to the theory that 'It all starts with changing the political system'.

Many of these reconciliatory reformists were in fact absorbed in Islamic banks and under the banner of allied *ulama* without antagonizing their governments. Hence, in a sense, this new alliance helps reformulate the power positions and power distribution in these countries. If we take as exceptions Sudan, Turkey, Pakistan and Iran, Islamic banks in other Muslim countries helped change the map of power distribution and brought about a new power centre. Although still small, this consists of a segment of the *ulama*, notably those who are involved in Islamization of the economic, finance and banking transactions, both on the research side as well as on the application side; a substantial component of the Islamic movement; new and rising Islamic capitalists, including bankers, entrepreneurs and professional executives; and a substantial portion of the non-antagonistic (to the Islamists), secularist intelligentsia who are categorized as professionals and bureaucrats.

SPECIAL CASES

The cases of Sudan, Turkey, Pakistan and Iran should be given special consideration because of the uniqueness of each of them.

In Sudan, the six domestic Islamic banks had, and are still having, an important role in shifting economic power from the traditionally rich class to a new class of Islamist entrepreneurs, those who are essentially either members or associates of the Islamic movement. The *ulama* play an important role in this association between bankers and rising new economic stars because of their close ties with the latter. Sudan has very few *shari'a* scholars outside the ranks of the Islamic political movement. Even those *ulama* who are not insiders in the movement have always maintained good relations with it.[27] The new power alliance in Sudan took an inseparable association with the Islamists. In other words, it only added an economic dimension under its fold. The *ulama–bankers* alliance helped create an economic base for the Islamic political movement consisting of upwardly mobile businessmen, newly affluent *ulama* and an empowered new class of Islamist CEOs. This is what really shook the traditional socio-political structure of Sudan in the 1980s and '90s and created a power base that extends from intellectuals to academics to financiers and businessmen. Islamic banks provided the financing seeds that grew in the soil of Islamic activists, but at the same time association with bankers did in Sudan what it has done in every other Muslim country, that is, it increased moderation and reconciliation among the Islamists. In the mid-1990s the government decided to Islamize the entire banking sector.[28] A new overall *shari'a* board was created at the central bank level to oversee the *shari'a*-compliance of the transactions of all banks. A test of the moderation effect of the alliance came with the split between Hassan al-Turabi and Lieutenant-General Omar Hassan al-Bashir. All the old guards of the Islamic movement sided with the government because they became reconciliatory, as a result of their long association with the Islamic bourgeois. Hassan al-Turabi was then left with only a group of frustrated university students!

In Turkey, four decades of harsh Kemalism were able to wipe out completely any Islamic political activism outside the domain of the *ulama*. Hence, the new Islamic political movement that is associated with the name of Necmettin Erbakan, under different party names, was from its inception allied with traditional *ulama*.[29] Therefore, Islamic banks in Turkey, very recent as they are, did not have any noticeable effect in changing the power composition of the *ulama* and Islamists. The Islamic banks' allied *ulama* are from the same rank and file as the political Islamists. In fact, there are few differences in the attitudes of traditional Turkish *ulama* and the political Islamists, especially vis-à-vis the neo-Kemalism and the anti-Islamic form of secularism adopted by the Turkish army and government. This is in spite of the presence of a powerful, but fragmented, Nursi movement outside the influence of Erbakanism.

Interestingly, Kemalism helped create a sort of unified stand between political Islamists and traditional *ulama* because, unlike the undeclared secularism of governments in the Arab countries, Kemalism indiscriminately antagonized all breeds of Muslims. Three of the five Islamic banks in Turkey have Saudi or Kuwaiti links.[30] All these special finance houses have strong ties with and members in MÜSİAD (Independent Association of Industrialists and Businessmen), which represents non-Kemalist national and Islamic businessmen. Although it is difficult to claim any direct association between Erbakanism and the Turkish Islamic banks, they are allied together in opposition to Kemalism. This perhaps explains why, after the fall of the Erbakan government in 1998, neo-Kemalists turned on Islamic banks (the special finance houses) to celebrate their victory with a toast of liquidation!

In Pakistan, the Islamization of the banking sector came from above, passing through the central bank, the Bank of Pakistan, with very little direct interaction between the *ulama* and the bankers. Although on several occasions the Islamic Ideology Council was called in by the government itself to give opinions on banking questions and to suggest Islamic solutions, the Pakistani government gave the Bank of Pakistan a free hand in interpreting the opinions of the Islamic Ideology Council, and in drawing the procedures for the application of the Islamic modes of financing without any interference from the *ulama* or from members of the Islamic political parties. The direct interaction between the *ulama* of Pakistan and its bankers had to wait until a few small private banks were licensed in the early 1990s. Even the latest decision of the Supreme Court (taken in the summer of 2000) on the elimination of interest from all transactions of the government and the banking system was left to the bankers and bureaucrats to implement without, necessarily, involving *shari'a* specialists; certainly the Islamists can always challenge any bureaucratic decision through the judiciary system.

In Iran, after the occupation of the American embassy in Tehran, the whole government fell into the hands of the *mullas* and the Islamic activists were marginalised.[31] When the Islamization of the banking sector came about, the *mullas* themselves carried it out and the government did not need to create any alliances. This may partially explain the general lack of trust the Islamic movement activists have towards the transformation that took place in the Iranian banking system. As one professor of economics, who returned to Iran in the early 1980s with overwhelming enthusiasm to serve the Islamic Revolution and later fled overseas for his life and safety, sarcastically put it: 'Since our government is Islamic, anything done by an Islamic government must surely be Islamic!'

CONCLUSION

The rise of Islamic capital may be looked at in the history of the Middle East and the Muslim World as the economic phase of independence that followed the political phase. The last three decades of the twentieth century witnessed the emergence of Islamic banks as growing centres of economic power in most Muslim and Arab countries. Islamic banks were accompanied by a new alliance with the *ulama*, or *shari'a* scholars. Such an alliance came about as a result of the pressing needs of the new Islamic bankers for legitimacy and recognition. While this alliance benefited its parties in several ways, its growth in many Arab and Muslim countries created two noteworthy effects on the socio-political scene: an enabling economic/political power was generated for the implementation of *shari'a*, even under adverse reactions from the dictatorial governments; and a gradual moderation effect on the political Islamists that allows for reconciliatory compromises with the prevailing regimes. The bankers' allied *ulamas* role as leaders of public opinion gained acceptance from both governments and Islamists. They were instrumental in bringing about these effects, yet it was, in a sense, a dialectical material development because Islamic bankers could not afford to ally themselves with either the Islamic intelligentsia or the political Islamists. After centuries of dormancy, the *ulama* have a new chance to play a crucial role in the development of events in their countries, without being brushed aside by political Islamic movements.

On the other hand, however, development of Islamic banking and Islamic capital in Sudan, Turkey, Iran and Pakistan took different paths, unique for each of these countries, with completely different outcomes with regard to the creation of new economic and political power centres and structures.

NOTES

1. The practice of *riba* is wholly condemned in the Koran and the *Sunnah*. The Muslim public, including those who are illiterate, have over time been antagonistic to those who deal with *riba* to the extent that neighbours and other community members would virtually boycott those who lend for interest, although the latter have always existed in Muslim societies.
2. The earliest of such writings go back to 1948 when Quraishi's *Islam and the Theory of Interest* was published in Karachi, followed by Maududi's *al Riba* and Sayyid Qutb's *Social Justice in Islam*. The publication that tackled the practical issues in running an interest-free bank was the article of Muhammad Uzair in 1956, which was followed by the late Muhammad Baqir al Sadr's *al Bank al La-Ribawi* in 1961.
3. It is interesting to record that the Islamic Cooperative Parliamentary Block in Syria was preparing a draft act for eliminating interest from the whole banking system in Syria, where all banks were state-owned since the nationalizations during the era of Nasser, when the coup of 28 March 1962 suspended the elected parliament that was

later dissolved by the Baath regime created by the coup of 8 March 1963.

4. In recognizing its effort in discovering a Malaysian style of Islamic banking, Tabung Hajji was given the IDB prize for Islamic Banking in 1990.

5. His later writings and lecturing invoked a vague notion of an overall social transformation and Islamization through the functions of Mit Ghamr-style Islamic banks.

6. Ahmed al Najjar was not politically involved and was never associated with the Muslim Brotherhood at any time. He remained on reasonable relations with the Egyptian regime until his death in Cairo in the early 1990s. However, this cannot be documented in published data and may never be documented in any future publication. The official government line regarding the closure of the Mit Ghamr banks is that it was a matter of violating procedures of registration and licensing, lack of ability to efficiently invest accumulated funds, and so on.

7. Ahmed al Najjar, *Manhaj al Nahdah al Islamiyyah* (Cairo: Mat ba'at al-'Ada, 1985).

8. There may be a political motive for the establishment of NSB as it came at a time when President Sadat needed the support of the Islamists in the crackdown on the Nasserites and the purge of the Arab Socialist Union, the only party in the country that Sadat inherited from Nasser.

9. It is interesting to note that even the theoretical writings never have any reference to *murabaha* until Sami Hamoud's dissertation that was published in 1976. As for the *ijara* (leasing) and especially *ijara wa-iqtina* (purchase/leasing), it only entered the theory of Islamic banking in the 1990s. (See Monzer Kahf, *al Ijarah al Muntahiyah bi al Tamlik* [lease leading to ownership], presented to the 12th annual meeting of the OIC *Fiqh* Academy, Riyadh, 22–28 September 2000.

10. This is despite the fact that two of the Gulf states, namely Kuwait and United Arab Emirates, have their own national institutions for foreign aid. Ideas in international politics always call for a multiplicity of instruments that serve overlapping purposes, because at any given time one vehicle may be more useful than the other.

11. Between 1974 and 2001 the IDB made small capital contributions in a handful of national Islamic banks. It started in 1981 with the establishment of the Bahrain Islamic bank, under the blessing of the Bahraini government and a capital participation from its Ministry of *Awqāf* and Religious Affairs. IDB is also a small shareholder in one Islamic bank in each of Malaysia, Bangladesh, Algeria, Turkey and Gambia. All requests for these contributions came through the countries' official representatives at the IDB and the contributions themselves make less that 10 per cent of the paid-up capital in each of these Islamic banks.

12. Ahmed al Najjar was instrumental in adding this clause. He was a member of the committee that prepared the first draft of the articles of agreement.

13. *Murabaha* was derived by Sami Hamoud from the *Kitab al Umm* of al Shafi'i. In 1976 Hamoud recommended it to both the IDB and the Dubai Islamic Bank. He later applied it in the Jordan Islamic Bank (1978) and proposed it to the Kuwait Finance House (1979). Sami Hamoud was honoured with the IDB prize in Islamic Banking in 1987 for his development of the *murabaha* mode of financing.

14. Changes involve three main areas: 1) the simple lending (*qard hasan*) provided by IDB to governmental non-profit institutions such as universities and some infrastructure that involved transfer of technology. These represented about 15 per

cent of IDB financing and they used to be conducted at a 2.5 per cent service charge to cover their administrative cost. The new policy suggested by the OIC *Fiqh* Academy calls for charging actual expenses, and if it were difficult to calculate expenses, then a percentage charge may be accepted provided it is calculated in a way that brings it the closest possible to actual expenses. The method adopted was to charge a percentage of administrative expenses of financing, not including any cost of money, calculated on the basis of moving averages for the past five years. The new charge was below 1 per cent for all concessional loans advanced prior to 1987. Since then the administrative cost calculated on a moving five-year average increased gradually. It was 1.27 per cent in 1999. After implementation of the new policy, a refund was made for extra charges levied on previous loans. 2) A few corrections in the proposed *ijara* financing. This allowed the Bank to start its leasing programme. Earlier the only mode of financing was *murabaha*. 3) Minor changes in the conditions of agency in the *murabaha* contract, called instalment sale. Later on, while establishing the IDB Islamic Banks Portfolio, the Bank relied on another *Fiqh* Academy resolution on the sale of packaged assets that consist of debts and physical properties.

15. It should be noted that, except for Sudan and Turkey, the twentieth-century Islamic movement in all Muslim countries has always been on poor terms with the *ulama*. Since Hassan Al-Banna in Egypt and Maududi in South Asia, the real raison d'être of the Islamic movement was that the *ulama* failed in discharging their responsibility in awakening the *umma*. At the same time, their relations with governments have always been volatile. Al-Banna declared in 1938 that a true test that the Muslim Brotherhood was on the right course would be visible expression of hostility from stooge governments and a corrupt *ulama* class.

16. Said al Martan, 'Transformation to Islamic Banking: the Experience of the NCB', paper presented at the Seminar on Islamic Banking, Casablanca, organized by the IRTI of IDB in cooperation with the Moroccan Association of Studies in Islamic Economics, April 1999.

17. While Islamic banks received a considerable image boost from the *ulama*, the so-called Islamic investment companies found it irrelevant to hire any *shari'a* advisers. These companies draw their clientele from two categories of people: those who could be reached by personal contacts and those who have an overwhelming desire for quick windfall profits to an extent that blinds them regarding potential risks. The first such company started in Saudi Arabia in the mid-1970s and it ended wiping out the savings of a large number of people while its owner/founder, al Ajhuri, was imprisoned in Makka for swindling the assets of thousands of middle-class savers. The same experience was repeated in Egypt, and on a smaller scale in Syria. In the late 1980s, abusing loopholes in the law, several companies were established in Egypt under the name of Islamic investment companies. They were able to collect huge savings from the public largely by offering a high rate of return that was derived from new savings deposited with them rather than profits. They mainly counted on the pyramidal cumulative effect of new deposits, with very little actual investment. In spite of the fact that Islamic banks and their associated *ulama*, as well as most academic Islamic economists and financiers, took a very strong stand against these companies, some outspoken Islamic activists in Egypt strongly defended them and attacked what they called 'the government conspiracy' against the Islamic investment companies.

18. Bank al Taqwa's management failed in 1998. The bank's report at the end of the year showed a loss of over 23 per cent of principal to both *mudaraba* depositors and shareholders. The *shari'a* board exceeded its limits in stating that the management did not violate the *shari'a* rules and went as far as stating that the board of directors and the management did their best and took sound finance and investment decisions, and the loss was a result of the South East Asian disaster as claimed by the management itself in its report. Facts were revealed in the year 2000, however, in a letter from the management indirectly indicating that in violation of well-established banking rules, regulations and wisdom, the management put most of its eggs in one basket, as it invested in one single project more than 60 per cent of the bank's assets.

19. Note that in Islamic history the *ulama* played leading and very critical roles in advising rulers and defending the general public against rulers' atrocities and sometimes against outside aggression. Islamic history is full of examples such as Ibn Hanbal, al Nawawi, Ibn 'Abd al Salam and Ibn Taymiyyah. In the past the *awqâf* was the main source of finance for Islamic as well as secular education. Starting from the time of Muhammad Ali in Egypt (1815 CE), the control on *awqâf* was transferred to the government. The *Awqâf* Act of 1856 in the Ottoman Empire extended the government authority to *awqâf* and made the *ulama* government employees. That made them lose their leadership status and gradually they took a position on the periphery of the political stage. Although the European invasion of the most of the Muslim land caused revolutionary reactions that were led in several instances by *ulama*, the majority of them remained invisible in a forgotten corner. The twentieth-century Islamic movement was in part a reaction to this dormancy, though it took a while to present itself as a substitute for existing regimes and rulers, while the Middle Ages' *ulama* did not pose any real threat to their rulers.

20. These stories come from the Sudan's Bank al Tadamun and Central Bank, respectively.

21. Most *ulama* come from the poor class. This is because of the structure of the education system in the Muslim countries. With the introduction of Western education and its emphasis on learning science, both resources of traditional Islamic education and job opportunities have become very thin. Since the beginning of the twentieth century, *shari'a* teaching has become the monopoly of poor children whose parents cannot afford to send them to public or private schools, as most *shari'a* schools provide meagre boarding facilities subsidized by charities and the remnants of *awqâf*.

22. Most Islamic banks take charge of distributing the *zakat* due on the shareholders' equity, and some of them obtain the consent of their depositors to deduct and distribute their *zakat* as well. This allows some Islamic banks to create sizable *zakat*-distribution departments that maintain relations with the poor and needy and with other local charitable agencies. This is very evident in the Nasser Social Bank and the Faisal Bank of Egypt.

23. There was a very critical (perhaps one must say accusative) paper at the seminar on contemporary *fiqh* and Islamic banks held by the School of *Shari'a* of the University of Jordan in 1993. One also finds similar expressions in some of the annual meetings of the OIC *Fiqh* Academy.

24. Othman Babikr, *Financing Micro Industries: the Experience of the Sudanese Faisal Islamic Bank* (Jeddah: IRTI, 1997).

25. Reports of 1998 and 1999 on these banks.
26. Although there is no statistical data to substantiate this assertion, a close examination of the lists of CEOs of Dar al-Maal al-Islami's central office and its affiliated
banks and of the Al-Baraka Group's banks especially in Tunisia, Algeria, Mauritania
and Bangladesh supports this claim.
27. The historical reason for this lies in the fact that although Belal, who was one of the
most renowned disciples of Muhammad, was from Sudan (Eritrians say he was from
their country), since the time of the great conquests in the middle of the seventh
century, when al Sarh led a Muslim army south from Egypt to close off Khartoum, no
place in Sudan had ever become a centre of Islamic learning. Islamic *shari'a* scholarship is new in Sudan; it only came about during the early period of the contemporary
Islamic political movement. This is not to say that Sudan has been less religious
than other Muslim countries. It has always had small schools of Koran and little *fiqh*
(Khalawi) throughout its cities and countryside that are centres for Sufi orders of
Khatmiyyah and the Ansar movement, which make the power bases of the two main
political parties in Sudan, al Ummah and al Ittihadi.
28. Banks in Sudan were all theoretically Islamized since 1983 with the famous set of
laws of implementing the *shari'a* enacted by President Nimairi. On the ground, however, no clear applicable instructions were ever issued to conventional banks, so they
continued business as usual. After 1989 the new management of the nationalized
banks that dominate about 80 per cent of the market, and of the central bank, took
the laws for the elimination of *riba* more seriously. In 1994 a new act that reorgan-
ized the whole banking system, including the central bank, was issued.
29. The Nursi movement, which fragmented later in different groups, was also born
under the influence of the *ulama*. A few Nursis went along with political Islam and
supported Erbekan while most supported other parties on the ground that the time
was not yet ripe for Islamic political activism.
30. Al-Baraka, Dar al-Maal al-Islami and the Kuwait Finance House had capital contribution in each of the first three banks.
31. The term Islamic activists is used in Iran to mean the groups that can be characterized as modern or enlightened political Islamists in a way that fairly describes
them as the counterparts of the Muslim Brotherhood, the Turkish Erbakanists, or, in
the sub-continent, Jamaat-e-Islami. They have two characteristics in common: they
are mostly intellectuals with no formal *mulla* training, and they are Islamic revivalists in a holistic sense, with the political aspect of Islam overblown. They generally
include disciples and followers of revivalists like Ali Shariati, Mahmud Talaghani,
Nawwab Safawi and Muhammad Behishti. Most of the members of the Mahdi
Bazagan's government were of this type. Unfortunately, at the time of writing, many
of them are now either in Iran, where they have been suppressed by the government,
or have fled to Europe and the United States.

2

Global Politics, Islamic Finance and Islamist Politics Before and After 11 September 2001

Ibrahim Warde

This chapter discusses the evolution of global politics, Islamic finance and Islamist politics over three periods: the later stages of the cold war (1973–89), during which the first aggiornamento of Islamic finance took place, the 'New World Order' that followed the end of the cold war (1990–2001) and the 'New New World Order' ushered in by the events of 11 September 2001. Each period was marked by different political alignments and priorities, different forms of Islamic finance and different types of Islamist movements.

Since its inception in the mid-1970s, Islamic finance was firmly embedded within the US-centred international economic order, under the aegis of Saudi-supported pan-Islamism. With the end of the cold war and the increased globalization of the economy, new sets of rules, norms and institutions emerged. The position of Islamic finance was paradoxical. On the one hand, Islamic finance thrived. Yet political Islam grew more diverse and complicated, and was designated in many influential circles as the most likely successor of Communism as the main enemy of the post-cold war era. The events of September 11th bolstered the 'Islam is the new enemy' view in the West, just as it fostered another Islamic revival. As the war against terrorism came to dominate world politics, many Islamic institutions came under attack (while demand for Islamic products grew unabated), and their integration in the global economy suffered a severe blow.

THE EARLY YEARS OF ISLAMIC FINANCE (1973–89)

Islam and the cold war

The rise of pan-Islamism can only be understood in the context of the 'Arab cold war' – which was itself rooted in the cold war pitting the United States against the Soviet Union.[1] Within the Arab and Islamic World, an increasingly wealthy Saudi Arabia emerged as a powerful ally of the Western camp at a time when Egypt had become a key Soviet client, and the use of Islam was rife with geopolitical overtones. In those years, the Muslim Brotherhood – the mainspring of most modern Islamist movements – were persecuted by Nasser's regime, as the stark geopolitics of the cold war – based on the principle that the enemy of my enemy is my ally – placed them squarely in the anti-Soviet, pro-US camp. Saudi Arabia offered refuge to key Islamist figures, and the seeds of a new transnational group were planted.

With US support, King Faisal sought to trump Nasser's pan-Arabism by founding in 1962 the first modern pan-Islamic movement, the Muslim World League, and used the pilgrimages to Mecca to forge ties with Islamic leaders, both inside and outside the Arab world. To oppose Nasser's message of Arab and Third World solidarity, he proclaimed the doctrine of Islamic solidarity.[2] In addition, he extended substantial amounts of aid to non-Arab Islamic countries in Asia and Africa, and embarked on a series of high-profile visits to Islamic capitals. Upon one such visit to the Shah of Iran in December 1965, the Saudi king was accused by the Egyptian press of using Islam 'as an instrument to combat Arab unity'.[3]

A number of events set the stage for an Islamic renewal, thus enhancing Faisal's position. The most dramatic was the crushing Arab defeat in the six-day war of June 1967. Significantly, in his first speech following the war, a humbled Nasser made a specific reference to religion.[4] In the soul-searching that followed, many of the principles that had governed Egypt's policy were called into question. It was then frequently said that the Arabs were punished for straying from the path of true Islam.[5] Egypt embarked on a more moderate course and Saudi Arabia's stature within the Islamic world grew. Then, in 1969, a deranged Australian set fire to the al Aqsa mosque in Israeli-occupied Jerusalem. In the aftermath, King Faisal, by then the unquestioned leader of the nascent pan-Islamic movement, called for an Islamic summit in Rabat, Morocco, at which it was agreed to form a permanent Islamic organization.

The Organization of the Islamic Conference (OIC) was created in 1970 – the year Nasser died. And unlike the June 1967 war, which was fought in the name of Arab nationalism, the subsequent October 1973 war (known as the Ramadan war in Arab countries and as the Yom Kippur war in Israel) was full of religious symbolism. It was, for example, code-named 'Badr' – the name of Muhammad's first decisive victory over the Meccans. By the mid-1970s, pan-Islamism had become a powerful movement, helped in no small part by the new-found wealth of Saudi Arabia. In such countries as Turkey, Indonesia, Malaysia and Pakistan, which until then had limited ties to the Arab World, Islamic solidarity became an important foreign policy theme, as a regional – and to a large extent Islamic – economy took shape: the oil-producing states of the Gulf became important providers of economic aid and major importers of manpower from the Middle East and South Asia. The rapprochement between Pakistan and the Persian Gulf states was especially significant for an understanding of Islamist politics and Islamic finance. It was in Pakistan that the bulk of the early research on an Islamic state – and Islamic banking – had been conducted.[6] And before Pakistan engaged in close cooperation with the US and Saudi Arabia to counter Soviet influence in Afghanistan, it played a key role in the Islamic revival.

Throughout the 1970s, as noted by Edward Mortimer, the Islamic revival was based on a division of labour, which would later have important geopolitical implications: 'While Saudi Arabia and other Gulf states provided the cash, Pakistan has provided much of the manpower, and much of the zeal, for the network of supranational 'Islamic' institutions that has developed [...] under the umbrella of the Organization of the Islamic Conference.'[7] Interestingly, it all started during the rule of Zulficar Ali Bhutto – to whom the labels of 'secular' and 'socialist' are usually affixed – who made numerous trips to oil-producing countries, emphasized the theme of Islamic brotherhood in his speeches and hosted the Islamic summit conference in Lahore, during which the idea of the creation of an Islamic bank was adopted. That summit also saw the reconciliation between Pakistan and the newly created Bangladesh, following an appeal in the name of Islam by President Anwar Sadat of Egypt.

In a sharp break with his predecessor's policies, during his period of office 1970–81, Sadat expelled Soviet advisers from Egypt and drew steadily closer to the United States. On the regional front, he entered into a close alliance with King Faisal of Saudi Arabia, who granted Egypt generous financial assistance and recognized its military role as the main confrontation state vis-à-vis Israel. Subsequently the King was to link his oil policy to the Arab–Israeli conflict.[8]

This linkage, combined to a new supply-and-demand picture,[9] led to the oil embargo of October 1973 against countries supporting Israel (including the United States), and to the quadrupling of the price of oil between October and December of that year. In what is commonly considered one of the most massive transfers of wealth in modern times, the mid-1970s were dominated by talk of a 'New World Order', more specifically of new relations between North and South and of Southern, and particularly Islamic, solidarity. Saudi Arabia suddenly became an immensely wealthy country. It is in that context that Islamic finance went from being a vague, somewhat utopian, idea to reality.

The first aggiornamento of Islamic finance

Following the creation in 1970 of the Organization of the Islamic Conference movement (OIC), research institutes focusing on Islamic economics and finance sprouted throughout the Muslim World. In the wake of the quadrupling in oil prices, the 1974 OIC summit in Lahore voted to create the inter-governmental Islamic Development Bank (IDB), which was to become the cornerstone of a new banking system inspired by religious principles. In 1975, the Dubai Islamic Bank, the first modern, non-governmental, Islamic bank came into existence.[10] In 1979, Pakistan became the first country to announce the full Islamicization of its banking sector.[11] It was followed in 1983 by the Sudan and Iran.

The first paradigm of modern Islamic banking was established in those years. Islamic jurisprudents reinterpreted a rich legal but pre-capitalist tradition to suit the requirements of the modern era. The main difficulty was that, although commerce had always been central to the Islamic tradition (Muhammad was himself a merchant), profits from 'pure' finance were viewed with suspicion. The Koran states, for example, that despite their superficial resemblance profits from commerce are fundamentally different from those generated by money-lending (2:275). More specifically, Islam prohibits *riba*. Literally meaning 'increase', the term has been variously interpreted – sometimes as usury (or excessive interest), more often as any kind of interest.[12]

While accepting the notion that 'time had to be priced', Islamic scholars objected to 'fixed, pre-determined' aspects of interest-based lending (which, incidentally, Islam shares with other religious traditions), which they perceived as unfair, for it often resulted in the lender taking advantage of the borrower.[13] In the early Islamic days, the dominant form of finance consisted in a partnership between lender and borrower, based on the fair sharing of both profits and losses – a logic similar to today's 'venture capital', where financiers link their fate to the firms in which they invest. For instance, in medieval Arabia, wealthy merchants financing the caravan trade would share in the profits of a successful operation, but could also lose all or part of their investment if, for example, the merchandise was stolen, lost, or sold for less than its cost.

A distinctive feature of Islamic banking was to be its focus on developmental and social goals. Profit-and-loss-sharing (PLS), or partnership finance, with its focus on cash-poor but promising entrepreneurs, held more economic potential than conventional, collateral-based lending, which favours established businesses. Islamic finance also promised to benefit local communities and draw into the banking system those people who had until then shunned '*riba*-based' finance. In addition, banks were to contribute to, as well as manage, '*zakat* funds'[14] earmarked for a variety of charitable and social purposes.

The first Islamic banks were committed to partnership finance – *mudaraba* (commenda partnership) and *musharaka* (joint venture) – though most of their operations consisted of 'cost-plus' operations such as *murabaha*, where the bank would purchase the goods needed by the borrower and then resell them to the borrower at a profit. As for the remuneration of deposits (cheque, saving or investment accounts), it was based on a profit-and-loss-sharing logic: investment accounts were remunerated based on the performance of specific investments and holders of savings accounts shared in the overall profits of the bank.

Saudi entrepreneurship and financing were essential in promoting the concept and in exporting it.[15] Prince Mohammad Al-Faisal (the son of King Faisal) created most of the Islamic banking infrastructure: he founded in 1977 the International Association of Islamic Banks, and financed the *Handbook of*

Islamic Banking, a 'scientific and practical encyclopedia for Islamic bankers' designed to become the definitive reference on the subject. He also created a network of 'Faisal Banks' throughout the Islamic world, in addition to the transnational Dar al-Maal al-Islami (DMI) Group based in Geneva. The other pioneer was Saudi businessman Sheikh Saleh Kamel, who founded the Dallah al-Baraka Group, which at one time had a presence in thirty-four countries.

Islamic finance and Islamist politics

Insofar as Islamic institutions had emphasized *zakat*, they played a role in the funding of Islamic charities, many of which took an active part in the propagation of the Saudi brand of Islam. Only in the Sudan did Islamic institutions become significant political players: the Faisal Islamic Bank, created in 1978, came to be controlled by the Muslim Brotherhood and in particular by Hassan al-Turabi, who later became the country's main powerbroker.[16] In a development that would later come back to haunt it, the same bank also entered into a short-lived joint venture with Osama Bin Laden, creating the Islamic Al-Shamal Bank.

Otherwise, Islamic finance was, in the context of the cold war, firmly embedded in the US-centered international political and economic order. In addition, the world of banking and finance is by nature oriented towards preferring the status quo, if not 'cowardly'. It craves stability and abhors uncertainty. In every new market they penetrated, Islamic banks established links with the local power structure, operated within the political, economic and regulatory framework, and worked within established oligopolies.[17] At the international level, the major Islamic banking groups, lacking experience and know-how, were keen on working with the major international financial institutions. The international capitals of Islamic finance were London, Geneva or the Bahamas, rather than Jeddah, Karachi or Cairo. As for the Islamic Development Bank (IBD), the initial cornerstone of the system, its statutes provided for coordination and collaboration with the International Monetary Fund (IMF) and other international organizations.[18]

After the oil shocks of the 1970s, the 'recycling' of petrodollars was undertaken by Western, and primarily American, banks. More generally, many countries involved in Islamic finance – especially those in the Gulf – belonged in the 'coupon-clipper' category, and had a stake in the stability of international markets, where they are heavily invested.[19] Paradoxically, the paucity of acceptable Islamic products also led Islamic banks to be heavily invested in foreign currencies and to have a large percentage of their deposits abroad.[20] The leading international banks were also instrumental in the very creation of Islamic banks.

Until the Islamic Revolution in Iran, Islamic finance and Islamist politics were, from an international relations standpoint, almost indistinguishable from

Saudi politics. To be sure, the hike in oil prices was, in certain circles, considered as an 'attack on the West'.[21] In reality, the main players involved – Anwar Sadat, King Faisal, the Shah of Iran – happened to be the strongest supporters of the United States and the West, all keen on having strong ties with the US-centered international economic order. The embargo was justified as a means to break a political deadlock. The price hike was justified in terms of achieving a more equitable distribution of wealth between North and South. On that issue, Saudi Arabia was decidedly a dove. Indeed, one of the lesser-known facts about what is generically considered an 'Arab' price hike, was that, at the fateful December 1973 meeting of the Organization of Petroleum Exporting Countries (OPEC) in Tehran, the two main hawks were Iran and Venezuela – both non-Arab countries and both at the time squarely within the US 'sphere of influence'.[22] The hawks saw no contradiction there, insofar as they considered the new prices consistent with the rules and logic of the free market. Perhaps a bit disingenuously, the Shah of Iran frequently reiterated his concern that the West was too dependent on oil, and that only significantly higher prices would lead to less waste and to a more resolute search for alternative sources of energy. Saudi Arabia had good reasons to lead the doves. It was sparsely populated and did not need all the additional income. Also, having the largest oil reserves in the world, it was worried that too steep a rise would encourage the development of alternative sources of energy, which in time could altogether supplant oil. Perhaps most importantly, Saudi Arabia, along with other Gulf states, was also heavily invested in international markets and was economically and militarily dependent on the United States. Crippling the US and the world economy would be self-defeating. When, in the following years, the Shah of Iran pushed for further price increases, Saudi Arabia refused to go along, for a time creating a two-tiered price system within OPEC.[23]

Overall, the relations between Saudi Arabia and the United States had been very close, although they were marred by differences over America's staunch support for Israel. The strong bilateral ties were reinforced by the official visits of Faisal to Washington in 1966 and 1971, as well as Nixon's visit to Riyadh in July 1974 at the height of the Watergate scandal and shortly before his resignation. In the context of the cold war, and despite the events of 1973, Saudi Arabia was firmly in the American camp. In the words of George Lenczowski,

> The two countries had a long history of mutual cooperation based on common concerns and complementary interests. Both were anticommunist and opposed to radical revolutionary movements anywhere in the world; both looked for stability and security in the Arabian Peninsula and the Persian Gulf; and both were interested that Saudi petroleum should flow uninterruptedly to the consumers in the industrialized democracies for the mutual benefit of the buyers and the sellers. The fact that a purely American company, Aramco, was the sole operator of oil fields on Saudi territory added to the closeness of this relationship.[24]

It was observed that, for King Faisal, as for his successors, 'the interests of Islam are in the last resort identified with those of the "free world" – which Faisal saw as the Christian world, ruled by "people of the book" – against those of atheistic communism'.[25] As for Sadat, he saw a 'commonality of interests between the Islamic states and the West: oil in exchange for technology and the common interest against the Soviet threat'.[26] Ideologically, both liberalism and economic Islam were driven by their common opposition to socialism and economic dirigisme.[27]

So despite policy differences over Israel and an oil policy that provided, among other things, for a gradual nationalization of Aramco, cooperation between the two countries actually increased, especially in military and financial matters. From 1974 onwards, the Saudis significantly increased their purchases of American weapons and chose to invest a significant part of their newfound wealth in US Treasury Bonds, while maintaining most of their deposits in American banks.[28] Indeed, at a time when the US encountered its first major economic difficulties since the Second World War , a trip to Saudi Arabia became a ritual for every incoming American Treasury Secretary.

In the late 1970s two major geopolitical developments further cemented the alliance: the Iranian Islamic Revolution of 1978–79,[29] and the Soviet invasion of Afghanistan in 1979. In those days predating the 'clash of civilizations' discourse (discussed later) and the perception of Islam as a monolith,[30] the US led a new anti-Communist alliance involving principally Saudi Arabia and Pakistan – which would result over two decades later in an unanticipated 'blowback'.[31] The Iranian Islamic Revolution – and its promotion of a radical, anti-American, Shiite-inspired Islam – had only touched a small minority of the Islamic world, and it was all the more reason to embrace the conservative, staunchly anti-Communist, pro-US brand of Islam represented by Saudi Arabia. The threat of radical Islam[32] made conservative Islamic regimes ever more dependent on the West.

Throughout the Reagan years, the crusade 'against Godless Communism' further cemented the ties between the US and Saudi Arabia. Hamstrung by both the post-Watergate restrictions on intelligence and a weak economy, the Saudis played a crucial, if behind the scenes, role, providing financing and intelligence help on such initiatives as Iran-Contra or secret operations against Hezbollah.[33] In Afghanistan, a US–Pakistani–Saudi alliance aimed at helping the anti-Soviet Afghan resistance seemed made in heaven: the US offered guidance, weapons and technical assistance, Pakistan micro-managed through its own Inter-Services Intelligence (ISI) the anti-Soviet resistance, while the Saudis handled financing and religious propaganda.[34]

In a 1998 interview, Zbigniew Brzezinski, former National Security Advisor in the Carter Administration, boasted that playing the 'Islamic card' was not simply an ad hoc response to the Soviet invasion. He asserted that he had conceived 'the secret operation which had the effect of drawing the Russians into the Afghan trap' six months before the entry of Soviet troops. Instilling a dose of religious fanaticism was necessary to justify a *jihad* or holy war against the Soviets. For the architect of that strategy, the rise of 'some unruly Islamists' was the price to pay for 'the liberation of central Europe and the end of the Cold War'. In the same interview, he asked rhetorically: 'What is more important: the Taliban or the collapse of the Soviet empire?' [35]

ISLAMIC FINANCE IN THE NEW WORLD ORDER (1990–2001)

Politics and finance in the New World Order

The year 1990 constitutes a convenient, if arbitrary, dividing line. The previous year had seen the fall of the Berlin Wall and the Soviet decision to withdraw from Afghanistan. In August 1990, Iraq's invasion of Kuwait touched off the first conflict of the post-cold war era. It was then that President George Bush first spoke of a 'New World Order'. On the economic and financial fronts, that year marked the beginning of the 'globalization decade': new global rules, norms and institutions emerged, with attendant impacts on Islamic politics and finance.[36]

In such an environment, the position of Islamic finance was paradoxical. On the one hand, a series of developments (discussed in the following pages) allowed Islamic finance to thrive. At the same time, however, in many influential circles, Islam was designated as the most likely successor of Communism as prime villain. The once-simple categorizations of Islam were blurred. Followers of Sunni Wahhabism, in contrast to those of Iranian Shiism, were supposed to be friendly to the West. But as the 'blowback' from the 'Afghan trap' started unfolding, a new radical form of Islamism appeared. The 'Afghan trap' may have served its purpose, but it had created a monster in the process, as 'Afghan Arabs' led by Osama Bin Laden went on a search for new holy wars.

The economic and financial fronts saw dramatic changes as well. Throughout the 1980s, both the regional economy that had taken shape a decade earlier and the cold war system were slowly disintegrating. Sovereign lending, through which banks recycled 'petrodollars' by lending them to governments, fell out of favour with the spread of the debt crisis (which had started in Mexico in August 1982). By 1990, it was clear that major new political and economic forces were at work. 'Globalization' and the 'New World Order' became shorthand for those transformations. The emerging global economy limited the options of national governments and imposed new norms and a new ideology.

Traditional views on development and the role of the state were discredited.[37] The new paradigm was strengthened by the collapse of Communism in Eastern

Europe and the implosion of the Soviet Union, which were interpreted as the victory, in the battle of ideas, of capitalism and the market economy over socialism and central planning.[38] Old dogmas regarding the respective roles of states and markets were turned on their head: government leaders were now seen as neither able nor willing to promote the public good; state controls could only encourage inefficiency, stifle entrepreneurship and delay reform. What came to be known as the Washington Consensus was conquering the world. The state, once seen as the provider of solutions, was now perceived as the major obstacle to development. All attempts at central planning, and even milder forms of industrial policy, were said to be doomed to failure. State-led policies, protectionism and import-substitution had to be replaced by privatization, deregulation and export-orientation.[39]

'Structural adjustment' policies became the order of the day: in exchange for international aid, countries had to conform to the dictates of the International Monetary Fund (IMF) and World Bank. The new orthodoxy included sound fiscal and monetary policies, reform of the public sector, the elimination of subsidies, the modernization of the supervisory and legal infrastructure, the liberalization of financial markets and the promotion of the free flow of capital and investment. A new trend of the 1990s was the 'rating' of countries by ratings agencies and other proxies, in order to reassure 'the markets' that reform was on track.[40]

The worlds of banking and finance experienced similar transformations. In the United States, the 1933 Glass-Steagall legislation had separated commercial and investment banking. Commercial banking was tightly supervised and interest rates, products and geographical markets were strictly regulated. The main source of profit came from interest income (the difference between interest earned on loans and interest paid on deposits). A mutually reinforcing combination of technological change and deregulation started in the US in the 1980s. It spread progressively to the entire world, greatly accelerating in the 1990s.[41] With the lifting of restrictions on capital movements, financial markets became increasingly interconnected and 'financial market regulators no longer held full sway over their regulatory territory'. [42]

Although Glass-Steagall was only formally scrapped in 1999, barriers separating various types of finance had been slowly but surely disappearing. Financial institutions reinvented themselves accordingly. Among the first to move away from traditional commercial banking were J. P. Morgan and Bankers Trust, the latter redefining itself as a 'risk manager' and creating a variety of new 'derivatives' designed to fulfil a variety of commercial and investment needs.[43] Soon, innovation in products and risk-management techniques took centre stage. Deregulation and technological change allowed the creation of a wide array of financial products. Traditional loans and other financial assets were securitized – that is, converted into tradable securities that can be bought and sold on the market. 'Financial engineers' were in a position to create an infinite variety of new financial products through a process of slicing and splicing. For example, the interest and principal components of a bond could be split and sold separately, or they could be combined with other instruments and packaged as a single product.[44]

During the same period, the Islamic World witnessed major political, economic, religious and demographic transformations: the emergence of new Islamic states following the collapse of the Soviet Union, the rise of 'Asian tigers' (principally Malaysia), a changing oil market, the emergence of new Islamic middle classes and the growing Islamic presence in the West. Most striking of all was the phenomenon of Islamic revivalism, which contradicted the dominant view that the march of secularization was inexorable.

There were many reasons for this revivalism: the vacuum left by secular ideologies, socialism in particular, that were discredited both politically and economically, as well as the moral outrage at the extent of oppression and corruption; the attempts by certain groups, especially among the lower classes and those traditionally underrepresented in government, to secure a place for themselves in the political arena; the identity crisis and the search for roots in a world dominated by commercialism and materialism and in settings where rapid demographic growth combined with poverty and unemployment to produce a sense of hopelessness. All these factors were intensified by economic problems and political demands. The decline in oil prices led to significant job cutbacks in oil-producing countries, falling remittances and the return home of migrant workers to dire economic conditions. Most governments, strapped for cash, embarked on austerity policies, which had the dual consequences of increasing discontent and providing Islamic movements with the opportunity to fill a vacuum. Schools and hospitals, along with a host of welfare services, were increasingly run by Islamic groups. Islam had also become, if not the language of protest, at the very least a means by which opposition could be expressed with minimal government interference.[45]

Throughout the Muslim World, the manifestations of religious sentiment had taken a variety of forms – ranging from demands for an Islamization of political life to a rise in 'pietism' – that did not attract much media attention. Thus, while Hamas, the Hezbollah or the Taliban were household words, few people outside the Islamic World have ever heard of the non-political Jamaat Tabligh, which, in terms of numbers and impact, far outstripped fundamentalist organizations.[46] Such aspects of the Islamic revival were reflected in increased emphasis upon religious observance (mosque attendance, fasting), religious programming on television, as well as dynamic *daawa* (missionary) movements aimed at converting non-Muslims, and also at bringing Muslims to deepen their religious knowledge and commitment.

Islam also played a growing role in civil society. Even, and at times especially, in those countries where political Islam was actively fought by governments, Islam had penetrated deeply within associations, ranging from trade unions to civic organizations to student groups, becoming part of the mainstream of society.[47] Even secular countries such as Egypt and Yemen responded by upgrading the role of the *shari'a* in the constitution.

The rise of Islamism was not necessarily incompatible with the values and ideology of the 'New World Order'. Two areas of convergence between the Islamist critique of statism and the Washington Consensus should be emphasized. First is the Islamic commitment to private property, free enterprise and the sanctity of contracts, in contrast to state-led economic policy and the arbitrary decisions that went along with a strong state bureaucracy. The Koranic emphasis on private property rights and Islam's positive view of commerce and profits were invoked to pursue policies of privatization and deregulation. Even fundamentalist Islamist regimes have, on occasion, openly embraced neo-liberalism. Thus, in the Sudan between 1992 and the end of 1993, economics minister Abdul Rahim Hamdi – a disciple of Milton Friedman and incidentally a former Islamic banker in London – did not hesitate to implement the harshest free-market remedies dictated by the International Monetary Fund. He said he was committed to transforming the country's statist economy 'according to free-market rules, because this is how an Islamic economy should function'.[48] In many countries, Islam became the tool of entrepreneurs seeking to get around restrictive regulation and an instrumental factor in privatization and deregulation – and the best excuse to disengage the state from the economy.[49] Insofar as financial liberalization is 'the process of reducing government control over the allocation of credit', [50] Islamic bankers were bound to make common cause with economic liberals. In countries such as Malaysia and Bahrain, governments used Islam as a tool of financial modernization – essentially as a way of countering the 'rentier' inclinations of the private sector and the anti-competitive leanings of the beneficiaries from the status quo.[51]

Second is the parallel between the 'privatization of welfare' (through reliance on *zakat*, philanthropy and other religiously-based redistribution schemes) advocated by Islamists and the downsizing of the state that was central to the new ideological consensus. Private virtue thus met efficiency: by helping the poor, the wealthy become better human beings; and the voluntary provision of charity reduces the need for public welfare organizations that are usually costlier to run. Islamic charities – ironically, given the future turn of events – were thus in tune with the ideological and political mood of the times.[52]

The second aggiornamento of Islamic finance

By the late 1980s modern Islamic finance seemed to be going nowhere. For one thing, the experiment had proved disappointing. More significantly, the transformation of global finance derailed the assumptions of the aggiornamento of the 1970s. Most of the ambitious cooperative and regulatory schemes devised in the early years of Islamic finance[53] were overtaken by events. Neither the infrastructure not the culture was propitious to profit-and-loss sharing. To many, Islamic finance appeared as an exercise in semantics: Islamic banks were really no different from conventional banks, except in their use of euphemisms to disguise interest.[54] The image of Islamic banks was also tainted by the failure of Islamic Money Management Companies (IMMCs) in Egypt in 1988 and by the collapse of the Bank of Credit and Commerce International (BCCI) in 1991.[55] It became common to dismiss Islamic banking as a passing fad, one associated with the oil boom and the fleeting belief in a 'New World Order'. In reality, Islamic finance was on the cusp of a major boom, albeit after undergoing major changes in both doctrine and practices: for most of the 1990s, Islamic finance experienced annual double-digit growth.[56]

Islamic finance grew more decentralized and diverse, reflecting the religious, political and economic transformations of the Islamic World. Religious reawakening, combined with the excesses of global finance, was bound to generate interest in a financial system rooted in traditional values. The sheer 'amorality' of contemporary finance has generated an interest in ethical approaches.[57] Insofar as Western or Judaeo-Christian finance had become thoroughly secularized (the religious origin of many financial institutions has long receded from the public consciousness),[58] the idea of Islamic finance struck a chord in a context of rising pietism.[59] Insofar as Islam held a positive view of economic activities while providing for a strict ethical framework, Islamic finance offered the potential for a fruitful compromise between finance and ethics.

A standard, if usually vague, demand by Islamic groups everywhere had been to Islamicize the financial system, or at the very least to allow for Islamic financial products. So typically, as banking laws were being overhauled, some provision was made to permit, if not promote, some form of Islamic finance. And following the breakdown of the Soviet Union, one of the hallmarks of newly independent Islamic states was the announcement of the creation of Islamic institutions.

In contrast to the first aggiornamento, which had been dominated by literal, legalistic and scholastic interpretations, the second aggiornamento focused principally on the spirit, or the 'moral economy', of Islam, in order to assess the compatibility of modern financial instruments with Islamic principles. Its modernist slant disavowed the view that whatever did not exist in the early days of Islam is necessarily un-Islamic.[60] Challenging common perceptions that Islam is rigid and fossilized, it emphasized those adaptive mechanisms – such as departures from tradition for reasons of local custom ('urf), public interest (maslaha), or necessity (darura) – that have allowed the religion to survive and thrive on every continent over the last fourteen centuries.

The transformations affecting politics, economics and finance happened to facilitate the growth of Islamic institutions. Where interest income was once the cornerstone of banking, its relative importance has steadily declined in recent years. As a result of competitive pressures and thinning margins, most financial institutions had increasingly been relying on fees and commission, rather than on interest income. On traditional banking operations – deposit-taking and lending – banks discovered that tacking on fees was as inconspicuous as it was lucrative. More significantly, banks were now engaged in financial operations – such as the creation and sales of derivatives and other new products – that did not directly involve interest. The downgrading of interest allowed sidestepping – to some extent – the most controversial aspect of banking and moving beyond debates about *riba*. Another factor was the convergence between the profit-and-loss-sharing logic of traditional Islamic finance and many modern financing techniques. Indeed, modern finance saw a sharp increase of risk-sharing arrangements, along the lines of the merchant banking or the venture capital model, where the financier is no longer a lender but a partner.[61] Financial innovation made possible by deregulation allowed the creation of specially tailored Islamic products. In the preceding years, financial institutions could only sell a narrow range of financial products. Now there were far fewer constraints on the products that 'financial engineers' could devise. The wide array of available products included mutual funds, and it was possible to envisage a product for every need, religious or otherwise.[62]

Whereas the early years of Islamic finance were dominated by Saudi Arabia,[63] and to a lesser extent Pakistan and Egypt, the second aggiornamento reflected the diversity of the Islamic World and its new geo-economics. Hence, the important roles played by Malaysia and by Islamic communities living in the West. In the new world of global finance, *riba* was no longer the central theological sticking point. Concerns over *gharar* (risk, uncertainty) drew the attention of scholars.[64] Islamic finance also became more pragmatic, and was increasingly converging with conventional institutions. By the 1990s, most conventional banks in the Islamic World started offering the option of 'Islamic windows'. Major Western institutions such as Citibank, HSBC and UBS developed significant Islamic departments or subsidiaries. In Europe and America, Islamic institutions were established in order to cater to local Islamic communities. Financial institutions in countries such as Malaysia (where Islamic finance is a tool of economic development and financial modernization) were aiming their increasingly sophisticated and diverse products at non-Muslims. And much of the new *ijtihad* on Islamic finance is conducted in cooperation between conventional and Islamic institutions, and often outside the Islamic World (at the Harvard Islamic Finance Information Program (HIFIP), for example). The fastest-growing segments of the industry proved to be outside traditional banking products and in areas of finance that were either initially dismissed as Islamically unacceptable – such as insurance or *takaful* – or that barely existed at the time of the first aggiornamento – Islamic mutual funds, for example. All those new possibilities explain why, in many Islamic countries, Islamic institutions were often more innovative and dynamic than their conventional counterparts.[65]

Not all the changes in the broader environment were positive. In certain respects, the incipient hostility of the 'New World Order' to Islam had direct and indirect impacts on financial institutions. In the pre-September 11th period the three main countries that have officially Islamicized their entire financial systems were subjected to a variety of financial sanctions. Iran and the Sudan have long held the 'rogue' label because of their alleged support of international terrorism. Pakistan was subjected to sanctions in 1998, following its response in kind to nuclear testing by India. Also, the advent of global regulation robbed national regulators of some of their previous autonomy. Central bankers in the Islamic World had to comply with the dictates of international bodies such as the Basle Committee on Banking Supervision of the Bank of International Settlements, the International Monetary Fund, the World Bank and the World Trade Organization. They were expected to impose new rules and norms (Basle or Cooke ratios, Core Principles of Banking Supervision, and so on) on the banks they supervised.[66]

Although most Islamic techniques had conventional counterparts, they did not always fit conveniently within existing regulatory regimes. The main financing techniques often implied specific contractual obligations and different levels of risk than their conventional counterparts. Islamic institutions considered that they should not be subjected to the same prudential ratios and capital requirements as conventional banks. Also, from the standpoint of ownership and control, many Islamic institutions could not comply with the 'comprehensive consolidated supervision by the home country regulator' requirements. Indeed, many Islamic financial institutions belonged to, or were otherwise associated with, transnational groups such as Geneva-based Dar al-Maal al-Islami (DMI) or the (now Bahrain-based) Dallah al-Baraka Group. Both are controlled by Saudi citizens, respectively Prince Mohammad Al-Faisal and Sheikh Saleh Kamel, but do not operate commercial banks in their home country.

Other regulatory complications were posed by the nature of interest-free banking. In the United States, for example, Islamic financial institutions have found it hard to comply with the Truth in Lending Act, the federal regulation that governs full disclosure of terms and costs in lending transactions. The law required the use of the term 'annual percentage rate'. Even replacing it, as some have suggested, by a 'profit participation rate' would be tricky since it would mean the endorsement of the 'fixed, predetermined rate' concept to which many Islamic scholars object. Similarly, those institutions trying to offer Islamic mortgages to their clients had to obtain special permission from regulatory authorities. The attitude of many Western regulators could be summed up in a famous statement by Robin Leigh-Pemberton, the former governor of the Bank of England, to the effect that Islamic banking is 'a perfectly acceptable mode of investment, but it does not fall within the long-established and well-understood definition of what constitutes banking in this country'.[67]

An additional reason for the increased scrutiny of Islamic institutions was that they had come to the attention of international regulators at the time of the Bank of Credit and Commerce International (BCCI) scandal in 1991. Though not an Islamic bank, the 'rogue' institution did have an Islamic unit, and enjoyed close links to Islamic banks. Regulators from seven countries coordinated the closing and liquidation of the bank, and much of the recent jurisprudence on global supervision stems from that case.[68]

Islam in the New World Order

During the Gulf War of 1991, although most Islamic governments were part of the US-led coalition, Islamic public opinion seemed deeply divided. The presence of foreign troops in Saudi Arabia, the birthplace of Islam, was especially controversial. Later that year in Algeria, the Algerian Islamic Salvation Front (FIS) was poised to sweep the Algerian parliament in the first open elections in the history of the country, when the electoral process was cut short, touching off a bloody civil war. Throughout the Islamic world, Islamic parties and organizations had burst upon the political scene. Some were part of the existing institutional and electoral system, others operated outside of it. Even secular Turkey had a year-long experience with an Islamist prime minister.

The growing visibility of radical Islamists led many theorists of the 'New World Order' to assert that Islam was on a collision course with the liberal values of the 'New World Order'.[69] A number of academics, pundits and policy experts posited the fundamental incompatibility between Islam and Western values. Fears over global Islam had started with the Iranian revolution, and were later greatly amplified with the demise of Communism and the search for a new enemy. In certain foreign-policy circles, given the threat vacuum, 'Islamic fundamentalism' was often designated as the most likely successor to world Communism as the 'single greatest threat' to American interests.[70]

The theme of Islam as new global enemy soon became fashionable in certain policy circles.[71] The influential journal *Foreign Affairs*, published by the Council on Foreign Relations, carried a debate: 'Is Islam a Threat?' (Judith Miller answered 'yes', Leon Hadar answered 'no').[72] The debate was given, if not theoretical and historical depth, at least academic cachet when Harvard University's Samuel Huntington wrote his famous *Foreign Affairs* article 'The Clash of Civilizations?', which argued that future conflicts would break out along civilizational lines, with Islam and Confucianism epitomizing those 'civilizations' that were inherently hostile to Western values.

The Huntington thesis, later expanded into a book, was appealing to foreign-policy experts who, since the end of Communism, had been frantically looking for a new foreign-policy doctrine. Anti-Islamic punditry became something of a cottage industry. Anti-US proclamations and declarations of *jihad* (or holy war) against the West by radical groups provided ample 'proof' of sinister designs. The 'threat' made good copy and was taken up by journalists who were quick to relay, even amplify, it, and 'experts', as many of them made a career out of 'explaining' its roots.

Since Islamic finance was neither well-known nor well-understood, those circles – as well as those people who found the notion of Islamic finance quaint – tended to make the assumption that its *raison d'être* was to fund terrorism.[73] For those who assumed that Islam had sinister designs, Islamic institutions could only look suspicious. In reality, as we saw, Islamic financial institutions were firmly embedded within the international status quo. There had been one instance where Islamic finance had been used to upset the status quo: it was in the Sudan, where Sheikh Hassan al-Turabi took advantage of his association with the Faisal Bank to build his power base. Other 'suspicious links' could be found, though they were primarily linked to the 'blowback' from the 'Afghan trap': Islamic institutions had surrounded themselves with a broad array of religious figures, a few of whom turned from friendly 'assets' into dangerous enemies.[74]

ISLAMIC FINANCE IN THE NEW WORLD ORDER

The post-September 11th era

The events of 11 September 2001 marked the beginning of a new era that seemed to justify the 'Islam is the new enemy' view. The attacks against the World Trade Center and the Pentagon, instantly interpreted as an 'act of war' committed by transnational Islamic fundamentalists, reordered priorities and transformed international relations.[75] The 'clash of civilizations' argument went mainstream, as anti-Islamic writers ranging from scholars, such as Bernard Lewis,[76] to policy entrepreneurs such as Daniel Pipes and Steven Emerson, and journalists such as Stephen Schwartz, exerted unprecedented influence on public opinion and policy-making.[77] Voices friendly to Islam were marginalized and subjected to unrelenting attacks.[78]

Although President Bush took pains to explain that the war against terrorism 'was not a war against Islam, a religion of peace', Islam was a religion under siege. In his 20 September 2001 speech to Congress, President Bush asked: 'Why do they hate us?' He foreclosed any discussion of US foreign policy when he uttered another famous line: 'if you're not with us, you're with the terrorists'. As a result, most debates have focused on the presumed essence of Islam and its problematic relations with the West, with the nineteen hijackers made to look like proxies for 1.2 billion Muslims worldwide. For Bernard Lewis, the root of Islamic rage and resentment could be found in 'the hatred of modernism and secularism'. In a bestselling book published shortly after September 11th, he revisited the rivalry between 'Islam' and the West: the Islamic civilizations, once dominant in science, mathematics and medicine, had turned into 'poor, weak, and ignorant' nations ruled by 'shabby tyrannies ... modern only in their apparatus of repression and terror'. The contrast between the Western values and Islamic ones was striking, since Muslim societies lacked any kind of freedom: 'freedom of the mind from constraint and indoctrination, to question and inquire; freedom of the economy from corrupt and pervasive mismanagement; freedom of women from male oppression; freedom of citizens from tyranny'.[79] But in a nation stunned by the attacks, such analyses sounded plausible, especially since broad, if unwarranted, generalizations (about 'the clash of civilizations', 'them' *versus* 'us', 'good' *versus* 'evil') were all admirably suited to a media culture characterized by soundbites and binary, Manichaean thinking.[80]

The war on terror and Islamic finance

Islamic finance, which had long been perceived as a moderating element in Islam,[81] found itself as never before in the crosshairs of law enforcement. The magnitude of the attacks of September 11th led to suggestions that 'sophisticated financial networks' were behind the attacks. In the 'new kind of war' against terror, the uniforms would be, in the words of Defense Secretary Donald Rumsfeld, 'bankers' pinstripes and programmers' grunge just as assuredly as desert camouflage'.[82] And indeed, the first battle took place on the financial terrain. On Sunday, 23 September, flanked by Treasury Secretary Paul O'Neill and Secretary of State Colin Powell, President Bush announced: 'We have launched a strike on the financial foundation of the global terror network.' A presidential decree simultaneously blacklisted twenty-seven individuals and groups. Since most assets linked to terrorism were outside the US, the President gave notice to the international financial community: 'If you do business with terrorists, if you support or sponsor them, you will not do business with the United States of America.' Similar announcements have since become routine, as more accounts were frozen and more financial regulations imposed.[83]

The template for the financial war was the money-laundering apparatus in place since the war on drugs of the 1980s. The rationale for the surveillance and control of financial flows was twofold: first, they could untangle money puzzles and yield a great deal of information about subversive and otherwise shadowy groups; second, the use of economic and financial tools – embargoes, asset seizures, and the like – would eventually 'take profit out of crime'.

More people learned about Islamic finance. A statement made by former National Security Adviser Sandy Berger, shortly after September 11th, epitomizes the general level of ignorance on the subject. The man who spearheaded during his tenure at the White House (1996–2000) the surveillance of Bin Laden's networks casually stated that it would be difficult to track down Osama Bin Laden's money because it was hidden in 'underground banking, Islamic banking facilities'.[84] And it took six months for Treasury Secretary Paul O'Neill, the official in charge of the financial war on terror, to 'learn', in March 2002 following meetings in Saudi Arabia, Kuwait and Bahrain, that Islamic banking was 'a legitimate way of doing business'.[85]

In a business where reputation matters greatly, the image of leading Islamic institutions suffered a devastating blow. At a November 2001 Islamic Banking Conference in Bahrain, the two leading figures in Islamic finance expressed dismay at the smear campaigns against their institutions. Prince Muhammad Al-Faisal declared: 'We all condemn the September 11th attack on the World Trade Center and Pentagon as a heinous crime, which has nothing to do with Islam or Muslims as a whole. The West is raising various questions. But these questions are not raised with us, but with "experts" who do not know anything about this.' Asked about the freezing of assets of some Islamic institutions, he said: 'If they wanted to do it merely on the basis of suspicion let them do it. Of course, it is fair to freeze anyone's assets if there is proof and there should be remedy if they do so without any proof.' As for Sheikh Saleh Kamel, founder of the al Baraka Group and chairman of the Council of Islamic Banks, he declared: 'The concept of Islamic banking is one of the creative methods of Islam to serve the economic and social welfare of Muslims. But some circles tried to use the September 11th attacks to launch a campaign under the false pretext that these Islamic banks are the source for financing terrorism.'[86]

Indeed, since the attacks of September 11th, a cloud of suspicion has been hanging over Islamic financial institutions. In a climate of generalized suspicion, Islamic banks – and more generally banks from the Islamic world – were considered guilty until proven innocent. 'Guilt by association' hit Islamic institutions from different sides. With every new list of 'suspect organizations' – which included banks such as Bank al-Taqwa, hawalas (money-transfer outfits) such as Al-Baraka Investment and Development Company, and Islamic charities such as Al-Wafa – there would be speculation as to who would be next. Press accounts that the US Treasury had asked foreign bank-regulators, including the Saudi Arabian Monetary Authority, to place Islamic banks under close surveillance kept such speculation alive.[87] Also, repeated attacks on Islamic charities (on the grounds that some charitable funds had ended up in the hands of terrorists) drew attention to the involvement of Islamic banks in the collection and distribution of zakat.

Islamic financial institutions were also affected in their dealings with international banks. As 'know your customer' rules were tightened, new rules on correspondent banking required that banks ensure that none of their correspondents was, wittingly or unwittingly, involved in financing terror. As international banks undertook a massive review of their correspondent relationships, Islamic banks were required to prove a negative, and many could not pass muster. (In addition, many leading international banks decided to refuse deposits from 'politically exposed' individuals, whose assets could in the future be confiscated. Following the embarrassing experience of having to trace and hand back fortunes of deposed leaders such as Ferdinand Marcos in the Philippines, Joseph Mobutu in Zaire and Sani Abacha in Nigeria, and to avoid costly information requests and seizure orders from law enforcement agencies, a few banks have even refused to deal with leaders from the Islamic world – including members of the once much-courted Saudi royal family.)[88]

Then there was the Saudi connection. Since September 11th, Saudi Arabia had been subjected to unrelenting criticism, first from the media and then from within the increasingly vocal neo-conservative wing of the US government. One revealing incident was a leak concerning a secret briefing by a Rand Corporation analyst to the Defense Policy Board, an advisory group of intellectuals and former senior officials.[89] The analyst, Laurent Murawiec, had stated: 'The Saudis are active at every level of the terror chain, from planners to financiers, from cadre to foot-soldier, from ideologist to cheerleader.' Calling Saudi Arabia 'the kernel of evil, the prime mover, the most dangerous opponent' who 'supports our enemies and attacks our allies', he suggested that the US 'target' its oilfields and overseas financial assets.[90] Despite the dubious credentials of the 'expert',[91] his affiliation with the prestigious think tank and the sponsorship of the influential hawk Richard Perle (the former Pentagon official who chaired the Defense Policy Board), the fact that the briefing took place – and that it was leaked – reflected the power of the anti-Saudi constituency within the US Administration.

Similarly, a report prepared by a self-styled 'nonpartisan' committee of 'experts on terrorist finances' sponsored by the Council of Foreign Relations in New York concluded: 'It is worth stating clearly and unambiguously, if only because official US government spokespersons have not: for years, individuals and charities based in Saudi Arabia have been the most important source of funds for Al Qaeda, and for years Saudi officials have turned a blind eye to this problem.' The committee, headed by Maurice R. Greenberg, chairman and chief executive of the American International Group, included William H. Webster, former director of the Federal Bureau of Investigation and the Central Intelligence Agency; David Cohen, deputy commissioner for intelligence of the New York City Police Department; and William F. Wechsler, former director for transnational threats at the National Security Council. One of its members, Stuart E. Eizenstat, a former deputy treasury secretary, expressly deplored the fact that the panel's conclusion was not more widely shared within the Administration, stating: 'There's always been a tendency to treat the kingdom with kid gloves because of its economic and strategic importance.'[92]

The new narrative mixed facts – Saudi Arabia had promoted its Wahhabi brand of Islam; it had generously funded Islamic groups worldwide and in particular the 'Afghan Arabs' who were behind the attacks; Osama Bin Laden himself came from a prominent Saudi family; and fifteen of the nineteen hijackers were Saudi citizens – with a new storyline – the Saudis paid off extremists so that they would stir trouble abroad and not on Saudi soil – that left out the geopolitical context explained earlier.[93]

It was only a matter of time before the question of financial compensation would arise. Daniel Pipes demanded that the Saudis disburse $100 billion.[94] New York Senator Charles Schumer suggested that $3.1 billion seized from Muslim charities should be used to compensate American victims.[95] On 15 August 2002, lawyers for relatives of 600 victims filed in US District Court in Alexandria, VA, what one of them called 'the lawsuit of the twenty-first century'. Leading figures of Islamic finance and major Islamic institutions – Prince Mohammad Al-Faisal and his Dar al-Maal al-Islami, Sheikh Saleh Kamel and his Dallah al-Baraka Group, the Al-Rajhi Banking and Investment Corporation and so on – were among eighty defendants accused of racketeering, wrongful death, negligence and conspiracy. (Other defendants included two Saudi Princes,[96] the government of Sudan, seven banks and eight Islamic foundations.) The fifteen-count lawsuit, modelled after action filed against Libya in the Pan Am flight 103 disaster, aimed 'to force the sponsors of terror into the light and subject them to the rule of law' by seeking 'an amount in excess of $1 trillion'. Other copycat suits followed. True to 'Sutton's Law',[97] they all included financial institutions and deep-pocketed Saudis among the defendants.

As a result of these developments, there was a dramatic slowdown in the integration of the major Islamic institutions in the global economy. Sheikh Saleh Kamel went as far as to call for a repatriation of Islamic funds, declaring: 'The West has always been hostile to Islamic banking, and 10 years ago, Al-Baraka Bank was even closed down in London. Therefore, it is time Muslim financial institutions and individuals bring back their money from the West to invest in Muslim countries and develop this industry in our region.'[98] The calls for repatriation of funds did not go unheeded. Islamic institutions suffered a blow, but demand for Islamic products has continued unabated, and the number of conventional institutions offering Islamic windows or Islamic products has kept growing, both inside and outside the Islamic World.[99]

Islamist politics after September 11th

Judging from the results of legislative and municipal elections conducted under relatively free conditions in the Islamic World between September and November 2002, political Islam is far from dead. In Pakistan, Turkey, Morocco, Algeria and Bahrain, moderate but dissident Islamist groups achieved, despite numerous obstacles, significant gains. In Bahrain's first elections in thirty years, Islamists managed, despite boycotts by leading Islamic groups, to win 24 of the 40 contested seats in the 80-member Parliament (the remaining 40 seats are filled by the ruler). In Algeria, where the Islamic Salvation Front, the over-whelming victor of the aborted 1991–2 elections, did not take part in the municipal elections, and other Islamist parties where banned, the Islah and other Islamist parties held their ground behind the resurgent National Liberation Front. In Morocco, where the most important Islamist party boycotted the elec-tion, the Justice and Development Party managed to triple its seats in Parliament, winning 42 out of the 325 seats. Moroccan political scientist Muhammad Darif explained these results in terms of a backlash: 'Arab and Muslim populations think the war against terrorism is nothing but a war against Islam, the culture of Islam, the Arab culture. The Islamist parties have been able to exploit this.'[100]

In Pakistan, a crucial ally in the war against terrorism, Islamist candidates won 78 out of 392 parliamentary seats. (In earlier elections, they were never able to capture more than 10 seats.) In the two provinces adjoining Afghanistan, the Muttahida Majlis-e-Amal, a coalition of Islamist groups opposed to the government's role in the US-led war on terror, won a majority of the votes. Similarly, in staunchly secular Turkey, the AK (Justice and Development) Party, a new political party with Islamic roots, managed to overcome institu-tional and political hurdles – albeit after recasting itself from Islamism to social conservatism, to win 360 out of 550 seats in Parliament, becoming the first party in years to be in a position to govern without a coalition partner.

These developments have caught the West by surprise. Indeed, it was assumed that the only choice was between secularism and radical Islamism. Many in the Bush Administration share Bernard Lewis's view to the effect that 'moderation' and 'pragmatism' are simply tactical ploys used by radical fundamentalists to attain power.[101] The nature of the political 'Islams' that will define the coming years will depend on the interplay among countless factors, some related to the Islamic World itself – the problems of persistent poverty, corruption and alien-ation, as well as the gap between rulers and ruled – and others related to the interaction between Islam and the West. On that front, suspicion reigns, and both camps include significant factions eager to turn the clash of civilizations into a self-fulfilling prophecy.

NOTES

1. Malcolm H. Kerr, *The Arab Cold War: Gamal 'Ab'd al-Nasir and his rivals 1958–1969* (Oxford: Oxford University Press, 1970).

2. Edward Mortimer, *Faith and Power: The Politics of Islam* (New York: Random House, 1982), p. 177–80.

3. George Lenczowski, *The Middle East in World Affairs* (Ithaca, NY: Cornell University Press, 1980), p. 603.

4. Nazih N. M. Ayubi, 'The Political Revival of Islam', in *International Journal of Middle East Studies*, December 1980, p. 489.

5. Mortimer, *Faith and Power*, p. 178.

6. Ibrahim Warde, *Islamic Finance in the Global Economy* (Edinburgh: Edinburgh University Press, 2000), pp. 112–17.

7. Mortimer, *Faith and Power*, p. 218.

8. Daniel Yergin, *The Prize: The Epic Quest for Oil, Money and Power* (New York: Simon and Schuster, 1991), p. 595; see also Ali D. Johany, *The Myth of the OPEC Cartel* (New York: Wiley, 1981); Sheikh R. Ali, *Oil and Power: Political Dynamics in the Middle East* (New York: Palgrave McMillan, 1987).

9. Yergin, *The Prize*, pp. 563–87.

10. There had been scattered attempts at interest-free banking in earlier years, such as the Mit Ghamr experiment in Egypt (1963–67), but they were usually short-lived as well as modest in size. See Warde, *Islamic Finance*, pp. 73–4.

11. It was, however, more a declaration of intent than of actual policies. Indeed, at the time of writing one can argue whether the Pakistani banking system is truly Islamic. See Warde, *Islamic Finance*, pp. 112–17.

12. Warde, *Islamic Finance*, Chapters 3 and 4.

13. Until recently, the Christian and Judaic traditions had comparable misgivings about interest. See Rodney Wilson, *Economics, Ethics and Religion: Jewish, Christian and Muslim Economic Thought* (New York: New York University Press, 1997).

14. *Zakat*, or alms-giving, is one of the 'five pillars' of Islam. The others are the profession of faith, daily prayers, fasting during Ramadan and, for those who can afford it, a pilgrimage to Mecca.

15. Somewhat paradoxically, Saudi Arabia – which relied heavily on its interest income – was ambivalent when it came to promoting Islamic finance at home. See Warde, *Islamic Finance*, pp. 207–8.

16. Warde, Islamic Finance, p. 212–13.

17. Clement M. Henry, *The Mediterranean Debt Crescent: Money and Power in Algeria, Egypt, Morocco, Tunisia, and Turkey* (Gainesville, FL: University Press of Florida, 1996), p. 125.

18. Hamid Algabid, *Les banques islamiques* (Paris: Economics, 1990), p. 122.

19. Alan Richards and John Waterbury, *A Political Economy of the Middle East* (Boulder, CO: Westview Press, 1996), p. 71.

20. Michel Galloux, *Finance islamique et pouvoir politique: le cas de l'Egypte moderne* (Paris: Presses Universitaires de France, 1997), p. 63.

21. See, for example, Jack Anderson with James Boyd, *Fiasco! The Real Story Behind the Disastrous Worldwide Energy Crisis – Richard Nixon's Oilgate* (New York: Times

Books, 1983), p. 256.

22. Lenczowski, *The Middle East in World Affairs*, p. 214.
23. Ibid. p. 607.
24. Ibid. p. 608.
25. Mortimer, *Faith and Power*, p. 180.
26. Ali E. Hillal Dessouki (ed.), *Islamic Resurgence in the Arab World* (New York: Praeger, 1982), p. 91.
27. Emmanuel Sivan, 'La revanche de la société civile', in Alain Gresh (ed.), *Un péril islamiste?* (Brussels: Editions Complexe, 1994), p. 28.
28. Lenczowski, *The Middle East in World Affairs*, p. 609.
29. Although the Iranian Islamic revolution was of momentous political import, its immediate impact on Islamic economics and finance was negligible. Iran had played no part in the Islamic finance experiment of the 1970s. When it did undertake, in 1983, the Islamization of its financial system, it was under conditions approximating autarky: the country was in the middle of a deadly conflict with Iraq (1980–88), and, still entangled in major lawsuits with foreign debtors and creditors, was a pariah in the international financial community.
30. The dominant literature on Islam in those years focused on the Shiite–Sunni divide. From a policy standpoint, Iran was perceived as a unique case: one of very few predominantly Shiite countries. Its relations with the US, and especially the US role in bringing the Shah back to power, was the key to its anti-Americanism. On that subject, see James Bill, *The Eagle and the Lion* (New Haven, CT: Yale University Press, 1988).
31. A CIA term referring to the negative unintended consequences of certain actions. See Chalmers Johnson, *Blowback: The Costs and Consequences of Empire* (New York: Metropolitan Books, 2000).
32. A few months after an Islamic Republic had been proclaimed in Iran, the Grand Mosque in Mecca was seized by religious extremists. Only the intervention of French and other special forces restored order. In 1981, Anwar Sadat was assassinated by an Islamist organization. The secular pro-Soviet regime of Syria had problems of its own with the Muslim Brotherhood, resulting in the Hama massacres of 1982. In the 1980s, 'Islamic terrorism' took centre stage. A number of terrorist incidents, inside and outside the Muslim World, were traced to Islamic extremists or to one of the other 'rogue states' (at various times the list included Iran, Iraq, Libya, Syria and the Sudan). In Lebanon, pro-Iranian Hezbollah attacked the US Marine barracks, causing the deaths of many soldiers, before engaging in a kidnapping campaign against Westerners.
33. Bob Woodward, *Veil: The Secret Wars of the CIA 1981–1987* (New York: Simon and Schuster, 1990).
34. John K. Cooley, *Unholy Wars: Afghanistan, America and International Terrorism* (London: Pluto Press, 1999).
35. *Le nouvel observateur*, 15 January 1998.
36. Clement M. Henry and Robert Springborg, *Globalization and the Politics of Development in the Middle East* (Cambridge: Cambridge University Press, 2001).
37. Deepak Lal, *The Poverty of Development Economics* (New Brunswick, NJ: Harvard University Press, 1985). See also Richard E. Feinberg and Valeriana Kallab (eds), *Adjustment Crisis in the Third World* (New Brunswick, NJ: Transaction Books, 1984).

38. Daniel Yergin and Joseph Stanislaw, *The Commanding Heights: The Battle Between Government and the Marketplace That Is Remaking the Modern World* (New York: Simon and Schuster, 1998).

39. Ibrahim Warde, 'Les faiseurs de révolution libérale', *Le Monde diplomatique*, May 1992.

40. Ibrahim Warde, 'Ces officines qui notent les Etats', *Le Monde diplomatique*, February 1997.

41. Martin Mayer, *The Bankers: The Next Generation* (New York: Truman Talley Books/ Dutton, 1997).

42. Richard O'Brien, *Global Financial Integration: The End of Geography* (New York: Council on Foreign Relations Press, 1992), p. 1.

43. Roy C. Smith, *Comeback: The Restoration of American Banking Power in the New Economy* (Cambridge, MA: Harvard Business School Press, 1993), p. 4.

44. Keith Redhead, *Financial Derivatives: An Introduction to Futures, Forwards, Options and Swaps* (New York: Prentice Hall, 1997).

45. John Esposito, *The Islamic Threat: Myth or Reality* (Oxford: Oxford University Press, 1991), pp. 132–6. See also Paul Salem, *Bitter Legacy: Ideology and Politics in the Arab World* (Syracuse, NY: Syracuse University Press, 1994), p. 260; Emmanuel Sivan, *Radical Islam* (New Haven, CT: Yale University Press, 1985); Gilles Kepel, *Muslim Extremism in Egypt: The Prophet and Pharaoh* (Berkeley, CA: University of California Press, 1986); Olivier Carré, *L'Islam laïque ou le retour à la Grande Tradition* (Paris: Armand Colin, 1993); Gilles Kepel, *La revanche de Dieu: Chrétiens, juifs et musulmans à la reconquête du monde* (Paris: Editions du Seuil, 1991); Gilles Kepel, *Jihad, expansion et déclin de l'islamisme* (Paris: Gallimard, 2000); Olivier Roy, *L'échec de l'Islam politique* (Paris: Editions du Seuil, 1992).

46. Yahya Sadowski, '"Just" a Religion: For the Tablighi Jama'at, Islam is not totalitarian', *The Brookings Review*, Summer 1996, Vol. 14 No. 3, pp. 34–5.

47. Esposito, *The Islamic Threat*, p. 132.

48. Judith Miller, *God Has Ninety-Nine Names: A Reporter's Journey through a Militant Middle East* (New York: Simon and Schuster, 1996), p. 144.

49. Leonard Binder, *Islamic Liberalism: A Critique of Developmental Ideologies* (Chicago, IL: University of Chicago Press, 1988).

50. Stephan Haggard, Chung H. Lee, and Sylvia Maxfield (eds), *The Politics of Finance in Developing Countries* (Ithaca, NY: Cornell University Press, 1993), p. 314.

51. See Georges Corm, 'Nouvel ordre regional, competition économique et injustices fiscales: A quand l'ajustement structurel du secteur privé dans le monde arabe?', *Le Monde diplomatique*, December 1994.

52. Ibrahim Warde, 'The Financial War on Terror', unpublished manuscript.

53. Mohammed Ariff (ed.), *Monetary and Fiscal Economics of Islam* (Jeddah: International Centre for Research in Islamic Economics, 1982).

54. Ibrahim Warde, 'The Revitalization of Islamic Profit-and-Loss Sharing: Lessons from Western Venture Capital', in *Proceedings of the Third Harvard University Forum on Islamic Finance* (Cambridge, MA: Harvard University, 2000).

55. Though not itself an Islamic bank, BCCI had set up in 1984 an Islamic Banking Unit in London, which at its peak had $1.4 billion in deposits, and had generally made heavy use of Islamic rhetoric and symbolism. More importantly, however, the collapse of the bank brought Islamic institutions into the international limelight

and raised questions about the management and regulation of transnational banks. Of BCCI's $589 million in 'unrecorded deposits' (which allowed the bank to manipulate its accounts), the major part – $245 million – belonged to the Faisal Islamic Bank of Egypt (FIBE). This amount was supposed to be used for commodity investments, though there was no evidence that such investments were ever made.

56. Warde, *Islamic Finance*, Chapters 4 and 5.
57. Ibrahim Warde, 'La derive des nouveaux produits financiers', *Le Monde diplomatique*, June 1994.
58. A couple of relatively recent examples illustrate the point. In late nineteenth-century Germany, Frederic Raiffesen, a Protestant, and in early twentieth-century Canada, Alphonse Desjardins, a Catholic, created mutual savings societies out of a moral/religious impulse (neither of them was a banker) to save poor farmers from the clutches of money-lenders. See Bernard Taillefer, *Guide de la Banque pour tous: Innovations africaines* (Paris: Karthala, 1996), p. 19.
59. Sadowski, '"Just" a Religion', pp. 34–5.
60. Frank E. Vogel and Samuel L. Hayes III, *Islamic Law and Finance: Religion, risk, and return* (The Hague: Kluwer Law International, 1998).
61. John W. Wilson, *The New Venturers: Inside the High-Stakes World of Venture Capital* (Reading, MA: Addison-Wesley, 1985).
62. See Ibrahim Warde, 'La dérive des nouveaux produits financiers', *Le Monde diplomatique*, July 1994.
63. A paradox worth noting is that although Saudi Arabia was instrumental in creating the modern Islamic banking system, it is one of the least hospitable countries to Islamic banks. The country has only one Islamic commercial bank, the Al-Rajhi Banking and Investment Corporation. Dar al-Maal al-Islami (DMI), the largest Islamic group, founded by Prince Mohammad Al-Faisal, a son of King Faisal, is based in Geneva, operates worldwide (through, among others, its 'Faisal Banks' subsidiaries), yet has no commercial operations in Saudi Arabia. To complicate things further, the DMI Group has nonetheless been a significant conduit of Saudi money and influence throughout the Islamic world. One possible explanation for the Saudi ambivalence is the fact that the issue could be politically, as well as religiously, explosive. Indeed, Saudi Arabia does not officially recognize the notion of interest, yet relies very heavily on interest income from its vast holdings. Recognizing certain banks as Islamic would also make all the other banks 'un-Islamic'. Saudi banks avoid the use of the word interest and describe their revenues as 'commissions', 'service charges' or 'bookkeeping fees'. See Peter W. Wilson, *A Question of Interest: The Paralysis of Saudi Banking* (Boulder, CO: Westview Press, 1991).
64. Warde, *Islamic Finance*, Chapter 3.
65. Roula Khalaf, 'Dynamism is held back by state control: As family dynasties stifle creativity in most of the industry, the Islamic sector is showing signs of the greatest vibrancy', *Financial Times*, 11 April 2000.
66. Warde, *Islamic Finance*, Chapter 10.
67. *Financial Times*, 18 November 1995.
68. Warde, *Islamic Finance*, pp. 184–7.
69. Samuel Huntington, *The Clash of Civilizations and the Remaking of World Order* (New York: Simon and Schuster, 1996), p. 70

70. For a more detailed discussion of the Islamic 'threat' in the New World Order, see Warde, *Islamic Finance*, pp. 214–20.
71. Alain Gresh, 'Quand l'islamisme menace le monde', *Le Monde diplomatique*, December 1993.
72. *Foreign Affairs*, Spring 1993.
73. Roland Jacquard, *Fatwa contre l'Occident* (Paris: Albin Michel, 1998), pp. 157–68.
74. Warde, *Islamic Finance*, pp. 214–23.
75. Bob Woodward, *Bush at War* (New York: Simon and Schuster, 2002).
76. Widely hailed as the 'preeminent expert' on Islam, Bernard Lewis was invited to the White House to 'explain' Islam.
77. Bernard Lewis, *What Went Wrong: Western Impact and Middle Eastern Response* (Oxford: Oxford University Press, 2001); Stephen Schwartz, *The Two Faces of Islam: The House of Sa'ud from Tradition to Terror* (New York: Doubleday, 2002); Steven Emerson, *American Jihad: The Terrorists Living Among Us* (New York: Free Press, 2002); Daniel Pipes, *Militant Islam Reaches America* (New York: W. W. Norton & Co., 2002).
78. Martin Kramer, *Ivory Towers on Sand: The Failure of Middle Eastern Studies in America* (Washington, DC: Institute for Near East Policy, 2001).
79. Bernard Lewis, 'The Roots of Muslim Rage', *The Atlantic Monthly*, September 1990.
80. Ibrahim Warde, 'Which God Is On Whose Side?', *Le Monde diplomatique*, September 2002.
81. Henry, *The Mediterranean Debt Crescent*, pp. 20–4.
82. *The New York Times*, 27 September 2001.
83. Warde, 'The Financial War'.
84. Gene J. Koprowski, 'Islamic Banking Is Not The Enemy', *The Wall Street Journal Europe*, 1 October 2001.
85. *The Wall Street Journal*, 12 March 2002.
86. *Gulf News*, 12 November 2001
87. *The Wall Street Journal*, 5 February 2002.
88. *The Guardian*, 17 July 2002.
89. *The Washington Post*, 10 July 2001.
90. *The Washington Post*, 6 August 2002.
91. Formerly associated with Lyndon La Rouche, Murawiec had no experience of the Arab world or Islam. See 'Le parcours atypique de Laurent Murawiec, consultant de la Rand', *Le Monde*, 12 August 2002.
92. *The New York Times*, 17 October 2002.
93. Schwartz, *The Two Faces of Islam*.
94. Daniel Pipes, 'Let the Saudis Pay for Terror', *The New York Post*, 15 April 2002.
95. *The Daily Star*, 27 July 2002.
96. In addition to Prince Mohammad Al-Faisal, his brother Prince Turki al-Faisal, the long-time head of Saudi intelligence, and Defence Minister Prince Sultan bin Abdul Aziz al-Saud.
97. Willie Sutton is the legendary bank-robber who, in answer to the question 'Why do you rob banks?', reportedly answered 'Because that's where the money is.'
98. *Gulf News*, 12 November 2001
99. Warde, 'The Financial War'.
100. *The New York Times*, 6 November 2002.
101. Judith Miller, *God Has Ninety-Nine Names*, p. 163.

3

The *Murabaha* Syndrome in Islamic Finance: Laws, Institutions and Politics

Tarik M. Yousef

INTRODUCTION

The observation half a century ago by Islamic intellectuals that in Muslim societies banking and finance, like other spheres of economic life, should be governed by religious tenets has undergone rapid transformation in the past few decades. Indeed, what began as an intellectual critique of Western-based financial systems by political movements in Muslim societies, and later on emerged as an area of research curiosity by Muslim social scientists, has now evolved into a broad field of academic and policy research across national and religious lines. Whereas early research dealt with the broad philosophical foundations of Islamic finance, recent analyses have employed greater conceptual and technical rigour to address specific problems of practical application. Even matters of legal interpretation, once the preview of religiously-trained scholars, have become a source of a rich exchange of views and counter-views across disciplinary lines.

Undoubtedly, much credit for this transformation is owed to the success of Islamic banks and financial institutions, which overcame the tests of survival in the 1970s to become dynamic pockets of financial development in the 1980s and integration into the world economy in the 1990s. At the turn of the twenty-first century, Islamic finance has become as much a project for Islamic intellectuals and capitalists as it is for financial and banking institutions across the globe.

Notwithstanding the progress made to date in the study and application of Islamic finance, the perceived disparity between the two domains remains wide. As has been widely noted, there has been a strong tendency in the literature to emphasize theoretical formulation over empirical analysis, with the consequence that the operations of Islamic financial institutions have been inadequately examined. The resulting gap in knowledge is all the more significant when the practices of these institutions are found to diverge in important ways from the intellectual doctrines underpinning their role in the economy. Perhaps the most vivid illustration of such a mismatch between theory and practice is found in the financing operations of Islamic financial institutions and, more specifically, the choice of instruments for extending funds to borrowers and investors.

According to prevailing interpretations of Islamic law, financial instruments should be based on the principle of profit-and-loss sharing and avoid predetermined or fixed returns. In modern terminology, equity contracts are permitted while debt contracts are prohibited.[1] Yet, evidence on current practice by Islamic banks suggests that the majority of financing operations are not based on equity. Rather, Islamic financial institutions have consistently favoured the use of the *murabaha* contract, an instrument that mimics the standard debt contract in conventional banking systems.

Not surprisingly, the appearance of an important departure from theory and religious doctrine has generated debate amongst legal scholars, and economics and finance specialists. The predominance of the *murabaha* represents a challenge to the very notion that Islamic finance would provide an alternative to interest-based conventional financial systems. And while there has been a tendency on the part of critics of Islamic finance to overplay the *murabaha* syndrome, defenders have been equally guilty of dismissing its significance for evaluating the contribution of modern Islamic capitalists. But what accounts for the *murabaha* syndrome? There is no shortage of explanations, ranging from the religious permissibility of the *murabaha* contract and the financial necessity of the instrument, to the economic rationality behind its prevalence. And while each of these perspectives offers a partial answer, individually they fail to provide a framework for understanding the systemic and comparative dimensions of the phenomenon. To what extent is the strong reliance on debt-like instruments in Islamic financial sub-systems any different from what takes place in conventional financial systems in Muslim countries and elsewhere? Do the determinants of financial structure, debt *versus* equity, in conventional systems provide a basis for understanding the practice in Islamic sub-systems?

In this chapter, we attempt to provide such a comparative framework for explaining the *murabaha* syndrome in Islamic finance. The observation that financial structures in Islamic sub-systems are no different from those in conventional systems establishes the necessity of a systemic examination of financial structure. Starting from the paradigm of corporate governance, we incorporate the insights of recent work on the systemic determinants of financial structure, including the role of law, institutions and politics. The empirical analysis places the *murabaha* syndrome into a broad national and international context, and sheds light on the constraints faced by Islamic capitalists in adhering to the goals of the equity-based model of Islamic finance. Following this Introduction, sections will, in order, illustrate the national and global dimensions of the *murabaha* syndrome; provide a conceptual framework; cover the empirical analysis; and discuss the implications for the future of Islamic finance.

FINANCIAL STRUCTURE IN ISLAMIC AND CONVENTIONAL SYSTEMS

We have referred to the *murabaha* syndrome as the strong and consistent tendency of Islamic banks and financial institutions to utilize debt-like instruments in the provision of external finance. Although we have singled out the *murabaha*, we have in mind other instruments that follow what is commonly known in the literature as the mark-up principle, in contrast to the profit-and-loss-sharing principle. We will refer to mark-up contracts, including the *murabaha*, as debt contracts, and profit-and-loss-sharing contracts, as equity contracts.[2] This typology is not only analytically convenient, it is also conceptually important. Researchers have for some time highlighted the parallels between mark-up and debt contracts on the one hand, and equity and profit-and-loss-sharing contracts on the other. Although obvious in the latter case, the similarities between mark-up and debt contracts deserve clarification. The salient feature of debt is not the payment of fixed returns; rather it is the transfer of control over the asset in cases of non-payment.[3] The control rights of mark-up contracts are equivalent to the control rights of debt contracts; in both cases, the bank retains ownership of the asset and can seize it if the borrower defaults. Under profit-and-loss-sharing contracts, the bank has no such direct claim on the asset, as it is in partnership with the entrepreneur.

The analytical convenience of the above typology lies in the fact that it allows us to draw on country-level indicators of debt and equity to compare financial structures in Islamic and conventional systems. Table 3.1 presents evidence on the *murabaha* syndrome in Islamic systems, based on the financing operations of eighty-one Islamic banks and financial institutions for the years 1994–95. The sample is drawn from the *Directory of Islamic Banks and Financial Institutions* and

Table 3.1: Modes of financing in Islamic banking, 1994–95

	Share of murabaha in total financing (%)	Share of mark-up instruments in total financing (%)
Middle East and North Africa	67.0	85.6
East Asia	44.7	70.4
South Asia	67.5	92.2
Sub-Saharan Africa	48.4	55.7

Notes: Share of *murabaha* in financing is derived directly from the information provided by banks and financial institutions. The share of mark-up instruments, which include the *murabaha*, is calculated by adding the *murabaha* and *ijara*; in some cases, it is calculated residually by subtracting the profit-and-loss-sharing instruments from the total.

covers most countries where Islamic banks operate. Our sample excludes government-owned institutions and those specialized in specific sectors of the economy, although the information presented below would not change significantly if the latter were included. We utilize two measures of the intensity of debt financing in Islamic systems: 1) the share of *murabaha* contracts; and 2) the share of mark-up contracts (*murabaha*, *ijara*, and the like) in total finance provided by the sampled institutions. Our working assumption is that, as proxies, the measured levels in our sample are representative of overall debt levels in Islamic systems.

As the information in Table 3.1 makes clear, the *murabaha* instrument alone accounts for between 45 per cent and 67 per cent of total financing in Islamic systems. Including other mark-up instruments raises the share of debt to between 70 per cent and 86 per cent. The dominance of debt applies to all other regions of the Muslim World, although banks in Sub-Saharan Africa and South East Asia have lower ratios than the Middle East and South Asia. Variations within and between countries are small, so that no particular banks or countries drive the aggregate ratio for any region. Similar tendencies towards debt financing have been found in previous work covering other time periods and samples of banks, including analyses that tracked specific banks, over a long period of time. The most well-studied case is that of Faisal Islamic Bank of Egypt, where, from the early 1980s onwards, the share of *murabaha* was no less than 75 per cent.

From the perspective of many Muslim scholars and outside observers, the figures presented above are at odds with the predictions of an equity-based Islamic model that is predicated on the profit-and-loss-sharing principle. But is the dominance of debt in Islamic finance unusual from the perspective of conventional financial systems? Ideally, one would prefer to compare the sample of Islamic banks with samples of conventional banks that engage in debt and equity financing operations at the national or international level. But such an approach is not feasible, since, unlike Islamic banks, distinct institutions offer debt and equity financing across much of the world for historical and regulatory reasons. This division of labour is also true in Muslim countries. Another approach that overcomes the data limitations is to examine financial structure at the aggregate national level by utilizing data on assets in banking systems and equity markets as proxies for debt and equity financing, respectively. This approach has the added advantage of allowing us to compare financial structure in Islamic and conventional systems within Muslim countries and between the latter and non-Muslim countries.

Table 3.2 presents two measures of financial structure for a sample of seventy-two countries across the world over the period 1980–95. We measure aggregate debt and equity levels, respectively, by credit to the private sector from domestic money banks and the value of stock market capitalization. The

Table 3.2: Financial structure from an international perspective, 1990–95

	Share of debt in external finance (%)	Debt-to-equity ratio
All countries	65.6	4.7
Muslim countries	64.1	3.3
Middle East and North Africa	69.2	5.0
South East Asia	57.2	1.9
South Asia	74.2	7.2
Sub-Saharan Africa	57.5	2.6
Latin America	70.4	7.6
OECD	65.2	3.7

Notes: External finance is defined as the sum of debt and equity financing in the financial system of the country. Debt is calculated as credit to the private sector by deposit money banks while equity is defined by the capitalization of the stock market. Thus, debt in external finance is given by the share of credit to the private sector by deposit money banks in external finance.

sum of debt and equity constitutes our proxy for total external finance.[4] Following the methodology in Table 3.1, we have constructed two indicators of the intensity of debt financing: 1) the share of credit to the private sector in external finance; and 2) ratio of debt to equity in the financial system.[5] The calculations in Table 3.2 reveal the dominance of debt in external financing is remarkably consistent across much of the developed and developing countries, including the Middle East and Muslim World. As a result, debt-to-equity ratios for most regions are close to the world average. The average debt-to-equity ratios in East and South East Asia and Sub-Saharan Africa, are much in line with the standing of Islamic sub-systems in the two regions in Table 3.1.

The composition of external finance in Islamic sub-systems appears to be no different from conventional systems. Such similarities have evoked considerable debate on the unique purpose and reformist credentials of Islamic capital. The critics and defenders, however, appear to miss an important conclusion that arises out of the global presence of the *murabaha* syndrome. The dominance of debt over equity across the world suggests that systemic factors might lie behind the convergence of Islamic and non-Islamic financial structures. In other words, the gap between the theory and practice of Islamic finance could be a function of variables that are contrary to the assumptions of theoretical models of Islamic finance and/or exogenous to the presumed intentions of Islamic capitalists. If so, then an investigation of the determinants of financial structure at the systemic level should shed light on the driving forces behind the dominance of debt over equity in Islamic finance and across the globe. At minimum, such an investigation would identify the parameters creating the divergence between the theory and practice of Islamic finance. This is the approach we follow in the remainder of this chapter as we seek to understand the *murabaha* syndrome.

EXPLAINING FINANCIAL STRUCTURE: LAW, INSTITUTIONS AND POLITICS

The past decade has witnessed the emergence of a new empirical tradition in the study of financial systems. Inspired by the four-decade debate on the advantages and disadvantages of 'bank-based' *versus* 'market-based' systems and the growing evidence linking financial development to economic growth, this new literature has sought to understand the determinants of financial structure and development. Much of this research has been made possible by the growing availability of comprehensive data sets on finance and other correlates for a large sample of countries representing the spectrum of advanced and developing countries. Researchers have moved beyond the earlier focus on the link between macro-economic variables and financial development to new areas of inquiry. The latter have ranged from the historical origins of financial systems, and the impact of legal traditions and institutional capacities on banking and capital markets, to the role of politics in the evolution of financial structures. As a result, there exists at present a large body of empirical work devoted to examining the nexus between financial development on the one hand, and law, politics and institutions on the other.[6]

The focus on systemic forces of law, institutions and politics stems from the belief that they directly or indirectly influence a fundamental problem conditioning financial development and structure: the agency problem, or what La Porta, Lopez-de-Silanes, Shleifer and Vishny call corporate governance.[7] As the authors explain, corporate governance deals with the ways in which suppliers of finance to corporations assure themselves of getting a return on their investment and that managers will not steal the capital they supply or invest it in bad projects.[8] Accordingly, the extent to which external finance is provided would depend on the existence of mechanisms that would resolve the agency problem. While market forces, reputation considerations and individual incentives may in theory be trusted to ensure corporate governance, in practice, financial systems across the world have employed legal and economic mechanisms to make possible the flow of funds between financiers and entrepreneurs. These mechanisms are in turn subject to the effect of legal tradition, regulatory institutions and political structures. For example, whether external finance is provided and what form it takes should be a function of how laws define the rights of creditors and shareholders, and how these rights are exercised.

The last observation is an important point of departure for the literature on law and finance, which has sought to link the prevalence of external finance to the origin and orientation of legal systems across the world. The role of legal traditions is relevant not only for the countries of origin, but also for the rest of the world where these traditions have been transplanted over the course of the last two centuries, either through colonialism or outright appropriation post-independence. Comparisons of protections afforded to investors under different legal traditions suggest an important divide between common law (English-speaking countries) and civil law (French, German and Scandinavian) countries. La Porta, Lopez-de-Silanes, Shleifer and Vishny find that, in general, common law countries provide entrepreneurs with greater access to external finance, debt and equity than do civil law countries.[9] When they compared specific legal indicators of investor and creditor protection across countries by legal tradition, the authors found that the common law countries do in practice extend greater rights to providers of external finance than civil law countries.

Although legal traditions may diverge in their propensity to protect owners of capital, the effectiveness of rules and regulations in practice is contingent on their enforcement. Whether laws affect financial systems is contingent on the extent of the Rule of Law in society since effective enforcement may compensate for weaknesses in legal protection for owners of capital. These considerations have given rise to what is known as the dynamic law and finance view. Among others, La Porta, Lopez-de-Silanes, Shleifer and Vishny examine the impact of the 'law and order tradition' of a country, based on assessments by foreign investors of the efficiency of the judicial system and Rule of Law, on external finance.[10] Beyond laws and their enforcement, the literature has studied the role of institutional quality and capacity in conditioning financial development. These institutions may directly affect the agency problem, as in the case of accounting standards and regulatory policies. Alternatively, the impact of institutions on corporate governance may be indirect through government corruption, red tape and risks to contracts. The empirical findings in this regard have shown that better institutions promote financial development and, as a direct consequence, the supply of external finance in all forms.[11]

The legal and institutional perspectives on corporate governance have been supplemented recently by another perspective that is rooted in the interaction between politics and finance, giving rise to what is called the politics and finance view. This view suggests that governments will only support financial policies and structures that are compatible with their political and economic goals. Alternatively, special interest groups in society could force the state into adopting policies that protect their financial advantage. In either case, the development of financial markets and availability of external finance hinges on the role of the state in the economy and the make-up of the ruling elite. Thus, in countries with strong centralized governments and/or elites drawn from the non-business class, the financial sector is underdeveloped. Similarly, democratic institutions and procedures – periodic and contested elections, protections for civil liberties and property, separations of powers, executive accountability and other constraints on governmental authority – strengthen government institutions and enhance the Rule of Law. This politics and finance view has drawn much empirical support from the recent wave of financial liberalization in the context of democratization in developing countries.

The new literature on law, institutions, politics and finance has demonstrated the importance of systemic influences in explaining cross-country patterns in financial development and structure. The agency problem and its resolution, once viewed from the perspective of individual market actors, is now examined from the perspective of the financial system as a whole. What has not received adequate attention is the composition of external finance – that is, the division of assets in financial systems between equity and debt, the counterpart to the concept of capital structure at the firm level. Whether legal traditions, political structures and institutional development should affect the composition, as opposed to prevalence of external finance, is not always clear.[12] For example, although common-law countries extend greater levels of debt and equity financing than civil-law countries, does it also follow that their financial systems would have higher levels of debt-to-equity ratios? The same question arises with regard to institutions and political structures. In other words, given the level of external finance, what explains its composition, the breakdown between debt and equity?

Specifically, given the empirical illustrations in the previous section, how can we explain the dominance of debt as a financial instrument across the world, the *murabaha* syndrome? Numerous theoretical studies have emphasized the role of the debt contract as a mechanism for solving the agency problem. The defining feature of debt is that creditors can exercise influence over managers, assume control of capital in case of default, and/or repossess assets and push a firm into liquidation. This feature may interact with the legal and economic environment in ways that enhance its effectiveness. For example, debt contracts promote greater concentration of control over entrepreneurs since typically large banks supply the financing in contrast to the dispersion of equity-holders in typical situations. Similarly, relative to equity, the clarity of creditor rights in debt contracts is often reflected in legal provisions which afford greater protection to the suppliers of finance than under equity contracts. Whereas most legal systems defer greater discretion to manager's vis-à-vis equity-holders, holders of collateral against debt obligations possess the right to liquidate these assets when contracts are violated.[13]

Because the debt contract also addresses the agency problem in environments characterized by informational distortions, debt should be favoured over equity in countries where the institutions protecting property and enforcing contracts are underdeveloped or where corruption and official red tape prevail. It is also true that where democratic institutions and procedures take root, they may serve as checks on corruption, improve transparency and reduce informational distortions. To the extent that democratization goes hand in hand with a reduced role for government in the economy, this would also reduce distortions in financial markets and spur the growth of equity financing. The upshot of this brief discussion is that the systemic influences of law, institutions and politics have as much to say about the composition of external finance as they have with regard to prevalence of it. This is the case because they influence the agency problem and favour one mode of financing over the other.

EXPLAINING FINANCIAL STRUCTURE: NEW EMPIRICAL EVIDENCE

When is debt favoured over equity? Do laws, institutions and polities affect the composition of external finance? To address these questions, we turn to direct empirical analysis of the cross-country data in Table 3.2. Through a series of parsimonious regressions, we will explore how country level indicators of legal tradition, institutional quality and political structure (independent variables) affect our two measures of debt dominance in financial structure: the share of debt in overall external finance and the debt-to-equity ratio (dependent variables). After examining the relationship for the entire sample, we will assess the position of Muslim and Middle Eastern countries relative to the rest of the world. It will be important to keep in mind throughout the analysis that we are not positing a causal relationship in a rigorous statistical sense between any of our variables. Rather, we are assessing here the strength of the statistical association between variables that are collectively endogenously determined; other studies have shown these statistical tests are not merely spurious correlations.

For each of the systemic influences, we consider three potential correlates. The legal variables consist of legal origin, an indicator of the orientation of the legal tradition, either common law or civil law; rule of law, an indicator of the effectiveness of the legal system; and private property, an indicator of the protections afforded to private property in a country. Whereas legal origin reflects the historical roots of the legal system, rule of law and private property are meant to capture dynamic legal influences, namely the effectiveness of the legal system. The institutional quality variables are expropriation risk, corruption, and bureaucratic quality. These variables capture different aspects of the government's ability to affect the business climate, including risks of confiscation, the prevalence of bribery and graft, and autonomy from political pressures.[14] The political variables consist of polity, an indicator of the democratic and autocratic tendencies of a political regime; system tenure, measured by the extent of democratic consolidation in the country's political system; and executive

Table 3.3: Law, institutions, politics and financial structure

	Dependent variable: Debt-to-equity ratio			Dependent variable: Share of debt in external finance		
A. Law and Financial Structure						
Legal origin	−3.06** (1.40)	−	−	0.144** (0.04)	−	−
Law and order	−	−0.88* (0.46)	−	−	−0.02 (0.14)	−
Private property	−	−	−1.51** (0.56)	−	−	−0.06** (0.02)
B. Institutions and Financial Structure						
Expropriation risk	−0.92** (0.44)	−	−	−0.02 (0.01)	−	−
Corruption	−	−1.34** (0.47)	−	−	−0.04** (0.02)	−
Bureaucratic quality	−	−	1.59** (0.64)	−	−	0.04** (0.01)
C. Politics and Financial Structure						
Democracy	−0.17* (0.10)	−	−	−0.001 (0.001)	−	−
System tenure	−	−0.08** (0.04)	−	−	−0.002* (0.001)	−
Executive constraints	−	−	−0.42* (0.21)	−	−	−0.01 (0.01)

Notes: This table summarizes the statistical relationship between the two measures of financial structure and the chosen set of legal, institutional and political variables. For each measure of financial structure, we have reported the coefficient and associated standard error from the following regression: $Y = \alpha + \beta X + \varepsilon$, where Y is the measure of financial structure and X is the explanatory variables listed in the first column above. *** and ** and * indicate statistical significance at 10 per cent, 5 per cent and 1 per cent respectively. See the Appendix table for data definitions and sources.

constraints, which captures the extent of limitations on executive authority. Each of these variables is explained more fully in the Appendix to this chapter.

The empirical results are presented in Table 3.3. For brevity, we only report the sign and significance of the relevant explanatory variables.[15]

We begin with the law and financial structure perspective in panel A. The evidence is supportive of the legal origin hypothesis: common-law countries on average have 14 per cent less debt in total external finance, and debt-to-equity ratios that are three times less. The extent of protection for private property has the expected impact on debt dominance in financial structure; the same is true for the rule of law variable, although the latter is not consistently significant. Panel B reports the empirical results for the institutions and financial structure perspective. All the estimated coefficients have the expected signs and are statistically significant. Higher levels of institutional quality go hand in hand with lower debt shares in external finance and smaller debt-to-equity ratios. On average, each unit improvement in the quality of institutions, as measured by the indicators, reduces the share of debt in external finance by 2 to 4 per cent. The political structure variables also have the expected signs but they are less significant and more sensitive to the choice of dependent variable compared to other correlates. Nonetheless, they suggest that democratization in general, and especially the consolidation of democratic institutions, goes hand in hand with less debt dominance in financial structure.

Notwithstanding the simplicity of the empirical approach, the results reported above are consistent with our working hypothesis that systemic forces outside the realm of finance condition not only the prevalence but also the composition of external finance. The *murabaha* syndrome prevails in countries with civil law traditions, weak institutions and non-democratic polities.

How do Muslim countries compare to the rest of the world? Specifically, which of the systemic influences examined above explains the tendency for the *murabaha* syndrome in this group of countries? Table 3.4 provides some tentative answers to these questions, where we have presented the correlates for each of the sampled Muslim countries together with other regional averages.

As far as legal origin is concerned, Muslim countries fall roughly in two categories: the Middle East, where the French civil-law tradition predominates, and the non-Middle Eastern countries that inherited the British legal tradition. The contrast between the two groups of Muslim countries, and between them and the rest of the world, is striking. However, Muslim countries in general do not stand out in this regard, as their legal systems conform to the world average. On account of legal orientation alone, we should observe a greater prevalence of the *murabaha* syndrome in the Middle East compared to the rest of the Muslim World and less in the latter relative to most other regions.

But while legal origin is not biased in favour of the *murabaha* syndrome in Muslim countries, the same is not true for the dynamic legal influences. In particular, the perceived effectiveness of law enforcement and the protection of private property in Muslim countries is slightly below the average for the sampled countries. Nonetheless, Muslim countries inside and outside the Middle East score above all developing countries except for East Asia. Within the Muslim World, Middle Eastern countries score higher, reversing the pattern of bias in legal origin between the two groups of countries. This reversal, however, is not quantitatively sufficient to overturn the advantage of non-Middle Eastern Muslim countries in legal tradition. In other words, on the basis of all legal

Table 3.4: Correlates of the *murabaha* syndrome in Muslim and non-Muslim countries

	Common law	Law and order	Private property	Expropriation Risk	Corruption	Bureaucratic quality	Democracy	System tenure	Executive constraints
Bahrain	0	4.5	5	8.0	3.5	4.0	−10	23	1
Bangladesh	1	1.4	2	4.9	0.6	1.2	−6	2.5	1.3
Egypt	0	2.5	3	6.3	2.3	2.6	−5.2	11.5	3
Indonesia	0	2.4	3	7.2	1.3	1.5	−7	20.5	2
Iran	0	3.3	1	5.0	3.2	2.5	−6	4.8	3
Jordan	0	2.6	4	6.1	3.3	3.0	−9.7	34.5	1.3
Kuwait	0	3.3	5	7.0	4.8	2.8	−8.3	10.5	2.7
Malaysia	1	4.1	4	8.0	4.4	3.5	4	17.5	5
Morocco	0	2.7	4	6.4	2.5	2.9	−8	26.5	2
Niger	0	3.0	3	5.0	3.5	3.2	−7	6.3	1
Nigeria	1	1.6	3	5.3	1.8	2.3	2.3	4.3	5
Pakistan	1	1.8	4	5.6	1.8	2.7	−6.5	5.7	1.3
Saudi Arabia	1	4.3	5	7.5	4.2	3.5	−10	6.8	1
Senegal	0	1.9	4	5.9	3.0	3.0	−1.2	9.5	3
Sudan	1	1.9	2	3.9	1.8	1.3	−7	6.8	3
Syria	0	2.3	2	5.0	2.3	2.1	−9	16.5	1
Tanzania	1	3.5	3	6.5	3.2	1.3	−7	11.1	3
Tunisia	0	2.8	3	6.0	3.0	3.0	−8.2	15.5	1
Turkey	0	3.1	4	7.0	3.1	3.3	1	5.8	3.5
Muslim countries	0.4	2.8	3.4	6.1	2.8	2.6	−5.7	12.6	2.3
Muslim MENA	0.1	3.0	3.4	6.2	3.2	2.9	−7.3	15.5	1.9
Other Muslim	0.7	2.4	3.1	5.8	2.4	2.2	−3.9	9.3	2.7
Sub-Saharan Africa	0.5	2.6	2.8	5.9	2.8	2.7	−4.4	12.6	2.6
South Asia	1.0	1.7	3.0	6.1	2.0	2.7	−0.4	18.0	3.5
East Asia	0.5	3.8	4.0	7.8	3.4	3.6	0.7	14.7	4.2
Latin America	0.3	2.6	3.3	6.1	2.5	2.4	1.5	13.9	4.2
OECD	0.3	5.5	4.7	9.4	5.3	5.5	9.4	45.7	6.7
World	0.4	3.5	3.6	7.1	3.5	3.4	0.8	22.0	4.1

Note: See Appendix 3.1, pp. 77–8, for numeric scales.

variables, we would expect a greater prevalence of the *murabaha* syndrome in the Middle East compared to the rest of the Muslim World. The debt ratios presented in Tables 3.1 and 3.2 are consistent with this prediction.

Comparisons within Muslim countries and between them and the rest of the world in the sphere of institutional quality follow those of the dynamic legal variables. Not surprisingly, the two sets of variables are highly correlated. Consistently, the Middle East enjoys a slight edge over the rest of the Muslim World. Similarly, Muslim countries collectively have lower levels of expropriation risk and corruption, and better scores of bureaucratic quality than other developing regions except for East Asia. When the legal and institutional variables are combined together to generate predicted debt ratios, the resulting figures are in line with the actual ratios in Tables 3.1 and 3.2. Moreover, the lower debt ratios for non-Middle Eastern Muslim countries appear to be driven by their common-law orientation, notwithstanding the lower scores on institutional quality.

Where Muslim countries appear disadvantaged is in the development of democratic institutions. Middle Eastern countries in particular have the lowest scores in the world on the polity indicator of democratic tendencies in political regimes; chief executives in the region have the least constraints on their authority. Although other Muslim countries do better, the Muslim World in general compares unfavourably with the rest of the world on these two scores of democracy. But on the most important correlate with financial structure, the consolidation of democratic institutions as captured by system tenure, Muslim countries, and especially the Middle East, are not far off from tendencies elsewhere in the developing world. The last observation is particularly important, as we saw earlier that system tenure was highly correlated with institutional quality; the same is not true for the polity indicator of democracy. This finding is consistent with the literature that has shown those standard measures of democracy are not strongly correlated with economic outcomes.

IMPLICATIONS FOR THE FUTURE OF ISLAMIC FINANCE

Thus far, we have examined the *murabaha* syndrome in Islamic finance through the prism of a systemic analysis of financial structures across the world. The premise underlying this approach has been that Islamic financial structures exist as sub-systems within larger systems that condition their operations and con-strain their development. Our evidence suggests that Islamic banks, as niche providers of capital, do not operate much differently from conventional banks. It is not surprising, then, that the prevalence of the *murabaha* syndrome in Islamic sub-systems mimics what is observed at the country and regional levels. These empirical regularities, we have argued, are a function of legal, institutional and political forces that are rooted in the historical processes of colonization, state formation and development. Taking these forces into account, the tendency towards debt-based finance in Muslim countries conforms to what is predicted theoretically and seen elsewhere in other comparable regions in the world. From this perspective, the apparent divergence between the theory of equity-based finance and the *murabaha*-dominated practice of Islamic institutions ceases to be a puzzle. If anything, given that the forces driving this divergence are exogenous to Islamic financial sub-systems, the absence of it would have stood out as an anomaly.

Where does this leave the equity-based model of Islamic finance? Does rationalizing the *murabaha* syndrome imply that the model is unsuitable for modern societies and should be abandoned in favour of a more flexible alternative? The answer clearly hinges on how we interpret the model. If we adopt a strict interpretation where debt-finance is prohibited in all forms, then the prospects of realizing this goal are not good, at least from the perspective of the empirical analysis presented above. According to the empirical results in Table 3.4, even the most institutionally developed country, scoring a 10 on the relevant correlates, would still extend close to 50 per cent of its external finance in the form of debt – and assuming a common-law legal system would lower this ratio to around 35 per cent. A handful of Muslim countries, including Malaysia and Saudi Arabia, have achieved this goal, exhibiting some of the lowest debt ratios in the world. But they, along with a few other countries, are an exception. How many Muslim or non-Muslim countries could lower debt ratios to these low levels, let alone eliminate all debt from the financial system?

Since the early 1990s, there have been some positive developments in several countries in the Middle East and the wider Muslim World. By and large, the quality of institutions (as evidenced by available scores) has improved in the 1990s relative to the 1980s, improvements that did not always take place in the context of democratization of political structures. This progress has coincided with financial liberalization and growth of capital markets, and especially equity markets that were buttressed by legal and regulatory reforms. On this basis, it may be reasonable to suggest that the institutional environment would support higher levels of equity finance, allowing Islamic sub-systems to edge closer to the ideal model. But the end road is unlikely to lead to the complete elimination of debt from the financial system, save for by government decree. And even with the latter, so long as it remains economically viable, the debt contract would continue to be utilized.

Perhaps this explains why even the most ambitious attempts to 'Islamize' the financial system by eliminating debt – as in Pakistan, Sudan and Iran – have thus far yielded limited results.

In the future, the overall institutional environment will be a more important determinant of the evolution of financial structures in Muslim societies than attempts to impose financial systems based on rigid religious interpretations. In fact, the case can be argued on economic grounds that a financial system offering both debt and equity will contribute more to social welfare than one that is restricted to either form. This is so because a system with the full menu of instruments will allow lenders and investors to fund more projects to more entrepreneurs while addressing their concerns with corporate governance. These considerations suggest an alternative to the strict interpretation of the equity-based model of Islamic finance, one that is founded on flexibility and aggregate welfare, goals that are not inconsistent with the objectives of the *shari'a*. The growing acceptance of the *murabaha* contract amongst scholars provides ample testimony for the emergence of a new doctrine on Islamic finance, one that is rooted not only in theological purity but also in economical viability. To the extent that such a reading reflects the evolution of Islamic economic thought, it demonstrates the pragmatic capacity of its ideologues and practitioners rather than their 'incoherence' and 'irrationality'.

Appendix 3.1: Data for cross-country analysis

Variables	*Description and Source*
Financial	
Debt	Claims on the private sector by deposit money banks as a percent of GDP; average for 1990–95.
Equity	Stock market capitalization as a % of GDP; average for 1990–95.
Debt-to-equity ratio	The ratio of credit to the private sector by deposit money banks and other financial institutions to stock market capitalization; average for 1990–95.
External finance	The sum of credit to private sector by deposit money banks plus stock market capitalization; average for 1990–95.
Legal	
Legal origin	Dummy variable taking the value 1 if the country's legal system follows the common law tradition and the value 0 if it follows the civil law tradition (French, German or Scandinavian). Source: La Porta, et al. (1997).
Rule of law	Measures of the tradition of law and order in a country. It ranges from 10, strong law and order tradition, to 1, weak law and order tradition; average over 1982–95.
Property rights	Rating of property rights on a scale from 1 to 5. The more protection private property receives, the higher the score. Source: La Porta, et al. (1998), using data from 1997 *Index of Economic Freedom*.
Institutional	
Expropriation risk	Assessment of risk of 'outright confiscation' or 'forced nationaliza-tion'. It ranges from 0 to 10, with lower scores indicating a higher risk; average over 1982–95.
Corruption	The level of corruption is scaled from 0 (high level of corruption) to 10 (low level), average over the period 1982–95.
Bureaucratic quality	Measures quality of bureaucracy. High scores indicate autonomy from political pressures and strengths and expertise to govern without drastic changes in policy or interruptions in government services; also existence of an established mechanism for recruiting and training; scores range from 0 to 6; average over 1982–95.
Institutions	A composite index of the above three institutional variables. The variables were scaled from 0 to 10 and averaged over the entire period.

Variables	Description and Source
Political variables	
Democracy	A composite index derived by subtracting the 'Autocracy' measure from the 'Democracy' measure in *Polity98*; ranges from –10 to 10, with high scores indicating greater democratic tendencies. In *Polity98*, each country is given a democracy and autocracy score depending on various factors such as competitiveness in executive and legislative selection and openness of political participation.
System tenure	Measures the consolidation of democratic institutions in a country through an assessment of executive election and tenure; higher scores indicate greater consolidation; average for 1980–2. Corresponds to the variable TENSYS in the *Database of Political Institutions*.
Executive constraints	Measures the extent of constraints on executives; ranges from 0 to 4, with 0 representing unlimited authority and 4 representing greater accountability by chief executives; average 1980–5.
Other variables	
Muslim	A dummy variable taking the value 1 if the country is a member of the Organization of Islamic Conference, and 0 otherwise.
MENA	A dummy variable taking the value 1 if the country belongs to the Middle East and North Africa region; includes Iran and Turkey and excludes Sudan.

NOTES

1. According to proponents of Islamic finance, profit-and-loss-sharing contracts are not only consistent with Islamic religious beliefs, they are also superior to debt-based financial instruments.
2. Mark-up instruments include the well-known *murabaha* and *ijara* contracts and other variants of them that are widely used.
3. This follows the incomplete contracts and control literature, which emphasizes the control rights over the asset that is conferred by financial instruments.
4. There are two limitations in using this measure. The first is that developing countries typically have large agricultural sectors, which do not borrow from the formal financial sector, thus including in GDP a large portion of the economy that does not finance investment via either debt or traded equity. The second is that numerator includes borrowing households in the private sector in standard reporting. Eliminating claims on the private sector held by non-bank financial institutions may remove most of the household sector, but the effect is uncertain across economies of different levels of wealth.
5. The alternative ratio of total commercial debt to listed equity, although imperfect, is a preferable measure of 'aggregate leverage'. The market capitalization ratio, or the value of listed shares divided by GDP, is typically used as a measure of stock market size, and is a proxy for the ability of corporations to mobilize capital and diversify risk. The ratio of total commercial debt to listed equity is therefore an approxima-

tion for the composition of capital in a country's domestic financial markets – a measure of financial structure.

6. Historically, analyses of financial structure have been confined to the US economy, often utilizing large sets of firm-level data. The theoretical foundation of this empirical literature was grounded in the classic Modigliani–Miller 'irrelevance' proposition which implied that, in perfect capital markets, a firm's cost of capital and its value are independent of its capital structure (Franco Modigliani and Merton H. Miller, 'The Cost of Capital, Corporation Finance, and the Theory of Investment', *American Economic Review*, 48(2), 1958, pp. 261–97; Franco Modigliani and Merton H. Miller, 'Corporate Income Taxes and the Cost of Capital', *American Economic Review*, 53(2), 1963, pp. 433–43). Departures from the assumptions of the Modigliani–Miller hypothesis provided the groundwork for testing various hypotheses on the determinates of capital structure that arise from economic, legal or institutional features of the financial system. The last decade saw the extension of this empirical tradition to the international setting in the OECD and developing economies. Again, the workhorse of these studies continued to be large data sets of firm-level information on capital structure. Notwithstanding the progress made in this regard, research to date has yet to establish satisfactory findings that relate theory to evidence in one country or across countries.

7. Rafael La Porta, Florencio Lopez-de-Silanes, Andrei Schleifer and Robert W. Vishny, 'Legal Determinants of External Finance', *Journal of Finance*, 52(3), 1997, pp. 1131–50.

8. Although extensions of the Modigliani–Miller proposition have dealt primarily with the effects of taxes and tax advantages of debt relative to equity, Jensen and Meckling demonstrated that agency costs of debt and equity also determine capital structure (Michael C. Jensen and William H. Meckling, 'Theory of the Firm: Managerial Behavior, Agency Costs, and Ownership Structure', *Journal of Financial Economics*, 3(4), 1977, pp. 305–60).

9. Rafael La Porta et al., 'Legal Determinants of External Finance'.

10. Rafael La Porta, Florencio Lopez-de-Silanes, Andrei Schleifer and Robert W. Vishny, 'Law and Finance', Working Paper 5661 (Cambridge, MA: National Bureau of Economic Research, 1996).

11. However, after controlling for differences in institutional quality, the origin of legal tradition maintains significant explanatory power, meaning that external finance is a function of both the legal origin and enforcement in a given country.

12. To our knowledge, only Demirgüc-kunt and Levine examine the systemic determinants of financial structure (Asli Demirgüc-kunt and Ross Levine, 'Stock Markets, Corporate Finance and Economic Growth', *World Bank Economic Review*, 10(2), 1996, pp. 341–69). However, their analysis is primarily concerned to differentiate between bank-based (debt dominated) and market-based (equity dominated) countries and is not rooted in the corporate governance framework.

13. Similarly, debt contracts promote greater concentration of control over entrepreneurs since typically large banks supply the financing in contrast to the dispersion of equity-holders in typical situations.

14. Unlike the legal and institutional variables, there is a big menu of political variables to choose from. We examined standard indicators in the Polity and Database of

Political Institutions databases. Our choice of variables reflected the strength of statistical association with the financial structure variables.

15. These statistical tests do not control for the level of income per capita in the country, as is customarily done in studies of financial development. While it is the case that richer societies are more financially developed as measured by the size of banking systems and capital markets, there is clear relationship between the level of income and the composition of external finance. In any case, controlling for income per capital does not change any of the reported coefficients.

4

Marketing Commodities Does Not Happen on Commodity Markets: The Egyptian Bursat Al-'Uqud and Oil Futures Markets

Ellis Goldberg

Discussions of Islamic finance usually turn, as in many of the papers in this volume, to the question of interest (*riba*). But charging interest is not the only point of contention between Islamic legal scholars and modern financial practices. Insurance is an additional area. Another, often neglected, aspect of modern financial practice that seems equally problematic from the viewpoint of contemporary exegetes of classical Islamic law is the market in financial paper that we usually refer to as the 'futures' market. The futures market (also called the commodities market) is a market in 'contracts calling for delivery of a standard quantity and quality of a commodity to a particular location during a specified period in the future'.[1] Because the contracts themselves are traded (rather than the goods they represent) most such contracts are cancelled before the delivery date and, in fact, most participants expect to cancel the contracts and have no intention of ever taking delivery.

Futures markets constitute important building blocks of the global financial system. As a consequence, the creation of viable financial structures in the Islamic world might be jeopardized if the content of Islamic law posed an impediment to their existence. Futures markets also constitute important building blocks in the structure of the production and marketing of many of the most important commodities in global trade, including energy, food and fibre. Again, if such markets are deemed to be in conflict with Islamic law, it might prove difficult to integrate the Islamic countries into a global system of production and trade. One conclusion to be drawn from the materials presented here is that where very powerful and concentrated economic interests exist they can protect crucial institutions from much public scrutiny and especially from any regulation by non-state Islamic jurists.

It is important, therefore, to recognize that in at least one Islamic country there was extensive experience with a futures market – Egypt. It is also important to recognize that Islamic countries today produce a commodity – oil – for which an important futures market exists. Consequently, there are two historical experiences to consider when we want to know how contemporary Muslim societies have dealt with futures markets in practice. In this chapter we will explore aspects of non-interference in the working of futures markets, first in a domestic futures market in Egypt tied to global markets, and second in the apparent decision of producing countries in the Arabian peninsula neither to engage in nor to oppose the working of a global futures market for oil. This is despite the expression of tremendous unhappiness on the part of many opinion leaders in Egypt, from the beginning of the twentieth century to its middle, with the futures market; there was never an attempt to deploy a specific vocabulary of Islamic criticism of its working even though such a criticism would have been consonant both with elite concerns expressed in secular language and with similar critiques expressed both in religious and secular language in Europe and the United States.

There is an Islamic contractual form for the present purchase of goods to be produced and delivered in the future: *salam* contracts. However, there were not in classical law and do not appear to be now any constructions of *shari'a* that allow the writing of contracts equivalent to those on commodity markets: for the purchase of uncertain quantities of goods at unknown prices in the future. In fact, it was and seems to remain illegitimate to buy and sell contracts exhibiting such uncertainties. There was an important debate about whether the state could pay interest (*riba*) on postal savings accounts and relevant *fatwas* were issued.[2] There do not appear to have been any *fatwas* or even any discussion about the selling of uncertain contracts in the future (*gharar*), which was an issue of great concern to the dominant social elite. Clearly, Islamic legal concepts were deployed only when they did not negatively affect powerful domestic interests.

A few words of warning should be offered. First, because futures markets as known and understood today did not exist before about 1860, these kinds of markets are not described in any of the classical Islamic legal materials on sale contracts. Second, the author makes no claim to have any particular knowledge about what constitutes Islamic law. Rather, in this chapter attention is focused on the kinds of claims that have and have not been made about what might be the content of Islamic law about these kinds of markets. Third, futures markets appear to be inseparable from trade in some – but not all – kinds of commodities, including (at the time of writing) currency, petroleum, grains and fibres. There are important theoretical arguments about why such markets exist at all, but the fact that they do appears to be linked to some structural or institutional characteristics of how the underlying goods are produced or traded. Fourth, the criticisms that we find in some contemporary Islamic legal literature about the functioning of futures markets are not unique to Islamic thought; they recapitulate criticism of the working of such markets in almost every setting in which they have occurred. Thus, the classic argument in Europe about the so-called *exception de jeu* (the idea that futures markets are a form of gambling) is quite similar to the expression of contemporary Islamic criticisms of such markets. Courts and legislatures in the US and Europe were long uncertain about whether obligations arising from futures contracts could actually be enforced or whether they were more akin to lost wagers. In both France and Germany, for example, futures markets were banned at various times in the nineteenth or twentieth centuries.

Existing research on Islamic law is fairly clear that futures markets as presently known are not consonant with Islamic law. Although contracts for future delivery are legal, the basic mechanism of the futures market is to allow participants to write contracts to deliver goods that they cannot and to offset the obligation to deliver by engaging in an offsetting contract to receive goods. At the time of writing, research by Islamic scholars indicates this is not permissible.[3] A decision by the Organization of the Islamic Conference Fiqh Academy indicates that, although it is possible to make an option contract it is not permissible to sell such contracts in a market.[4] Part of the problem for Islamic scholars is precisely that markets in contracts (as opposed to markets in goods) are relatively novel and that they present a variety of complex problems of law and equity. There appears to be some dispute about whether options themselves are permissible, although some authoritative opinion inclines to the idea that they are not.[5]

Islamic scholars are not alone in having difficulties with markets for contracts. Although political scientists have recently spent much time discovering how states create the rules that make markets work, they have shown relatively little interest in the mechanics of how formal markets work. The growth of a global market for commodities has been accompanied by the growth of financial markets linked to those commodities and the total value of contracts traded for goods is invariably far larger than the total value of the goods themselves. Such financial markets in contracts for commodities have a life of their own and can, on occasion, influence the production and distribution of the underlying commodities themselves. Although it might be possible to produce commodities without 'commodity markets', it has not been done since the mid-nineteenth century. Egyptian farmers, whether peasants or landowners, did not simply grow cotton for the mills of Lancashire; they also produced the raw material for the financial markets of Alexandria and Liverpool. By the beginning of the twentieth century, the role of the futures market had become central to the production and pricing of Egyptian cotton and on occasion the financial markets could dramatically affect what happened in the fields.

Commodities may, by definition, be goods produced for markets, but commodity markets refer specifically to formal spot and futures markets, which in

Egypt were located in Alexandria. 'Commodity markets' are not, of course, markets for commodities or at least not markets for the commodities whose names they nominally bear. There are three kinds of contracts or markets associated with commodities markets: forward, spot and futures. A forward market, as its name suggests, is a market for delivery of a good at some distant time; a spot market is a market for immediate delivery; a futures market is a market in contracts for forward deliveries. The contemporary literature on Islamic finance finds no problem with spot markets which are easily assimilated to the idea of 'hand to hand' delivery, or with forward markets that appear to conform to the concepts of *salam* or *mu'ajjal* contracts. It is the existence of contracts that, both in practice and in theory, are never intended to lead to delivery and whose fluctuations alone provide access to wealth to well-informed traders that creates a real problem.

Because futures markets are financial markets in contracts for commodities, they have a life of their own. Although many commodities are marketed without 'commodity markets', where they exist futures markets play crucial roles in the production of many internationally traded goods. Commodity (futures) markets closely approximate the ideal type of market, and such markets increase the efficiency of market structures domestically and internationally because they vastly expand the contacts between buyers and sellers.[6]

There is significant disagreement about how to explain – or at any rate, how to model – what commodities markets do because they are centres of speculation as well as exchange. The two major theoretical approaches to explaining why there are commodity markets (and therefore what they do) can be summarized as theories of insurance[7] and theories of transaction cost reduction.[8] The most useful approach for understanding Egypt is embodied in an aphorism by Meeker that provided the basis of Williams's approach: that short sales are debts in goods rather than money.[9] By implication, then, markets do not simply exchange goods for money but turn goods themselves into a kind of credit-money. The advantage of this approach is that it sheds more light than any of the others on why control of the futures markets was as crucial as the control of the country's banks (and thus interest rates). In some ways, because of the absence of a fully developed central bank (and a consequent lack of political control over elements of both interest-rate policy and exchange-rate policy), political control of the commodity markets was even more important in Egypt than in other agricultural countries.

Although political scientists have recently spent much time analyzing how states create the rules that make markets work, they have shown relatively little interest in the mechanics. This is doubly surprising because the volatility associated with speculation in these markets is politically important and because of the central role these markets play in organizing much of the world's trade in raw materials and (at the time of writing) finance. Only because the political consequences of volatility on organized futures markets has emerged as a contemporary issue in the international political economy is any attention paid to such markets at all and usually then in the context of discussions about central banking systems. Volatility, speculation and the desire for political control over markets that are dominated by traders with no commitment to the underlying structures of production have long been consequential wherever such markets emerged – from American grain production to Brazilian coffee.[10] Most controversial of all the activities that occur on futures markets is the routine selling of 'uncovered' short sales, in which a speculator guarantees to deliver goods that he does not own, never intends to own and consequently never intends to deliver.

To recapitulate: the organization of futures markets for primary commodities such as cotton and wheat by the 1860s facilitated the movement of far larger quantities of agricultural goods over much longer distances than ever before. As the volume of trade grew sufficiently large, it was increasingly desirable (efficient) to make contracts for the delivery of standardized commodities. Such standard-ized contracts used an existing type of good as the basis for trading in all other similar goods and therefore also implicitly in the services (transportation, cleaning, processing) required to transform non-standard into standard goods. Selling (or going short) on a contract confers an obligation to deliver a good and buying (or going long) a corresponding obligation to receive it. Thus, any position may be cancelled by buying the opposite position: an obligation to deliver cotton can be eliminated by purchasing an opposite position to receive. Unlike speculators, who intend to cancel all their positions before a specified delivery date, farmers must always dispose of their goods and processors must always purchase them. Because futures contracts ultimately come due on the spot market, the definition of the standard confers a certain market power on the traders who organize markets because they can always deliver the specified grade instead of the grade desired by processors or available from farmers. Con-tracting for future deliveries provided insurance to both suppliers and consumers and thus allowed both sides greater security to make fixed investments.

The liquidity necessary for futures markets requires the existence of entre-preneurs who specialize in risk and speculation. 'Dealings in cotton,' as Herbert Knox Smith wrote in submitting a report on the organization of American markets to the House of Representatives in 1908, 'must always be accompanied by risk, either to the producer, the merchant middleman, the speculator, or the spinner ... It is a general principle that much of the risk should properly be borne by the speculative class'.[11] Because of the many functions of commodity exchanges, they are, like banks, far too important to be allowed to work unregu-lated and the coalitions engaged in their regulation will include producers, speculators themselves and (probably) processors. To allow them to be regulated solely in the interests of farmers, for example, is no less unsound than allowing banks to be regulated solely by the interests of borrowers.

An active futures market links producers and consumers through contracts between private parties made in a financial market with a clearing house facility. The futures market itself, through price discovery, lowers the spread between buyers and sellers in distant markets, although clearly such markets can only exist once transport costs (as in the nineteenth century) have become a small part of the value of goods produced in different parts of the globe. The issuance of export permits by the state, as in early nineteenth-century Tunisia for olive oil, should in no way be confused with a futures market even if the permits themselves are tradeable.[12]

EGYPTIAN FUTURES MARKETS FOR COTTON

At the beginning of the twentieth century, the Alexandria spot and futures markets were central to the production and pricing of Egyptian cotton, and when financial markets dramatically affected what happened in the producing areas there were demands for further regulation of their activities. So important was the issue of regulatory control of these markets that, in at least one instance, powerful landowners were willing to cede some control over cropping decisions in return for more regulatory authority over the commodities markets. They did this rather than, for example, attempting to mobilize an 'Islamic' assault on the market, as was occurring more or less contemporaneously in regard to both charging and paying interest. To understand the story of the futures markets in the political economy of Egypt until the middle of the twentieth century, it is therefore appropriate to review the origin and organization of these markets and then turn to the debate that was had over how to save Egyptian commercial agriculture at the beginning of the Great Depression.

The futures market, or 'contracts market' as it was called in Arabic (bursat al-'uqud), was a private organization whose members were drawn from the cotton-exporting agencies in Alexandria and the ranks of professional speculators. The spot market (also known as Minet al-Bassel) was where delivery actually occurred. From its foundation in 1860 until the Depression, the spot market (unlike the futures market, which had been subject to government regulation since 1909) was a wholly private company and neither growers nor government officials served on its governing board. The organization of both markets was a constant concern and growers, no less than spinners, had an ambivalent relationship with it. The growers were frequently in conflict therefore with the representatives of the cotton merchants over the rules governing the sale of future contracts and spot transactions. The link was that futures contracts could ultimately be brought to the spot market for delivery. The emergence of an efficient market in futures was essential for the growth of the cotton industry but it often exacted a heavy price from parties that traded in it.

Egyptian growers and English spinners alike understood that they were well-served by the existence of such markets. What each side bitterly resented, however, was the price of having an institutionalized futures market: the profits made by brokers and the occasional fortunes of speculators. Futures markets were originally private businesses owned by brokers who consequently made rules that benefited themselves in the short term. Their rules did not always make for more efficient trading between buyer and seller.

Future contracts also played several roles in regulating relations between growers and buyers. Large landowners sold contracts for future delivery 'on call'. By financing for the coming crop, they thereby decreased the cost of credit for large growers. They were also believed to provide an incentive to increase the quality of the crop because the full size of the premium would depend on that quality. These contracts allowed them to deliver cotton on any day during the month specified for delivery in the contract. The contract or delivery note was known as a *filière* (*filyara* in Arabic) and these were, like contracts on all commodity exchanges, what made up the market rather than deliveries. Trading in notes occurred by successive endorsements on the *filière* itself.

Until 1917 the basic contract traded on the futures market for delivery was defined as Fully Good Fair Brown (*Mit Afifi*) Cotton, but that year a specific contract was introduced for *Sakel*. The sudden shift away from long-staple to extra-long-staple that appeared to result in ecological yield collapse also caused dramatic effects on the integrity of Egypt's agricultural markets.[13] Specifically, the new contract was introduced to make futures trading more efficient given insufficient supplies of *Mit Afifi* and the danger of substituting inferior grades of cotton for superior ones in the spot market where it was the basis. The Ministerial Decree of 14 June 1920 introducing the two types of contracts simply confirmed the shift already made in the marketplace.

Futures contracts provided cheap financing for the large landowners. Large growers in Egypt, as in the United States, sold their cotton 'on call'. Alexandria brokers who contracted to sell cotton to spinners abroad matched those sales with contracts to buy cotton in the future. Up to a contractually defined date, growers could choose when to complete the sale or 'fix' the price with premiums or deductions for quality relative to the standards set by the Bourse. In exchange for an immediate cash payment that financed the crop and the right to choose when to complete the sale, the seller guaranteed delivery and agreed to mark the final payment ('points on' or 'off') to an as yet unknown future Alexandria spot price. At fixing, the parties settled any difference between the cash advance and the spot price at the time of completing the sale. Exporters reportedly tried to balance their on-call sales to spinners with their on-call purchases from farmers and their success at managing the risk entailed was crucial to their profits. Besides the obvious financial importance of these contracts, they were believed to give growers an incentive to improve quality and earn the maximum number of points 'on'.

Producers and processors constantly worried and complained about the risks of speculation and the danger that the speculative 'tail' appeared to wag the productive 'dog'. The most extreme concern, widely voiced in the first two meetings of the International Cotton Federation, was the threat of a corner associated with insufficient supplies of the raw material. The spinners considered, and rejected, several plans to create their own stockpiles or to enter existing futures markets to depress prices. The failure of attempts to corner the market in 1905 (the Sully corner) and the expense and institutional difficulty of creating a counter-corner were replaced by continuing fears about the possible effects of speculators accentuating market volatility.[14] Despite constant complaints by Yusuf Nahas about the inequity of on-call purchases, the legitimacy of the futures markets was never challenged in reference to Islamic law or *shari'a*.[15] Clearly, in this case Nahas was at odds with members of the association he directed. Strictly speaking, trading on the Alexandria bourse in on-call options was completely legal, as was the taking of interest. Islamic law did provide a possible arena from which to challenge the futures markets and the short sales that are necessarily required for them to work. Short sales were illegal, after all, for periods in the nineteenth century in Germany and France,[16] as were options in Illinois. The reasoning behind voiding such contracts was, as would be the case in *sharia*, that the contracts amount to a wager, and their defence (as might also be the case in *shari'a*) was that such contracts were too useful for commercial practice to be voided.[17]

As with other institutions in Egypt, there was a distributional consequence to the working of commodities markets. Egyptian peasants who owned fewer than five feddans could not legally mortgage their land and thus were forced to contract higher-interest loans from local lenders; likewise, they could not write contracts for forward delivery. Before the creation of the state-run *halaqas* by Lord Kitchener in 1912, such peasants sold cotton directly to small merchants who re-sold cotton to the large export houses.[18] After 1912, the state provided much of the institutional infrastructure to bring the global market to poorer peasants in regard to the daily spot price, but not in regard to financing the crop.[19]

Concerned as Egyptian landowners and the officials of the organization that frequently represented them were about the organization of commodities markets, they made few attempts to wrest control of the spot market and extend control over futures until the Great Depression that hit Egypt with great severity in 1930. Retrospectively, most accounts of the Egyptian political economy focus on 1930 as the year of tariff autonomy and the first steps toward protective tariffs for industrialization. The finance minister, Ahmad Abdel Wahhab, issued a memorandum to propose dramatic institutional transformations guided by government policy to restore the agricultural sector, and especially the large commercially oriented landlords, to prosperity. Because the report was presented as a technical discussion, the full political implications have been largely misunderstood. The memorandum discussed both technical aspects of demand for Egyptian cotton[20] and advanced a compromise to sectoral conflict over tariff reform,[21] but it was also an attempt to transform the nature of social investment in reputation and the institutional framework in marketing.

The Ahmad Abdel Wahhab memorandum explicitly laid out 'the coordination of the efforts of the State and of the growers' as its programmatic core.[22] Such coordination itself was not new; what was new was that Ahmad Abdel Wahhab sought to transform the nature of that cooperation away from the older policy of investment in reputation to segment the market and reap a monopoly rent. Advocating what he called the 'principle of "mass production"', Ahmad Abdel Wahhab's policy was remarkably similar to the kind of competition envisaged by Alfred P. Sloan at General Motors: it was to bracket existing grades of American cotton with Egyptian cotton at competitive prices. Specifically, Ahmad Abdel Wahhab argued for a policy designed 'to produce a fifteen million qantar crop of which 9/10ths can be utilized by spinners who are now using higher grade American types, while we should be able to preserve a difference in tensile strength amounting to 20 or 30 percent – a result which would put our cotton in an absolutely impregnable position'.[23] Such a crop sold 'at a price slightly higher than that of American' would have a sufficiently large demand that it would never go unsold.

To accomplish his goal, which required the subordination of growers to regulation and the acceptance by a large group that they would cease to grow the most valuable cotton, Ahmad Abdel Wahhab had to promise them something in return beyond simple coordination. The proposals in the memorandum went far to win the cooperation of the Agricultural Union. This they had to do because without the grower's cooperation no agricultural policy would work on the ground. Ahmad Abdel Wahhab had to resolve a problem of partisan competition with the Wafd. Just prior to the Depression, the Wafd Party had intervened in the economy through the futures and spot markets to maintain a premium price for Egypt's longest-staple cotton. Although Egyptian governments intervened in cotton markets throughout the 1920s, there were two periods of massive intervention: 1926 and 1930. In the spring and summer of 1926, on the verge of an election, the government of Ahmad Ziwar announced its willingness to preserve the premium between Egyptian and American cotton prices that was briefly on the verge of disappearing. The formation of a coalition government with the Wafd in June 1926 reinforced the policy of buying cotton on the spot market as well as on the futures market and led to a government stockpile of nearly half a million cantars at a cost of more than L.E. 3 million.[24] The intervention planned by the coalition government on its own in late 1926 was even more extensive: 'purchasing all contracts offered and taking delivery of the cotton'.[25] Luckily, prices rose without the government actually having to take delivery. In November 1929 a caretaker government headed by Adli Yakan announced that it would purchase spot and futures contracts. On 23 December 1929, as a new Wafd government prepared to come to office in a week, Mustafa Maher, the outgoing Finance Minister (and former president of the General Union), announced that the government was willing to set a fixed price for January and February contracts (*Sakel* and *Ashmuni* respectively) and a higher price for the March and April contracts (technically called a '*contango*'). Because distant months usually sell for less than nearer ones (the technical term is 'backwardation'), the government was offering a riskless arbitrage opportunity and the Wafd extended this in February to the May and June contracts. By May, the Wafd government was buying Sakel and Ashmuni at prices higher than those prevailing in the spot market.[26] It is not surprising then that nearly 3 million cantars was tendered from farmers and from arbitragers in the futures market. These were costly operations for the government. Taken in conjunction with the role of Yusuf Nahas and Hamdi Sayf al-Nasr in the leadership of the Agricultural Union from its foundation until the 1930s, such policies established the Wafd as the party of agricultural price support[27] in contradistinction to its opponents such as Isma'il Sidki.

Ahmad Abdel Wahhab therefore had to bring the growers round without destroying the fiscal balance of the country in the process, a task made more difficult by the willingness of earlier governments to manipulate the markets for political advantage and economic stability. In his memorandum Ahmad Abdel Wahhab proposed a policy that, by limiting acreage, both contravened the preferences of the General Union and the analytic framework deployed to support those preferences by its general secretary, Yusuf Nahas. His was not a technical argument about optimal tariff policy or even about elasticity of demand (Hansen) but an attack on an important interest group. His attack on 'the theory that holds that Egyptian cotton … has its own special market separate from that of other cottons' was aimed specifically at Nahas. Ahmad Abdel Wahhab may have set the government down a new policy, but he was not the first to propose such a policy. Three years before the memorandum's publication, Victor Mosseri, speaking at the 1927 Cairo meeting of the International Cotton Federation, had argued for redirecting government policy away from attempts to maintain high prices. These, he asserted, stimulated new production and also encouraged the search for substitute fibres. 'Far from agreeing without further investigation to this tempting palliative which is extremely dangerous,' Mosseri said, 'the prudent man will seek his salvation in a sound and efficient policy, viz., the *reduction of the cost of production and not the reduction of acreage*' (italics in original).[28] Mosseri, himself a large landowner as well as an agronomist, was proposing a very different approach to Egypt's role in global trade than Nahas's.[29] Mosseri's approach was, however, premised on continued high levels of investment in reputation. Mosseri himself championed the use of biological research and government regulation to create a system of pure seedlines. This he counter-posed not only to acreage limitations but also to the creation of districts in which only one type of cotton could be grown.[30]

Ahmad Abdel Wahhab's proposal was far more pointed than Mosseri's remarks in its claim to repose on 'natural and permanent elements … inherent in the production of cotton' so as to accord with the 'well known and quite elementary proposition of economics that it pays every country best to grow the crops for the production of which it is most highly favored'.[31] Although the policy had been enunciated earlier, Ahmad Abdel Wahhab's analysis followed largely (but not wholly) from an article then under publication by Costantino Bresciani-Turroni, which presented quantitative evidence that the global cotton market was largely dominated by American production. Abdel Wahhab alluded to the problem of substitution away from Egyptian cotton production and to the emergence of a Japanese industry that had shifted to using Indian cotton (instead of American) for coarse fabric.[32]

What could Ahmad Abdel Wahhab offer in return for a restriction of the extra-long staple acreage so that its production would stabilize at the level of about 1.5 million cantars in the northern Delta? What he proposed was to realize a long-standing goal of the Agricultural Union: to link them directly to spinners in Europe and thereby circumvent the Alexandria General Produce Association. He proposed that the spot market in Minet al-Bassel be placed under the supervision of the government rather than of the AGPA and that, in addition to the appointment of a government commissioner for the market, the growers be given seven seats on the Bourse Commission, where previously no growers had sat, and that growers would henceforth sit on the committee to determine grades for cotton at delivery.

With the passage of time, the impact of these proposals has become less well understood. As early as 1915, criticisms about the monopoly power of AGPA in creating types in a market whose existence depended not on physical merchandise but 'could only arise from a conventional understanding among traders, from some regulation' were voiced.[33] Teymur, a former trader, argued that the AGPA abused its right to fix cotton types and called for establishing a formal role for growers and the state and thus limiting 'an autonomous power totally sheltered from public power'.[34] In a letter to Makram Ubayd, who served as the

Minister of Finance in the Wafd government during the first half of 1930, Nahas identified the absence of government control over the spot market and the consequent absence of government control over the standardization of cotton types as crucial steps to enhance the situation of the growers.[35] British staff at the Embassy and personnel in Barclays also specifically noted that there would be significant objections to creating standard types because these would undermine – if not completely destroy – the links between the largely foreign exporters and their clients abroad, the spinners. In exchange for limiting the amount of Sakel that could be grown, Ahmad Abdel Wahhab proposed to create a coalition between growers and the state to displace the export houses and to achieve the policy that Nahas had long sought: to place the producers in direct contact with the buyers. In his first comments on the Ahmad Abdel Wahhab proposal, in fact, Nahas noted that the growers had finally succeeded in their decade-long struggle to subordinate the spot market to the government. Nahas's criticisms, several of which were adopted at the 1921 Milan meeting of the International Cotton Federation, were phrased in terms of ending 'pure' speculation on the futures exchanges; but a careful reading of Nahas's own response to critiques (from Jules Klat, for example) make it clear that Nahas's primary objections were twofold: the acutely felt danger of a corner and the problem of speculative losses that insolvent speculators could not be forced to cover.[36] In the memorandum, therefore, Ahmad Abdel Wahhab suggested (and to some degree the growers agreed) that increased influence by growers over commodities markets was worth the price of decreased control over their own cropping decisions.

What are the contemporary implications of this story? This matters because one of the world's most important commodity markets is centered on a good produced in countries that happen to have large Muslim populations and that, in several important cases, claim to be guided by Islamic law. Let's begin with a speculation. Why, despite the expression of heartfelt moral condemnation of such speculation and their desire to regulate the commodities markets in the name of the national economy, did Egypt's large landowning cotton growers not enlist the aid of the *ulama*? Here, as indicated at the beginning of this paper, the question is not what Islamic law actually is. A more tractable question is when do coalitions between religious authorities and prominent social and political actors form? If it is true that, at least historically, Islamic law emerges out of requests for judgments by interested parties (Jackson, Coulson, Tyan) rather than from the need to enunciate public policy, an answer already suggests itself. Shaykh Muhammad Abdu's *fatwa* legalizing interest payments on postal deposit accounts was a decision rendered on behalf of interested actors. It appears the landowners (growers) never sought a *fatwa* about the futures market. This was despite the framing of their (the landlords') critiques in a vocabulary quite similar to that of contemporary theorists regarding inadmissibility of such markets as a valid form of Islamic financial institution. The emergence of a public policy literature on financial institutions that aims to subject them to the requirement that they be congruent with expert orientations towards Islamic law may be what is important about the new discourse on Islamic financial institutions. Clearly, for a prolonged period, Egyptian Muslims engaged with commodities markets felt the primary role of the state was to regulate them rather than subordinate them to a legal discourse. If a review of the commodities market in Egypt shows anything, it may be that the issue is not what kinds of contracts are sanctioned by classical (or even post-classical) Islamic legal scholarship. The crucial and substantive issue is where the emergent discourse on Islamic public policy fits with the existence of institutions designed to enhance economic exchange. This is, in a sense, to restate an old chestnut. It may also be a way of asserting that renewed vitality in debates on Islamic law will arise from their confronting the same kinds of issues about how the rule of law shapes institutions for human needs. The question for the present is whether the governments of oil-producing countries should be engaged in the futures markets for petroleum.

GLOBAL MARKETS FOR OIL

A very different experience with markets is the emergence of commodity markets for petroleum and derivative products in the 1980s. Many of these markets are located in the US, although the primary goods on which they are founded are produced in large measure in the Middle East.[37] Unlike Egyptian cotton producers who sought increased control, Arab oil producers appear to have been quite wary of having anything to do with futures markets. This is so without, however, any open discussion about the role of such markets for Arab oil producers or where they fit into Islamic law. These markets were created as the large integrated oil firms were being undone by the nationalizations of the 1970s and appear to be important and now well-rooted institutions in global trade. One question is whether it is, in fact, wise for producers to stand wholly apart from them, given that for some periods of time the financial tail can wag the productive dog. Although the nationalized firms have attempted to recreate the experience of integrated firms by investing in marketing and other 'downstream' activities, it seems likely global oil markets will resemble markets for other commodities in the twenty-first century to a greater degree than they resemble the production and marketing of oil in the first half of the twentieth century.

Globally integrated commodity markets for cotton were organized in the nineteenth century, but there were no such markets for oil for most of the twentieth century. This is because the dominant trend in the oil industry was towards vertical integration and the formation of tightly closed firms, rather than open markets for a large number of small producers, as was the case with cotton. In vertically integrated industry, the firm internalized uncertainty about prices. Centralized decision-making processes allowed the companies to absorb adverse shocks that affected different stages of production, from the lifting of the oil from the ground to the ultimate sale to the final consumer. Despite the dismantling of Standard Oil in 1911, large firms continued to have high levels of integration. The technological and implicit capital requirements of the industry led it to become a highly concentrated one, dominated by the so-called 'Seven Sisters' firms that were completely integrated vertically.

The discovery of oil in the Middle East in the first half of the twentieth century only increased the predominance of the large integrated companies, as did the rewards of collective action. The discoveries in the Arabian Peninsula were exceptionally large and the companies demanded exceptionally long concession agreements that gave them nearly full property rights over the oilfields. The firms employed contractual and informal means to share ownership and to co-ordinate price and production levels. The resolution of collective action problems was, of course, the other face of the absence of price competition and prices remained stable for long periods. Any changes in the market were managed either internally between the different segments of production, or externally with the other companies.

The integrated oil companies used artificial transfer prices to benefit their own downstream industries, and sold the remaining crude to other refineries at high prices to minimize the profit obtained by this segment of the productive chain.[38] Transfer prices, used mainly for accounting purposes, did not reflect the marginal costs of the different sub-processes and 'posted' prices, although ostensibly public, really existed to establish the tax liabilities of the producing firm. By definition, these prices were not efficient in an economic sense. These prices allowed the firms to transfer profits between different stages of production according to the changing conditions in the market or to transfer profits to government tax-collectors. Firms sometimes charged artificially high prices to their own refineries and thereby deterred new entrants to that segment of the market. The adjustment of crude supply and refined products was done within these companies without any intermediate market intervention.

The high fixed downstream costs, as well as the high costs for storage, led the refineries to look for the most stable sources of crude. The integrated oil companies operated with excess capacity in order to refrain competition. This intentional excess capacity in the downstream segment of the industry was controlled in the upstream segment. 'To have lifted crude above the downstream capacity of the company would have meant selling at arm's length.'[39] This would have meant greater competition downstream. Refineries were willing to pay a premium for this stability, which the major integrated companies were ready to accept.

The appearance of independent oil producers in the Middle East did not initially affect the structure of firms or markets because they, like the majors, signed long-term supply contracts. The new players did disrupt the existing equilibrium between the large companies and the host governments. The 'independents', as they were called, were willing to increase the prices paid to the host governments. Because they only had interests in oil extraction, they also sold increasingly to non-integrated refineries downstream.[40] Thus, although the mechanisms linking producers to consumers had not changed, greater competition generated more entrants into the downstream segment of the market. Paradoxically, nationalization was the catalyst for change, for in its wake there was increased competition on the supply side, long-term contracts became less common and the oil firms, now consumers as well as producers, increasingly turned to the spot market as an important source of supply.[41]

The threats to the integrity of the integrated firms was initially seen as destabilizing and chaotic but, of course, there were other methods to deal with the uncertainty in the oil industry: market solutions. Such solutions require markets, and the integrated firms had long been hostile to markets. Thus, early attempts to create commodity markets for oil products had failed. In the nineteenth century, the Petroleum Exchange had attempted to create a market for physical oil.[42] Another attempt, in 1935, to create a market for oil futures for West Texas Intermediate (WTI) had also failed. Other attempts were made after the brief Arab oil embargo of 1967, and in 1971 the New York Cotton Exchange introduced a propane contract, which was not successful. In 1974 another attempt to deal with crude oil was made. During the '70s, the Forward Contract Exchange Company in Amsterdam started trading in motor spirit and gas oil. The failure of these attempts to create markets casts some light on the possible causes of the later dramatic successes. As Horsnell and Mabro put it, 'markets are historical phenomena. They emerge at a particular moment ...'[43] More producers were needed and it was imperative that they not be able to coordinate their activities as easily as had the companies.

Nationalization of oil production in the 1970s was widely perceived at the time as a blow to the role of markets in the global economy. Because prices went up, and because resources were transferred from consumers to producers, it was widely believed at the time that the nationalizations were the prelude to a major shift in global power. There is no doubt that the intentions behind nationalization were to enhance the power of the producing states and to increase the flow of rents to their treasuries. The impetus for nationalization of petroleum resources has in every case been to provide a larger flow of resources to the state. Thus, one early demand for nationalization was couched in the need to provide jobs. Abdullah Tariki wanted nationalization to expand Saudi employment in the oilfields dramatically and to increase the income of oil workers. He considered it an injustice that the Abadan refinery in Iran alone employed 30,000 workers (three times the number of Aramco employees) and that Egypt employed 4,827 employees per million tons of oil produced, while Saudi Arabia employed only 139 Saudi Arabians per million tons.[44] Tariki also argued that patterns of employment, as well as wage levels, could be significantly changed to benefit Saudi nationals from nationalization, as he believed had occurred in Egypt and Venezuela.[45]

In relation to these three goals – expansion of the workforce, state-mandated wage increases and substitution of nationals for expatriates – the experience of other countries was not positive. In Mexico, the state-owned company Pemex (which had nationalized the oil industry in 1938) 'subsidized the rest of the economy through such various means as paying higher than necessary wages to its workers, and providing a variety of social services such as "paving roads, building schools, providing water systems and other public works ..."'[46] The result was an oil industry that was characterized even in 1967 as suffering from 'production declines, inefficiency, red tape and corruption'.[47] While it is true that such expenditures result only because Pemex was there to exploit the oil reserve, one question is whether the income flows from oil were themselves used in a socially efficient manner. The indications even before the surge in OPEC prices drove the oil companies back to Mexico were that an integrated state monopoly was not very efficient. Labour unions tied to the state seem only to give the labour union bureaucracy a reason to participate in inefficient state allocations of resources, although labour unions operating in a free labour market would presumably ensure that the price of labour did not slip so low that uneconomic substitutions of labour for capital occurred.

What is surprising is that neither the worst fears nor the best hopes of those in the early debate on nationalization were realized. The nationalizations broke apart the industry and created the possibility for disaggregating these firms and thus allowing the creation of more nearly efficient markets at each stage of the process. Although oil still generates significant rents, these flows are far smaller than appeared likely in the 1970s and the strategic importance of nationalization has been quite small. The paradoxical consequence of nationalization was to spawn new market institutions and thereby to hasten the transformation of oil into a mere commodity and limit the ability of producers to reap all the benefits they expected. The role formerly played by integrated firms is now played by spot and futures markets for crude oil and oil products. The dim outlines of such a possible transition could be seen in the history of British Petroleum, which became a leader in refining after 1951 because it no longer had a main source of production in Iran. That is to say, even such an early effect of nationalization was to reinforce specialization among the multinationals. From the 1960s onwards, property rights in oil were no longer vested in the company but companies had to pay for oil as an input into their processes, as independents already existed in the US. Having to start charging market prices, to governments, BP had already moved to the criterion of unit profitability. Countries now become one 'unit' of a firm owning the asset of what's in the ground.

One of the most important results of the chain of events discussed previously was the creation of a set of markets for oil and its products. More importantly, these markets lead to the creation of financial markets where the uncertainty of the oil market could be diversified away. The previously integrated companies sold part of their downstream industries by their own volition.[48] The disintegration of the oil industry also created increasing specialization. However, these specialized companies became increasingly vulnerable to shocks, as they lost diversification. The increased volatility created the need for hedging. This uncertainty became an attractive opportunity for financial intermediaries, not only for those who had been trading in other commodities, but also for financial institutions.

Financial markets created instruments to hedge the risk for companies that needed oil and by the 1980s the financial markets were mature enough to undertake this function. The increased number of participants in the market not only generated competition, but also the necessary liquidity for the appearance of financial instruments that had crude oil as its underlying asset. The increased competition did not come for free: there was an increase in the uncertainty of supply of oil to the markets. And again, the solution lay in the financial markets. The conditions were set for a more transparent trading system for the oil industry.

For the financial markets to operate, there had to be a relative homogenization of quality and sufficient participants in the market to create a reliable market at any point in time. Commodities markets such as the International Petroleum Exchange (IPE) and New York Metal Exchange (NYMEX) created standardized contracts with sufficient liquidity to create an independent competitive market in financial contracts. Nationalization allowed the creation of futures markets for both crude oil and refined products, as it externalized a market that had been within the integrated firms. The increased number of participants meant a higher liquidity and therefore a more transparent price-setting mechanism. As the market gained the liquidity needed, and the increased volatility meant higher pay-offs, purely financial agents appeared on the scene. Traders from other areas entered the market. With the traders, came the speculators, who increased the number of participants, diversifying it even further. By 1987, financial intermediaries and professional traders already accounted for 50 per cent of the transactions dealing with oil.

The number of sweet crude oil futures contracts traded in NYMEX ballooned during the first couple of years. During the first full year of trading (1984), the average monthly rate of growth was 18.32 per cent. The corresponding annual growth was an astounding 254 per cent! In little over three years, the number of contracts had increased tenfold. The open interest at the end of January 1985 was 73 per cent larger than a year before (63,458 in January 1985 *versus* 23,168 in January 1984). An increasing trend, although not as strong, continues into the twenty-first century and higher liquidity has also been witnessed in the refined products, such as heating oil and unleaded gasoline.

Some authors have argued that high interest rates made inventory maintenance very expensive,[49] but it seems more plausible to argue that the creation of these markets allowed a global decrease in the inventory levels, as the refiners could rely on the spot market for their crude oil supply. The worldwide inventories of crude oil do not support the claim that inventories have decreased. Instead, it seems that they have shown a small tendency to increase between 1973 and 1986. In the US, however, the level of inventories of crude oil has, at the time of writing, arrived to a range between 800,000 and 950,000 barrels since mid-1985. The maturity of the financial markets in the US would explain how financial instruments have replaced the need for physical inventories. The existence of both crude and refined oil products allowed the refiners to keep just-in-time inventories. The possibility of selling refined products to the market also allowed the refiners to work to capacity without concerns about the uncertainty in price. As the use of financial instruments rose, the size of the inventories fell. The financial instruments replaced the need for inventories.

Saudi Aramco produced state revenues greater than its own requirements, therefore contributed to national expenditure and investment patterns. The Third Development Plan called for 'maximizing domestic value-added from crude oil production through domestic hydrocarbon industries', as well as for reducing the 'percentage share of physical infrastructure in total investment after completion of the continuing commitments from the Second Plan period'.[50] When he was Planning Minister, Hisham Nazir indicated Saudi Arabia planned to make investments in Saudi Arabia sufficient to allow it to produce 5 or 6 per cent of world requirements for certain key petrochemicals, such as polyethylene.[51] Whether such investments in Saudi Arabia (rather than outside) are as financially compelling as they are politically is open to question, as is the problem of whether internal Saudi pricing for Saudi-owned (or largely Saudi-owned) firms is based on international prices or politically set.

The question for the Saudi state, however, was really where to take its profits and to determine what financial and industrial structure maximized the overall level of profits of the industry available to the state and society, regardless of how the state then chooses to allocate its share. This required balancing price and market share.

To ensure the maximum profits, it was important that Aramco and other

Saudi entities not be insulated from world market prices nor be unable to respond because of the rigidities built into the long-term pricing structure of Aramco contracts. A variety of experiments were undertaken in this regard. Thus, sometime in 1983 Norbec was created to deal with spot sales and a growing inventory of unsold oil through the creation of a large physical reserve. Norbec administered a floating storage capacity estimated to be 50 million barrels of oil.[52] Norbec had the ability to place single cargoes with buyers on short notice through numerous and growing numbers of contacts and provided Saudi Arabia with new potential to respond to changes in the oil markets and even affect them. Over time, the Saudis discovered that controlling huge volumes of oil in physical storage was unnecessary and uneconomical. But even if they do not actively participate in futures markets, their existence made it possible to decrease the size of physical inventories.

The issue of nationalization had been on the table since the Mexican nationalization in 1938, but oil companies had been able to avoid it by slowly increasing payments to government. The integrated oil companies were able to collude and avoid large payments to the producing countries. The appearance of the independent oil producers and the Iranian case made nationalization a real threat. The emergence of OPEC as a forum to discuss oil issues for producing countries allowed countries to share their experiences dealing with the oil companies. The wave of nationalization spread across the world, and oil companies were left without the extraction capacity. The irony of all this is that, despite the fears of policy-makers in the US and the hopes of the holders of assets in the ground around the world, nationalization weakened the degree of oligopolistic control over petroleum.

The dis-integration of the oil industry generated a loss of internal information for the companies. This informational loss had to be compensated by a market that could provide new information. This loss of information also hurt OPEC, as the dispersion of information as well as the dispersion of control within the industry made the policing task of OPEC more difficult. The decentralized structure of the market was capable of generating information for price-setting. The need for hedging and managing price risks further on gave rise to the forwards and futures markets. The efficiency of the prices in crude oil markets since then has improved.

Nationalization created more fragmented and therefore more competitive markets that, at least in light of the predictions commonly made in the 1970s about ever-rising oil prices, benefited consumers of crude oil and its products. The producer countries possibly considered that they would be able to extract the rents the integrated oil companies had been extracting from oil. The increased number of participants in the market did not allow this to happen, and the end result was the creation of a more transparent market.

The national firms are primary producers. The question is whether they – including those in the Persian Gulf countries – should become major participants in the futures markets. There has been significant demand within the futures markets for one or another grade of Saudi crude to become the marker. At the time of writing, these markets are pegged in relationship to a rapidly diminishing production of Dubai crudes in regard to the Gulf, as well as to Brent and West Texas. Although it would make sense to peg these markets to Saudi production, to do so would involve Saudi Aramco in the global futures markets to a far greater extent than at present.

At present, none of the Gulf states participates actively in the futures markets, and within the Kuwaiti national oil company opinions about them are divided. Some officials wish to enter these markets in order to counteract market volatility. Others, who do not wish to enter such markets, claim that volatility is not an issue because the only window of uncertainty is a period of roughly thirty days. This is not convincing, given that even minor changes in price have a large effect on cargoes of half a million barrels.

More convincing is the argument that the political impact of being active in the futures market inhibits the Gulf producers. Domestically, the inevitable losses would become the source of politically motivated attacks on the national firms and in such a context it seems plausible to imagine the invocation of an argument grounded in Islamic law against such involvement. If this is so, then it makes it apparent that the crucial questions about Islamic law may be less grounded in law than in the political context in which the invocations of such laws occur. It would clearly be worth further research, however, to understand why producers of such a volatile commodity have avoided entry into these markets that are, at the time of writing, the primary substitute for the collapse of a system based on integrated firms. Such a research agenda would also have the advantage of highlighting what is clear to most participants but still hidden from politically motivated policy-makers – that oil today is sold in markets that are far more transparent and efficient than at any time in the last hundred years.

The historical experience of producers in Muslim countries with futures markets is suggestive but not decisive. Where individual producers are small relative to world demand, and where futures markets can provide attractive financing, as in early twentieth century Egypt, futures markets were a fixture of the local political economy. Where local production is a large fraction of traded goods, and where financing is available in other forms (frequently through trades of future production for present investment), producers have chosen not to engage in activity on large and liquid futures markets. This suggests two further conclusions. The first is that the situation of producers rather than their religious commitments governs their entry into such markets. The second is that, despite the claims of contemporary economists such as Douglass North, the existence of institutions that could, in theory, serve the needs of market participants does not necessarily mean those participants will use them.

NOTES

1. Jeffrey Williams, *The Economic Function of Futures Markets* (Cambridge: Cambridge University Press, 1986), p. 2.
2. Jacques Berque, *Egypt: Imperialism and Revolution* (New York: Praeger, 1972), p. 217; Maxime Rodinson, *Islam and Capitalism* (New York: Pantheon, 1973), pp. 148, 149.
3. Fahim M. Khan, *Islamic Futures and their Markets: with Special Reference to their Role in Developing Rural Financial Markets* (Jeddah: Islamic Development Bank, 1995), p. 51.
4. Khan reports Decision 65/17 of the Seventh Annual Meeting of the *Fiqh* Academy, ibid. p. 65.
5. Frank E. Vogel and Samuel Hayes L. Hayes III, *Islamic Law and Finance: religion, risk, and return* (The Hague: Kluwer Law International, 1998), p. 164, and the allusion to the *Fiqh* Academy.
6. Alfred D. Chandler Jr, *The Visible Hand: The Managerial Revolution in American Business* (Cambridge: Belknap Press, 1977).
7. J. M. Keynes, *A Treatise on Money*, Vol. II (London: Macmillan & Co., 1930); J. R. Hicks, *Value and Capital* (Oxford: Clarendon Press, 1946); Leland L. Johnson, 'The Theory of Hedging and Speculation in Commodity Futures', in *The Review of Economics and Statistics*, 27(3), 1960, pp. 139–51; Jerome L. Stein, 'Cobwebs, Rational Expectations and Futures Markets', in *The Review of Economics and Statistics*, 74(1), 1992, pp. 127–34.
8. Holbrook Working, 'The Theory of Price of Storage', in *American Economic Review*, 39(6), 1949, pp. 1254–62; Lester G. Telser, 'Futures Trading and the Storage of Cotton and Wheat', in *The Journal of Political Economy*, 66(3), 1958, pp. 233–55; Lester G. Telser and Harlow N. Higinbotham, 'Organized Futures Markets: Costs and Benefits', in *The Journal of Political Economy*, 85(5), 1977, pp. 969–1000; Jeffrey Williams, 'Futures Markets: A Consequence of Risk Aversion or Transaction Costs', in *The Journal of Political Economy*, 95(5), 1987, pp. 1000–23.
9. J. Edward Meeker, *Short Selling* (New York: Harper & Brothers, 1932).
10. Robert H. Bates, *Open-Economy Politics* (Princeton: Princeton University Press, 1997).
11. United States Bureau of Corporations, *Summary of the Report of the Commissioner of Corporations on Cotton Exchanges* (Washington, DC: Government Printing Office, 1908), p. v.
12. Khelifa Chater, *Dependence et mutations précoloniales: la Regence de Tunis de 1815 à 1857* (Tunis: Publications de l'Universite de Tunis, 1984), p. 336. The existence of an 'export-raj' and other forms of mercantilist economic institutions long predates futures markets and largely moves to increase the arbitrage opportunities available to exporters by decreasing public information and restricting the right to sell of local producers.
13. M. Zaki Abd el-Motaal, *Les Bourses en Egypte* (Paris: Libraire Genérale de droit et de jurisprudence, 1930), p. 413.
14. Joseph Nahas, *Al Qutn Fi Khamsin 'Am* (Cairo: Dar al-Nil, 1954); International Federation of Master Cotton Spinners' and Manufacturers' Associations, *Official*

Report of the International Cotton Congress, 1927; Bent Hansen, Egypt and Turkey (Oxford: Oxford University Press, 1991), pp. 52–3.

15. The Islamic contractual form for the present purchase of goods to be produced and delivered in the future is called salam. There were not then and are not now any provisions of shari'a law to write contracts for the purchase of uncertain quantities of goods at unknown prices in the future nor was it legitimate to buy and sell contracts exhibiting such uncertainties. There was an important debate about whether the state could pay interest (riba) on postal savings accounts and relevant fatwas were issued. There do not appear to have been any fatwas or even any discussion about the selling of uncertain contracts in the future (gharar), which was an issue of great concern to the dominant social elite.

16. Meeker, Short Selling.

17. Williams, The Economic Function, pp. 176–7.

18. E. R. J. Owen, Cotton and the Egyptian Economy (Oxford: Oxford University Press, 1969), p. 218.

19. Halaqas provided, in return for a nominal fee, access to an official weighing machine, information (the daily opening price in Alexandria) and a place in which to exchange cotton. They were also used to distribute seed, which was not simply an 'improvement'. See ibid.

20. Bent Hansen, The Political Economy of Poverty, Equity and Growth (Oxford: Oxford University Press, 1991), pp. 92–4.

21. Robert L. Tignor, State, Private Enterprise and Economic Change in Egypt 1918–1952 (Princeton: Princeton University Press, 1984).

22. Ahmad Abdel Wahab, Memorandum on the Bases of a Stable Cotton Policy (Cairo: Government Press, 1930), p. i.

23. Ibid. p. 14.

24. Ibid. p. 51; Yunan L. Rizk, Tarikh al-wizarat al-misriyyah 1878–1953 (Cairo: Al-Ahram Strategic Studies Center, 1975), p. 296.

25. Abdel Wahhab, Memorandum, p. 51.

26. Foreign Office Records, London: FO 371 14647.

27. Nahas, Al Qutn Fi Khamsin 'Am.

28. International Federation of Master Cotton Spinners', Official Report, p. 219.

29. Mosseri was one of the rapporteurs of the 1910 government Cotton Commission, as well as the author of at least eight technical papers, including one on drainage.

30. International Federation of Master Cotton Spinners', Official Report, pp. 208, 209.

31. Abdel Wahhab, Memorandum, pp. 2, 19.

32. He understood that the Japanese could spin Indian yarn on ring spindles; he believed that the crucial innovation by the Japanese was spindle design rather than cotton blending (Ibid. p. 13).

33. M. Hussein K. Teymur, 'De la nécessité d'une réforme de la bourse de commerce d'Alexandrie', L'Egypte Contemporaine, 21, 1914, p. 69.

34. Ibid. p. 65.

35. Nahas, Al Qutn Fi Khamsin 'Am, pp. 218, 220.

36. International Federation of Master Cotton Spinners' and Manufacturers' Associations, Official Report of the XVIII International Cotton Congress (Manchester: The Cloister Press, 1938).

37. Much of the world's oil is produced and sold domestically; the Middle Eastern oil-producing companies are dominant in internationally traded oil.

38. Brian Levy, 'World Oil Marketing in Transition', in *International Organization*, 36(1), 1982, pp. 113–33.

39. David Hawdon, *The Changing Structure of the World Oil Industry* (London: Croom Helm, 1986), p. 35.

40. Levy, 'World Oil Marketing'.

41. Telser and Higinbotham, 'Organized Futures Markets', p. 987.

42. J. E. Treat and B. L. Treat, 'The Future of "Futures"', in Robert G. Reed III and Fereidun Fesharaki (eds), *The Oil Market in the 1990s: Challenges for the New Era* (Boulder, CO: Westview Press, 1989).

43. Paul Horsnell and Robert Mabro, *Oil Markets and Prices: The Brent Market and the Formation of World Oil Prices* (Oxford: Oxford University Press, 1993), p. 3.

44. Abdullah Tariki, 'Nationalization of the Arab Petroleum Industry is a National Necessity', in *League of Arab States, Fifth Arab Petroleum Congress: Papers and Discussion* (Cairo, 1965), pp. 116–17.

45. Ibid. pp. 115–16.

46. See George Philip, *The Political Economy of International Oil* (Edinburgh: Edinburgh University Press, 1994), pp. 299–300. This problem continues at the time of writing, with significant over-staffing, and was dramatically enhanced when the trade union was given the right to allocate drilling contracts. See Mary Ann Tétreault, *Revolution in the World Petroleum Market* (Westport, CT: Quorum Books, 1985), p. 115.

47. Philip, *The Political Economy*, p. 294.

48. Levy, 'World Oil Marketing'.

49. See Treat and Treat, 'The Future of "Futures"'.

50. Cited from the Plan in Richard P. Mattione, *OPEC's Investments and the International Financial System* (Washington, DC: Brookings Institution, 1985), p. 62.

51. Ibid. p. 85.

52. *Saudi Arabia*, (London: Economist Intelligence Unit, 1988), p. 18.

5

Financial Performances of Islamic *versus* Conventional Banks

Clement M. Henry

The purpose of this chapter is to gain a better understanding of the competitive advantages and disadvantages of Islamic banks compared to their conventional counterparts operating in Muslim countries. The '*murabaha* syndrome' described by Tarik Yousef in Chapter 3 suggests that Islamic banks labour under a major disadvantage: long-term financing with *mudaraba* or *musharaka* seems far riskier than the medium- or long-term lending of conventional banks. The Islamic financial instruments presuppose a high degree of trust between business partners, whereas conventional banks can maintain hands-off relationships with their clients, subject to minimal monitoring of their businesses. Without the trust, Islamic financiers would undergo far higher monitoring costs than conventional banks because their long-term 'lending' takes the form of an equity-like investment in the business that would otherwise be 'borrowing' funds from a conventional bank. The Islamic bank cannot afford to be a sleeping partner sharing in the profits of the enterprise because the latter may manipulate its profits and losses at the expense of the bank.

Islamic finance does not yet seem to have resolved this moral hazard problem, for its financing activities remain largely confined to short-term trade financing or leasing. Consequently, Islamic banks would appear to be at a major disadvantage in competing with the conventional banks. The latter may mimic any 'investment' operation of the Islamic bank, but the converse is not true. Conventional banks may generate revenue in many ways from which Islamic banks, unable to charge fixed predetermined interest rates, are excluded. In other words, conventional banks enjoy tremendous advantages over Islamic banks in their ability to place the funds they raise from the general public.

Yet, as shown in Table I.1 of our Introduction, Islamic finance has been growing steadily since the 1970s in countries that are still served by conventional banks. They obviously enjoy one clear-cut competitive advantage in Muslim countries over conventional banks: many, probably a large majority of Muslims, believe that the fixed interest offered to depositors is a form of *riba* and hence illicit. Substantial numbers of them apparently prefer to put their savings into Islamic rather than conventional banks. In wealthy Muslim countries the effects may be dramatic. One international consulting firm estimated in 1999 that conventional banks in Saudi Arabia were losing 2 per cent of their collective deposits annually to new Islamic funds and that these were growing at an annual 15 per cent.[1] In 2002 there seemed to be much room for growth because close to 30 per cent of the Kingdom's commercial bank deposits were non-interest bearing.[2] The driving force behind the Islamic finance movement seems to be the supply of funds rather than the demand for them by businesses in the region.

Possibly, if the faithful are ready to pay a premium, the cost of funds that Islamic banks pay out in the form of profit-sharing to their 'investors' may be less than the interest expenses incurred by conventional banks to attract deposits. Despite their disadvantages in placing funds, they may receive them at less cost and manage to keep up with the conventional banks in overall profitability. Arguably, the shareholders of an Islamic bank, like the depositors, may be willing to pay a premium for their faith and not demand the conventional bankers' rate of return on their investment. In the long run, however, the faithful would probably be unwilling to undergo losses. How viable, in fact, is Islamic banking in the various local Middle Eastern commercial banking markets? Do its special advantages in raising funds from the public offset its disadvantages in placing them? Can these banks keep up with conventional banks in competitive national markets?

AN OVERVIEW OF THE LOCAL MARKETS

These markets already display considerable variation in their acceptance of the new Islamic financial institutions, as Table I.1 of the Introduction indicated. If the Sudan is excluded, there was a fair correlation between the market share of the Islamic banks and the per capita income of their home countries. Egypt, Jordan and Yemen had a bit more Islamic market share than their per capita GDP would predict, whereas a number of countries, most noticeably Libya and Oman in Figure I.1 of the Introduction, had much less. The present inquiry, however, tries to focus not necessarily on the countries that have been the most penetrated by Islamic finance so much as upon those that may display relatively fair playing fields for competition between Islamic and conventional banking.

One factor to be taken into account in the selection of cases is the extent of the private sector in banking. Where government banks have an official monopoly, as in Iraq and Libya, Algeria until the mid-1990s, and Syria until 2001, there is little room for private financial enterprise, whether Islamic or conventional. Even in the Islamic Republic of Iran, it was necessary in 2000 to encourage a private sector for Islamic finance to develop. Egypt and Tunisia practise a veneer of economic liberalism and tolerate limited private activity in their banking sectors. However, their states very largely control their respective systems, as is evidenced by the huge proportions of total assets that their banks deploy. Assuming with LaPorta[3] that holding a 20 per cent stake puts the government in command of a bank, their governments in the mid-1990s respectively controlled over 80 per cent of the total assets of the Tunisian banking system and 96 per cent of Egypt's. The latter has selectively encouraged private Islamic banks, but they generally stand a better chance of developing in relatively liberal economic climates featuring strong private sectors and a plurality of competing banks across both public and private sectors.

The present analysis of financial performances draws on some data from Egypt prior to 1991, when the Faisal Islamic Bank of Egypt suffered major reverses. But the government's overwhelming presence in the commercial banking sector limits any meaningful comparisons between the different types of financial institution. Since 1997, moreover, one of the top two state banks, Bank Misr, has raised more funds in its specialized Islamic banking branches than the largest Islamic bank. Since the Islamic branches do not disclose their operations as an independent profit centre, there is no way to compare their performance with that of a conventional bank. The Islamic branches may simply collect funds that the bank then lends out in conventional ways.

Islamic banks would seem to have better opportunities to compete and to expand their shares of the market in relatively open, liberal economies than in closed ones. Since 1995, the Heritage Foundation, a right-wing American foundation, has published an *Index of Economic Freedom* in cooperation with the *Wall Street Journal*. Figure 5.1 presents the average score of each MENA country that has Islamic banks on 9 of the 10 indicators (excluding low taxation rates that may attract foreign investment but do not necessarily indicate a liberal economic climate). The more open the economy is perceived to be, the lower its score. Bahrain leads the MENA countries on this indicator and indeed became the principal centre of Islamic finance in the late 1990s.

It cannot be argued from the available evidence, however, that economic liberalization has actually enabled Islamic banks to expand their beachheads in the conventional banking system. The trouble is that liberalization is also strongly associated with per capita wealth. When regressions of per capita GDP and our modified *Index of Economic Freedom* are run on Islamic bank deposits, the wealth effect washes out any impact of economic liberalization. Appendix 5.1 reports the results, excluding Sudan and the countries that do not allow any Islamic banking (Iraq, Libya, Morocco, Oman and Syria). It is interesting to note that within this restricted sample Algeria, Lebanon and Tunisia still each 'deviate' about one standard deviation below the Islamic banking share of deposits that their respective per capita incomes and degrees of economic liberalization would predict. Algeria and Tunisia reflect the closed economic environments of financially repressive regimes, whereas in Lebanon Christians still retain substantial

Figure 5.1: Islamic share of commercial bank deposits by a country's degree of economic openness

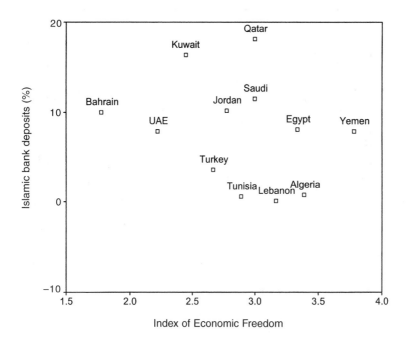

wealth and influence in the banking system. In these settings where Islamic banks have miniscule shares of the market, comparisons with conventional banks would make little sense.

Another way of looking at the competitive environment of Islamic banks is to examine the total amount of credit, as a proportion of GDP, which the commercial banking system provides to the private sector. While Islamic banks also engage in trade financing for public-sector enterprises, their prime customers are private enterprises and households. Figure 5.2 locates their most promising private-sector markets for financing in the GCC countries, Jordan, Egypt, and to a lesser extent in Turkey.

The biggest anomalies, again, are Tunisia and Lebanon, which display relatively generous credit to the private sector (as a percentage of GDP). Two countries not included, because they do not have Islamic banks, are Morocco and Oman, which are positioned close to Tunisia with respect to both economic openness and credit to the private sector. They would appear to be relatively well-placed for Islamic banking but have steadfastly refused entry to such banks. As Commander of the Faithful, King Hassan was unwilling to permit an Islamic alternative to the banks he indirectly controlled through various conglomerates during

Figure 5.2: Islamic share of commercial bank deposits by credit to the private sector

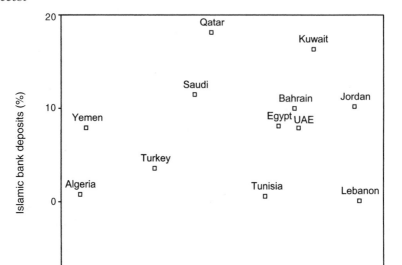

Credit to private sector

his reign, 1961–99. An Islamic alternative might challenge the Commander's religious authority, as well as discredit his conventional financial institutions.

In reality, Saudi Arabia may be an even greater anomaly despite the respectable 11.5 per cent showing of its single Islamic bank, Al-Rajhi Banking and Investment Corporation (ARABIC) and an additional undisclosed market share of dedicated Islamic branches of the Kingdom's largest bank, the National Commercial Bank. Islam's two big transnationals, Al-Baraka and the Faisal Group, both of which are principally owned by Saudis, have unsuccessfully tried for over a decade to obtain commercial banking licences in Saudi Arabia. As in Morocco, one reason for their failure may be that monarchy, so reliant on Islam for its legitimacy, does not wish to run the risk of de-legitimating itself by association with the rest of the banking system. Al-Rajhi received a licence after new laws prevented money-changers from accepting deposits. This big, well-established money-changer was given its licence as a normal commercial bank but then claimed on its own, backed by a religious advisory board, status as an 'Islamic' rather than a conventional commercial bank. Its astonishing success may be the real reason why the transnationals have not been given licences. Their conventional competitors, now including major royal investors like Prince Walid al-

Talal, do not wish to see their profitable enterprises undermined. Some, like the Prince's Saudi American Bank (SAMBA), have established Islamic windows to capture some the growing Islamic sector of the market. As pious, profit-seeking customers gradually shift their funds from non-interest bearing accounts to Islamic investments, conventional banks are devising new Islamic products to satisfy their depositors. In 1999, SAMBA was estimated to have captured 4 per cent of this new market,[4] although it also still enjoyed a substantial share of non-interest bearing deposits – some 21.5 per cent of its total deposits in 2001.[5]

To conclude this overview of the local commercial banking markets, the most promising prospects seem to lie in Saudi Arabia, most of the other GCC countries, Jordan and, with the reservations noted above, Egypt. Although the Turkish commercial banking system seems less penetrated by Islamic banks and generates less private-sector credit (as a percentage of GDP) than the others, it operates in a relatively open economy (see Figure 5.1) and has tolerated the presence of up to six 'special finance houses' in business since 1986. In these market environments that seem relatively open to Islamic banking, we may best observe the distinctive competitive advantages and disadvantages of Islamic banks by comparing their performances with those of conventional banks.

SAUDI ARABIA

With monotonous regularity, since 1990 Al-Rajhi Banking and Investment Corporation (ARABIC) headed the list of GCC banks in total profits, over competitors almost twice its size, such as Saudi Arabia's (with Prince Walid al Talal and Citibank) Saudi American Bank (SAMBA), and the even larger but poorly managed National Commercial Bank. SAMBA caught up with ARABIC in 2000 and posted substantially greater profits than ARABIC in 2001,[6] but in profitability, the ratio of net income to total end-of-year assets, ARABIC's 3.0 per cent was still ahead of SAMBA, although only barely. Two years earlier, ARABIC topped most of the world's commercial banks and beat everybody in the MENA except a handful of nimble investment banks – half of which are also Islamic.[7]

The reason was obvious. ARABIC pays no interest on its current accounts and enjoys a loyal clientele. Unlike most Islamic banks, it pays out only a very small proportion of its profits at the end of the year to the depositors – or 'investors' as they are called, who in other banks hold 'investment deposits' or 'investment savings accounts'. Although ARABIC also carries a relatively small proportion of funds deposited by other banks on its balance sheet, there is no evidence on its income statement that it incurs any interest expenses. Clearly, ARABIC benefits – much more than SAMBA – from the Saudi propensity for non-interest bearing accounts. Remove SAMBA's interest expenses, which amounted to over 3 per cent of its total assets in 1998, and it would have been earning 5.4 per cent on them compared to ARABIC's 3.7 per cent.[8] SAMBA would appear to be the more efficient money machine, but ARABIC has a far lower cost of funds. Similarly, the Riyadh Bank would have earned 4.7 per cent rather than 1.7 per cent on its end-of-year assets.

Arguably, however, the recent momentum in the GCC favouring Islamic banking endangers ARABIC's profits as much as the conventional banks' because depositors seem to be breaking away from their habit of parking funds in non-interest bearing accounts. Data for all of the Saudi banks are not available, but Riyadh Bank indicated in the notes to its 1999 Annual Report that about one-third of its deposits are still 'non-commission sensitive', and *Middle East Economic Digest* reported in 2001 that about 30 per cent of all commercial bank deposits were non-interest bearing. In this respect, Saudi Arabia may be less competitive compared to more demanding publics that expect to earn profits – not interest, of course – from their savings. But Saudi Arabia is changing, even if there are few signs to date of 'the potential cannibalization of deposit bases as funds move off balance sheet'.[9]

Meanwhile other banks like SAMBA are catching up with ARABIC because they benefit more from declining interest rates, which diminish their cost of funds without necessarily passing these 'savings' on to their borrowers. Yet the decline of interest rates can also aversely affect Islamic as well as conventional banks on the 'asset' side of their ledgers. ARABIC's profits diminished by 21 per cent in 2001 because the slow business climate reflected in lower interest rates made it more difficult for the Islamic bank than for others like SAMBA to 'invest' its cost-free funds.[10] Indeed, other Saudi banks with relatively high proportions of non-interest bearing accounts were facing prospects of diminished profitability in 2002. Their lending rates were diminishing without a corresponding reduction of costs.

The future of the Islamic movement may depend on its ability to compete in profits distributed to investment depositors with the interest offered by conventional banks or the profits offered through their Islamic windows. In the more financially demanding climates of the MENA, such as Kuwait or Jordan, the fertile fields of non-interest bearing deposits may be smaller than in Saudi Arabia, though they do exist. In 1998 and 1999, for instance, the Jordanian National Bank reported non-interest bearing accounts amounting to over 15 per cent of its total deposits.[11] But they constituted only 0.1 per cent of the deposits of Kuwait's leading conventional bank, the National Bank of Kuwait[12] and about 10 per cent of the Commercial Bank of Kuwait's.[13] Obviously, more systematic data would be useful but most banks do not yet disclose such matters online or even in their written annual reports – pending stronger regulations about financial disclosure. The *Middle East Economic Digest* reported in 2001 that Kuwaiti banks held an average 15 per cent of their deposits in non-interest bearing accounts, about half the Saudi average.[14]

KUWAIT

The other large established Islamic bank in the GCC is the Kuwait Finance House (KFH). Its depositors expect 'profits', and indeed the KFH regularly posts the annual rate of returns on its various types of investment accounts at the end of the year. No Islamic bank can promise a specific rate of return but, like track records of mutual funds for small investors in the United States, they try to gain reputations for profitability. Table 5.1 compares the average interest rates offered by conventional banks for various kinds of time deposits with the information posted by the KFH in a recent annual report. The latter's categories unfortunately do not specify the type of currency and are therefore not strictly comparable, but the comparison shows that KFH paid a bit less for its short-term deposits than the average conventional bank rate but a bit more, some years, for deposits held for twelve months.

Despite paying customers for their deposits at pretty much market rates, KFH outperformed all the rest of Kuwait's big commercial banks in 1998 and 1999. Its return on assets reached 2.51 per cent at the end of the century – well above the norm of 1.53 per cent collectively achieved by the top 65 banks in the GCC states.[15] KFH's consistent profitability – with steady returns above 2 per cent in the late 1990s – suggest that Islamic banks can survive competition with conventional banks even when depositors combine piety with financial acumen. A closer examination of its balance sheet and income statement, however, indicates that KFH may have enjoyed special advantages. It is 49 per cent owned by the

Table 5.1: Rates of return on Islamic investment accounts and interest rates, 1996–2001

Short-term deposits	1996	1997	1998	1999	2000	2001
KFH rates of return	4.66	4.75	4.80	4.50	4.42	3.50
KD interest rates	6.49	5.96	5.87	5.27	5.43	3.70
USD interest rates	5.24	5.26	5.08	4.86	5.99	3.33
Over one year	1996	1997	1998	1999	2000	2001
KFH rates of return	6.22	6.33	6.40	6.00	5.89	4.67
KD interest rates	6.67	6.22	6.24	5.66	5.85	3.97
USD interest rates	5.49	5.55	5.10	5.10	6.33	3.37

Sources: Central Bank of Kuwait and Kuwait Finance House *Annual Reports*, 2001.

Table 5.2: The earnings and net income of the Kuwait Finance House and the National Bank of Kuwait (KD million)

	KFH 1997	KFH 1998	KFH 1999	NBK 1997	NBK 1998	NBK 1999
Assets	1,581	1,669	1,769	4,118	3,835	3,797
Capital	128	169	192	369	381	397
Deposits	1,185	1,262	1,335	2,434	2,360	2,287
Earnings	122	132	134	330	313	298
Cost of funds	52	58	60	197	182	150
Net income	36	42	44	73	80	93

Sources: Annual reports of the banks and *Middle East Economic Digest*, 14 June 2002.

government, and some ministries encourage their employees to deposit their salaries in the bank, assuring it a steady stream of funds.

It is instructive to compare KFH's financial statements with those of the National Bank of Kuwait (NBK), the country's flagship conventional bank. Table 5.2 compares the earnings and net income of the KFH and NBK, the latter being a much larger institution in terms of assets, customer deposits and paid-up capital. KFH has a relatively lower cost of funding than NBK, reflecting the fact that its pious depositors are prepared to accept somewhat lower returns than conventional bank depositors – it was paying them 1.1 per cent less, on average, than NBK in 1997. This makes it relatively more profitable.

Table 5.3 provides a comparison of key financial ratios for the KFH and NBK over the period from 1997 to 2001. It is apparent that the KFH earned a higher net income on its assets during the early part of the period, but after 2000 NBK caught up. NBK made provisions against non-performing assets that were written off over the period, reducing the value of the bank's total assets as Table 5.2 shows. Once this restructuring was completed, the NBK was able to achieve comparable returns to those of the KFH, despite the latter's lower cost of funding. By the later part of the period, it is clear that the KFH was unable to maintain the very high ratio of net income to capital achieved earlier in the 1990s. To some extent this reflected the need for the bank to increase its capital-to-assets ratio to improve capital adequacy, as in 1997 this was barely acceptable under the Basel capital adequacy requirements that are enforced by the Central Bank of Kuwait. Nevertheless, NBK also increased its capital adequacy over the period while being able to actually improve its net income-to-capital up to 1999, although in 2000 and 2001 it slipped behind the KFH on this measure.

KFH had a relatively stronger base of customer deposits than NBK, which

Table 5.3: Key financial ratios for the NBK and KFH (%)

Kuwait Finance House	1997	1998	1999	2000	2001
Net income/assets	2.3	2.5	2.5	2.4	2.2
Net income/capital	28.5	24.9	23.1	21.9	21.4
Capital/assets	8.1	10.1	10.9	10.7	10.1
National Bank of Kuwait					
Net income/assets	1.8	2.1	2.4	2.5	2.4
Net income/capital	19.9	21.0	23.4	20.2	20.1
Capital/assets	9.0	9.9	10.5	12.2	11.7

Sources: Annual reports of the banks and *Middle East Economic Digest*, 14 June 2002.

relied more heavily on the deposits of other banks for its funds. But KFH also had to work harder for its returns than NBK. A substantially greater proportion of its total assets were tied up in various forms of Islamic financing, risk assets comparable to NBK's loans and advances to customers. KFH generated about as much gross revenue as NBK, proportionate to their respective assets, but it did so by deploying an extra quarter of its total assets in risky transactions. This difference is only partly explained by netting out a bizarre liability on KFH's balance sheet, 'deferred revenue'. KFH appears to have a riskier profile than NBK, yet it was also less capitalized until 1998 and is still so with respect to risky assets which may have adverse implications when the new Basel capital adequacy accords are introduced in 2004. In other words, KFH's capital-to-risky-assets ratio is still much lower than NBK's. KFH also carries more provisions for losses (as a percentage of risky assets) than NBK, but capital and provisions constituted only 21 per cent of KFH's *mudaraba* and leasing assets in 1996 and 1997, compared with NBK's 35 per cent to 37 per cent in 1998 and 1999. The Islamic bank's 49 per cent government ownership perhaps offsets the added the risk. KFH can be relatively confident that the government would bail it out in any emergency. Indeed, in the wake of the Suq al-Manakh crisis of 1982, the KFH's return on assets plummeted from over 2 per cent to zero, and the government rescued it in 1984. Despite its higher return on capital, it distributes slightly smaller returns to shareholders in the form of dividends.

Good government connections and loyal customers have enabled the KFH to compete successfully with Kuwait's flagship conventional bank. Like ARABIC in Saudi Arabia, KFH is a success story. Elsewhere in the Gulf, the Islamic commercial banks have performed less well but have kept their substantial market shares. The pioneer, Dubai Islamic Bank, had to be bailed out in 1999 because of an internal embezzlement scandal but had survived over two decades with returns on assets of less than 1 per cent. In Bahrain and Qatar the financial performances were better – usually over one per cent – but hardly earthshaking. Despite its mediocre return of 1.14 per cent in 1999, however, the Bahrain Islamic Bank (BIB) ranked fifth in the *Middle East Economic Digest's* efficiency index, converting 45 per cent of its gross earnings into net income.[16] Like ARABIC, BIB seems to have benefited from the low cost of funds acceptable to pious depositors. Other small Islamic investment banks, however, did much better. Not only were the International Investor of Kuwait and First Islamic Investment Bank of Bahrain among the top six in efficiency in 1999, they also ranked among the top five in returns on assets, earning from 4.6 up to 17.8 per cent. There was clearly much money to be made from devising new Islamic instruments for a pious and financially sophisticated clientele disenchanted with non-interest bearing deposits in conventional banks.

The wealthy can perhaps afford to satisfy their consciences by taking more risks for slightly less returns in Islamic banks than in interest-bearing accounts. Those who are pious, in the sense of refusing interest, have no alternative except to store their funds in non-interest bearing accounts, donate the interest to charity, or avoid banks altogether. The affluent depositors of the GCC countries are a relatively promising market for Islamic banks. But in the rest of the MENA, with much less per capita wealth and less use of banks generally, Islamic banks seem to have fewer advantages. There will always be a pious minority ready for an alternative to non-interest bearing accounts, but the less wealthy and more risk-averse potential investors may prefer to keep those small savings under the mattress if they do not earn competitive market returns. The case of the Jordan Islamic Bank (JIB) illustrates some of the dilemmas of Islamic finance in the less affluent countries of the MENA.

JORDAN

An affiliate of the al Baraka Group, the Jordanian Islamic Bank opened its first branch office in 1979 and sustained its momentum until the mid-1990s. There is clearly strong demand in Jordan for Islamic banking. JIB claimed over 800,000 accounts in 2001 – quite a substantial number for a country with a population of only five million. The highly respected Arab Bank, the oldest privately-owned bank based in the Arab world as well as one of its largest, opened up a new Islamic bank in 1998 to compete with JIB. It also has plans to extend to other developing Islamic finance nuclei in Egypt, Yemen and the GCC countries, where Arab Bank owns conventional branches or affiliates. There are clearly markets to be won, but small Islamic banks that do not enjoy either strong government protection or a major ally like the Arab Bank may be in trouble.

Figure 5.3: Jordan Islamic Bank's market share

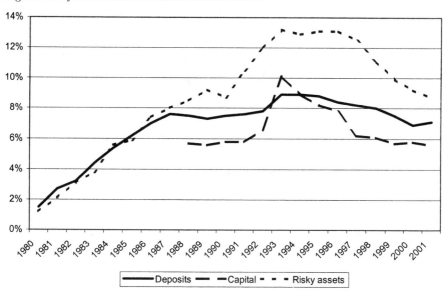

Sources: Jordan Islamic Bank *Annual Reports* and Central Bank of Jordan *Monthly Statistical Bulletins,* various years.

Figure 5.3 pieces together what happened to JIB over the years. There was rapid expansion of its market share of deposits in the early years of its operations but from 1987 onwards its share seems to have flattened out. Despite an infusion of capital in 1993, it could not sustain its ambitious efforts to mobilize ever-greater shares of commercial bank deposits. It continued in the latter 1990s to add more branches but their productivity declined after 1994: each branch on average generated fewer deposits and revenues. Between 1999 and 2001, the bank tripled its number of cash offices to sixteen while reducing its investment in new full-service branches to expand its deposit base. In 2001, the bank finally arrested the trend of losing market share to other commercial banks, but it clearly had difficulty keeping its 'profit rates' paid to depositors in line with prevailing interest rates.

JIB's financial statements reveal serious weaknesses. In its earlier years JIB did fairly well, keeping up with and even in 1985 and 1989 surpassing the average returns on equity of Jordanian public shareholding companies in the financial sector. Between 1989 and 1992, its net income before taxes as a percentage of stockholders' equity outperformed the average return of financial enterprises traded on the Amman Stock Exchange. Although it seems to have been taxed more heavily in the late 1980s than its competitors, its net income after taxes

Table 5.4: Gross earnings-to-asset ratios for second-tier Jordanian banks (%)

	Jordan Islamic Bank	Cairo-Amman Bank	Ahli Bank
1992	5.2	5.0	N/A
1993	5.3	4.8	6.6
1994	5.9	5.2	6.4
1995	5.4	5.9	7.8
1996	5.5	7.1	7.2
1997	4.7	N/A	N/A
1998	4.9	N/A	8.3
1999	3.9	N/A	7.7
2000	3.5	N/A	7.7
2001	3.8	N/A	N/A

Sources: Annual reports of Jordan Islamic, Cairo-Amman and Ahli Banks.

return on equity also kept up with them until 1993. Even in these halcyon years, however, its returns on total assets were mediocre, never even reaching the 1 per cent attained in 1982. During these years, moreover, JIB does not appear to have been as fully capitalized as the average bank.

Figure 5.3 indicates, for instance, that in 1989 the bank's share of capital, reserves and allowances to cover investment losses (provisions for non-performing loans in other banks) was only 5.6 per cent of the total recorded by the Central Bank of Jordan. Yet JIB held a full 9.2 per cent of the total risk assets – loans and other forms of financing outstanding to private and public entities, excluding the central government. Like KFH, it had to work harder for its revenues than conventional banks. Arguably, then, the bank should have been more fully capitalized than other banks to cover the additional financing risks. Islamic banks like to claim that their depositors are, in fact, like stockholders sharing in the bank's profits, but the depositors, like bank regulators, may see it differently.

JIB seems not to have enjoyed any special advantages of cheap sources of funds. Table 5.4 compares its gross earnings (profits after paying off its depositors or 'investors') with the spreads of conventional banks. The two banks, Cairo-Amman and Ahli, were selected because of their comparable medium sizes and relatively mediocre financial performances. Like JIB's, Cairo-Amman's return on assets never exceeded 1 per cent in the early and mid-1990s, and Ahli only did marginally better before falling into the red in 1999.

The data for the cost of funds in Table 5.5 reflects the returns paid to depositors. The Cairo-Amman was paying its depositors even less than JIB – possibly because of low market rates on the West Bank, where Cairo-Amman enjoyed a virtual monopoly until 1995. Ahli was paying out substantially more

Table 5.5: Cost of funds for second-tier Jordanian banks (%)

	Jordan Islamic Bank	Cairo-Amman Bank	Ahli Bank
1992	4.4	3.6	N/A
1993	4.2	2.0	4.6
1994	4.8	2.6	4.9
1995	4.0	3.5	6.5
1996	3.9	4.1	6.5
1997	3.7	N/A	N/A
1998	3.7	N/A	6.8
1999	3.1	N/A	6.0
2000	3.2	N/A	N/A
2001	2.7	N/A	N/A

Sources: Annual reports of Jordan Islamic, Cairo-Amman and Ahli Banks.

than JIB after 1994. In 1999, it lost part of its own capital but still paid depositors 6.6 per cent on average – more than twice as much as JIB. Of course, this 'flexibility' of Islamic banks is cited as one of their strengths: in hard times they are less likely to go bankrupt. But then they are likely to lose depositors. In 1995, JIB reached its high-point in deposits: its share of the market would then steadily decline, even before the Arab Islamic Bank entered the market in 1998.

It seems that JIB simply could not pay depositors well enough to keep them. The number of them grew but the average size of deposits declined, suggesting that JIB's expanding branch network might be tapping into small savings that would otherwise stay under the mattress. But most of the depositors probably expected to earn at least as much as they would from a savings account at a commercial bank – 4 to 5 per cent in the late 1990s.[17] JIB diminished its returns roughly in line with market rates, but its savings accounts earned only 2.13 per cent in 1999[18] compared to the national average of 4.19 per cent. The distribution to these savings accounts increased in 2000 and 2001 to 2.16 per cent,[19] and the national average diminished to 3.76 per cent by the end of 2000 and to 2.9 per cent at the end of 2001.[20] JIB continued to lose market share, down from 7.5 per cent in 1999 to 6.9 per cent in 2000, but then slightly recovered in 2001. The bank simply could not generate enough revenues to meet the going rates.

The explanation was simple: either JIB was undercharging customers for Islamic financing or growing proportions of those risky assets were not being paid off (or had perhaps been lost). JIB's returns on risky assets plunged in the late 1990s; by 1995, they were already lower than the interest rates received by the mid-sized commercial banks. Although these were second-tier banks, with relatively anaemic returns on assets, they were generating substantially greater gross earnings in the mid-1990s. In its worst year, 1999, Ahli generated twice as much as JIB, and the Islamic bank seemed again, as in the early 1990s, to be undercapitalized and over-weighted with risk assets. Although its share of the commercial banking system's deposits had contracted to 7.1 per cent in 2001, its share of the banking system's capital was only 5.6 per cent, whereas it still held 8.7 per cent of the risk assets (or loans) despite efforts to manage them and write off non-performing ones. Its net income in 2001 plummeted to only 0.1 per cent of its average total assets and the capital of the bank actually decreased during the year. Despite lower interest rates being paid by other commercial banks, it seems that it had to spend some capital to protect its base of depositors. Perhaps competition with the Arab Islamic Bank would oblige JIB to contract further and write off any non-performing assets so as to regain profitability. A number of other Islamic banks have faced similar problems.

For years, for instance, Faisal Islamic Bank of Egypt (FIBE) has stagnated, for reasons Samer Soliman explains in Chapter 12. In more difficult straits than JIB, the Egyptian bank lost market share and generated scarcely enough revenue to pay off its depositors. In the mid-1980s it was so desperate to generate revenue that it lent hard currency to the Central Bank of Egypt for importing commodities; then, when Egypt's foreign exchange situation improved, it lent out funds to the Bank of Credit and Commerce International (BCCI), which offered it higher than market rates. The collapse of the BCCI in 1991 initially cost FIBE some 20 per cent of its balance sheet. Most of the funds were eventually recovered, and in 1999, for the first time in almost a decade, FIBE claimed a small profit (0.3 per cent of its total assets). But meanwhile its deposits did not keep up with inflation between 1995 and 1998, and FIBE held on to barely 3 per cent of the market (down from 9.7 per cent in 1986, see Table I.1 of Introduction). Like JIB, it simply could not generate enough earnings to distribute adequate 'profits' to depositors, much less to shareholders of the bank. Like JIB, however, the bank survived and in fact had 3.5 per cent of the market for commercial bank deposits at the end of 2000.

The Islamic banks in Egypt and Jordan did not enjoy as much support as their Kuwaiti counterpart among major elements of their respective governments and Islamist political oppositions. The political relationships are discussed in further detail in the country studies on Kuwait, Jordan and Egypt. In Jordan and especially Egypt, the banks kept their distance from Islamist political parties and associations in order to stay in the good graces of their respective governments. Differences in their respective political environments may help to explain why the Jordan Islamic Bank's financial performance was so much weaker than that of the Kuwait Finance House. JIB did not enjoy the political connections that facilitated KFH's ability to generate revenues comparable to those of a strong conventional bank. The KFH, it should be recalled, paid about 1 per cent less returns to its depositors than the National Bank of Kuwait, and it held a much higher percentage of risky assets than the conventional bank despite being less capitalized. Assured of government support in the event of major losses, it could afford a riskier profile than Kuwait's flagship conventional bank. It may be the political connections as much or more than any technical differences between Islamic and conventional banks that condition their respective financial performances.

TURKEY

If so, Turkey presents an ideal laboratory for testing the proposition that changes in the political climate may affect the financial performance of Islamic banks. Under special legislation encouraged by Prime Minister Turkut Özal, two 'special finance houses', al Baraka and Faisal, were established in 1985. These two Saudi–Turkish joint ventures represented Islamic banking's two principal multinationals, Sheikh Saleh Kamel's Al-Baraka Group and Prince Mohammad al-Faisal's Dar al-Maal al-Islami. They were joined in 1989 by Kuwait Turkish Evkaf, a joint venture between the Kuwait Finance House and Türkiye Vakiflar Bankası. Vakiflar is a small public-sector bank with historical ties to Turkey's religious endowments. Subsequently, Turkish private investors founded three special finance houses: Anadolu Finans in 1991, Ihlas Finance House in 1995, and finally Asya in 1996.

Very briefly, to anticipate Feliz Baskan's in Chapter 10, these special finance houses enjoyed various privileges, continued after President Özal's death in 1991 until April 1994, when the Central Bank rescinded some of them.[21] In the 1995 legislative elections, however, the National Welfare Party, Turkey's Islamist political party, won 23 per cent of the vote to become the largest party represented in Turkey's Parliament. Its leader, Necmettin Erbakan, became prime minister until the Turkish military ousted him from power in 1997. He was disbarred from politics, with the banning of his party in 1998, but the Virtue Party quickly took its place in Parliament and contested the 1999 elections, where it did not fare as well as in 1995. Virtue in its turn was abolished in 2001 and gave rise to two new Islamist parties, Contentment and the Justice and Development Party. Not only did the military crack down on the political Islamists, by 1999 they were also attacking religious orders, Islamist business groups and the special finance houses. A new Paragraph 6 of Article 20 of the Banks Law No. 4389 integrated the latter into Turkey's commercial banking system in 1999 and eliminated the special privileges accorded to the special finance houses in Decree Number 7506 of 16 December 1983.[22]

Until 1998, in short, the special finance houses enjoyed a relatively favourable political climate, although it may already have begun to deteriorate after the dismissal of Erbakan's government in February 1997. As Baskan explains in Chapter 10, the special finance houses had expanded their branch networks primarily in the cities where the political Islamists had electoral strength. The military's persecution of the political party may consequently also have begun to put pressure on the special finance houses before 1999, to the extent that they were perceived as being associated with the party or having enjoyed special favours from a pro-Islamist government. After 1999, if political connections really did materially condition the financial performances of these banks, the negative effects should show up on their balance sheets and income statements.

Turkey experienced a major banking crisis in November 2000, followed by a severe foreign exchange crisis in 2001 that adversely affected the financial performance of virtually every commercial bank in the country. Declines in the special finance houses' overall returns on assets, spreads and capital adequacy could therefore be ascribed as much to general economic conditions as to the deteriorating political climate for businesses marked with an Islamic tendency. Indeed, amid the mounting foreign exchange crisis the Banking Regulation and Supervision Agency (BDDA) revoked the licence of the largest of them, İhlas Finance House, on 10 February 2001, after it was discovered that it had siphoned off over $1 billion to its parent holding company.[23]

No balance-sheet analysis can neatly isolate political from macroeconomic effects, much less plain mismanagement, but the available Turkish data still offer possibilities for controlling macroeconomic effects by comparing different categories of commercial banks. The Central Bank publishes monthly statements of the aggregated balance sheets and income statements of the special finance houses, and the Banks Association of Turkey (BAT) presents yearly analyses of the conventional banks by type of enterprise, whether commercial or investment, private or public sector or under government receivership (the eleven Turkish banks, including those that failed in November 2000, that are managed by the Deposit Insurance Fund) or foreign, as well as presenting the performance ratios of each bank. It is possible, using the BAT data, to compare the special finance houses as a group with other commercial banks with respect to profitability, capital adequacy and spreads by constructing equivalent ratios for the special finance houses.

Compared to the entire set of Turkey's conventional banks, the special finance houses perform reasonably well, although their market share of deposits has dramatically diminished with the collapse of the İhlas Finance House, which held about 40 per cent of the special finance houses' total assets. As Table I.1 of the introduction indicated, the market share of the special finance houses declined by about half, from 3.5 to 1.8 per cent, between the end of 2000, when the İhlas Finance House was still in business, until the following November. Some of this decline resulted from the general panic that seized many of the hundreds of thousands of depositors in the special finance houses when they realized that they did not enjoy the deposit insurance that protected the small depositors in conventional banks. Deposits diminished in absolute terms despite inflation and reached a low of 1.64 per cent of the market in May 2001 before recovering somewhat. The drop was even more precipitous than Table I.1 indicated because the six finance houses had been attracting around 3.9 per cent of Turkey's commercial bank deposits between March and November 2000.

Despite mounting concerns in Turkey about the solvency of the entire financial system, however, the special finance houses remained profitable until 2001. As of 31 December 2000, the six houses collectively claimed a net return of 0.6 per cent on their average of total assets held during the year, and if the ailing İhlas Finance House is excluded, the net return of the remaining five houses was 1.5 per cent. These numbers compared favourably with those of the entire banking system, with the entire commercial banking system, and with the public sector commercial banks, which respectively lost 2.8, 3.2 and 0.5 per cent of their average total assets. The five surviving finance houses even did a little better than the private-sector commercial banks that were not in receivership. The healthy ones averaged a 1.1 per cent return on their average assets. Table 5.6 presents the 'return on average assets' data by type of bank for the years 1990–2000, beginning when three of the special finance houses were already well-established yet still enjoying a special legal status.

Table 5.6: Net income as a proportion of total assets for Turkish banks (%)

	1990	1991	1992	1993	1994	1995	1996	1997	1998	1999	2000
The Turkish banking system	2.5	1.9	2.2	2.8	1.4	2.9	3.1	2.7	2.3	−0.5	−2.8
Commercial banks	2.6	2.0	2.3	2.9	1.6	3.0	3.1	2.6	2.1	−0.8	−3.2
State-owned commercial banks	2.0	0.5	1.7	2.4	0.0	0.2	0.7	0.6	0.7	1.2	−0.5
Privately-owned commercial banks	3.2	3.1	2.5	3.2	2.4	4.9	4.6	3.8	4.7	4.4	1.1
Banks under the Dep. Insur. Fund									−72.7	−88.9	−47.6
Foreign banks	3.0	5.7	6.6	4.2	7.3	6.4	5.5	5.7	6.0	6.8	0.7
Development and investment banks	1.8	1.4	1.3	1.8	−1.1	2.2	3.7	2.9	5.8	6.0	4.8
Special finance houses	2.8	1.9	1.8	1.2	0.7	1.2	1.8	2.1	1.9	1.2	0.6
without İhlas Finance House											1.5

Sources: Banks Association of Turkey, Central Bank of Republic of Turkey, *Quarterly Bulletins*

On average, the special finance houses were about as profitable in their early days as the entire banking system, and they tended to perform slightly better than the state-owned commercial banks, albeit not as well as the privately-owned ones. In the mid-1990s, their profitability declined slightly, possibly reflecting their loss of special privileges in 1994. Profitability rose again in 1996, possibly reflecting the more favourable political environment for the Islamists, with the Welfare Party's leader now serving as prime minister. Despite his dismissal from power in 1997, however, the special finance houses continued to perform relatively robustly until 1999. Their profitability then deteriorated, but then so also did that of the entire Turkish banking system, which operated at a loss in 1999 and 2000 under the burden of bank failures (eleven banks with 12.9 per cent of the total bank deposits were managed by 31 December 2000, under the Deposit Insurance Fund). Any political fallout from the dismissal of the Erbakan government in 1997 and subsequent attacks on Islamist business groups, discussed below in the Turkish case studies, does not seem to have affected the profitability of the special finance houses. They seem to have weathered the banking crisis of November 2000 as well as the privately-owned commercial banks. With the collapse of İhlas, however, they lost much of their deposit base, and their ratio of overdue receivables to placements (analogous to the commercial banking percentage of non-performing loans) rose dangerously, to 24.7 per cent by November 2001, higher than that of the entire banking system's 18 per cent and much more than the private commercial banking sector's 4.9 per cent.

Irrespective of the gyrations of Turkish domestic politics, the special finance houses were structurally more vulnerable to a prolonged financial crisis than the conventional private banks. Careful comparisons of the balance sheets and income statements of the Islamic with the privately-owned conventional commercial banks present a picture resembling those of Kuwait and Jordan. The Islamic banks had to work harder, with greater exposure to risk, than their conventional counterparts. They had to invest more of their assets than the conventional banks in risky 'placements', and consequently were more vulnerable to a serious deterioration in the business environment. Table 5.7 presents the relevant data. The commercial banks had a much lower portion of their assets accounted for by lending to the private sector, the equivalent of the special finance houses' placements, largely because the banks lent a major part of their funds to the government itself.

The special finance houses consistently carried far more risky assets on their balance sheets than the conventional banks. The percentage of 'placements' of the former's total assets were up to double those of the loans in the privately-owned banks. In 2000, placements constituted 76.2 per cent of the special finance houses' collective balance sheet, whereas loans made up only 37.7 per cent of private banks' total assets. Thus, the Turkish houses worked at least as hard, relative to conventional banks, as their Jordanian and Kuwaiti counterparts. Yet the special finance houses were undercapitalized compared to the conventional banks. For twice the risk they were supported by only half the capital: in 2000 the special finance houses' total shareholders' equity amounted to a mere 7.1 per cent of their total assets, whereas bank capital covered 14 per cent of the assets of the private banks. The Turkish finance houses appeared to have riskier structures than either their Kuwaiti or Jordanian counterparts. They also had relatively little liquidity compared to conventional banks, since so much of their collective balance sheet was carrying risky placements. The liquidity of the special finance houses seems to have diminished in the late 1990s, as they struggled to earn returns on as much of their assets as possible – at least until 2001, when the business climate worsened and their 'overdue receivables' skyrocketed. Until then the special finance houses apparently did not have appreciably more overdue receivables than the banks' non-performing loans, and their provisions were about as adequate.

Table 5.7: Asset ratios of the special finance houses and commercial banks compared

	1990	1991	1992	1993	1994	1995	1996	1997	1998	1999	2000	2001
Special finance houses												
Placements/ assets	69.0	67.9	74.1	77.9	69.9	71.1	72.8	71.9	72.9	75.3	76.2	51.3
Overdue	2.6	2.8	1.2	N/A	N/A	N/A	N/A	N/A	4.4	4.4	5.7	24.7
Liquid/total assets	10.0	13.9	11.5	N/A	N/A	N/A	N/A	N/A	7.9	8.0	4.8	17.8
Spreads/assets	6.0	6.5	4.5	5.8	4.8	5.3	5.9	7.7	5.9	6.4	7.2	N/A
Cost of funds/ investments	25.1	20.6	18.5	18.8	15.4	13.9	16.6	18.3	13.9	16.4	13.7	18.3
Commercial banks												
Loans/assets	43.0	39.8	39.8	40.5	39.8	39.1	43.6	44.7	41.4	33.5	37.7	32.5
Non-perform/ loans	2.6	2.7	2.3	1.8	2.6	1.8	1.6	2.0	2.4	3.6	6.1	4.9
Liquid/total assets	42.5	43.0	44.0	38.4	42.7	46.0	37.7	41.7	43.5	39.0	36.5	36.4
Spreads/assets	6.0	7.4	7.6	9.2	7.8	9.8	10.0	10.3	12.5	9.8	6.7	N/A
Cost of funds/ loans	20.4	18.7	18.0	14.0	15.5	18.2	17.9	17.8	19.3	18.4	13.2	16.0

Sources: Banks Association of Turkey, Central Bank of Republic of Turkey, *Quarterly Bulletins*.

Their vulnerability arose from the spreads, the difference between a conventional bank's interest earned on loans and paid on deposits, or between the profits of an Islamic bank's investments and those profits distributed to its depositor/investors. As Table 5.7 shows, the spreads as a percentage of average total assets of the special finance houses were generally lower than those of the commercial banks. Their cost of funds as a percentage of investments regularly exceeded that of the commercial banks (with respect to loans) until the mid-1990s. Over the years, these costs would mount, not because the special finance houses paid higher 'profit' rates than the banks' prevailing interest rates, but because they had to carry more deposits than the conventional banks to support their heavier investment (loan) portfolios. Yet their profits on the average of portfolio investments held over the year tended to be substantially less than the interest income received by the commercial banks for their averages of loan holdings. Table 5.7 points to major reductions in these spreads in 1994–95, just those years when the special finance houses were most suffering from the government's decision to rescind their special status. By 1997, however, the special finance houses almost caught up with the commercial banks before business slowed for them in 1998.

The year 1998 perhaps reflected the consequences of a troubled political scene. In that year the Welfare Party was shut down, giving rise to the Virtue Party. Perhaps, if political Islamists and politically minded businesses had been generating good business for the special finance houses, their troubles also got reflected in poorer financial performances. Perhaps the problem of the poor spreads was as much political as structural. If the special finance houses were able to finance longer-term investment at higher prices, they would be less in need of overextended balance sheets. But the 1995–97 rises in profits came to an end in 1998, even while the commercial banks were enjoying their best year. By the turn of the millennium, the special finance houses 'caught up' only in the sense that the commercial banks' revenues and spreads also declined sharply. Perhaps the easiest way to see this structural or possibly political disadvantage of the special finance houses is to compare their ratio of profits to profit distributions with the conventional banks' ratio of interest income to interest expenses. The special finance houses were always at some disadvantage, though least so in 1997 after the political Islamists had enjoyed over a year in power.

Their other Achilles heel was a serious rise in operating expenses. These expenses were substantially less, as a proportion of total assets, than those of the conventional banks in the early 1990s, but by the end of the decade they had traded places: while the conventional banks tightened their belts and reduced employee expenses, the special finance houses splurged – even while keeping their employee expenditures below those of the conventional banks. Special finance house branches worked harder and on average carried twice the deposits and processed three times the loans of the conventional banks. Yet their overall operating expenses were greater.

By November 2001, the special finance houses appeared, at least on average, to be approaching insolvency. They had contracted their portfolios of placements to 51.3 per cent of total assets but still carried substantially more risky assets than the conventional banks. About one quarter of the special finance houses' collective portfolio was 'overdue', and their collective equity and provisions could barely cover two-thirds of it. Al-Baraka and Anadolu Finans seemed to be in particularly dire straits, whereas Faisal, bought out by a Turkish shareholder and renamed the Family Bank, still prospered.

CONCLUSION

Whether in Jordan, Kuwait, or Turkey, three of the most favourable environments for Islamic banking, it seems that Islamic financial institutions always needed special help and privileges if they were to survive in competition with conventional banks. There is no doubting the existence of a niche market for these innovative companies, since many Muslims distrust conventional banks. But so far there have been few synergies between political Islam and these financial institutions that could enable the latter – by covering some of the monitoring costs associated with domestic investment – to generate the necessary revenues to pay their investor/depositors competitive rates without carrying too heavy a portfolio of risky investments. The one instance of relative success is Kuwait. Yet even the Kuwait Finance House displayed a much riskier and exposed financial profile than its principal competitor. The KFH's prime defence was its government ownership. Another possible illustration of synergy between financial and political Islamism may be that of the special finance houses in Turkey during the 1995–97 years when the Welfare Party achieved power. But this experiment was too short to be conclusive. Short of special political conditions, it seems that Islamic banking suffers the structural effects of incurring greater risk for domestic lending than the conventional banks. In the absence of major economic reform and consequent reduction in monitoring costs, which would benefit Islamic more than conventional banks, it may be more interesting to view the former (and conventional banks, too, for that matter) as vehicles for mobilizing overseas investment or 'capital flight'.

Appendix 5.1: Regression of per capita GDP and economic openness on Islamic bank deposits

Variables Entered/Removed[b]

Model	Variables entered	Method
1	Index of economic Freedom, per capita GDP 1998[a]	Enter

[a] All requested variables entered
[b] Dependent variable: Islamic bank deposits

Model Summary[b]

Model	R	R square	Adjusted R square	Std. error of the estimate
1	0.731[a]	0.534	0.431	0.04436

[a] Predictors: (Constant), Index of Economic Freedom, per capita GDP 1998
[b] Dependent variable: Islamic bank deposits

ANOVA[b]

Model		Sum of squares	df	Mean square	F	Sig.
1	Regression	0.020	2	0.010	5.162	0.023[a]
	Residual	0.018	9	0.002		
	Total	0.038	11			

[a] Predictors: (Constant), Index of Economic Freedom, per capita GDP 1998
[b] Dependent variable: Islamic bank deposits

Coefficients[a]

Model		Unstandardised coefficients		Standardised coefficients		
		B	Std. error	Beta	t.	Sig.
1	(Constant)	−6.13E−02	0.103		−0.593	0.568
	Per capita GDP 1998	6.347E−06	0.000	0.856	2.989	0.015
	Index of Economic Freedom	2.713E−02	0.031	0.252	0.879	0.402

[a] Dependent variable: Islamic bank deposits

Casewise Diagnostics[a]

Case number	VAR00004	Std. residual	Islamic bank deposits	Predicted value	Residual
3	Algeria	−1.207	0.01	0.0615	−0.0535
84	Jordan	1.438	0.10	0.0382	−0.0638
93	Lebanon	−1.205	0.00	0.0545	−0.0535
163	Tunisia	−1.047	0.01	0.0525	−0.0465

[a] Dependent variable: Islamic bank deposits

NOTES

1. Diane B. Glossman, *Citigroup: Saudi Arabia – A Special Case*, Lehman Brothers, 7 October 1999, pp. 17–18.
2. 'Special Report: Standing at the Crossroads', *Middle East Economic Digest*, 21 December 2001, p. 27.
3. Rafael La Porta, Florencio Lopez-de-Silanes and Andrei Shleifer, *Government Ownership of Banks*, National Bureau of Economic Research Working Paper No. 7620, 2000.
4. Glossman, *Citigroup*, pp. 17–18.
5. 'Non-Interest Bearing Accounts', *Middle East Economic Digest*, 11 May 2001, p. 28.
6. 'Special Report Banking: How they rank', *Middle East Economic Digest*, 14 June 2002, p. 28.
7. *Middle East Economic Digest*, 23 June 2000, p. 40.
8. Saudi American Bank (SAMBA), *Saudi Arabia: Investors' Guide*, MEED Money, 1999, pp. 16–17.
9. *Middle East Economic Digest*, 14 June 2002, p. 2.
10. Ibid.
11. Jordan National Bank, *Annual Report*, 1999.
12. http://www.nbk.com/nbktoday/data/annualrep99.pdf
13. http://www.banktijari.com/index_ht.html
14. 'Non-Interest Bearing Accounts', p. 28.
15. *Middle East Economic Digest*, 23 June 2000, p. 40.
16. Ibid., p. 38.
17. Central Bank of Jordan, *Monthly Statistical Bulletin*, Table 21, http://www.cbj.gov.jo/docs/bulletin/21.html, 28 August 2000.
18. Jordan National Bank, *Annual Report*, 1999, p. 30.
19. Jordan National Bank, *Annual Report*, 2000, p. 32; and 2001, p. 27.
20. Central Bank of Jordan, *Monthly Statistical Bulletin*, Table 22, http://www.cbj.gov.jo/docs/bul_1_e.html
21. 'Our step children: special finance institutions', *Turkish Daily News*, 13 February 2001, http://www.turkishdailynews.com/old_editions/02_14_01/scanner.htm
22. Central Bank of the Republic of Turkey, *Annual Report*, 2001; Clement M. Henry, *The Mediterranean Debt Crescent: A Comparative Study of Money and Power in Algeria,*

Egypt, Morocco, Tunisia, and Turkey (Gainesville, FL: University Press of Florida, 1996), pp. 94, 126.

23. 'Ihlas Finans outlines liquidation plan', *Turkish Daily News*, 14 February 2001, http://www.turkishdailynews.com/old_editions/02_14_01/econ.htm

6

Capital Flight through Islamic Managed Funds

Rodney Wilson

In much of the Islamic World finance is asymmetric, as private wealth is, at least in part, generated locally but then invested in Western markets, a phenomenon which is referred to as capital flight. In contrast, Muslim governments mostly fail to raise sufficient revenue to cover their expenditures, and as a result they become dependent on international borrowing to fund their deficits. There is, in other words, varying degrees of private affluence and this is by no means confined to the oil-exporting states of the Gulf; at the same time there is public squalor and run down and decaying public services. To what extent can Islamic finance help solve these imbalances? Is the application of *shari'a* law a help or hindrance to the development of domestic financial intermediation and national financial markets in Muslim countries?

As Islamic finance is by definition primarily of concern to Muslims, its adoption might be expected to result in capital markets of the Islamic World becoming segmented from global markets based on conventional finance. Indeed, Islamic markets might be ghettoised, which might imply losing out on some of the potential gains from globalisation, such as economies of scale in financing and lower transactions costs. On the other hand, global capitalism is often viewed as exploitative from a Muslim developing country perspective, with the gains from international financial integration unfairly distributed.

In this chapter the direction of Islamic investment is analysed. Financial flows through the Islamic Development Bank (IDB) are examined, as these involve recycling within the Muslim World, but the main focus is on outward portfolio investment flows, especially those through managed funds. There is relatively little Islamic foreign direct investment, reflecting the failure of indigenous multinational companies to develop in most Muslim countries where governments are resistant to competing local centres of economic power beyond their control. The Islamic managed fund industry remains modest in scale, with assets worth less than $10 billion, but it is qualitatively significant, as its experience demonstrates the constraints in redirecting Muslim capital flows to emerging Muslim markets.

ISLAMIC CAPITALISTS AND THE STATE IN THE MIDDLE EAST

Governments in the Middle East have not only failed to attract significant amounts of Western capital through foreign direct investment, they have also been unwilling and unable to create the conditions for domestic Islamic capital accumulation. Ironically, it is in the much more liberal conditions of Western markets that Islamic capital is starting to flourish, and where most Islamic wealth creation is occurring as a result of outward portfolio investments. Domestic economic liberalisation in the Middle East is a necessary precondition for capital flight to be reversed, and for Islamic investors to feel that they are stakeholders in their own economies, rather than being globally footloose and nationally rootless. Governments and Islamic investors both recognise the links between money and political power, but while governments in the Middle East use their influence to monopolise resources, Islamic investors need more diverse, competitive structures and the economic space to pursue their own entrepreneurial activities. In this respect, their needs are no different than those of Western capitalists.

Though frustrated by their own governments, a number of leading Muslim businessmen have nevertheless profited from agency rights they have obtained from the state, and enjoyed its protection of their monopoly privileges to initiate their wealth. Any patronage system, partly because of its inherent inefficiencies, is limited in its ability to transform millionaires into billionaires. For more serious wealth accumulation Islamic investors have therefore had to look beyond the state at the global marketplace, hence the trend towards capital flight. Saad Eddin Ibrahim referred to Saudi Arabian entrepreneurs as 'lumpen capitalists', believing that by the 1970s, as a result of the oil boom, they no longer were traditional merchants, but yet at the same time they had not become entrepreneurial in the Western sense of taking risks with their capital.[1] Nevertheless, far from being a parasite and reaping profits without work, Ibrahim sees the Saudi entrepreneur as a 'cultural broker par excellence', interpreting the socio-political environment of the Kingdom to the outside world and vice versa.[2]

Contemporary Islamic capitalists are also cultural brokers, in the sense of acting as intermediaries between societies that are guided by shari'a law and the wider global economy that is largely based on Western modes of capital accumulation. Whereas in the 1970s and early 1980s, when there was much profit to be made in government contracts, especially in the Gulf, the Islamic capitalists relied on the state, by the 1990s, with a weakening economic role for the state, Islamic capitalists were seeking alternatives. One was to look at investment opportunities in booming Western markets, and profit from channelling capital – both their own and that of others for whom they acted as intermediaries – towards these markets. Labelling such activity involving capital flight as Islamic finance made it more acceptable, especially if respected *shari'a* scholars could be persuaded to endorse the practice.

MUSLIM BELIEFS AS A CONDITIONING FACTOR IN INVESTMENT BEHAVIOUR

A religion can get its teachings respected and enforced either by having government acting on its behalf or by persuading individual believers to act in accordance with their faith, or by some mixture of the two. Political Islamists advocate the former, by having governments enforce *shari'a* law in all areas of human activity, including the financial sphere, as with Iran's Islamic banking laws of 1983. An alternative, and arguably preferable, approach is to support the provision of Islamic financing facilities to ensure that individual believers can manage their finances in accordance with Islamic teaching, while at the same time permitting conventional financial institutions to continue functioning. Such a dual system is found in the majority of countries with substantial Muslim populations, with the growth of Islamic finance driven by market forces rather than government dictate. In such a dual system, whether to use Islamic financial services is a matter of personal moral choice in a marketplace where there are differentiated products, some with ethical as well as purely financial characteristics. There are many parallels here between the ethical finance industry and Islamic financing, with marketing using moral suasion to appeal to conscience and stressing social benefits rather than simply private returns.

Muslim investors could be better served by Islamic economists and finance specialists than they have been up to the time of writing. In their discussion of Islamic economic agents, Farhad Nomani and Ali Rahnema focus on consumer behaviour, the stress being on moderation, but they remain silent on investor behaviour.[3] Ibrahim Warde does not treat the behaviour of savers and investors explicitly, although he does discuss problems of moral hazard in an Islamic context in relation to debt,[4] and there is a brief acknowledgement of the difficulties investors face in emerging markets.[5] The only discussion of Islamic investment funds has been by Muhammad Taqi Usmani, who serves as *shari'a* advisor to numerous Islamic banks and conventional banks offering Islamic financing and asset-management facilities.[6]

Although the message of Islam is universal, most have taken national rather than internationalist perspectives, and have little to say about issues such as capital flight. Umer Chapra[7] refers to capital flight from Iran as one factor whose legacy adversely affected the Islamic banking system, but there is no discussion of country risk perceptions as a cause of capital flight. Chapra also correctly diagnoses the causes of the Asian financial crisis of 1997 as the mismatch between reliance on short-term dollar-denominated debt and longer-term lending in local currencies, which affected Muslim countries such as Malaysia and Indonesia, but there is no attempt to provide a specifically Islamic critique.[8] There is, for example, the issue of whether government imposition of capital controls is justified. On the one hand, such controls may prevent Muslims, admittedly the wealthy, from exporting their capital and earning potentially higher and less risky returns. On the other hand, controls may help maintain the value of the currency, keeping down the price of imported foodstuffs and other basic commodities for the poor, and ensure that local savings at least are deployed into national investments.

There has also been surprisingly little written by Islamic economists on economic cooperation between Muslim countries. Although Munawar Iqbal expressed his frustration that surplus funds from some Muslim countries and their citizens were not deployed in other Muslim countries lacking resources for development, he did not analyse why this was the case.[9] Similarly, Masudul Alam Choudhury applied the principles of *taweed* and brotherhood to Islamic economic cooperation, but failed to suggest how such a programme of cooperation could be implemented in any practical sense apart from in the sphere of Islamic trade financing.[10]

DEVELOPMENT ASSISTANCE AS A MEANS OF PROPAGATING ISLAMIC LAW

Islamic finance was viewed as a potential unifying factor by the Muslim governments meeting under the auspices of the Organisation of the Islamic Conference (OIC) in 1973 and subsequently. The OIC was established as a forum for political dialogue between Muslim states on matters of mutual interest, including relations with the West and the rights of Muslims in Palestine. Some of its proponents, notably the government of Saudi Arabia, saw it as an alternative to the secular Arab League, which had been used, wholly unsuccessfully by Nasser, as a vehicle for Arab unity, including economic unity. Rather than focusing on trade relations, as the Arab League had done, the OIC in the economic sphere emphasised financial relations, partly because trade between Muslim states was only a small proportion of their total trade, most of which was with the West, and it was recognised from the ill-fated experiences of the Arab Common Market and the Arab Economic Unity Council, that it would be difficult to change this reality.

With the oil price increases of 1973–74, Saudi Arabia had vastly increased financial resources at its disposal, which could potentially be used to further the regime's international relations objectives, namely secure recognition as the guardian of the holy sites of Islam and counter criticism from both Arab nationalists and political Islamists that it was too closely involved with the

United States. There was a continuing tension between the Kingdom's dependence on Western oil markets and the United States as a military protector, and
its desire for legitimacy as a defender of the *shari'a* law in the eyes of both
Muslim governments and Islamist groups, at home and abroad, who were at best
openly suspicious of Western and Zionist intentions, and, more often, virulently
opposed to western secularist values and the threat they posed to the Islamic
World. In the majority of Muslim countries, governments either ignored or
suppressed such Islamist groups, but Saudi Arabia, a regime based on Wahabbi
credentials, could not embark on a policy of suppression, especially as many of
its own citizens shared the views of these Islamist groups, and, in some cases,
were prepared to offer them financial backing in their struggles with their own
regimes or the West.

Egypt depicted the 1973 war as a victory for the Arab cause due to the efforts
of its soldiers in crossing the Suez Canal and establishing a bridgehead in Sinai.
Sadat argued that the oil price increases, which benefited Saudi Arabia but not
Egypt, had come about through its sacrifices, and therefore it was entitled to
financial recompense. Other Arab states without oil, notably Jordan and the
Sudan, asserted that they were being forced to pay more for oil imports from their
Arab neighbours, and more distant Muslim states such as Pakistan and Malaysia
voiced similar concerns. Saudi Arabia's response was to support the founding of
the Islamic Development Bank (IDB), with itself as the major shareholder.

The remit of the IDB, which was established in 1975, was to foster economic
development and social progress in Muslim countries in accordance with the
principles of the *shari'a*. The bank has financed trade within the Islamic World
and numerous projects in Muslim countries, but over a quarter of a century of its
impact has been, at best, limited. Funds have been recycled within the Muslim
World, but the results were modest in relation to the aspirations of the OIC.
The initial paid-up capital was only $750 million, of which Saudi Arabia sub-
scribed $200 million, a modest sum in relation to its financial resources at that
time.[11] By 2000, the paid-up capital of the IDB was almost $8 billion, which seems
impressive but is modest in relation to the financial resources of major global
organizations such as the International Monetary Fund, which is capitalised at
$290 billion. Saudi Arabia's share of IDB capital is $2 billion, a substantial but
by no means overwhelming commitment.

The IDB does not finance projects in Saudi Arabia, but the Kingdom has
benefited indirectly, as almost one-third of the trade financing by the IDB has
been for oil imports, with one of the original aims of the new institution being
to assist poorer Muslim countries without oil resources to pay for their essential
imports, especially after the oil price rises of 1973–74. The IDB has approved
trade financing arrangements worth over $15 billion and project finance valued
at more than $6.5 billion, as well as 340 technical assistance operations.[12] In

recent years, trade financing has involved a diverse range of commodities, including industrial intermediate goods ($3.2 billion), vegetable oil ($900 million), refined petroleum products ($769 million), fertilisers, phosphoric acid and potash ($465 million), rice and wheat ($459 million) and cotton ($367 million). Although these figures seem large, they refer to cumulative financing over the 1975–99 period, which averages out to approximately $1 billion per annum, a much smaller amount. By comparison, World Bank funding amounts to $17 billion per annum.

The IDB attempts to set an example by using *shari'a*-compliant financing methods, with much of the trade financing being offered through *murabaha*, mark-up funding with the bank purchasing goods on behalf of the importer and reselling them at a premium. Project finance has become increasingly important for the IDB in recent years, with much of the funding provided through leasing, (*ijara*) hire purchase (*ijara wa-iqtina*) and advance purchase financing (*istisna*). Almost one-third of project finance has been for public utilities such as power generation plants, electricity transmission, and water treatment and distribution facilities, with over $1.5 billion used in this way between 1995 and 1999. Social projects account for a further quarter of the total, including schools and hospitals, with around $1.2 billion disbursed over the same period. Other project funding at this time was for transport and communications ($1 billion), industry ($850 million) and agriculture ($800 million).

With over twenty-five years' operational experience, it is appropriate to ask to what extent the IDB has achieved the objectives of its founders, and Saudi Arabia in particular. Clearly, with Muslim countries experiencing some of the lowest growth rates in the developing world, it has not been successful in foster-ing economic development. Nor has it achieved much in terms of encouraging the application of Islamic law in the field of commerce; indeed, some of the states it has supported generously, notably Turkey, at least until the 2002 elec-tions became more secularist than ever, although it has permitted the special finance houses to operate, two of which, Al-Baraka Türk and Faisal Finance, are backed from Saudi Arabia. There have also been some benefits to Saudi interests in Egypt, notably with the establishment of the Faisal Islamic Bank of Egypt, although arguably this more accommodating attitude towards Islamic finance was more opportunistic on the part of the Egyptian government rather than because of any deeper commitment. More significantly, the IDB has acted as a vehicle for the improvement of Saudi–Iranian relations since 1997, with Iran subscribing an additional $1 billion to the bank as a concrete indication of its willingness to participate in pan-Islamic World projects in collaboration rather than in competition with its Arab neighbours.

The other important OIC organisation is the *Fiqh* Academy, based in Jeddah, which brings together experts in Islamic jurisprudence. Since 1986 it meets annually shortly after the end of Ramadan, the sixteenth meeting being held in Mecca from 5 to 10 January 2002.[13] Since its inception it has become arguably the most authoritative source of modern Islamic law and its *fatwas* are more widely accepted than those from any other source, at least in the Sunni Muslim World. This is partly because of the wide range of those represented at the meetings and the specialists in disciplines such as medicine and economics, who are on the fringes but often called to give expert advice. The resultant *fatwas* are respected, as not only are the rulings published but also the reasoning behind them. Consequently, the authority of alternative sources of Islamic law, notably Al Ahzar in Cairo, has tended to be undermined. This has not so much enhanced the position of the Saudi Arabian government in relation to the Egyptian authorities, but rather strengthened pan-Islamic law in relation to state laws.

THE EXTENT OF CAPITAL FLIGHT

The lower-income Muslim countries in the Arab World, South Asia and South East Asia all maintain controls on capital movements, with varying degrees of restriction on foreign exchange transfers to fund investment abroad. Capital still moves abroad illegally, usually either through black market foreign exchange dealings, or the retention of hard currency earnings by exporters or migrant workers. These earnings are subsequently invested abroad rather than remitted into domestic currency. Due to their illegal nature, it is difficult to estimate the extent of such transactions, although they are undoubtedly a significant source of capital flight.

Saudi Arabia and the Gulf states have no restrictions on capital movements by local nationals, and their currencies are freely convertible and stable against the United States dollar. As a consequence, substantial amounts of private wealth are held abroad, as Table 6.1 shows, drawing on Saudi American Bank

Table 6.1: Saudi and Gulf high net worth individual wealth abroad

	Amount $ billion	Individuals	Average per individual $ million
Saudi Arabia	700	85,000	8.235
UAE	266	60,000	4.433
Kuwait	163	40,000	4.075
Other Gulf	65	15,000	4.333
Total	1,194	200,000	5.970

Source: Saudi American Bank 2001 extrapolations from 1995 Merrill Lynch/Gemini Consulting Study.

estimates.[14] The funds are mostly held in the United States, with perhaps over a quarter in Europe and the remainder in Asian markets, mainly Japan and Hong Kong. Funds are invested in equities, managed funds, government and corporate bonds, and residential and commercial property. The weighting of each investor's portfolio is determined by attitudes towards risk, financial market conditions and whether the fundholder is more concerned with receiving income or capital gains. Most of the investments are managed professionally, either through private banking or fund management groups.

In most respects, the investment behaviour of the estimated 200,000 high net worth individuals from Saudi Arabia and the Gulf is little different from that of their counterparts elsewhere. Their aim is to generate income and wealth from their assets which benefits their families and themselves, where the funds are invested being a less important consideration. How funds are invested is for many more crucial than where, as most Saudi Arabian and Gulf citizens, like Muslims elsewhere, are concerned about deriving income from interest, even though for the majority this concern does not translate into positive action. Some cleanse or purify interest income by donating it to charitable causes; others invest part of their funds in a *shari'a*-compliant manner to ease their conscience, while investing the remainder conventionally. In this respect, Islamic investors are little different to Western ethical investors, who tend to adopt a partial approach rather than deploying all their funds ethically.

The professional advisors involved in the management of the assets of Saudi Arabian and Gulf investors are often instructed to place the funds in accordance with *shari'a* law. It is these instructions that have resulted in the growth of Islamic banking activity in international markets, notably London and Bahrain, where leading Western banks such as HSBC, Deutsche Bank, ABM Amro, Citibank Group and Merrill Lynch all offer Islamic financial products. Private banks are prepared to construct bespoke Islamic portfolios on their client's behalf, if they have sufficient funds to invest to justify the cost. Where portfolios include equities, investment in companies involved in alcohol production or distribution or pork products are excluded, as indeed are conventional banks because of their interest dealings, even though paradoxically the same banks are managing the funds. For clients with lesser amounts of funds to invest, Islamic mutual funds, the focus here, have become an acceptable alternative. Such 'off the peg' Islamic investment appeals to those who have insufficient funds to qualify for private banking services, or who do not wish to pay the fees levied for a personalised 'tailored' product.

THE GLOBAL ORIENTATION OF ISLAMIC FUNDS

As of December 2001, there were 105 Islamic mutual funds, of which 86 were equity funds and 16 were balanced or secured funds, the other three being Islamic bond funds offered by Malaysian institutions.[15] The funds are classified geographically, as Table 6.2 shows, with a preponderance of global equity funds, although North American, Asian and emerging-market funds are also significant. As most of the global equity funds hold over half their assets in the United States, the extent to which they are truly global is debatable.

This geographical emphasis is both a reflection of equity market realities and client perceptions. There are two major client groups, the dominant group being those residing in the Gulf, where there are no capital controls, as already indicated, and investors are free to deploy their funds anywhere. The second group is investors in Malaysia, Indonesia and to a lesser extent those in other Asian countries, who are primarily focused on their domestic markets, although some have access to dollar funds which they wish to invest globally.

There are also two factors explaining the direction of portfolio investment flows of fund management groups offering designated Islamic products. The first relates to the supply of available equity stock, which can be used to construct an equity portfolio to serve clients' needs. As dollar-denominated stock is sought, the United States is clearly the prime destination for portfolio flows, followed by dollar-denominated stock quoted in other markets. The second relates to the demand side, and that is ultimately a marketing issue. Clients are looking for a global spread, with a concentration on North America, as they know that stock quoted on the New York Stock Exchange and NASDEQ account for over one-third of the global total by stock value. Despite the setbacks of 2001 and 2002, there is an underlying confidence in the long-term resilience of the North American markets.

Table 6.2: Categorisation of Islamic mutual funds

Type	Number
Global	33
North America	10
European	5
Asian	18
Emerging market	12
Small companies and technology	8
Balanced or secured funds	16
Islamic bonds	3

Source: www.failaka.com/Funds.html

Table 6.3: Economic indicators for Muslim countries

Country	GNI $ billion 1999	GNI, ppp $ per capita 1999	Growth % 1990–99	Investment % GDP 1999	Debt $ billion 1999
Egypt	86.5	3,460	2.4	23	30.4
Indonesia	125.0	2,660	3.0	24	150.1
Iran	113.7	5,520	1.9	18	10.3
Jordan	7.7	3,880	1.1	21	8.9
Malaysia	76.9	7,640	4.7	22	45.9
Morocco	33.7	3,320	0.4	24	19.1
Pakistan	62.9	1,860	1.3	15	34.4
Saudi Arabia	139.4	11,050	−1.1	19	N/A
Syria	15.1	3,450	2.7	29	22.4
Turkey	186.5	6,440	2.2	23	101.8
UK	1,403.8	22,220	2.1	18	N/A
US	8,879.5	31,910	2.0	20	N/A

Source: World Bank, 2001.

Note: GNI is gross national income, GNP is gross domestic product and N/A is not available.

Islamic-designated funds might be expected to invest a greater proportion of their funds in the financial markets of Muslim countries – indeed, they are often criticised for not being more proactive in promoting inter-Islamic World portfolio investment flows, and taking money out, rather than directing it to cement greater Muslim World economic solidarity. One problem is that the restricted size of stock markets in Muslim countries reduces their absorptive capacity. Simply pouring more funds into these markets would increases price-earnings ratios to levels that could not be sustained.[16]

Another problem is country risk uncertainties, not so much with political stability but rather with inconsistent and poorly implemented macroeconomic policies that have failed to create the conditions for sustained economic growth. Ultimately, the returns in financial markets reflect economic success and, as Table 6.3 shows, many of the economies of the Islamic World are extremely small, with very low growth rates and high levels of debt.

Even the United Kingdom's economy is over seven times the size of Turkey's, the largest in the Muslim World, a factor that is inevitably reflected in the size of its capital market. Furthermore, although the economic growth rate in the UK and the US was not especially impressive for the 1990–99 period, and even less impressive subsequently, the absolute increase in gross national income per capita from a higher base is numerically much greater than that from a lower base.

Global market volatility has inevitably had an adverse impact on Islamic funds. Conditions in major international equity markets, especially the New York

Figure 6.1: Total Islamic fund assets, year end, $ million

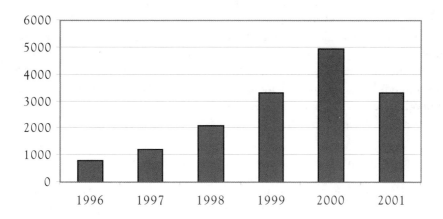

Source: Failaka International, *www.failaka.com* 2002.

Stock Exchange and NASDEQ, have been difficult since the spring of 2000, with the prices of overvalued high technology stock falling first, but then a more widespread retreat as the United States economy slowed down, and then a further across-the-board fall since the events of 11 September 2001 and the move of the American economy into recession. This has adversely affected the performance of global Islamic funds, which, as already indicated, are heavily exposed to US markets, and technology stock in particular. One estimate suggests the value of assets in Islamic funds has fallen from $5 billion in early 2000 to $3.3 billion by February 2002, as Figure 6.1 shows.[17] Even those Islamic funds exposed to other markets have been adversely affected in so far as stock prices in these markets have been correlated with those on Wall Street. There are exceptions, notably Saudi Arabian stocks, which have performed well, partly due to

Table 6.4: Islamic funds

Year	Number	Year	Number
1993	9	1998	62
1994	13	1999	78
1995	17	2000	85
1996	29	2001	98
1997	41	2002	105

Source: Failaka International, *www.failaka.com* 2002.

some repatriation of funds after 11 September 2001, but even Malaysian equity prices have moved in line with those in North America and Japan.

Of course, the post-millennium setback in stock prices mirrors other similar falls in the past, and many predict recovery by 2003. The record number of Islamic funds, as Table 6.4 shows, illustrates confidence in the future, although there has been a slowdown in new offerings as market uncertainty has deterred banks and fund management groups from launching as many Islamic funds. The seven funds launched in 2001 include two of the Malaysian Islamic bond funds and other new fund launches have focused on those where capital is at less risk, rather than on equity growth.

INTERNATIONAL MANAGEMENT AND SPONSORSHIP OF ISLAMIC FUNDS

Most Islamic funds focus on clients from the Gulf and, to a lesser extent, Malaysia. There are relatively few investors of high net worth or even those in the upper-middle-income category in other Muslim countries, and those who are in this group tend to have international earnings which can be invested and managed anywhere in the world, rather than through domestic financial institutions. Therefore, this category of footloose rich from the Muslim World can be targeted from London, Geneva or New York as easily as from their home bases. There are also relatively few higher-income earners who are potential investors in Islamic funds amongst the Muslim populations of most Western countries, with the possible exception of a minority of Muslims in the United Kingdom and the United States. Many of the more wealthy Muslims in the West are closely integrated into their adopted countries and simply use conventional financing facilities, having relatively little interest in Islamic finance.

Some promoters of Islamic funds, notably the international banks, have targeted the very wealthy and offered managed funds as a lower-cost alternative to a privately managed portfolio, which is more labour intensive to monitor and administer, overheads that can only be justified for those with at least $250,000 to invest. Lower thresholds can be offered for managed funds, as they are administered and monitored on a pooled basis, with the costs spread over several, or in the case of popular funds, many clients. In the Gulf, the target clients for Islamic fund promoters are not only the most wealthy segments of society, but rather upper-middle-income bank clients who want additional avenues for their capital beyond savings deposits. Such deposits are not well-regarded by the devout, as they feel obliged to purify their income by giving away any interest-based returns to charity. Their main hesitation with respect to managed funds is the knowledge that their capital is at risk, even though in the medium to long term the hope is for capital gains.

The top twelve leading Islamic managed funds are listed in Table 6.5, with the Al-Ahli Global Trading Equity Fund offered by the National Commercial

Table 6.5: Leading Islamic managed funds

Fund	Promoter	Established	Minimum investment	Annual fee %	Total assets $ million
Al-Ahli Global Trading Equity	National Commercial Bank	1995	$2,000	1.75	640.0
Alfanar Investment Holdings	Permal Asset Management	1997	$5,000	2.00	171.0
Takaful Global Fund	Keppel Insurance	1995	S$4,000	1.50	94.3
Al-Dar World Equities	Pictet & Cie	1998	$100,000	1.50	45.9
UBS Islamic Fund – Global Equities	UBS Islamic Fund Management	2000	$100,000	2.04	33.8
Citi Global Portfolio	Citi Islamic Investment Bank	1997	$10,000	1.81	33.8
Al-Rajhi Global Equity	Al-Rajhi Banking and Investment Corporation	1996	50 shares	1.5	30.0
Dow Jones Islamic Index	Wafra Investment/ Al Tawfeeq	1999	$10,000	1.5	22.5
SAMBA Global Equity	SAMBA Capital Management	1999	$2,000	2.15	16.0
Al-Bait Global Equity	Securities House	2000	$50,000	1.75	15.0
Al-Baraka Global Equity	Al-Baraka Investment Bank	1997	$25,000	1.50	11.1
Global Equity 2000 Sub Fund	First Investment Company	2000	$10,000	1.50	11.0

Source: Failaka International, *www.failaka.com* 2002.

Bank of Saudi Arabia being by far the largest. This is a retail fund with a only a modest minimum investment of $2,000 required, the target market being National Commercial Bank account-holders, including those with limited incomes. Permal Asset Management of London promotes Alfanar Investment Holdings mainly to wealthy private investors in the Gulf, its link with Saudi Economic and Development Company (SEDCO) generating most of its business. Keppel Insurance of Singapore markets the Takaful Global Fund, the target group being wealthy investors from Brunei, Malaysia and Indonesia. The funds promoted by Pictet & Cie and the UBS from Geneva are aimed at private banking clients of high net worth, with minimum investments required of $100,000. Several Islamic banks in the Gulf, in return for a booking fee, recommend these funds.

Table 6.6: Five largest Islamic fund managers

Manager	Country	Assets, $ million
Wellington Management	United States	553
Permal Asset Management	United Kingdom	336
Deutsche Asset Management	Germany	134
Gulf International Bank	Bahrain	122
Pictet & Cie	Switzerland	98

Source: John Bauer (SAMBA Capital Management), 'Islamic equity funds: investment and marketing issues for fund managers', paper presented to *The International Islamic Finance Forum*, Dubai, 18 March 2002.

Table 6.7: Five largest Islamic fund sponsors

Sponsor	Country	Assets, $ million
National Commercial Bank	Saudi Arabia	935
SEDCO	Saudi Arabia	336
Keppel Insurance	Singapore	98
The International Investor of Kuwait	Kuwait	83
Rashid Hussain Berhad (RHB) Unit Trust Managers	Malaysia	57

Source: John Bauer (SAMBA Capital Management), 'Islamic equity funds: investment and marketing issues for fund managers', paper presented to *The International Islamic Finance Forum*, Dubai, 18 March 2002.

To be viable and cover their costs in the longer term, managed funds typically need to have assets under management of at least $50 million. Only three of the 105 Islamic funds are in that category at the time of writing, but the industry is new and much will depend on how much funding they attract during the upturn of the next economic cycle when international markets recover. Funds administered from Malaysia and the Gulf have lower administrative costs than those managed from major international financial centres such as London. However, as much of the money is invested in Western markets, those with knowledge and experience of these markets are usually the best managers. Therefore, many Islamic funds are promoted by leading Western fund management groups, Wellington of the United States being the market leader in terms of assets managed, as Table 6.6 shows.

Wellington manages the Al-Ahli Global Trading Equity Fund and the much smaller Al Kawthar Fund promoted by the National Bank of Kuwait, as well as the Caravan Fund promoted by the Commercial Bank of Qatar. They also manage their own Hegira Global Equity Fund, but most of their Islamic fund assets derive from their links with the National Commercial Bank. Permal, a London subsidiary of Worms & Cie, a Paris-based conglomerate that grew out of a Swiss private wealth management group, look after the Alfanar Funds on behalf of SEDCO. Permal Asset Management is based in the United States, but it is the London subsidiary that manages the Alfanar Funds, although the latter are incorporated for tax and regulatory purposes in the British Virgin Islands. Deutsche Asset Management handle the secured funds offered by the National Commercial Bank, one of which is global and the other focused on European investment. Gulf International Bank is the only Arab-based fund manager of significance, as it manages the National Commercial Bank's Al-Ahli Asia Pacific and European Equity Funds. Wisely, the policy of the National Commercial Bank is to engage several Western fund managers so that their relative performances can be assessed on behalf of their Islamic investors.

As Table 6.7 shows, the only other institution apart from the National Commercial Bank that has enjoyed success in attracting high-value investments into Islamic funds is SEDCO. This company is largely owned and managed by the Bin Mahfouz family, who were the founders and main owners of the National Commercial Bank until its takeover by the Saudi Arabian government and management reorganisation in 1997. This followed the departure of Khalid Bin Mahfouz, Osama Bin Laden's brother-in-law, who was accused of misuse of his position and being involved with Islamic militants and doubtful religious charities.[18] Khalid Bin Mahfouz was stripped of his Saudi Arabian citizenship while abroad but he had already acquired Irish citizenship in 1990 under a dubious deal involving the sale of passports under former Prime Minister Charles Haughey that is being investigated by the Moriarty Tribunal[19] and the Flood Enquiry.[20]

SEDCO was established in 1976, but it was largely concerned with distribution, equipment leasing and real estate management.[21] Since 1998, it has become more involved in investment management and the ambition of its chairman, Mohammad Bin Mahfouz, is for the company to become the premier Islamic investment institution. With assets of over $336 million already under management, it has made significant progress in this direction.

There have been three reactions by the Islamic fund management industry to the global stock market volatility of 2000 and 2001. The first is increased interest in a more diverse range of markets, including those of Muslim countries, with more domestic Islamic funds being marketed to local citizens. The second consequence is, as already noted, more interest in Islamic equity funds with lower risks that aim to produce a reasonable dividend stream, rather than focusing on capital growth. Such funds invest in utilities or retailers rather than high technology companies, and are less subject to price volatility. Islamic funds of this type include the Al-Rajhi Balanced Funds, the Al-Ahli Secured Funds offered by the National Commercial Bank, the Al Hilal Fund promoted by the Abu Dhabi Islamic Bank and the Faysal Shield Fund offered by the Shamil Bank of Bahrain.

The third reaction has been the emergence of more Islamic funds that are either based on Islamic bonds or on investment in real estate or other forms of property. The returns from property investments derive from the rental income, which is usually more stable than dividend income. There would also appear to be scope for the development of 'with profits' bonds, similar to those offered by insurance companies in the West, where returns are linked to equity performance but there is a degree of protection from downside risks. Bonuses, once declared, cannot be taken away but do not fully reflect capital gains and dividends payable. There is a revisionary bonus paid on maturity but penalties for early exit, usually within a five-year period. Islamic 'with profits' bonds may appeal to many Muslim investors investing for the medium term in uncertain financial conditions, providing they are prepared to sacrifice liquidity.

In the aftermath of the events of September 11th and the tragic consequences for Afghanistan and the Palestinians, there is a desire by Islamic investors to rethink their strategies for asset management and, if possible, to do more to help their fellow-believers in the Muslim World. Translating preferences into realities is not so easy, but as change can come in the longer term it is instructive to examine the flows from the Gulf to two Muslim markets to illustrate the opportunities and difficulties.

PORTFOLIO INVESTMENT FLOWS FROM THE GULF INTO EGYPT AND MALAYSIA

It is unlikely that there will be a sudden flood of Gulf funds into markets such as those of Egypt or Malaysia, as there are restrictions on capital movements out of both countries which deter inward investors, and Egypt's ability to maintain the value of its currency is questioned as the tensions since September 11th have caused tourists to think again about visiting the country, with arrivals well down on 2000 and fewer advance bookings. Around 20 per cent of Egypt's hard-currency earnings are accounted for by tourism, mostly from Europe and the United States.

There is only one specialist Saudi Arabian fund that invests in Egypt, the Al-Rajhi Egyptian Fund that is managed by EGF Hermes in Cairo, although the Al-Rajhi Middle Eastern Fund also has around 22 per cent Egyptian exposure, the other major investments being in Turkey and Saudi Arabia (22 per cent each), and Jordan, Morocco, Lebanon and Bahrain (8.5 per cent each).[22] Both these Al-Rajhi funds are small, with a mere $10 million each under management. The Al-Ahli Arab Equity Fund offered by the National Commercial Bank of Saudi

Arabia invests in Egypt and other Arab League countries, but this is not marketed as an Islamic fund, and there is no screening of investments for *shari'a* compatibility.

There is no specialist Islamic fund in the Gulf focused on Malaysia or Indonesia, although the Al-Ahli Asia Pacific Trading Equity Fund, which is offered by the National Commercial Bank, and managed by the Gulf International Bank, does have some exposure to the Kuala Lumpur market. The Al-Ahli South East Asia Fund has even greater Malaysian exposure, but it is not a designated Islamic fund. The Arab-Malaysian Unit Trust has marketed the Tabung Ittikal Arab-Malaysian Fund to Gulf investors since 1993, but the trust has no Gulf presence, its offices being in Kuala Lumpur.

LOCAL INVESTMENT IN THE SAUDI ARABIAN MARKET

The major investment in Muslim markets is simply domestic investment with Saudi Arabians and Malaysians investing in Islamic funds that offer a portfolio of local stock that has been screened for *shari'a* compliance. If investors have future anticipated liabilities in riyals or ringitt, then they will also want to have assets denominated in these currencies. The banks or fund promoters also have an advantage in their local markets, as they can manage the funds themselves, given their knowledge of their own market, rather than relying on international banks or fund management groups.[23] Leading local Islamic funds in Saudi Arabia include the Al-Rajhi Local Share Fund, the Al-Ahli Saudi Riyal Murababaha Trading Fund and the Al-Ahli Saudi Trading Equity Fund marketed by the National Commercial Bank,[24] the Riyadh Equity Fund marketed and managed by the Riyadh Bank and the Al Arabi Saudi Company Shares marketed by the Arab National Bank.

As Figure 6.2 shows, there has been a very rapid rise in the numbers of investors in Saudi Arabian mutual funds in recent years, with almost 100,000 individual investors participating by 2001, more than double the 1997 figure. Most of these investors are bank clients with current accounts who are reluctant to open savings accounts that earn an interest-based return. Bank clients could, of course, switch to the Al-Rajhi Banking and Investment Corporation, which provides investment accounts on a *mudaraba* basis, but in practice there is much bank account inertia in Saudi Arabia, as in most other countries. Furthermore, even within Al-Rajhi, most clients simply have current accounts that yield no return.

The National Commercial Bank has played the leading role in Saudi Arabia's mutual fund industry since the 1980s and it accounts for over half of the total funds under management. Its first fund was launched in 1979, the Al-Ahli Short Term Dollar Fund. It largely invested in United States government securities and highly rated corporate bonds, and was conventional rather than Islamic in

Figure 6.2: Numbers of investors in Saudi Arabian mutual funds

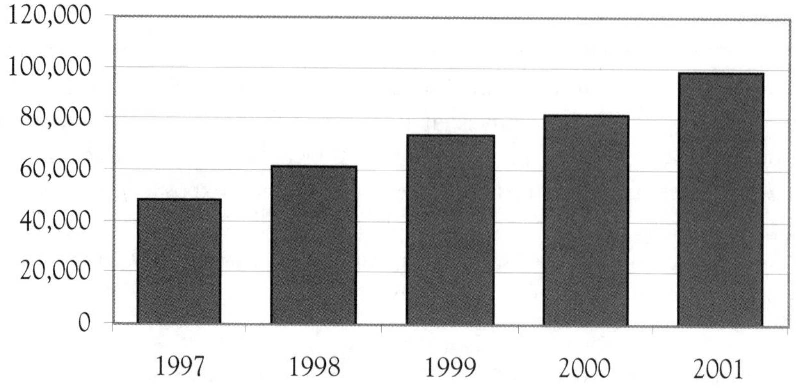

Source: National Commercial Bank, *Market Review and Outlook*, Jeddah, 1 February 2002, p. 5.

character, as returns were interest-based. In 1987 the National Commercial Bank launched its first Islamic fund, the Al-Ahli International Trade Fund, which provided investors with capital preservation but an income stream from short-term *murabaha*-based trade transactions. This was, to some extent, a response to the change in status of the Al-Rajhi to a banking and investment corporation providing Islamic financial services, as the National Commercial Bank, as the leading bank in the Kingdom, also wanted to stress its Islamic credentials, even though it was a conventional bank.

As Table 6.8 shows, the total assets of Saudi Arabia's managed funds amounted to almost $10.7 billion by 2001, of which $4.6 billion was categorised as non-interest – or, in other words, Islamic. The assets of Islamic-designated managed funds exceed that of any other single category, with the Al-Ahli Global Trading Equity Fund offered by the National Commercial Bank being the largest Islamic mutual fund in the world, with funds of over $640 million under

Table 6.8: Saudi mutual funds, 2001

	Assets, $ million	*Investors*	*Funds*
Bonds	46	434	10
Money market	2,490	27,680	19
Non-interest	4,616	44,107	18
International stock	2,969	23,232	57
Local stocks	324	1,216	12
Total	10,687	99,147	13

Source: National Commercial Bank, *Market Review and Outlook*, Jeddah, 1 February 2002, p. 6.

Figure 6.3: Islamic *versus* money market funds in Saudi Arabia, $ million

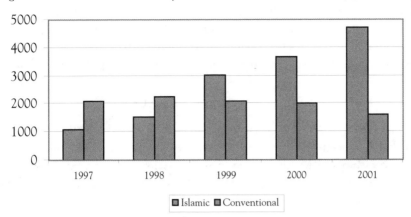

Source: National Commercial Bank, *Market Review and Outlook,* Jeddah, 1 February 2002, p. 5.

management. The value of the units in the fund has doubled since inception in January 1995, although there was a loss of 20.9 per cent in 2000 and a marginally smaller loss in capital values in 2001. The last profitable year was 1999, when the units increased in value by 27.3 per cent. The Al-Ahli Global Trading Equity Fund has two-thirds of its investments in the United States and around one-quarter in Europe, with the remainder in Japanese equities.

Although the Al-Ahli Global Trading Equity Fund has the largest assets, most of the Islamic funds in Saudi Arabia are based on short-term trading instruments, usually *murabaha* mark-up contracts or *salam* commodity sale contracts. It is meaningful, therefore, to compare Islamic fund assets with those of money market funds, given their emphasis on income and liquidity. Figure 6.3 shows that the value of Islamic funds exceeded that of money market funds by 2001, the latter category being the least acceptable from an Islamic perspective, given the interest-based nature of the income. The Al-Ahli International Trade Fund has been the most successful of the Islamic funds that were viewed in Saudi Arabia as an acceptable alternative to money market funds. It largely invests in metals and soft commodities, with an annual fee of only 0.75 per cent, but with a high minimum investment of over SR 250,000 ($66,667). Returns are paid monthly directly into investors' bank accounts. Although non-interest based, returns fell from 4.81 per cent in April 2001 to 3.96 per cent in June, and by September were below 3.8 per cent.

The largest local equity fund in Saudi Arabia is the Al-Ahli Saudi Trading Equity Fund. Its aim is to produce capital growth through investment in Saudi-listed stock, mostly in industrial and cement production, with this actively managed fund applying a higher management charge of 1.75 per cent annually, but with a relatively modest minimum investment of SR 5,000 ($1,333). The Al-Ahli Saudi Trading Equity Fund has over SR 30 million ($8 million) under management, making it the largest local fund in the Kingdom, although its size is modest compared to that of Islamic global funds. It has produced a return of 22 per cent since its inception in 1998, and a return of 6.1 per cent for 2000.

LOCAL INVESTMENT IN MALAYSIA

In Malaysia, the leading local Islamic managed fund is the RHB Mudarabah Fund that has been operating since 1996. This is the largest Islamic fund in Malaysia, with over RM 194 million ($51 million) being managed on behalf of 2,800 investors.[25] Almost 10 per cent of its funds are invested in Telekom Malaysia, a further 10 per cent in local technology stock and a third in diverse trading services, with 7 per cent in both property and construction. The timing of the launch of the fund was unfortunate, immediately prior to the 1997 crisis, and the fund has lost over 20 per cent of its value since inception. In 1999, there was a return of over 36 per cent, but this was followed by a capital loss of almost a quarter of the fund's value in 2000. The other significant local fund in Malaysia is the Amanah Saham Bank Islam Fund, which has been successfully promoted by Bank Islam Malaysia to its own depositors as an investment vehicle that can result in capital appreciation. Unfortunately, it is difficult to outperform the market, and investors in this fund, which was instigated in 1994, have fared less well in recent years than prior to the Asia financial crisis.

As local Islamic investors in Malaysia have been deterred by the poor performance of the Kuala Lumpur Stock Exchange, three of the fund management groups have launched Islamic bond funds that aim at capital preservation and a regular non-interest based income. The Islamic bond market in Malaysia developed in the 1990s with the issue of government and then corporate notes based on *al bai bithamen ajil*, the sale of goods on a deferred-payments basis. Usually the notes were issued to cover equipment financing, the client settling by instalments that provided the income stream on which the security could be based. Although there are objections in the Gulf amongst *shari'a* scholars to *bai al dawn*, the sale of debt, as it is argued that those owing money should know their creditors, in Malaysia it is argued that as long as those being financed know in advance their debts will be traded, the issue of debt securities is legitimate.

The RHB Islamic Bond Fund was launched in Malaysia in August 2000, with a minimum subscription of only RM 1,000 ($265), a single buying and selling price, no entry fees and disbursements of dividends twice each year. Total dividends of 6 per cent were paid out during the first year of operation, and the fund attracted over RM 14 million ($3.7 million) from 400 investors during the first six months of its operations.

IDENTIFYING THE BEST PERFORMING FUNDS

Investors in Islamic mutual funds have to identify their financial objectives when deciding what funds to invest in, as some may want low-risk investments, capital preservation and a regular income from their funds, while others may be prepared to accept a higher level of risk in anticipation of capital gains, with much less stress on income. Age and family commitments may be important factors in determining attitudes towards risk and returns, as clearly it would be foolish for an investor with a modest income and many financial outgoings to invest heavily in high-risk technology stock or volatile emerging markets.[26]

The reference points for price performance for Islamic investments are increasingly the Islamic indices provided by the FTSE and Dow Jones.[27] FTSE has a global Islamic index with sub-components for the Americas, Europe, the Pacific Basin and South Africa, while the Dow Jones has its general Islamic market index, with more focused indices for the United States, Canada, Asia/Pacific, Europe and the United Kingdom.[28] In addition to its geographical indices, the Dow Jones has Islamic indices for technology stock and extra liquid securities. Both FTSE and Dow Jones screen out stock whose core activities are related to conventional interest-based banking, alcohol, tobacco, gaming, insurance, pork production (and pork distribution), or other activities deemed offensive under Islamic law. A financial screen is also applied, as companies are excluded if their interest-bearing debt-to-assets ratio is equal to or greater than one-third. The Islamic objection here is that companies that are too heavily dependent on *riba*-based financing should be excluded, but that some dependence is permitted on pragmatic grounds, otherwise there would be no acceptable companies to invest in.[29]

In practice, the movements of Islamic indices is closely in line with their conventional counterparts, the major exclusions affecting performance being the stocks in conventional banks. When bank shares are doing well, there is an underperformance of the Islamic share universe, and when the conventional banking sector is performing relatively badly, the converse occurs. It is arguably appropriate to use these indices to compare the performance of Islamic dollar-denominated global equity funds, but they are not relevant for looking at the performance of equity markets in Muslim countries.

The more relevant indices for these purposes are the Standard and Poors International Finance Corporation (S&P/IFCI) emerging market indices for Muslim economies, as shown in Table 6.9, which cover Egypt, Indonesia, Malaysia, Morocco and Turkey. As the table shows, 2001 was disappointing for all these markets, but 2002 saw a marked recovery in Malaysia and Indonesia. Egypt was emerging market of the year in 1999, but subsequent performance has been poor. Saudi Arabia is not included in these indices, as foreign portfolio investment flows into the Kingdom are not permitted, with the exception of

Table 6.9: S&P/IFCI price indices for Muslim emerging markets, %

	2001	January to June 2002
Egypt	–35.1	–3.2
Indonesia	–12.0	71.2
Malaysia	–7.8	15.2
Morocco	–14.7	–9.9
Turkey	–64.2	–23.4

Source: *www.spglobal.com/indexmainemdb2000.html*

those from other GCC countries, in line with a policy of maintaining local ownership of companies. Non-GCC investors can only invest indirectly in Saudi Arabia by purchasing shares through specialist Saudi funds, the Saudi American Bank being the sole provider of such a fund at the time of writing. The Saudi American Fund is not classified as Islamic.

In many respects, the Saudi Arabian stock market is, with Malaysia, one of the two most interesting in the Islamic World because of its size. The capitalization of the market exceeds $100 billion, and there are 76 listed companies. This means it is the largest market in the Middle East, with the value of stock exceeding that of even the Russian market. A new electronic trading system, *Tadawul*, started functioning on 6 October 2001, enabling customers of the Kingdom's ten commercial banks to trade at most branches throughout the country.[30] The market index rose by 11 per cent in 2000, and although in 2001 conditions were less favourable, with a modest fall in prices, the rise in trading volumes from January to the end of September exceeded 39 per cent.[31] The post-September 11th period witnessed gains for Saudi Arabian shares as modest amounts of capital were repatriated, with the market reaching an all-time high by June 2002, but prices subsequently fell back owing to increasing uncertainty during the build-up to the war against Iraq.

CONCLUSIONS

The Islamic mutual fund industry is largely focused on Western stock markets, rather than the emerging markets of the Muslim World. The flow of funds mirrors that of high net worth individuals from Saudi Arabia and the Gulf; indeed, those of more modest means are more likely to be risk-averse and wish to have their funds invested in more mature Western markets, rather than Muslim emerging markets.

There is, nevertheless, much political disillusionment amongst Saudi Arabian and Gulf nationals with the United States following the war in Afghanistan and the deterioration in the situation of the Palestinians. In addition, the harassment of Saudi Arabian and Gulf students in the United States since 11 September 2001, many of who come from wealthy families, has fuelled resentment. The freezing of bank accounts and other financial assets of those who are not involved in any way in supporting terrorism has also, inevitably, caused much antagonism.[32] Often this has arisen because of mistaken identities and confusion over names, as many in Saudi Arabia and the Gulf have similar or even identical names, but such explanations are seen as just another manifestation of Western ignorance.

Fund managers and private bankers have noticed an increasing coolness towards investment in the West, and the United States in particular, amongst their Gulf clients since October 2001; but although there is a desire to invest in other Muslim countries and at home, the financial constraints remain for the reasons illustrated here with respect to Egypt, Malaysia and Saudi Arabia. There may be increasing flows of official development assistance through the IDB, but the ending of private capital flight and the repatriation of funds invested in the West will only occur if present hostilities remain for a protected period of years. Ironically, the position is even more difficult for Islamic funds, as conventional bank shares are dominant in Muslim stock markets in Saudi Arabia, the Gulf and Jordan. Holding such shares is *haram*, as far as investors are concerned who wish to respect *shari'a* law.

NOTES

1. Saad Eddin Ibrahim, *The New Arab Social Order: A Study of the Social Impact of Oil Wealth* (Boulder, CO: Westview Press, 1982), p. 8.
2. Ibid. pp. 10–11.
3. Farhad Nomani and Ali Rahnema, *Islamic Economic Systems* (London: Zed Books, 1994), pp. 84–91.
4. Ibrahim Warde, *Islamic Finance in the Global Economy* (Edinburgh: Edinburgh University Press, 2000), pp. 154–8.
5. Ibid. p. 176.
6. Muhammad Taqi Usmani, *An Introduction to Islamic Finance* (The Hague: Kluwer Law International, 2002), pp. 93–101.
7. M. Umer Chapra, *The Future of Economics: An Islamic Perspective* (Leicester: Islamic Foundation, 2000), p. 291.
8. Ibid. pp. 317–18.
9. Munawar Iqbal, 'Financing economic development', in AbulHasan M. Sadeq, Ataul Huq Pramanik and Nik Mustafa Hassan (eds), *Development Finance in Islam* (Kuala Lumpur: International Islamic University Press, 1987), pp. 118–19.
10. Masudul Alam Choudhury, *Islamic Economic Co-operation* (London: Macmillan, 1989), pp. 66–89.
11. Rodney Wilson, 'Saudi Arabia: the Islamic Development Bank's role as a pan-

Muslim agency', in Rodney Wilson (ed.), *Islamic Financial Markets* (London: Routledge, 1990), p. 200.

12. IDB *Annual Report*, 2000, www.islamic-banking.int
13. www.islamiq.com, 24 December 2001.
14. Brad Borland (Chief Economist, Saudi American Bank), 'Outward flows, inward investment needs in the GCC', *Arab Banker*, Vol. XVI No. 2, Autumn 2001, p. 50.
15. Excluding the Mutajarah Fund launched in November 2001 by Towry Law International, which is managed by the Swiss Alternative Investment Strategies Group and marketed by the International Investor of Kuwait. See *New Horizon*, No. 114, November 2001, p. 17 (*New Horizon* is published by the Institute of Islamic Banking and Insurance in London, www.islamic-banking.com). A listing of the Islamic funds compiled by Failaka International is published in *New Horizon*, No. 119, May 2002, pp. 8–9.
16. For a discussion of some of these issues, see the proceedings of the Islamic mutual funds conference held at the University of London's School of Oriental and African Studies in November 2001, www.Islamic-banking.com/lectures/conf_soas_report.php#top
17. Failaka International, *Islamic Equity Funds: Analysis and Observations on the Current State of the Industry*, 2002, www.failaka.com
18. Kevin Dowling, 'The ties that bind: Barclays, a bin Laden relative, Carlyle and the BCCI boys', *Online Journal*, 3 November 2001.
19. Mark Sage, 'Bin Laden's brother in law an Irish citizen', *PA News*, 4 October 2001.
20. www.ireland.com/special/tribunals/flood/
21. SEDCO owns Al-Jazira Equipment Company and Auto World, the leading vehicle leasing company in Eastern Province of Saudi Arabia, the Universal Shelves Industrial Company supplying warehouse equipment, and Eimar Arabia, a Jeddah-based project management, real estate marketing and property management company. Its relations with Worms & Cie not only involve Pemal, but also the French hotel group Accor, in which Worms & Cie own a stake. Accor manages SEDCO properties in Saudi Arabia, including the Sofitel, Novotel Elaf Al-Huda and Mercure Elaf Ajyad in Makka and the Mercure Grand Al-Bustan in Jeddah.
22. www.alrajhibank.com.sa/egyptiansharesfund.htm
23. Said Al-Shaikh, 'The mutual funds market in Saudi Arabia', *NCB Economist*, Vol. 10 No. 2, March/April 2000, pp. 5–12.
24. www.ncb.com.sa/islamic-banking/long-term-funds.asp
25. www.rhb.com.my/non-shockwave/links/14html
26. 'Monitoring the performance of Islamic equity funds', *New Horizon*, No. 103, October 2000, p. 6.
27. Dow Jones now offers its own Islamic index fund. See *New Horizon*, No. 114, November 2001, p. 8.
28. www.dowjones.com/corp/index-directory.htm
29. Taqi Usmani, *An Introduction to Islamic Finance*, pp. 93–4.
30. *New Horizon*, No. 114, November 2001, p. 20.
31. Ayham Zekra, 'Arab stock markets: trading influenced by events after an optimistic start', *Arab Banker*, Vol. XIV No. 2, Autumn 2001, pp. 56–8.
32. Editorial, 'A witch hunt in the making', *Islamic Banker*, No. 68, September 2001, pp. 2–3.

PART II
Case Studies

7

Interest Politics: Islamic Finance in the Sudan, 1977–2001

Endre Stiansen

The Islamization of financial legislation in the Sudan was undertaken in secrecy and haste. But whatever the prelude, from August 1983 no court could enforce interest-based contracts. After only a few months, it became apparent that the legal reform (supplement to the Civil Procedure Act) and subsequent efforts to correct the deficiencies (supplements to the Civil Transaction Act and circulars from the Bank of Sudan) were only moderately successful. Banking continued much as before, and it took more than fifteen years before the Government resolved to enforce the prohibition of *riba*, defined as all forms of interest.[1] Yet, in the recent history of the Sudan it is difficult to underestimate the overall impact of Islamic finance. This is because the political aspect always has been more important than the economic aspect of Islamic finance.

The chapter is divided into four parts. The first presents a survey of the history of Islamic finance in the Sudan. The second addresses the politics of Islamic finance in the 1970s and 1980s. In the third part, the most common Islamic contracts are examined, and in the fourth and final part, the focus is on Islamic finance in the 1990s.

HISTORY AND EVOLUTION

While some traditional Sudanese methods of finance resemble contracts that are part of the standard repertoire of contemporary Islamic financial institutions,[2] formal financial institutions did not emerge until after the Anglo-Egyptian conquest of the Mahdist State, and the legislation regulating the financial sector was based on British laws and practice. Two factors are worth noting with regard to the development of formal financial institutions. First, the Post Office Savings Bank, in the pre-independence period the only bank that sought to develop a popular profile, was concerned not to offend Muslim sensitivities on the *riba* question, and depositors had the right to refuse to accept 'a dividend proportional to the amount of his deposits'.[3] Of course, this was just another way of saying that depositors could decline the interest that their money on account earned. Second, most people, whether in the growing urban centres or in the rural districts, did not deal with formal financial institutions, so for the majority of the population financial intermediation was regulated according to traditional norms. The status of non-written contracts posed a problem for the courts. On the one hand, the courts could and would prosecute defaulters, and protected private property rights. On the other, the courts did not recognize all contracts as valid, and the civil transaction act included provisions against forward-purchase contracts, even though such contracts (called *shayl*) remained dominant in the agricultural sector.

Islamic finance did not emerge in the Sudan before the late 1970s. To some extent, the establishment of Islamic banks reflected developments in the Gulf countries, and the tremendous increase in oil prices in the early 1970s, which produced enormous private fortunes in the Gulf countries and provided entrepreneurs with the required capital. Local factors were at play as well. Many Sudanese Muslims did not feel comfortable with the national banking system because it revolved around interest-based contracts. They were looking for non-interest alternatives, and some were familiar with attempts at establishing Islamic financial institutions elsewhere in the Muslim World.[4] Moreover, ever since independence in 1956, influential members of the political establishment had advocated the adoption of an Islamic constitution, and it went without saying that the reconfiguration of the fundamental law of the land would force the alignment of the financial legislation with (their conception) of Islamic laws and values. Finally, the 1971 nationalization of the largely foreign-owned commercial banks was seen as a policy failure, and the government began to encourage financial institutions to establish branch offices in Khartoum. Hence, the introduction of Islamic finance served multiple interests.

ISLAMIC FINANCE: THE 1970S AND 1980S

The Faisal Islamic Bank of Sudan (FIBS) was the first distinctly Islamic financial institution to set up offices and do business in the Sudan.[5] Established in 1977 by a special Act of Parliament, the bank was registered as a public limited company under the Company Act of 1925, and commenced operations in 1978. The unprecedented parliamentary Act gave the bank very valuable concessions, such as tax exemptions on all assets and profits, as well as employees' salaries and pensions, and complete freedom to transfer and use its own foreign currency deposits. Headquartered in Khartoum, the bank pursued an aggressive growth strategy and over four years, from 1979 to 1982, increased its equity (paid-up shares and re-invested profits) by more than 350 per cent – in the same period the average growth rate was 70 per cent – making the bank much better capitalised than other commercial banks.

The rapid growth was also reflected in share of commercial bank deposits: in

1979 it did not hold more than 4 per cent of the total but by 1982 this share had increased almost fourfold to 15 per cent; concurrently, the share of total advances increased from 3 per cent to 8 per cent. The bank's return on capital was very impressive. From a reported net profit of LS 1 million in 1979, it increased to LS 21 million (also net) in 1982 – the latter figure amounting to more than the paid-up capital and 40 per cent of total equity funds. The bank kept around 30 per cent of annual profits, while paid-out dividends gave shareholders roughly 25 per cent return on their investment. In a marked contrast to conventional commercial banks, the FIBS charter specified that 10 per cent *zakat* should be deducted from net profits and distributed to the poor and needy.

Unlike the existing 'Faisal banks', the Sudanese bank was from the start designed to have a broad ownership structure. The prospectus received a tremendous welcome and shares were oversubscribed several times, with the result that the Government allowed the increase of the authorized capital from LS 6 million to LS 40 million. Bank equity was distributed according to an agreed key, giving 40 per cent to Sudanese nationals, 40 per cent to Saudis and 20 per cent to Muslims from other countries. Shares were paid either with local currency or dollars. The Sudanese shareholders included the crème de la crème of the political and economic elites (President Nimairi, Sadiq al-Mahdi and Hassan al-Turabi were all shareholders).

The initial success of the FIBS triggered the establishment of more Islamic banks. These new banks were not necessarily set up to offer interest-free banking – in an interview, one leading banker confessed that his bank merely included 'Islamic' in the name for PR purposes.

A striking feature of the formative phase of Islamic finance in the Sudan was how closely the different banks were associated with different political groups. The Sudanese Islamic Bank (established in 1983) had close ties to the al Khatmiyyah Sufi order and therefore also to the Democratic Unionist Party; the general manager was the son of one of *Sayyid* Ali al-Mirghani's *khalifas* and the chairman of the board of directors, Muhammad Uthman al-Mirghani (*Sayyid* Ali's son) was the patron of the Democratic Unionist Party. The Tadamon Islamic Bank had very close links to the Muslim Brotherhood. Even though it did not use Islamic in the name, the Al-Baraka Investment and Development Company (also established in 1983) belonged to the 'Islamic segment' of the financial sector, since it operated on a non-interest basis. It was fully controlled by a Saudi family; however, the managing director was a leading member of the Muslim Brotherhood. Notably, the Umma Party did not have its 'own' bank.[6]

The FIBS was the political bank par excellence. The battle for control of the bank began even before it was incorporated in the Sudan, and the outcome the result of a determined effort by the Muslim Brotherhood led by Hassan al-Turabi.

In the context of Sudanese politics, the Muslim Brotherhood is a relative newcomer,[7] and it is a distinctly modern party with a clear ideology, unlike the Umma Party and the DUP that rely on the support of the Ansar movement and the al Khatmiyyah respectively. (Hence, it is a party similar to the Sudan Communist Party; a party the Muslim Brotherhood saw as its own antithesis.) Other important differences from the two main parties are that the Muslim Brotherhood's core support is in the urban areas and among people with higher than average education. Throughout its history, the Muslim Brotherhood has given emphasis to agitation on university campuses and in secondary schools.

The Muslim Brotherhood, neither as a movement nor as individual members, did not have access to the same resources as the traditional parties. To some extent, this reflected the membership profile (throughout the 1960s, the stereotype of a Muslim Brother being a schoolteacher or clerk was not too far off the mark) and the socio-political structure of the Sudan that favoured members of the old establishment. The relative balance between the different groups began to change in the 1970s. The nationalizations in the early phase of the Nimairi era hit the Ansar movement particularly hard, but also the DUP suffered from being in the political wilderness. As important, the massive migration of Sudanese – both professionals and labourers – to the oil-producing areas was significant, since virtually all improved their material conditions and some men of humble origins made great fortunes.

The Gulf and Saudi Arabia also provided venues for important contacts. In the present context, it is interesting to note that exiled members of the Sudanese Muslim Brotherhood belonged to the circle around Prince Muhammad Al-Faisal, and their influence may explain why, as early as 1972, he expressed an interest in investing in the Sudan.[8] The Prince was at this time building the Geneva-based Dar al-Maal al-Islami Group. While his first initiative was rebuffed, the association between conservative Saudi businessmen and exiled Sudanese continued, and only a few years later, after the process of National Reconciliation had got under way, exiled Sudanese returned with capital and political ideas.

Information from different sources suggests Sudanese Muslim Brothers saw the FIBS as an important vehicle to reach political and economic objectives.[9] Initially, the Muslim Brotherhood was faced with two challenges. First, the movement had few members with the necessary experience to run the bank and experienced professional bankers (without political agendas) were recruited to the most senior positions. Second, the sympathizers with the Muslim Brotherhood did not fully control the board of directors and therefore had to forge alliances with other shareholders to be able to wage decisive influence.

The battle for control took place both in bank offices and in the boardroom. In the main office, as well as in branch offices, the Muslim Brotherhood used its position to recruit other members of the movement to jobs with the bank, and colleagues known to be critical or hostile to the movement were forced out. In the boardroom, strategic alliances gave the Muslim Brotherhood confidence, and from 1979/80 they were strong enough to push their own agenda. This caused an open confrontation at a crucial board meeting. The managing director failed to get the required support and he resigned. Shortly afterwards, some of his closest advisers also left the bank. The new managing director, who had been the deputy director, was a Muslim Brother, and within a short period of time all of the senior management came from the movement.

The battle was fierce because the bank's lending and investment profile was at stake. Members of the movement favoured other members of the movement, and political criteria carried more weight than the quality of the business proposal. Often it was enough that a senior member of the movement recommended somebody for a 'loan'. Members of the board of directors were among those who benefited, and the lack of normal procedure could go unchecked because the FIBS Act effectively shielded the bank from scrutiny from the Bank of Sudan.

The bias in favour of the Muslim Brotherhood did not go unnoticed. Businessmen, some of them shareholders, complained that they could not receive finance from the bank. On this point, it is important to notice that boardroom battles took place in other Islamic banks as well, but the ideological implications were less prominent than in the case of the FIBS. Internal audits and audits by the Bank of Sudan revealed that in many banks, members of the board of directors and/or senior management monopolized borrowing, and the default rate on such loans was in general very high.

THE CONTRACTS

Islamic banking in the Sudan relies on a limited number of contracts.[10] Since 1983, the most common contract has been *murabaha*, but banks also offer standard contracts such as *musharaka* and *ijara*. Remarkably, the *mudaraba* has never been of more than marginal importance. Over time there has been a noticeable change in the relative importance of the different contracts, and some contracts that were wholly absent have become part of the standard repertoire. Two developments are worth describing in some detail.

The *musharaka* contract has steadily gained in importance, and Bank of Sudan records from mid-2000 indicate that *murabaha* and *musharaka* contracts are of equal importance, as measured against the total volume of financial transactions in the formal sector of the economy – both account for about 35 per cent.[11] Given that some ten years earlier *murabaha* contracts may have accounted for 80 per cent (or more) of the total, this is an important change in the cumulative investment profile of the financial sector because *murabaha* contracts are primarily used for short-term deals, while *musharaka* contracts are better suited for long-term investments. Put differently, a *murabaha* contract is particularly well-suited to finance imports and exports, and the *musharaka* is more a vehicle for equity finance.

Government pressure has been the major factor behind this shift towards more *musharaka* finance. Two objectives have guided Government policy in this regard. One objective has been to reduce what de facto was the continuation of interest-based lending through widespread use of synthetic *murabaha* contracts. Another aim has been to increase long-term finance. If a shift towards more long-term capital investments indeed is taking place, this represents a radical break with the banking tradition that was established during the Condominium period. As in all other areas dominated by British-style banks, the emphasis was on short-term lending in the form of standing overdraft facilities. This pattern of banking continued after independence and well beyond the introduction of Islamic financial legislation. Bankers have expressed strong reservations about the Government's preference for the *musharaka* contract, because they see this contract as much more risky than the *murabaha* that commonly can be secured against liquid assets. (Of course, the item financed through the *murabaha* contract represents additional security as long as the bank retains title.) In this connection, it is worth mentioning that, among bankers, the limited use of the *mudaraba* contract, which from many perspectives may be seen as the ideal Islamic financial instrument, is explained by reference to the high-risk level owing to the absence of security.

A radical change in the nature of agricultural finance led to the introduction of *salam* contracts in the early 1990s.[12] As mentioned above, the *salam* contract resembles the traditional *shayl* contract, and for this reason its introduction represented an unexpected development. Some thirty years previously, government had established the Agricultural Bank of Sudan (ABS) specifically to give farmers an alternative to *shayl* finance from village merchants. *Shayl* was seen as a highly exploitative form of lending because the so-called 'lender' used his monopoly position to take advantage of the so-called 'borrower'.[13] The motivation for the use of *salam* contracts, however, was clear enough. From the point of view of Islamic law, there is no doubt that it is a legal contract, and as a forward contract it provides farmers with finance when they need it most.

In the history of Islamic finance in the Sudan, no contract has given rise to more controversy than the *salam* contract. The debate centres around two issues. First, farmers have felt they have a rightful claim on part of the profits the banks realise when prices are good. To some extent, this claim was accepted by the Bank of Sudan's *shari'a* council, which, in an important *fatwa* capped the profit of government banks at 30 per cent above the *salam* price; for balance, the same *fatwa* said that farmers should return some of the *salam* price if the market price fell to the *salam* price less one-third. Second, *salam* contracts have commonly been secured against real estate (in addition to the crop itself) and in cases of default, which became increasingly common at the end of the 1990s, the banks have taken farmers to court to recover their losses. Legal action of this kind is almost without precedence in the Sudan, and the real danger of mass eviction, or mass arrests, caused a moral outrage in agricultural areas. Remarkably, people even began to compare the (Islamic) *salam* contract unfavourably with the traditional *shayl* contract.[14]

With regard to contracts, it is interesting to note both sectoral differences and differences among banks. The *salam* contract is exclusively used in the agricultural sector of the economy; incidentally, it is becoming less common even here and in 2000 the contract accounted for less than one-fifth of the total volume of agricultural finance. By far, *murabaha* is the most versatile contract, since it is used in every sector of the economy; for import and export trade its share is 80 per cent and 100 per cent respectively. Some banks do not employ certain contracts, such as *salam* and *muqawala* (contract finance), and some rely almost exclusively on *murabaha* contracts. Particularly the foreign banks that specialise in import/export trade stay away from all contracts except the *murabaha*, but in July 2000 even the Nilein Bank, a government-owned institution with a strong position in the industrial sector, reported that *murabaha* contracts accounted for 94 per cent of the total volume of transactions. The Government's stated aim has been to bring down the share of *murabaha* contracts to one-third of the total volume of finance, and hence these examples point to serious discrepancies between banks' preferences and the official policy.

ISLAMIC FINANCE: FROM 1989 ONWARDS

The military coup of 1989 radicalised the Islamization process in the Sudan. Even though it took some time before the Islamists in the armed forces, who executed the coup, and the National Islamic Front admitted their partnership, the close connection became clear enough when Lieutenant-General Omar Hassan al-Bashir began to appoint members of the movement to important positions. Hassan al-Turabi, of course, emerged as the ideologue of the 'National Salvation' revolution.

The new government gave immediate attention to the financial sector. This was in part to reverse the democratic government of Sadiq al-Mahdi's attempts at loosening up the interest ban by allowing the banks to charge 'compensatory rates' on loans, and pay similar rates on deposits. The leading members of the *shari'a* boards of the Islamic banks had vigorously protested against the compensatory rates when they were introduced in 1987, but the Prime Minister, who had the support of the Bank of Sudan, overruled their views.[15]

Another concern was the common practice in the business community of observing the letter but not the spirit of the law. Irrespective of the use of compensatory rates, conservative bankers and observers of the financial sector had for a long time complained that interest-based contracts continued to dominate in the financial sector. The prevalence of synthetic *murabaha* contracts was the core problem. Purists have always viewed the *murabaha* with a great deal of scepticism because it is so easy to camouflage interest. In the Sudan, they have had good reason to worry. Commonly, a *murabaha* contract would not fix the bank's profit margin (mark-up or *murabaha* margin), but set a flexible (that is, non-fixed) repayment schedule that let the time factor determine the cost of finance. Moreover, banks would demand security other than the commodity itself, and almost never take physical possession of the commodity. Combined, these factors ensured that most *murabaha* contracts were nothing but interest-bearing loans that were secured against liquid assets.

In 1993, the Bank of Sudan's *Sharia* Council issued a *fatwa* designed to curb abuses.[16] The *fatwa* established key requirements that had to be met in order for a *murabaha* contract to be legal. The most important are as follows:

1. the client must submit an application that in detail describes the commodity to be purchased;
2. the bank must buy the commodity (the first transaction) on its own account and physically take possession of it;
3. the client has the right to refuse to accept the commodity when the bank offers it to him (the second transition).

The *fatwa* broke with established commercial practice, and bankers in particular found it difficult to accept that customers should have the right to walk away from what previously had been viewed as legally binding contracts. On one point, the *fatwa* made a concession to established business practice. The *Sharia* Council recognised the opportunity costs of money, and therefore accepted that the profit margin (mark-up) could be set against the length of the repayment schedule.

The streamlining of the financial contracts did not improve bank performance from the early 1990s up to the time of writing. Several factors contributed, and it is useful to differentiate between those that can be considered external to Islamic finance as a system, and those that directly relate to the modalities of the system. With regard to the latter, it is possible to further sub-divide between the modalities of Islamic finance, and factors that were unique to the Sudanese experiment.

To start with the 'external factors': by all indicators, the Sudanese economy was in dire straits throughout the 1990s.[17] Nothing makes this clearer than a survey of the annual rates of inflation. On average, the rate of inflation exceeded 50 per cent and in some years went into triple digits.[18] In the context of a rapidly depreciating currency, it was not surprising that real per capita income fell, and the number of people living below the poverty line increased steadily, exceeding 90 per cent at the end of the decade.[19] Moreover, production of vital cash crops in the agricultural sector declined and, as a result, the volume of exports shrunk. The situation in the world market aggravated an already difficult situation, since the world price for the most important Sudanese export commodity, cotton, stayed depressed while the most important category of imports, petroleum products, on average remained relatively high. The result was a gradual worsening of the terms of trade. Again, there were aggravating factors: the international unpopularity of the military government caused a drying-up of transfers (aid and concessionary loans) from abroad, which led to an increase in the inflationary pressures in the economy, since the government compensated by borrowing from the central bank. Finally, it is impossible to (over)estimate the real impact of the civil war on the Sudan's economic performance during the 1990s.

These factors can all be considered external to Islamic finance as a system, and for obvious reason they – each element on its own or combined, as was the case – seriously undermined the banking system's ability to stay solvent. However, it is possible to point to some factors that can be considered as internal to the system. The *murabaha* contract, as mentioned the most popular financial technique, is the most salient case in point. As indicated in the previous section, the fundamental problem relates to the issue of 'time value for money',[20] or more specifically how to penalise customers/'borrowers' who do not honour the agreed repayment schedule. If a contract is left open-ended, it becomes equivalent to a loan at interest, and hence it will be illegal under Islamic law. Similarly, penalties imposed as sanctions after defaults are not legal because they are the equivalent of interest.[21]

This feature of the *murabaha* contract created obvious moral hazard problems. While it is impossible to present accurate figures, in interviews bankers and others with good knowledge of the Sudanese financial sector expressed the view that many businessmen took advantage of the legal 'loophole'. The only recourse available to the banks was to take the client to court. Since there is no doubt that a *murabaha* contract is binding on the customer/'borrower' once he has received (that is, taken physical possession of) the commodity in question, the bank would win the case but because of the general prohibition of *riba* the court could not order payment of more than the original amount. The high rate of inflation, and the notoriously slow legal system, added to the advantage of the customer/'borrower'.

The last category of factors that will be discussed here relates to the nature of Islamic banking in the Sudan. As mentioned, each of the Islamic banks had close ties to particular groups and the many new commercial banks that emerged in the 1980s were also associated with their own groups. A characteristic feature of banking in the Sudan has been that the major shareholder and the members of the board(s) of directors have monopolised the banks' available capital resources. During most of the 1990s, when the money market was tight, this was particularly important. Since the biggest shareholders also nominate the members of the board(s) of directors and appoint the senior management, they met few restrictions from within the banks themselves. If these 'loans' had been repaid to the banks with a profit and at the agreed time, this would have been more a legal than an economic problem, but many banks experienced default rates on these loans that were extremely high. In principle, Bank of Sudan had the legal means to act on fraudulent and corrupt practices by bank managers and owners, but in fact it did little. One reason for the inactivity may have been lack of resources, but more likely it shied away for another reasons. The politicisation of the Bank meant that, as the central bank, in order to fulfil its mandate as controller of the financial sector, it would have to challenge people with vested interests in the system. Towards the end of the 1990s, the Bank of Sudan introduced guidelines that set tighter restrictions on loans to members of the boards of directors and prohibited fresh loans of credit to indebted clients. While much needed, it can be said that these measures towards better bank supervision and improved regulations came too late.

Agricultural finance presents a special case, also with regard to whether the high default rates here should be viewed as internal or external to Islamic finance as a system. What is certain is that the sector saw very high default rates in the 1990s; some bank managers reported that they only recovered about 50 per cent of their agricultural investments.[22] Particularly, *salam* contracts were exposed. Under normal circumstances, rainfall and other factors that determine production will decide whether or not a farmer is capable of servicing his bank obligation. Fluctuations in the weather determined output in the agricultural sector of the Sudan in the 1990s, and in bad years farmers were not in a position to hand over whatever they had sold through a forward contract (*salam*). Clearly, such defaults cannot be blamed on the Islamic system. Yet there was an 'Islamic' factor at play as well. As indicated, many farmers felt the banks were making excessive profits, and demanded their share. If they failed to reach an understanding, their most effective sanction was to refuse to harvest even if it meant defaulting. References to Islamic principles of equity and fairness justified such action. As mentioned, the Government accepted this moral economy argument, but it did not really solve the problem of default. This was because farmers now had an incentive to delay harvesting as long as it took for prices to rise, even if it meant breaking the terms of the contract.

The combined effect of external and internal factors proved quite devastating. Some ten years after the 1989 revolution, the International Monetary Fund reported that in 1998–99 as much as 18 to 19 per cent of bank credit was considered as 'non-performing', and this is very high even in the context of other developing countries.[23] Moreover, other indicators suggest a fundamental lack of confidence in the banking system, and as a whole the economy is characterised by a very low level of financial intermediation. That is to say, banks have very limited, indeed declining, deposit bases and credit to the private sector has contracted steadily, from 1993 in real terms and from 1999 even in nominal terms.[24]

CONCLUSION

The Sudan's experiment with Islamic finance is a paradox. By economic criteria, the experiment has not been a success, and by all measures the financial sector is extremely weak. But by political criteria, Islamic finance has achieved considerable success. The banking law of the land is based on principles derived from the Koran and the *Sunnah*, and there has been a real transfer of wealth to groups associated with the incumbent regime. Whether viewed together or separately, these factors demonstrate the power of interest politics.

NOTES

1. It says something about the complexities of the Islamization process that it was not the government that introduced the laws, but the government three times removed that made the decision to change the nature of banking. In the relevant period, the Sudan has had the following governments: 1969–85, Nimairi's one-party state; 1985–86, a military-led transitional government; 1986–89, a democratically elected government with Sadiq al-Mahdi as Prime Minister; and from 1989 to the time of writing, a military government under Lieutenant-General Omar Hassan al-Bashir. From 1996, Lieutenant-General Omar Hassan al-Bashir has been President, but the election did little to change the nature of the government.

2. To give two examples, the ancient *shayl* arrangement is quite similar to *salam*, and *mudarabas* are well-documented in the historical sources going back several centuries.

3. The Post Office Savings Bank Regulations, Paragraph 7. The POSB was modelled on the postal savings bank system in the UK.

4. The Egyptian Mit Ghamr savings bank was known among some Sudanese.

5. This and the next two paragraphs draw heavily, but not exclusively, on Elfatih Shaaeldin and Richard Brown, *Towards an Understanding of Islamic Banking in Sudan: The Case of Faisal Islamic Bank* (Khartoum: Khartoum University Press, 1985).

6. Some associate the Saudi-Sudanese Bank with the Umma Party (and thus, by extension, the Ansar movement), but political affiliation is much less obvious than with the other Islamic banks. The SSA is 60 per cent owned by Saudi Arabian nationals and institutions, and Saudi Arabian Airlines is the single largest shareholder. The bank did not use Islamic contracts until *after* the Islamization of 1983.

7. The Muslim Brotherhood (*al-Ikhwan al-Muslimun*) has, as a movement, gone through several phases and contested elections under three different names. In 1954, the movement was founded as *al-Ikhwan al-Muslimun*, and it was basically an ideological copycat of the Egyptian Muslim Brothers. The Muslim Brotherhood fought the 1965

elections as the Islamic Charter Front, and the 1986 elections as the National Islamic Front. It is important to note that the movement has experienced several schisms, and Hassan al-Turabi's line has been severely criticized from within the movement.

8. Mansour Khalid, *The Revolution of Dismay* (London: KPI, 1985), p. 63.

9. I base my account of the attitude of the Muslim Brotherhood to the FIBS on a number of interviews with people with intimate knowledge of the bank's operations in the late 1970s and early 1980s. Due to the sensitive nature of the information, I cannot – at least for the time being – name my sources.

10. The most common contracts used by Islamic financial institutions are described in virtually all books on Islamic banking and finance. Hence, I have found it super-fluous to include elaborate descriptions in this chapter.

11. Bank of Sudan, weekly surveys, mid-2000.

12. This change, as well as a detailed examination of the contract, is discussed in Michael Kevane and Endre Stiansen, '"Removal of Injustice": Market Logic Versus Moral Economy in Islamist Sudan', paper presented at the Annual Meeting of the African Studies Association, Nashville, 16–19 November 2000.

13. I am using 'so-called' because commonly both the *shayl* and the *salam* contracts are misconstrued as a particular type of a loan.

14. Personal interviews, Sinnar and Khartoum, October–November 1999.

15. This development, as well as the debate between Sadiq al-Mahdi and the *shari'a* boards, is discussed in Endre Stiansen, 'Islamic Banking in the Sudan: Aspects of the Laws and the Debate', in Endre Stiansen and Jane I. Guyer (eds), *Credit, Currencies and Culture: Financial Institutions in Africa in Historical Perspective* (Uppsala: Nordiska Afrikainstitutet, 1999), pp. 108–12.

16. Ibid, 112–13.

17. For a survey, see Ibrahim A. Elbadawi, 'The tragedy of the civil war in the Sudan and its economic implications', in Karl Wohlmuth (ed.), *African Development Perspectives Yearbook: Empowerment and Economic Development in Africa* (Münster: Lit, 1999), pp. 545–65.

18. World Bank, *Development Indicators*, Washington, DC, 1999.

19. United Nations Development Programme, 'The Sudan: Human Development Report', n.d. (This report has not been released, and I rely on first-hand information from one of the principal authors. The team of researchers collected most of the material for the final report in 1998–99.)

20. It is important to note that Islamic law, as developed in the classical period, recog-nises a 'time value for money', and hence price differentials, determined by repayment schedules, are perfectly legal. For a discussion, see Frank E. Vogel and Samuel L. Hayes III, *Islamic Law and Finance: Religion, risk, and return* (The Hague: Kluwer Law International, 1998), pp. 201–14.

21. Some Sudanese banks tried to introduce monetary penalties, but in general such sanctions were considered illegal.

22. Private interviews, 1999, 2000.

23. Alexei Kireyev, 'Financial Reforms in Sudan: Streamlining Bank Intermediation', International Monetary Fund working paper (WP/01/53), May 2001, p. 9. The information given here must be considered to be conservative estimates. The IMF report uses the term 'nonperforming loans', but this is a misnomer, given that the

banks do not 'lend' but rather 'invest'. In interviews, people with an excellent knowledge of the balance sheets of both private and public banks said that in their view only a couple of the banks operating in the Sudan would be considered solvent by conventional criteria.

24. Ibid. p. 17.

8

The Kuwait Finance House and the Islamization of Public Life in Kuwait

Kristin Smith

INTRODUCTION

In the mid-1970s the Arab countries of the Gulf made a dramatic entrance onto world financial markets. In a single year oil prices quadrupled, precipitating the most rapid transfer of wealth in the twentieth century. As a result of this infusion of petrodollars, many Gulf citizens who previously had no dealings with formal financial institutions had their first introduction to banking.[1] It quickly became apparent, however, that the institutions and norms of Western finance were at odds with the prevailing belief amongst many Gulf citizens that interest is forbidden by Islam. This combination of wealth and piety made the Gulf an ideal market for the revival of Islamic banking. By appealing to religious values, entrepreneurs adapting Islamic financial principles to modern banking institutions were able to break into largely oligarchic banking sectors, and succeeded in making the Gulf the geographic centre for Islamic commercial and investment banking that it is today.

The religious injunctions against interest opened the banking sector to new business competition, but it likewise embroiled it in the broader political debate within Gulf societies over social values and identity. For the early entrepreneurs in Islamic finance in the Gulf were seeking more than profits; they were often political activists in the Muslim Brotherhood movement and were eager to use the structural power of bank ownership to expand their influence. By linking local religious norms to global capitalist practice, Islamic entrepreneurs were able to bring Islam to a prominent position in contemporary public life.[2] And due to the natural links between finance and politics in the patrimonial rentier societies of the Gulf, they also gained a powerful resource for political battles.[3]

No state in the region demonstrates the successful synergy between economic activity and Islamist politics better than Kuwait. As seen in Clement Henry's analysis, Kuwait is among the top three countries in terms of Islamic share of commercial bank deposits, currently around 15 per cent of the market. It owes this ranking to its sole Islamic bank, the Kuwait Finance House (KFH), which has been one of the most successful and influential institutions in the Islamic finance industry. Established in 1977, KFH grew rapidly to become the second-largest bank in the country in terms of deposits, assets and profits, just behind the venerable National Bank of Kuwait (NBK). However, these statistics alone fail to communicate the influence of KFH. Commercially, KFH is one of the largest owners of real estate in the country, and its commercial sector leads consumer lending with approximately 30 per cent of the market, most notably in automobiles.[4] Politically, KFH is one of the most visible institutional expressions of the Islamic movement in Kuwait, and it is widely perceived as serving the movement's interests through its linkages among business, government, and charitable associations. In ways both implicit and explicit, KFH uses its links with political Islam to protect and expand its business, and its business links to expand and protect the interests of political Islam.

How has KFH achieved this success? Unlike many of the cases under examination in this volume, Islamic finance in Kuwait has received considerable support from the government. KFH was established with a 49 per cent government share in capital[5] and it has enjoyed perks not afforded other banks, most significantly freedom from Central Bank regulation and protected monopoly status as Kuwait's only Islamic bank. As the first bank in Kuwait not under the control of the country's liberal merchant elite, KFH has played an important role in reaching out to the more traditional segments of the population. The political support the bank has received can be traced in part to its ability to mediate with this important constituency, and in part for its provision of financial services to the ruling family away from the watchful eyes of the merchants. More broadly, though, KFH is a concrete expression of the de facto alliance between the ruling family and the Islamic movement, an alliance that has grown in substance along with the growing weight of the conservative worldview in the country as evidenced through popular institutions such as the parliament, food cooperatives – and the market itself. Islamic finance in Kuwait, then, embodies the growing Islamization of public life in Kuwait under the benign gaze of the Kuwaiti government.

This chapter presents an analytic history of Kuwait's only Islamic bank – the KFH. The first two sections examine the political context that led to the establishment of the KFH. This is followed by a study of the bank's economic and marketing strategies, with an emphasis on the synergies that are generated between the bank's pursuit of profit, and the Islamists' pursuit of political power. Of particular interest is what may be called the socio-politics of KFH: by relating financial activities to religious values and beliefs, KFH both reflects and leads a growing Islamization of Kuwaiti society. Finally, in this chapter it seems appropriate to question the future of KFH and of Islamic finance in Kuwait: specifically, will KFH's defence of its standing as Kuwait's only Islamic bank hinder the advance of the Islamic marketplace?

THE POLITICS OF FINANCE: OIL PATRONAGE AND OLIGARCHIC BANKING IN KUWAIT

While economists write about financial markets as being relatively autonomous of political institutions, political scientists have long noted the political roots of financial systems and their integral position in state-building. Collectively their works recognize that the historic accommodations made between economic and political elites are reflected in financial institutions and determinative of the fundamental nature of the state.[6] Thus, to understand the political significance of the financial sector in Kuwait, one needs to examine the historical relationship between the Kuwaiti ruling and merchant families.[7]

The Kuwaiti polity was born through an understanding between merchant families that harvested pearls from the Gulf and traded with India and East Africa, and the ruling Al-Sabah family. The Al-Sabah were selected as the leading political family and were expected to provide protection from marauding tribes for the small trading settlement in the northern Gulf. The power of the Al-Sabah was constrained, however, by their financial reliance on the merchants. The merchant families were able to leverage this financial position into political influence, forcing the acceptance of the Gulf region's first and only parliament back in the 1930s.

The discovery of oil fundamentally altered the power relationship between these two groups. As the revenue from oil exports accrued directly to Kuwait's rulers, the Al-Sabah were freed from their financial reliance upon the merchants. Nonetheless, the merchant families still retained enough social cohesion to force a compromise on the Al-Sabah: the merchants renounced their claim to participate in decision-making in exchange for a large share in the oil revenues and promises of government restraint in the private sector.[8] This assured the continued dominance of the merchants in the transformed economy of the state.

The regime had various ways of passing oil wealth along to the merchants. One of the most important means was through land-distribution schemes and the speculation on land prices that followed. Beginning in the 1950s, the government acquired land from Kuwaitis at deliberately inflated prices. From 1951 to 1979, the government spent approximately 8 per cent of total oil revenues and 11 per cent of public expenditure for this purpose; incredibly, in the peak year of 1967 over 85 per cent of oil revenues went to the Land Acquisition Program. In total, nearly $7 billion was transferred to Kuwaiti citizens in this manner, with the greatest beneficiaries being the merchants and the Al-Sabah family itself.[9] Another mechanism for transferring wealth to the merchants was through the stock exchange: in 1963, 1973, 1975, 1977 and 1982 the government intervened to halt downturns or crashes of the market, supporting prices and making good the losses suffered by shareholders. One of the more secure ways for the merchants to amass wealth was through the holding of exclusive agency contracts, as foreign companies were obliged to take on local partners to distribute and service their goods. Ministries and embassies usually provided the contacts, but the banks were also a source of the introduction that would bring an exclusive distribution monopoly. Contracts with the government were also a source of patronage, as merchant-owned companies were hired to expand state infrastructure during the boom years and beyond.

The banks were key intermediaries – and beneficiaries – in the circulation of this oil patronage. The 1960 Commercial Companies Law had banned expatriates entirely from finance and banking, and the ruling family likewise minimized state interference in the sector. This left the banks in the hands of Kuwait's elite merchant families, who organized themselves into competing clans and used the banks to service their own businesses.[10] Thus, they were well-positioned to profit from the management of real estate and land deals, and the general business resulting from oil patronage. The government also turned a blind eye to the banks' speculative practices and bailed them out when they got into financial trouble.[11] Bank ownership, then, was key to the merchants' hold on the Kuwaiti economy. The next section will examine how the Islamist movement broke this oligarchy by establishing their own bank.

POLITICAL CONTEXT: RULING FAMILY, MERCHANTS AND THE BEDOUIN/ISLAMIST COUNTERWEIGHT

Clearly, Kuwait's banking system is intimately linked to the politics of the state, acting as a conduit of patronage from the ruling family to its political constituents. Any change in the banking system should therefore reflect a political shift in the state.[12] The emergence of Kuwait's first Islamic bank thus signals important political changes in the emirate. The purpose of this section is to examine these political shifts that resulted in the establishment of KFH in 1977.

As noted in the previous section, Kuwait's power structure can best be described as oligarchic; the Al-Sabah have preserved their family's right to rule, while acknowledging the privileged place of the prominent merchant families in the economic life of the emirate. However, the introduction of oil wealth brought new players to this political game. Before oil, the political reach of the Al-Sabah was limited to the walled area of Kuwait City, along with some alliances with the surrounding Bedouin tribes. The establishment of borders under the British gave a new territorial reality to Kuwait, and the growing cash flow fuelled by oil exports attracted Bedouin tribes who began to settle around the city, oasis villages and oil installations of the emirate. In the Bedouin, the Al-Sabah saw potential conservative allies and a natural counterweight to the politically sophisticated and increasingly demanding merchant and urban population. The ruling family therefore encouraged them to settle by providing government housing, services, and employment. Then, in 1961 and again in 1967, the government undertook a mass naturalization programme, enfranchising tens of thousands of Bedouin.[13] The growing political power of this conservative element was formally consolidated in 1981, with the reshuffle of Kuwait's electoral constituencies to favour the outer tribal areas.[14]

The shift to the tribal constituencies outside Kuwait City was coupled with a lenient attitude towards a rising Islamist movement within the urban constituency of Kuwait. The need for additional labour in the 1950s and '60s had led to the importation of workers from socialist Arab states. These migrant workers often brought their radical pan-Arab politics with them. Their support for socialism and Arab unity eventually spread to Kuwaiti nationals, and a vocal opposition to the measured politics of the Al-Sabah regime emerged in the 1975 National Assembly.[15] The Kuwaiti government, alarmed over the volatile mix of the opposition's rhetoric and the large Palestinian expatriate community working in Kuwait, dissolved the parliament for the first time since liberation and began casting about for new allies to counter the Arab nationalists. It found them in the Islamist forces.[16]

Up until this time the Islamic organizations had not been very active in the political life of the emirate. Their main organization – the Social Reform Society – was formed in 1962 to act as a philanthropic charitable organization. It had ties with the Muslim Brotherhood but had not played a role in opposition politics in Kuwait apart from mobilization on some social issues. In 1975, the Islamic organizations did not condemn the dissolution of the parliament, and were rewarded with the ruling family appointment of the chairman of the Social Reform Society, Abdel Aziz al-Mutawwa', to the position of Minister for Religious Endowments (awqâf).[17] With the encouragement of Egyptian Islamists, entrepreneurs from Kuwait's Islamic societies had been working since the late 1960's to be allowed to open an interest-free financial institution.[18] Although initially reluctant owing to the novelty of the concept, the ruling family became more cooperative owing to the changing political reality; with the encouragement of the Ministry of Awqâf and the good favour of the ruling family, KFH was finally established through an Emiri decree in 1977.

The Al-Sabah's search for new allies – using the Bedouin to counter the merchants, and the Islamists to counter the Arab nationalists – laid the political context for the acceptance and spread of Islamic banking. As will be shown in the next section, the interests of these two constituencies began to intersect as the Islamists found in the socially conservative and economically marginalized Bedouin a receptive political audience – and an under-tapped banking market.

ISLAMIC BANKING, KFH STYLE

The establishment of KFH gave the Islamists access to the political patronage filtering through the financial system from above, and it also linked them to an important constituency on the ground: the Bedouin, whose financial needs had been neglected by the merchant-centered commercial banks. In this section, there is an examination of how KFH developed services that appealed to this newly urbanizing population, along with Kuwait's growing middle class.

By promoting the virtues of interest-free banking and denouncing Kuwait's 'interest' banks for bleeding Kuwaiti consumers of limited income, KFH rapidly gained acceptance amongst Kuwait's conservative population. KFH immediately established branches in Kuwait's less wealthy outer constituencies – three of their first four branches were located outside of Kuwait City – and was flooded with new depositors.[19] KFH offered customers no-risk current accounts, but most customers chose to place funds in savings accounts based on the *mudaraba* principle of managing depositors' funds on a profit-and-loss basis.[20]

By 2003, bank deposits at KFH totaled 1.8 billion KD (nearly $6 billion), a sum representing 15 per cent of the market in Kuwait – one of the highest market shares of any Islamic commercial bank in a national market. Yet this actually

Figure 8.1: KFH customer deposits

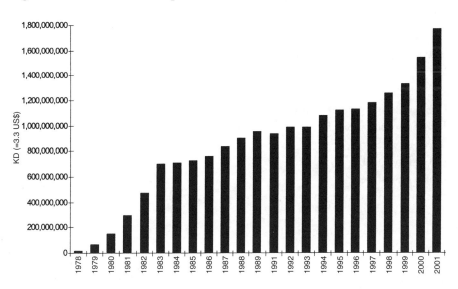

Sources: Kuwait Finance House, *Annual Reports,* 1979–2001; Institute of Banking Studies, *Financial Operating Report 1997–2000,* 11th edition, Kuwait.

underestimates the attraction of the Islamic bank, as KFH puts no minimum balance restrictions on opening accounts and tends to draw a higher portion of its customers from Kuwait's lower-income brackets. This means that a much higher percentage of Kuwait's citizens bank at KFH; the bank's assistant general manager of the banking sector informed me that KFH has the highest share of government salary deposits at 37 per cent – a significant statistic as over 90 per cent of the workforce of Kuwaiti nationals is employed by the government.[21]

With so much money at hand, the problem for KFH has been finding the means to profitably deploy these funds in accordance with Islamic guidelines and with Kuwait's limited economy; in fact, during the recession following the collapse of the informal Suq al-Manakh stock market, KFH actually stopped accepting deposits as it was unable to invest all of its funds.[22] A comparison of the asset portfolios of KFH and the National Bank of Kuwait (NBK), Kuwait's premier conventional bank, reveals some of the impediments to investing in compliance with Islamic legal principles, but it also shows KFH's resourcefulness in overcoming these restrictions.

The first point to note is KFH's challenge in managing liquidity – a problem shared with all other Islamic banks. The main tool for doing this among conventional banks is the inter-bank market, but Islamic banks cannot participate in this, as it is interest-denominated. Instead, KFH along with other Islamic banks, engages in international commodity transactions based on the *murabaha* contract that have a lower return – around 1.8 per cent. Similarly, KFH cannot purchase fixed-interest government treasury bills or bonds, which are another form of secure investment for conventional banks.

Table 8.1: Comparison of asset portfolios, KFH and NBK, 2001, %

	NBK	KFH
Cash and deposits with banks	25	3
International *murabaha*		25
Treasury bills	8	
Government bills	12	
Government bonds	5	
Lending and receivables	35	50
Investments	12	17
Land, property and equipment	1	1
Leased assets		2
Other assets	2	2
Total	100	100

Source: National Bank of Kuwait and Kuwait Finance House, *Annual Reports*, 2001.

Still, even without these outlets KFH has been able to generate impressive profits. KFH has the highest return on equity of any Kuwaiti bank,[23] and the value of owners' equity has increased rapidly over the past decade: after being the lowest of all Kuwaiti banks in 1990, by the end of the decade it had the second highest value just behind NBK.[24] Essentially, KFH has been forced to work harder to employ its funds, and to make up for the low returns on the international *murabaha* transactions. From Table 8.1 above one can see that KFH has a higher asset share in both receivables and in investments than its competitor, NBK.[25] KFH's ability to generate this business came about through its innovate adaptation of Islamic financial instruments to Kuwait's changing social structure and economy.

One defining characteristic of Islamic banking is its attempt to keep finance linked to real goods. KFH applies this principle literally by keeping large inventories of real estate, automobiles and other products in demand by Kuwaitis. One KFH manager told me that KFH will import anything its customers want within the bounds of Islam, 'from needles to aircraft'.[26] Therefore, KFH is something of a hybrid between a bank and a trading company. This concrete link with tradables opened up a unique marketing opportunity for KFH – one of which they took full advantage.

In the oil boom years of the 1970s and '80s, per capita income increased dramatically and Kuwait's consumer landscape completely changed.[27] Flush with oil money, the state had been passing on its wealth through increased government spending and expanded state employment that benefited the general population and especially the tribal regions. As Bedouin began to settle in government-subsidized housing next to wealthier citizens, their needs and expectations began to rise. There was a demand for financing to help purchase homes, building supplies, cars, furniture and other consumer durables. Thus, there existed a need – and an opportunity – for an understanding financial intermediary to step in between the steady flow of funds from the state to this new constituency.

KFH played this role. By capitalizing on the Islamic bank's standing outside of banking regulations and thus its freedom to participate in both banking and trading activities, KFH became an innovative facilitator of consumption, marketing both goods and financing together.[28] KFH took advantage of government subsidies in the land market and invested heavily in real estate; by 1983, almost 60 per cent of KFH assets were held in commercial and residential plots, buildings and large lands.[29] Its investments in the sector were so substantial, however, that it became the largest holder of real estate in the country, and many began to accuse the bank of driving up prices.[30] KFH responded by diversifying into other commodities; by the end of the 1980s, the percentage of its assets in land and real estate had dropped to 37 per cent.[31]

At the time of writing, KFH's trading sector, which comprises cars, housing materials, furniture and other products, is 25 per cent of its business, and generates an enormous 50 per cent of net profits.[32] Through car showrooms and slick brochures marketing building supplies, furniture and electronics, KFH provides financing at the point of sale, placing customers on installment plans consistent with the Islamic *murabaha* instrument. This strategy of focusing on consumer finance made good business sense, as the government had created an entirely new consumer base with its employment of the Bedouin and the urban middle class. KFH actively catered to this market segment by offering special prices and facilities for government workers; it was likewise the first Kuwaiti bank to negotiate with the government the direct deposit of government salary checks.[33] KFH was also able to use this business to increase its depositor base by demanding that customers bank with KFH, or face higher costs on their *murabaha* facilities and mortgage financing.[34] Thus, with cheques arriving reliably from government coffers to KFH accounts, payments for *murabaha* facilities could be deducted directly at the beginning of the month, greatly reducing KFH's default risk.

KFH's emphasis on consumer financing has garnered criticism. Its trading activities became so extensive that there were again protests of unfair competition, this time from Kuwaiti merchants who accused the banking behemoth of using its market position to pressure them into working through KFH.[35] Others have complained that KFH is encouraging unhealthy spending habits; it is estimated that 83 per cent of Kuwaitis are in debt, with most of their arrears concentrated in housing, cars, furniture and other consumer items marketed by KFH.[36]

Clearly, KFH's effect on Kuwait's domestic economy is profound, but its influence does not end there. The market power gained by KFH, and its increasing linkages with the Bedouin, had consequences for Kuwaiti society beyond the financial realm. Politics has been defined as the authoritative allocation of resources and values.[37] We usually associate such 'political' acts with governmental institutions, but KFH is a private-sector institution that combines these two activities, providing funds while simultaneously promoting a particular vision of social organization and interaction. The next two sections examine the political role KFH has assumed through its allocation of resources and values.

ECONOMIC AND POLITICAL NETWORKS ENTANGLED: KFH IN POLITICS

The rise of KFH mirrors the rise of Islamist politics in Kuwait. Although it is difficult to assign a direct cause-and-effect link between the two, it is clear that having the structural power of a financial institution has provided certain benefits to the political movement, and a powerful means of promoting its socio-religious agenda. At the same time, having the support of a political movement in Kuwait has given KFH some market opportunities as well.

There is a strong correlation between KFH's economic penetration of the Bedouin market and the Islamist political penetration of Kuwait's outer, more tribal districts. The Islamists entered Kuwait's formal politics in 1981, taking their first two seats in the pro-government National Assembly that followed the dissolution of the rancorous 1977 Parliament. It is difficult to track the Islamist rise in popularity throughout the 1980s, as the National Assembly was dissolved for a second time in 1986 and was not reinstated until after the Gulf War in 1992. The elections that year, however, as well as the subsequent two elections, have shown a sharp increase in the influence of the Islamist factions in Kuwait.[38] At the same time, it is clear that the popularity of the Islamists has shifted from its urban origins to a more tribal constituency.

By superimposing the rise in KFH's receivables (that is, *murabaha* facilities) on a bar graph showing the rise in Islamic political influence in the National Assembly, one can clearly see the correlation: KFH benefited from the spread of Islamic politics into the outer constituencies, and perhaps contributed to it as well.

A good example of the mix between Islamist business and politics can be found in the Kuwaiti food cooperatives. Each Kuwaiti neighbourhood has its own food cooperative that is communally run, each one administered by a board elected through a general assembly. The general assemblies of the cooperatives are a good reflection of Kuwaiti populism, as nearly a quarter of all Kuwaitis are

Figure 8.2: Islamicist politican and economic power

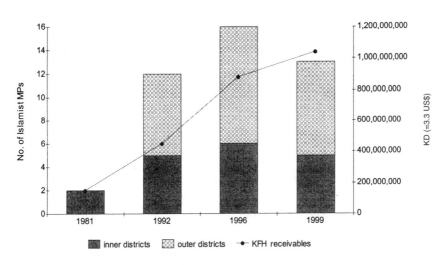

Source: Data on KFH receivables is taken from Kuwait Finance House *Annual Reports.*

members. The cooperatives are also an extremely profitable network of businesses, generating total revenues of nearly 10 billion KD ($33.3 billion) and representing 75 per cent of the Kuwaiti food market.[39]

At first, KFH tried to enter into the foodstuffs business directly, placing on the market its own products, such as Islamically-slaughtered beef and chicken. This proved problematic, however, as it placed KFH in direct competition with food import businesses and the small merchants who were the natural customer base of the bank.[40] They therefore decided to switch strategies, moving from direct sales into promoting themselves as a financing intermediary between the small merchants and the cooperatives. At the time of writing an estimated 70 per cent of these importers are now customers of KFH.[41]

KFH had not been as successful, however, in the competition for the business of the cooperatives themselves. All of the banks were competing furiously both to win the cooperatives as depositors, and to be allowed to place bank branches in their stores, which would position them for the profitable quick-cash retail business. After trailing the conventional banks in this competition, KFH's fortunes improved when Islamist candidates began standing for election on the cooperative boards and eventually took over the management of most of them.[42] After these political successes, the new Islamist boards – supported by lobbying from the general assemblies against interest banking – shifted their bank accounts to KFH. Through promotions and public community campaigns, KFH also gained business from the cooperatives for its affiliate companies; International Turnkey Systems (ITS), a KFH-owned technology firm, won nearly 70 per cent of the cooperative business in cash registers and inventory systems and drove the previous leader in the market out of business.[43]

It is widely rumoured that KFH repays the Islamist politicians in kind, putting its considerable resources behind their election campaigns. Although there is no evidence of direct funding of candidates, KFH can use its considerable resources – money, real estate and jobs – to influence elections. There were accusations during the 1996 campaign for the National Assembly that KFH was working with the government-directed charity Zakat House to offer lower-priced *murabaha* facilities and housing in certain strategic outer districts where Islamist candidates faced close elections. Although a specially appointed governmental committee to probe the allegations cleared Zakat House of buying elections, charges that KFH uses its financial influence in parliamentary elections persist.[44] KFH is likewise said to offer its extensive land holdings for use as venues for Islamist campaign rallies.[45] But one of its greatest political resources is its standing as one of the largest private-sector employers of Kuwaiti citizens. With unemployment becoming a critical issue with Kuwait's youthful population, jobs mean political leverage; this has given KFH influence both in the university, where student Islamist parties campaign on the promise of entry-level jobs for supporters, and in the National Assembly, where employment is one of the most important forms of patronage given by MPs to their constituents.[46]

Concerns about KFH's political influence extend beyond Kuwait, owing to its association with Kuwait's charities. Since the oil boom of the 1970s, Kuwait has witnessed a proliferation of private charitable associations, most of which have an Islamic character and many of which are associated with Islamist political trends in the country. These associations prevail upon Kuwaiti social conscience and upon the Islamic religious pillar of alms-giving to collect millions of dollars in aid for programmes around the Islamic World. These primarily fund humanitarian projects, although a sizeable percentage of donations go towards more explicitly religious activities and many emphasize support for Islamic political causes. It has long been suspected that a small portion of this money may be diverted to violent Islamic opposition groups in places such as Egypt, Algeria and Afghanistan.[47] The US government appears to have confirmed these suspicions by placing the Afghanistan and Pakistan branches of one Kuwaiti charity on the list of organizations whose assets are to be frozen due to their suspected links with Al-Qaida.[48]

Because Islamic charities would find it inappropriate to place funds in interest-bearing banks, KFH has become a hub for the financial activities of these groups, which hold over 100 accounts there.[49] Newspapers are full of advertisements asking that people deposit contributions directly to open accounts held at KFH, or to take advantage of KFH campaigns allowing donations to be transferred by phone. In addition, KFH makes its own direct contributions to Islamic charitable campaigns, both in Kuwait and abroad. Certainly, the vast majority of these funds are for legitimate charitable purposes, but suspicions remain owing to the political cast of some of Kuwait's charities, and most importantly owing to the fact that KFH remains outside of the supervision of Kuwait's Central Bank.

This fact has crystallized all of the fears of Kuwait's liberals, and has become their main point of attack, especially in the polarized post-September 11 political environment. In an extraordinary interview, the outspoken former Kuwaiti Ambassador to the United States, Sheikh Saud Nasser Al-Sabah, criticized his country's timid response to the September 11th attacks, and its lukewarm support of the United States-led war against terrorism. He provocatively asserted that this measured stance was due to the fact that the country had been 'hijacked' by Islamic groups, which have taken over a number of organizations to use as covers to carry out their pursuit of political influence and power. He specifically pointed to KFH and charged that Islamist activists were using it, along with the charitable societies to seize power in Kuwait through their control of financial means.[50]

Sheikh Saud's accusations reflect in part the bitter rivalry between the liberal camp and the Islamists over political influence and business networks, and the resentment the liberals feel towards KFH as a prominent institutional reflection of the Islamic trend. Yet its hyperbolic tone likewise reveals the alarm liberals feel over the erosion of their vision of Kuwaiti society, which was grounded in a broad scope for personal liberties and a staunchly pro-Western outlook and lifestyle. The spread of conservative Islamic norms has been substantiated in a survey conducted over the past ten years by KFH's main conventional competitor, the National Bank of Kuwait. This research was prompted by concern over the popularity of KFH, and the request by NBK's own customers for financial intermediation in line with *shari'a* law. By asking a number of behavioural questions, NBK has been able to track the fortunes of the Islamic trend. Over the ten-year period, they have found that the percentage of Kuwaitis polled who can be classified as 'liberals' has been declining and now stands at less than 15 per cent. By contrast, the percentage of 'Islamics' has been growing, so much so that a new category – 'modern Islamic' – had to be created to account for the shift from 'moderate' to 'Islamic'. The two categories of Islamics now account for some 55 per cent of those answering the survey.[51] For liberals, KFH's role in promoting this shift in values in Kuwaiti society is perhaps more disturbing than its business success.

BANKING WITH A MESSAGE: THE SOCIO-POLITICS OF KFH

The previous two sections have demonstrated how Islamic entrepreneurs, with the support of the Kuwaiti government, have been able to employ Islamic finance in their pursuit of profit and political influence. However, Islamic financiers have done more than exploit existing Islamic belief and sympathy; they have actively used the institutionalization of Islam in finance to proselytize and bring new adherents to their worldview. This section examines how both the institutional presence and market power of KFH promote the Islamization of public life in the emirate.

The first place KFH can influence public values is through the example it sets with its own employees and places of work. KFH is known to show preference in hiring to Kuwaiti nationals, especially the devout young Kuwaiti men from the Islamic trend.[52] At KFH main offices there is an attempt to foster a religious communal environment; prayer times are announced throughout the building, and employees often gather in the halls to pray together. Smoking – and, of course, alcohol – is prohibited. And both employees and customers at the main headquarters are exclusively male, including receptionists.

KFH does cater to women at its commercial sites, such as the car showrooms and at special ladies banking divisions, but everything is done to facilitate the separation of the sexes. Special offices staffed by women employees are set up to handle transactions with female customers, and certain days are set aside every month when women can view showrooms without the presence of men. Indeed, it is an interesting fact that KFH is increasingly focusing on women as a target market segment; special promotions are directed at women, gifts are offered and educational talks given by KFH employees at Kuwaiti schools are treated as opportunities to market Islamic financial products among the predominantly female teachers.[53] So although integrating women into the work force and economy, KFH simultaneously promotes gender segregation within society.

KFH's market presence offers other mechanisms for promoting an Islamic lifestyle, sometimes in surprising ways. KFH owns several rental buildings that are known by Kuwaiti residents as being 'Islamically run', and people whose lifestyles may be incompatible with this avoid them. KFH also segregates its apartment buildings, some for bachelors and others for families, and public spaces such as swimming pools are gender segregated. Thought is given to the proper Islamic way of life even in the design of the apartments. The chairman of the KFH-owned Al-Enma'a company informed me that KFH builds 'Islamic flats' which place the kitchens near the bedrooms so that wives will not have to pass through the public salon while their husbands are entertaining friends and colleagues.[54] Islamic restrictions extend as well to KFH's commercial properties. Its biggest holding – the Al-Muthanna shopping mall and residential centre in downtown Kuwait City – is anchored by the French family department store Prisunic, selected because of its specialization in children's clothing as KFH customers have larger than average families.[55] Storeowners located in the mall are told in their contracts not to use display mannequins, which are seen as a violation of the Islamic prohibition on the depiction of the human figure.

Alongside its market power, KFH's institutional presence within Kuwaiti society provides many opportunities for networking amongst like-minded individuals and organisations. KFH contributes to schools, charities and cooperatives, and fosters close relations with these social institutions. KFH has been especially interested in education, sponsoring field trips to KFH, scholarships encouraging students to study Islamic economics, Islamic competitions (Koranic memorization, and the like), and the establishment of private Islamic schools. KFH is particularly active around religious holidays, donating sacrificial animals for religious feasts to the needy, and organizing pilgrimages to Mecca for its employees. And KFH reaches out to society at large through its monthly publication, Al-Noor, which has a circulation of over 10,000 inside Kuwait and in other Arab countries such as Jordan and Yemen.[56] In print for twenty years, Al-Noor has evolved into a glossy magazine covering issues of special interest to the Islamic community and the Islamic consumer. It has a particular focus on women and children, as half of the publication is devoted to Islamic family life.

And it, of course, keeps its readers informed about the activities and special promotions of KFH itself.

Through its activities and its very presence, then, KFH has promoted the Islamic trend in Kuwait – the advance of which translates into a growing demand for Islamic financial products. The success of KFH in both creating and responding to the Islamic consumer is substantiated in a study by the Institute of Banking Studies in Kuwait. Their survey of 1,000 Kuwaiti residents showed that 50 per cent had used Islamic financial products, and of the non-users 50 per cent intended to do so in the future. The survey also revealed that KFH dominates the market for Islamic financial products, as 89 per cent of the users had turned to KFH for their Islamic financial needs.[57]

It may be that KFH has been too successful in nurturing Islamic banking and expanding the demand for Islamic financial products. With so much demand, there have been mounting pressures to open up the sector by allowing both conventional banks and other new entrants to establish Islamic banks. However, the means for this expansion, namely a new Islamic banking law, has been held hostage to the long unresolved issues of KFH's regulatory status.

THE FUTURE OF ISLAMIC FINANCE IN KUWAIT: KFH MONOPOLY OR THE ISLAMIC MARKETPLACE?

Since its creation in 1977, KFH has enjoyed the protection of being Kuwait's only Islamic bank. By the 1990s, however, a number of political and economic forces coalesced in support of the enactment of a new Islamic banking law that would set out the regulatory framework for Islamic banking in Kuwait and allow for new competitors in the market.

The main promoter of this legislation has been the Kuwaiti Central Bank, which has grown increasingly unhappy with its inability to regulate KFH.[58] As KFH deposits have grown so has its economic impact on the country. Yet owing to its creation under a special Emiri decree, which left it outside of Central Bank regulation, the Central Bank cannot demand financial information from KFH nor impose standards for liquidity and reserve requirements or a host of other regulations deemed necessary to secure the stability of the banking system. KFH has been cooperating with the Central Bank on a voluntary basis, but there is no law to force its compliance with Central Bank wishes. This omission is deemed by many economic observers to be courting disaster. Although KFH insists that, in keeping with Islamic law, its depositors' accounts are not guaranteed, no one believes that Kuwait's second-largest bank could fail without a huge impact on Kuwait's economy and enormous costs to the state. The Central Bank, then, would like to see KFH come under its regulation, and to sharply curtail many of KFH's commercial ventures, which it sees as putting depositor funds at unacceptable risk.[59]

The liberal camp in Kuwait also wants KFH to be regulated and has backed the Central Bank in its calls for a new Islamic banking law. Liberal politicians and pundits view KFH as an extension of political Islam and would like to see it cut down to size. At the same time, prominent merchants outside of the Islamic movement fear the threat KFH represents to their primacy in business; they support Central Bank legal restrictions on the Islamic bank that would curtail its encroachment into their commercial activities.[60]

Still, the calls for a new Islamic banking law represent more than just opposition – they also represent opportunity. Since Kuwait's liberation following the 1991 Gulf War, the demand for Islamic financial products has exploded. NBK has already entered the Islamic mutual fund business through its Kawthar fund, but it would like to be able to accept Islamic deposits as would other Kuwaiti banks. At the same time, a large number of Islamic investment houses – some catering to modest *murabaha* consumers and others to high net worth investors – have entered the Kuwaiti market; there were ten different companies in Kuwait by the beginning of 2000 with total capital reaching KD 235 million.[61] Yet they are likewise prevented from offering commercial banking services, owing to the absence of an Islamic banking law.

This final group is most significant, as it represents a split within the Islamic movement itself over the best way to develop the Islamic finance industry in Kuwait. Although many are dedicated to KFH, seeing it as Kuwait's most visible example of the application of Islamic law to public life and an institutional asset to the movement, others believe that the goals of the Islamic movement – not to mention the Islamic consumer – would best be served by opening up Islamic finance to more competitors, thereby encouraging the expansion of the Islamic marketplace in Kuwait.[62]

It is within this political and economic context that the National Assembly entered discussions about the drafting of a new Islamic banking law. Ironically, the initiative began under Ismail Al-Shatti, an MP from the Islamist Constitutional Movement and in 1992 chairman of the Finance Committee.[63] Al-Shatti had presided over the settlement of the Suq al-Manakh debt crisis, which resulted in government compensation to Kuwaiti banks, including a half billion KD pay-out to KFH. He became convinced of the dangers of lack of transparency and regulation and thus provided the government with a budget and time frame to study the best way to regulate Islamic finance. In 1994, a government committee made up of representatives of the Ministry of Finance, the Central Bank and KFH directors met with the Finance Committee to discuss the matter. Divisions quickly emerged, however, between the Central Bank view on the necessity of regulation and KFH's reluctance to submit to the Central Bank. When the Ministry of Finance appeared to be taking the Central Bank's view of the matter, the KFH representatives took the opportunity of a prayer break to lobby the Islamist MPs on the parliamentary Finance Committee to get them to postpone the matter.[64]

This early intervention presaged KFH's strategy over the next decade: content with the status quo, KFH has been eager to use its influence with Islamist politicians to stall the implementation of a new law as long as possible. In 1997, the Central Bank finally brought a proposal before the National Assembly, which not only would end KFH's monopoly, but would also significantly curtail its business activities. It was immediately met by a rival proposal, drafted by KFH and submitted by five sympathetic Islamist MPs, defending KFH's current business practices. The differences between the Central Bank and KFH views are sharp and rooted in mutual distrust. KFH believes the Central Bank to be hostile to Islamic finance and set in positions that would undermine the success of KFH. The Central Bank, meanwhile, believes KFH to be a dangerous maverick institution that threatens Kuwaiti financial stability. The specific issues of contention have been:[65]

1. Central Bank regulation: it was understood that any new Islamic banking law would give the Central Bank the authority to supervise and regulate. The Central Bank is adamant that any new Islamic banking law be written as amendments to existing banking regulation and require that all Islamic banks, including KFH, come under its jurisdiction. KFH has come to accept the inevitability of Central Bank regulation, but has worked first to stall, and then to limit, the Central Bank's ability to interfere in its current business practices.
2. Commercial activities: the initial Central Bank draft law sought to end KFH's ability to conduct non-financial activities – KFH would only be able to buy property at the immediate request of a customer instead of holding inventories, and its real estate holdings would be limited to 25 per cent of the bank's capital and reserves. KFH views this as tantamount to shutting down the bank, as 80 per cent of its profits come from its trading and real estate sectors.[66] Still, in anticipation of future changes, KFH has been spinning off many of its commercial activities as separate businesses.
3. The nature of competition: the conventional banks would like to be able to open Islamic windows, which would require the least effort on their part to break into the Islamic banking business. KFH opposes this; the managing director of KFH sent a memo to each of the MPs on the Finance and Economic Committee expressing the dangers of allowing Islamic windows and branches, and urging the committee to allow only new Islamic banks or the complete conversion of conventional banks to Islamic banks.[67]

The existence of the two opposing draft laws with political sponsors to defend them essentially left the matter deadlocked in the National Assembly, and there was essentially no movement on the Islamic banking law for five years. A number of factors converged to end this stalemate and allow for the passage of a compromise draft law out of the Finance and Economic Committee in November 2002. One was the aforementioned flourishing of the Islamic finance sector, which increased both the need for regulation and the interest in opening new Islamic banking institutions. Specifically, in addition to the expected pressure from the Banking Union on behalf of influential conventional banks such as NBK, the MPs on the committee began to hear from the new Islamic investment companies, which established their own lobbying committee to press for the law's immediate passage.[68] Perhaps even more influential was the changed economic and political circumstances caused by the September 11th attacks and the ensuing financial war against terrorism. Concern from the United States and reluctance in the international financial community to deal with Middle Eastern/Islamic banks greatly added to the urgency of bringing KFH under proper regulation. With this changed context and years of studying the issues at hand, the MPs in the Finance and Economic Committee finally decided to take the initiative in finding a compromise between the KFH and Central Bank draft laws.

The National Assembly finally passed the law in April 2003, thereby ending KFH's monopoly and bringing the bank under Central Bank regulation. Still, it leaves so many details open that in some ways this can be seen as the beginning, not the end, of the struggle between KFH and the Central Bank. The committee draft allows for the application of new banks and for conventional banks to open Islamic branches, not windows. It likewise splits the difference in the battle over KFH's non-financial activities, allowing KFH's direct investment in whatever commercial activities it likes, but with ceilings set by the Central Bank in order to limit risk. The exact nature of the Central Bank's regulation of the Islamic banking sector was likewise left undefined. Thus, the new law will be an important step in the expansion of the Islamic financial marketplace in Kuwait, but the extent of its impact on KFH will be subject to future negotiations – and political battles – with the Kuwaiti Central Bank.

CONCLUSION

The emergence and expansion of Islamic finance in Kuwait came about through a favourable domestic confluence of government support, popular sympathy and innovative marketing. It is worth asking if powerful international currents could spell trouble for the industry and KFH in particular. The aftermath of the attacks of September 11th, especially the ensuing financial war against terrorism, has raised suspicions of all things Islamic. As mentioned in the last section, the changed international context is largely responsible for the recent movement in the National Assembly on the long-frozen Islamic finance law that will spell the end of KFH's monopoly. And as is readily apparent in the attack by Sheikh Saud Nasser Al-Sabah, Kuwait's liberals are eager to use the new international environment as leverage to shift the domestic balance of power in their favour and to limit the influence of the Islamists.

Despite these challenges, KFH and the Islamic finance industry are well-placed to survive and even prosper. Indeed, the initiative to pass a new Islamic banking law is a tribute to KFH's achievement in bringing acceptance of Islamic finance to Kuwait. Over time, the KFH has been able to use the favour of the ruling Al-Sabah to build a popular network of charities, businesses and social organizations that rival those of the liberal elite. The Islamists have succeeded in drawing upon these networks to gain influence in many ministries and in the National Assembly, where, with the support of traditionalist MPs, they can often martial a tribal–Islamist–populist coalition comprising a majority. The influence they wield in important institutions like KFH gives them access to jobs and financial resources that can further be used to garner support for the movement, particularly among Kuwaiti youth. In short, the expansion of economic and political participation in Kuwait through the broader inclusion of Bedouin and the middle class more generally has effected a growing Islamization of public life in Kuwait. And as evidenced by KFH itself, the movement has achieved an impressive degree of institutionalization within Kuwaiti society. With such deeply embedded social roots, the demand for Islamic financial products seems assured.

NOTES

1. Informal money-changers were prevalent, and Western banks were used by the commercial elite.
2. For an interesting discussion of the global commodification of Islam, see Armando Salvatore, 'The Genesis and Evolution of 'Islamic Publicness' under Global Constraints', *Journal of Arabic, Islamic and Middle Eastern Studies*, Vol. 3 No.1, 1996, pp. 51–70.
3. On the links between patrimonialism and finance in the Middle East, see Jean Francois Seznec, *The Politics of Financial Markets in Saudi Arabia, Kuwait, and Bahrain*, PhD dissertation, Yale University, 1994; and Clement M. Henry, *The Mediterranean Debt Crescent: Money and Power in Algeria, Egypt, Morocco, Tunisia, and Turkey* (Gainesville, FL: University Press of Florida, 1996).
4. Commercial sector statistics from an interview with Fawaz Al-Uthman, Deputy Assistant Manager and Operation Manager, Commercial Sector, Kuwait Finance House, 7 December 1999.
5. When one considers both direct and indirect ownership through agencies, the government ownership share in KFH is closer to 60 per cent today.
6. Classic works on finance and state-building include Alexander Gerschenkron, *Economic Backwardness in Historical Perspective* (Cambridge: Belknap Press, 1962); and

John Zysman, *Governments, Markets, and Growth: Financial Systems and the Politics of Industrial Change* (Ithaca, NY: Cornell University Press, 1983).

7. I use the term 'merchant families' to refer to a self-aware corporate class represented by the Kuwaiti Chamber of Commerce and Industry (KCCI); it is not meant to signify just anyone participating in trade.

8. Jill Crystal, *Oil and Politics in the Gulf: Rulers and Merchants in Kuwait and Qatar* (Cambridge: Cambridge University Press, 1990).

9. Ghanim Al-Najjar, 'Decision-Making Process in Kuwait: The Land Acquisition Policy as a Case Study', PhD dissertation, University of Exeter, 1984, pp. 103–6.

10. Kuwait's largest bank, the National Bank of Kuwait (NBK) is dominated by the al-Bahar, al-Sayer and Al-Khorafi families, who represent the prominent Sunni tribes originally from Saudi Arabia. Another large bank, the National Commercial Bank (NCB), represents the interests of families originating from modern-day Iraq, such as the al-Wazzan and al-Marzouq. The prominent Shiite merchant families – Behbehani et al. – own the Al-Ahli Bank. Prior to its independence, Kuwait's financial sector was primarily in the hands of British overseas banks. For a history of banking in the emirate prior to independence, see Rodney Wilson, 'Financial Development in the Arab Gulf: The Eastern Bank Experience, 1917–1950', *Business History*, Vol. 29 No. 2, 1987, pp. 178–98.

11. With the boom of the petrodollar-fed informal stock market of Kuwait in the early 1980s, bank board directors often forced their own banks to make large loans to themselves against pledges of shares. When the market collapsed in 1982, the government bailed out the banks, buying bad loans with long-term treasury bonds and providing deposits to maintain liquidity. See Seznec, *The Politics of Financial Markets*, p. 212.

12. This follows the suggestion of Gwenn Okruhlik to make explicit the linkages between state strategies of expenditure and the political consequences for particular social groups: 'Rentier Wealth, Unruly Law, and the Rise of the Opposition: The Political Economy of Oil States', *Comparative Politics*, April 1999, pp. 295–300.

13. Crystal, *Oil and Politics*, p. 89.

14. Changes in Kuwait's election laws are discussed in Mary Ann Tétreault, *Stories of Democracy: Politics and Society in Contemporary Kuwait* (New York: Columbia University Press, 2000), pp. 108–10.

15. Crystal, *Oil and Politics*, p. 92.

16. Shafeeq Ghabra, 'The Islamic Movement in Kuwait', *Middle East Policy*, May 1997, p. 2. This was a common strategy throughout the Middle East at this time. Sadat did the same thing in Egypt, releasing members of the Muslim Brotherhood imprisoned under Nasser; they later assassinated him.

17. Ibid. p. 2.

18. Early supporters of an Islamic bank in Kuwait are discussed in an article on Aisa Abdu, an Egyptian promoter of Islamic finance in the Gulf. See Muhiaddin Attiyah, 'Aisa Abdu: One of the Important Scholars of Islamic Economics in the Contemporary Era', *Contemporary Muslim*, Februrary 1984, pp. 120–3. (Arabic)

19. *Al-Qabas*, 3 September 1979. Besides the main office, branches were established in Jahra, Riqa and Fahaheel. Kuwait Finance House, *Annual Reports*, 1979–80.

20. Savings accounts are available, from which Kuwait Finance House (KFH) invests a

minimum balance throughout the month and pays returns at the end of the year. The majority of KFH customers, however, choose to put their money in three-month or one-year revolving fixed accounts in which a higher percentage of the balance is invested, but customers are not allowed to withdraw funds prematurely without penalties. For more details on the legal basis of Islamic financing structures, see Frank E. Vogel and Samuel L. Hayes III, *Islamic Law and Finance: Religion, risk, and return* (The Hague: Kluwer Law International, 1998).

21. Interview with Wa'el Al-Qatami, Assistant General Manager, Banking Sector, Kuwait Finance House, 25 June 2002.

22. *Al-Qabas*, 25 December 1984, p. 15.

23. Institute of Banking Studies, Kuwait, *Financial Operating Report, 1997–2000*, 11th edition.

24. Statistic from an interview with Hamid Hamoud Al-Ajlan, Kuwaiti commentator on Islamic finance, 13 June 2002.

25. KFH's investment portfolio differs considerably from NBK, as they invest the majority of their funds in property, while NBK invests more in securities.

26. Interview with Sulaiman Al-Braikan, Chairman, Al-Enma'a Real Estate Co. and Assistant General Manager, Business Development, Kuwait Finance House, 7 December 1999.

27. The growth in revenues was indeed impressive: in the 1970s, oil income increased from $963 million to $9 billion. Shafeeq Ghabra, 'Kuwait and the Dynamics of Socio-Economic Change', *Middle East Journal*, Summer 1997, p. 2.

28. For an overview of Kuwait Finance House's consumer finance business in the 1980s, see Rodney Wilson, 'Kuwait: Islamic Financing for a Consumer Society', in Rodney Wilson (ed.), *Islamic Financial Markets* (London: Routledge, 1990), pp. 129–53.

29. Kuwait Finance House, *Annual Report*, 1983.

30. Kuwait Finance House claimed to be seeking price stability in the real estate market (*Al-Qabas*, issue 5471, 1983, p. 7). It was rumoured that the ruling family was using KFH to maintain high prices in land and real estate in order to protect the value of its own extensive holdings.

31. Kuwait Finance House, *Annual Report*, 1989. Real estate remains a strong portion of KFH business, representing 17 per cent of KFH's assets and generating 30 per cent of net profits.

32. Profit figures are from an interview with Muhammed Said AbdulWahab, Department Manager, Financial Control, Kuwait Finance House, 26 June 2002.

33. Interview with Fawaz Al-Uthman.

34. Interview with Wa'el Al-Qatami.

35. *Al-Qabas*, 15 March 1986, p. 22.

36. 'Debt and dishonour', *Gulf Business*, October 1999, p. 31. It is interesting to note that Kuwait Finance House's competitors among the Islamic finance houses have taken the consumer finance craze even further by offering *murabaha* facilities for marriages and even for vacations to London!

37. David Easton, *The Political System: An Inquiry into the State of Political Science* (New York: Knopf, 1953).

38. Political parties are illegal in Kuwait but there are informal political groupings within the National Assembly which function very much like parties. This, together

with the fact that most of the fifty MPs are listed as independent, makes it difficult to accurately count each group's standing in the National Assembly. The numbers listed in the graph should be taken as estimates and include some MPs with Islamist political leanings.

39. Interview with Saad Al-Barrak, Chairman, ITS Systems, December 1999.
40. Interview with Ahmed Al-Muleifi, former Kuwait Finance House manager and MP in the National Assembly, December 1999.
41. Interview with Adnan al-Bahar, Chairman, The International Investor of Kuwait, 29 June 2002.
42. Shafeeq Ghabra, 'Voluntary Associations in Kuwait: The Foundation of a New System?', *Middle East Journal*, 45, Spring 1991, p. 208.
43. Interview with Saad Al-Barrak.
44. 'Panel to probe Zakat House', *Arab Times*, 24–25 April 1997; 'Probe clears Zakat House of buying '96 election', *Arab Times*, 23 July 1997; 'Ten plus ten equals zero', *Al-Qabas*, 21 April 2001, p. 20.
45. Interview with MP Hussein Al-Qallaf, December 1999.
46. Interview with Kuwait University Professor of Political Science, Dr Ahmed Al-Baghdadi, 18 June 2002.
47. *Al-Hayat*, 15 May 1994, p.1.
48. 'Kuwait questions Islamic charity on allegation of funding terrorists', AP, 29 December 2001.
49. *Al-Talia*, 18 May 1994, p. 6.
50. *Asharq Al-Awsat*, 13 October 2001, p. 1. In a response, the head of the Islamic Reform Society, Abdel Aziz al-Muawwa', denied the Islamic groups were trying to take over the country and countered that those who criticize them 'don't know their way to the mosque'. *Al-Siyassah*, 18 October 2001, p. 7.
51. Interview with Faten Abu Ghazala, Assistant General Manager, Marketing Division, NBK, 30 June 2002. The NBK survey was conducted with a sample group of 1,000 and has a margin of error of +/– 3 per cent.
52. From its earliest days, the Kuwait Finance House has trumpeted its reliance on Kuwaiti labour and expertise – a rarity in Kuwait's expatriate labour economy. *Al-Qabas*, 30 October 1978.
53. Interview with the Kuwait Finance House's Director of Commercial Sector, Fawaz Al-Uthman.
54. Interview with Suleiman Al-Breikan.
55. Wilson, 'Kuwait: Islamic Financing for a Consumer Society', p. 151.
56. Interview with Mohammed Al-Owaied, Chief Editor, *Al-Noor*, 25 June 2001.
57. Institute of Banking Studies, Kuwait, 1998.
58. The Kuwait Finance House is regulated to a limited degree by the Ministry of Commerce.
59. Interview with Salah El-Kholy, Assistant Manager, Supervision Department, Central Bank of Kuwait, November 1999.
60. For more insight into the competition between liberal and Islamist businessmen in the Gulf, see Pete Moore, 'Rentier Fiscal Crisis and Regime Stability: Business–State Relations in the Gulf', *Studies in Comparative International Development*, Vol. 37 No. 1 , Spring 2002, pp. 34–56.

61. Interview with Hamid Hamoud Al-Ajlan.
62. Kuwait's Higher Consultative Committee to Work for the Completion of the Implementation of *Shari'a* Law submitted a memo to the Finance and Economic Committee of the National Assembly accepting the necessity for the Central Bank to supervise and regulate Islamic finance and urging a rather liberal policy of allowing conventional banks to offer Islamic financial products. *Al-Watan*, 5 June 2000, p. 14.
63. Although an Islamist politician, Al-Shatti has a number of reservations about the Kuwait Finance House, which he laid out in a editorial in *Al-Qabas*, 6 April 2000, p. 33.
64. This account of the committee meeting was provided in an interview with Ismail al-Shatti, 29 June 2002.
65. Gleaned from interviews with liberal MP Abdel Wahab Al-Haroun, Chair of Finance and Economic Committee, and Islamist MP Dr Nasser Al-Sane, June 2002.
66. Interview with Muhammed Said AbdulWahab.
67. Letter from the Managing Director of the Kuwait Finance House, Bader Mukheizeen, to the Head of the National Assembly, Jassem Al-Khorafi, 11 May 2002.
68. From an interview with Dr Nasser Al-Sane, Member of Kuwait National Assembly, 16 June 2002. He mentioned the Gulf Investment House, Al-Usuul, and The International Investor of Kuwait as those lobbying for a new Islamic banking law.

9

Jordan: A Case Study of the Relationship between Islamic Finance and Islamist Politics

Mohammed Malley

The main contention of political Islamists is that Islam is a complete way of life that encompasses rules and regulations, not only for spiritual and moral uplift, but also for how to establish and maintain political, economic, social and other systems. This was the first of twenty basic principles that Hassan Al-Banna, the founder of the Muslim Brotherhood, stated in a treatise[1] he wrote to explain the understanding of Islam held by his movement, which was the first Islamist organization of the modern era and the largest and most well-known of those groups until the 1990s. Al-Banna believed that the main role of his movement, and of Islamists in general, was to re-establish those aspects of the comprehensive Islamic religion that had been lost or destroyed before, during or after the colonial era. The establishment of Islamic banks in the second half of the twentieth century could be seen as a practical application of the ideological view that Islam contained within it an alternative means of running economic and financial affairs.

The ties between Islamic banks and Islamic movements have not, however, been as strong as might be expected. In this chapter, the role Islamists played in the early history of the Jordan Islamic Bank (JIB) is examined, as well as the ongoing relationship and kinds of interaction between Islamists and both the JIB and the Arab Islamic Bank (AIB). The economic agenda of the Islamic Action Front Party is also discussed, as is that of Islamist activists in professional organizations and other aspects of civil society.

THE ROLE OF ISLAMISTS IN THE ESTABLISHMENT OF THE JORDAN ISLAMIC BANK

The 1970s was a decade of extensive institutionalization for Islamists in Jordan.[2] In the aftermath of the 1967 war, the popularity of Islamic movements and Islamism as an ideology increased dramatically throughout the Arab World, including Jordan. By siding with the monarchy in Jordan's 1970 civil war, the Muslim Brotherhood in Jordan began enjoying an almost semi-official status in the 1970s, a status that enabled it to establish numerous new charitable, educational and healthcare institutions in the Kingdom.

It was in this milieu of both increased popularity and increased institutionalization that many Jordanian Islamist leaders and intellectuals began discussing
the concept of 'Islamic economics' and thinking about the possibility of
establishing Islamic financial institutions in Jordan and elsewhere. The books
and articles of the Pakistani Islamist intellectual Abu'l-A'la Mawdudi, who had
been writing about Islamic economics since the 1940s, were widely discussed
among Islamists in Jordan in the 1970s. The success of the Mit Ghamr savings/
investment houses in the Egyptian countryside were also looked to by Islamists
as proof of the feasibility of Islamic banking.[3]

The Mit Ghamr houses were established in Egypt in 1963 by Ahmed al
Najjar. While al Najjar was not himself an Islamist, the institutions he established worked on the principle of interest-free financing and many members of
the Egyptian Muslim Brotherhood worked and invested in them. The Mit
Ghamr experiment came to a quick end in 1967 when the banks were liquidated by the Egyptian government.[4] The short-term experiment was influential,
however, as Islamists perceived it as having provided a practical example of
Islamic banking in the modern era. The banks fuelled the aspirations of Islamists in Jordan and elsewhere to establish a more enduring Islamic alternative to
the prevailing economic and financial institutions.[5]

The establishment of two Islamic banks in 1975 also encouraged Jordanian
Islamists. In that year, the Organization of the Islamic Conference established
the Islamic Development Bank in Jeddah to finance government projects in the
Muslim countries and the Dubai Islamic Bank was established in the United
Arab Emirates. These two banks were dedicated to working on Islamic prin-
ciples, but it was still unclear at the time exactly what that entailed.

The person who perhaps did more than any other to provide substance to the
concept of Islamic banking in the 1970s was Sami Hamoud, a Jordanian economist who had been working at the Jordanian National Bank since 1956.
Hamoud was not himself a member of any Islamist organization, nor did he have
any outwardly Islamist tendencie.[6] His father, however, was an Islamic scholar
who had always encouraged his son to use his knowledge of economics and
finance to devise methods of interest-free banking. After working at the National
Bank for a number of years, and witnessing many of the shortcomings of an
interest-based financial system, Hamoud became convinced that an interest-
free system was not only feasible, but also ultimately more just and superior to
conventional banking methods. Believing that all the earlier writings about
Islamic banking were superficial, Hamoud became determined to write his PhD
dissertation on the concept of interest-free banking and how it would work in
the modern world. Published in 1976, the dissertation was widely viewed as the
most substantial academic piece on Islamic banking that had been written until
that time.[7]

After finishing his PhD, Hamoud began feeling out of place at the National Bank and started actively advocating for the establishment of an Islamic bank in Jordan. The idea was still new and seemed risky from the perspective of other bankers. When Hamoud took his idea to Abd al-Majeed Shoman, the head of Arab Bank, Jordan's largest and most well-respected bank, the latter wished him luck but was himself unwilling to invest any of his own resources to work with Hamoud in turning his idea of an Islamic bank into reality. Nevertheless, Abd al-Majeed Shoman's children established the Arab Islamic Bank (AIB) in 1998. At the time of writing, the AIB is Jordan's second-largest Islamic bank and the only real competition to JIB. However, in the mid-1970s the Shomans' and other bankers were still not willing to take the risks inherent in establishing a new kind of bank that would work on principles very different from conventional banking practices. Initially, the chief of Jordan's Central Bank, Mohammed Saeed al-Nabulsi, was also very hesitant about even allowing for the establishment of an interest-free bank in Jordan.

Hamoud was, however, strongly supported in Islamist circles and the Muslim Brotherhood began using its institutions and its connections in royal and governmental circles to help bring Hammoud's ideas into reality. Ishaq Farhan, the most prominent member of the Muslim Brotherhood in the National Consultative Council at the time, noted that the Islamists in that semi-parliamentary institution played an important role in advising the government to permit the establishment of an Islamic bank.[8] Sheikh Ibrahim Zaid al-Kilani, one of the most prominent leaders and Islamic scholars within the ranks of the Muslim Brotherhood, invited Hamoud to be a guest on a weekly television show that Sheikh Ibrahim Zaid al-Kilani hosted. Hamoud ended up coming back for four consecutive weeks to discuss Islamic banking. The show played a tremendous role in popularizing the movement for the establishment of an Islamic bank in Jordan.

The establishment of an Islamic bank would require a special law that would have to be passed by the Council of Ministers. The Minister of *Awqâf* at the time, Kamil al-Shareef, was a prominent member of the Muslim Brotherhood. After the airing of Sheikh Ibrahim Zaid al-Kilani's show, Shareef adopted Hamoud's plan as his own and, according to Hamoud, became one of his closest and most trusted advisors.[9]

Shareef convinced Hamoud to establish a Preparatory Committee that would serve as an official organizational body calling for the establishment of an Islamic bank in Jordan. In a process that largely repeated itself later when the Arab Islamic Bank was established in 1998, those working to establish the Jordan Islamic Bank in the mid-1970s worked to both appease and gain the support of the Islamists, while at the same time being very careful to remain independent of the Islamists and thus not seem to pose any threat to the political regime. In establishing the Preparatory Committee for the JIB, Shareef deliberately advised Hammoud to choose members who did not have strong political party or ideological affiliations. Shareef knew that if the bank was seen as too closely connected to the Muslim Brotherhood, or any other Islamic political party, it would be much more difficult to obtain a licence.

Shareef nominated Yousef al-Mbeideen, a respected lawyer known for his piety and strong Islamic beliefs yet who was not connected to any Islamist party, to be the second member (along with Hamoud) in the Preparatory Committee. Mbeideen was highly respected in both governmental circles as well as in Islamist circles[10] and, with his legal skills, proved to be an adept partner to Hamoud. Hamoud and Mbeideen then jointly chose six other members to serve on the Preparatory Committee. While at least three of those members had some ties to the Muslim Brotherhood, none were considered political leaders of the movement and were known more for their technical skills and business acumen than their participation in the Islamic movement. Dr Mohammed Saqr, a Harvard-graduated economist, was one of the most prominent economists in Jordan, and Sa'd al-Din and Misbah al-Zumeili were from a very wealthy business family that provided a substantial amount of economic support to the bank in its early years.

Hamoud's dissertation, the four-part television series on Islamic banking and the establishment of the Preparatory Committee, attracted attention in Saudi Arabia. The Saudi Prince Mohammad Al-Faisal invited Hamoud to the Kingdom to discuss the bank and while there Hamoud also met Sheikh Saleh Kamel. Prince Mohammad and Sheikh Saleh Kamel were both interested in the idea of Islamic banking and promised Hamoud they would support his endeavour by investing the full 40 per cent of initial capital that Jordanian law would allow to be invested by non-Jordanians. Prince Mohammad also followed Hamoud's visit with a visit of his own to Amman, where he met the Jordanian Crown Prince Hassan. Prince Hassan responded favourably to the idea of an Islamic bank in Jordan and soon thereafter the issue was brought to the Council of Ministers. In May 1977, the Council of Ministers agreed to permit the establishment of an Islamic bank. However, an interest-free institution could not operate under the legal codes that governed how other banks operated, so the Council also asked the Preparatory Committee to prepare a blueprint for a Special Law that would detail the rules and regulations under which the Islamic bank would operate.

The Preparatory Committee formed a *Fatwa* Committee, including mostly Islamic legal scholars, but also some economists and lawyers responsible for devising a blueprint for the new law. As in the Preparatory Committee, there were some Islamists in the *Fatwa* Committee, including most notably Ibrahim Zaid al-Kilani, but again there seems to have been a deliberate attempt to choose *shari'a* scholars who were acceptable to both the government and the general masses and who were not too closely linked to Islamist groups or parties. The *Fatwa* Committee held fifteen meetings from 6 July until 11 September 1977. During the meetings, the scholars discussed the kinds of contemporary financial transactions that were Islamically permitted. The Islamic scholars were not in full agreement on all the issues but after heated debates the *Fatwa* Committee issued a blueprint for a law that was approved by the official Jordanian *Fatwa* Agency and later the Jordanian Central Bank and Council of Ministers, which passed a temporary law entitled 'The Jordan Islamic Bank Law for Finance and Investment: No. 13, 1978'.

The final law included some controversial matters that some claimed violated the *shari'a*. These issues influenced Prince Mohammad Al-Faisal to back out from his earlier commitment to the bank,[11] but Sheikh Saleh Kamel quickly agreed to cover the full 40 per cent of the non-Jordanian capital that he and Prince Mohammad had earlier agreed to split among themselves.

In June 1978, a meeting was held by those who were committed to becoming initial shareholders in the bank. Interestingly, the meeting was held in the auditorium of one of the most prominent schools run by the Muslim Brotherhood and the meeting was chaired by Misbah al-Zumeili, who had ties to the Muslim Brotherhood. However, the Founders Committee that was elected at that meeting, like the earlier Preparatory Committee, had some Muslim Brotherhood members but no prominent leaders from the movement or other Islamist movements. The Founders Committee completed the remaining requirements for the bank to become registered and obtain a licence, including finding shareholders willing to invest JD 4 million in initial capital. The bank became officially registered on 28 November 1978 and obtained a licence permitting it to begin its work on 26 March 1979. The first *shari'a* advisor for the bank was Sheikh Abd al-Hameed Al-Saih, who had closer ties to the Palestine Liberation Organization than any Islamist group but who was well-respected by Islamists as well as the public at large.

In reviewing the role of Islamists in the establishment of the Jordan Islamic Bank, it is clear that they played an important supportive role. The importance of the backing of prominent Muslim Brotherhood leaders like Ishaq Farhan, Kamil al-Shareef, and Sheikh Ibrahim Zaid al-Kilani, as well as the financial support of the al-Zumeilis, cannot be underestimated. Their assistance, advice and lobbying on behalf of the bank, as well as their deliberate work through their mass media outlets to popularize the bank and give it legitimacy, probably played a decisive role in helping the bank gain early support and ultimately come to fruition. However, the Muslim Brotherhood itself recognized that being too closely linked to the bank, might lead to apprehension in some government circles, and thus it accepted playing a secondary role in the actual decision-making and leadership of the bank and never attempted to make the bank an institution of their movement. While many Muslim Brotherhood members were among the initial shareholders in the bank, they did not constitute a sizable enough portion to control General Assembly votes nor does it appear that they ever tried to use their votes to support any Brotherhood or other Islamist agenda.

When the Arab Islamic Bank (AIB) was established in the late 1990s, the Islamists played a less central role. With the backing of the conventional Arab Bank, the AIB did not need nor did they seek the help of Islamists in gaining the necessary governmental approval to become registered in 1997 and begin operations in 1998. Nor did the Islamists have any meaningful influence over the Banking Law of 2000, which restructured many aspects of banking in Jordan and included a major section that formalized the laws regulating Islamic banks in Jordan.

The support of the Islamist leadership for the establishment of the AIB did, however, prove important in helping the bank gain legitimacy. The Arab Bank, Jordan's largest and most respected bank, financed the establishment of the AIB as an independent Islamic bank whose dealings were wholly separate from those of the conventional banks. While many Muslims were distrustful of an Islamic bank that was owned by a conventional bank, the AIB was able to get the support of important segments of the Islamist leadership, thus providing their bank with the legitimacy it needed to be recognized as a true Islamic bank. It was the two most notable international Islamic scholars linked to the Muslim Brotherhood, Yusuf al Qaradawi in Qatar and Faisal Mawlawi in Lebanon, who wrote the most convincing *fatwa* stating that the financial transactions undertaken by AIB were Islamically legitimate.[12] The leader of the Muslim Brotherhood in Jordan, Abd al-Majeed Thuneibat, also sent a letter of congratulation to the bank when it officially opened and Muslim Brotherhood leaders have taken the official position that the AIB is a legitimate Islamic bank that should have the support and patronage of Islamists in the country.

THE ISLAMIST VIEW OF ISLAMIC BANKING IN JORDAN

From the time Islamic banks were first established in Jordan, political Islamists have been keen to ensure their success and have often looked to them as points of pride, especially during the years when the banks were doing well. Political Islamists pointed to the success of Islamic banks in their speeches and in numerous newspaper and magazine articles as proof that Islam was a complete way of life that could not be restricted to the merely spiritual realm and that it could also provide economic solutions to the country's problems. The success of such banks gave concrete weight to the assertions of the Islamists that Islam as a religion was suitable for modern times in all aspects of life.

This does not mean that the political Islamists have always been supportive of everything done by the Jordan Islamic Bank and the Arab Islamic Bank. There are deep frustrations amongst Islamist leaders and even more so at the grassroots Islamist level regarding the inability of the Islamic banks to realize many of the expectations that had been set out for them. There is a feeling that the banks could do much more in terms of providing social services, such as interest-free loans to the needy or to students, and that they should concentrate their investments in areas that better promote Islam, such as Islamic schools, or what they see as national security interests, such as agriculture, while avoiding dealing with the West.

Dr Mohammed Saqr, a member of the Muslim Brotherhood who served on both the Preparatory Committee and the Founding Committee of the JIB in the late 1970s and maintained close relations with the bank ever since, was himself very critical of the bank during a conference on investment opportunities in Jordan in the summer of 2001.[13] He noted that the bank was too traditional, not innovative enough and, most importantly, did not in any way serve the developmental role that it potentially could. He derided the bank for investing outside Jordan rather than fulfilling its responsibilities towards helping Jordanian development and noted that the bank had never even come close to fulfilling the early hopes that it could serve a developmental role similar to the role played by German banks, or even Bank Misr in early twentieth-century Egypt. Saqr noted that, while Bank Misr was a conventional bank, its founder Talaat Harb had some Islamic inclinations and that those inclinations led him to use his bank to help develop and industrialize Egypt, an Islamic responsibility that Saqr noted was just as important as the legalistic prohibition of interest.

Jamil Abu Bakr, the spokesman for the Jordanian Muslim Brotherhood, noted that while the Muslim Brotherhood continued to support both the JIB and the AIB, the group hoped the banks would do much more in terms of helping to industrialize Jordan.[14] He noted that the banks had not adequately fulfilled their role of undertaking innovative studies and research in the fields of Islamic economic and financial practices. Ali Abu Sukur, a prominent member of the Muslim Brotherhood and the general secretary of the Jordanian Engineers Association, criticized the JIB for not using its extensive resources to buy land and ensure the country's agricultural resources remained in Jordanian hands.[15] Saud Abu Mahfudh, another prominent leader of the Muslim Brotherhood and the editor of Jordan's Islamist newspaper al-Sabeel, said that both the JIB and AIB failed to play any social or developmental role in Jordan whatsoever and that while their activities were not forbidden – they did not deal in interest – they were not really true 'Islamic' banks because they did not fulfil any other Islamic conditions besides the prohibition of interest.[16]

One of the best references for how political Islamists viewed the JIB during the banks halcyon years in the late 1980s and early 1990s is the 1990 doctoral dissertation of Ramadan Shallah, who, a few years after he wrote the dissertation, became the leader of the Palestinian Islamic *Jihad* movement. Shallah was very critical of the JIB for not providing enough social services and for not undertaking its developmental responsibilities. He was also critical of some managerial aspects of the bank, especially the fact that the bank had at the time only one *shari'a* advisor, rather than a *shari'a* board or committee, and that the board of directors of the bank could at any time appoint or dismiss the advisor, whose salary was also set by the same board. Shallah pointed out that such a status threatened the independence of the *shari'a* scholar to give correct judgments without undermining his own position.[17]

Despite his criticisms, Shallah went out of his way to show how the bank was successful and was playing an important role in helping Jordan solve some of its major economic problems. Jamil Abu Bakr, while criticizing some aspects of the bank, also acknowledged that the bank was in general doing a good job and that the dreams many Islamists had for the bank were perhaps unrealistic under the circumstances. The main thesis of Shallah's dissertation echoed this sentiment. He ultimately concluded that the difficulties the bank was facing were the result of governmental restrictions that had established what he called 'a hostile and unencouraging environment' that put the bank at a severe disadvantage with respect to conventional banks.

A decade after Shallah completed his dissertation, Islamists seem to be less forgiving of the bank's shortcomings. In looking at the poor performance of the JIB since the mid-1990s, Islamists are now more likely to blame mismanagement at the bank itself than governmental restrictions on Islamic banking activities. Abdul Lateef Arabiyyat, the leader of the Islamic Action Front Party, said that his party had worked to pressure the Central Bank to deal with Islamic banks in a manner that would be less discriminatory but acknowledged that the major reasons for the bank's poor performance lay not in governmental dealings, but with mismanagement, lack of expertise and lack of vision by the bank itself.[18] Arabiyyat said that the bank dealt with its customers and depositors in a less professional manner than other conventional banks.

A frustrated Islamist small businessman echoed these sentiments, saying that the JIB took its customer base for granted and treated them poorly.[19] The businessman said that the only reason Islamist businessmen use the JIB is because they consider other banks forbidden Islamically and that loans from the JIB always end up much more expensive than loans from conventional banks. The businessman said the central problem with the JIB was more with their administrative shortcomings and mismanagement than with any state laws, regulations or restrictions hindering Islamic financial practices.

Political Islamists are not the only ones to complain about the administrative shortcomings and mismanagement at JIB. The general perception of the JIB within Jordanian society has become very negative since the mid-1990s. The belief that the bank uses an Islamic veneer to coerce Muslims into dealing with it is widespread, and most non-Islamist Jordanians asked about the bank asserted that it takes and gives interest under the guise of different names. Islamists and non-Islamist Jordanians were very critical of the high mark-ups charged by the bank, the bank's unwillingness to engage in any even remotely risky ventures, and the relatively low 'profit' margin the bank returns to customers.

One major difference between Islamists and non-Islamists, however, is in the general view of who controls and manages the JIB. Many non-Islamists assume that the bank is an institution of the Muslim Brotherhood, while Islamists are very quick to point out that the JIB is in no way connected to their movement. Islamists now recognize that association with the bank carries more negative than positive baggage and that while they will continue dealing with, advising and working for the success of the bank, they want to make it clear that the bank's shortcomings are due to the human faults of its managers and not to the Islamic movement or to the inability of Islamic economic principles to work in the modern world.

Many Islamists were quick to point out that while the bank itself did not have any political affiliation, it historically had many more business dealings with the Palestine Liberation Organization than it did with the Muslim Brotherhood or any Islamist groups. Saud Abu Mahfudh noted that many top administrators of the JIB were or had earlier been members of Palestinian nationalist groups such as Fatah and the Popular Front for the Liberation of Palestine (PFLP), while none of them were members of the Muslim Brotherhood. He noted that while Musa Shehadeh, the general manager of the JIB since 1982, had become a devout Muslim who prayed regularly, he had earlier been a member of the radically secular PFLP. Saud Abu Mahfudh pointed out that, in the early years of the bank, the JIB did not hire any known member of the Muslim Brotherhood, even for minor clerical positions.

Many Islamists were also very critical of the JIB's largest stockholder, Sheikh Saleh Kamel. While some Islamists noted that Sheikh Saleh Kamel is a generous benefactor who has been willing to support the building of mosques and other charitable causes, others asserted that he was only interested in profit and were quick to point out that a famous satellite television station he owns is far from Islamic.

Just as there are conflicting views within Islamist circles about the JIB, there are conflicting views about the only other Islamic bank in Jordan, the Arab Islamic Bank (AIB). While some Islamists expressed wariness about the Islamic nature of the AIB, others were supportive, noting that competition might force the JIB to become more efficient and innovative. Jamil Abu Bakr noted that, while some members of the Muslim Brotherhood were against the AIB on the grounds that it was too closely linked to a conventional bank and thus the source of its money and the methods with which it invested depositors' funds was suspect, the Muslim Brotherhood as an organization encouraged its establishment and believed that competition would be good for Islamic banking in general. Saud Abu Mahfudh, who has worked extensively with both the JIB and the AIB, noted that the AIB was much more professional and easier to work with than the JIB. Ali Abu Sukur said most of the JIB's shortcomings would probably be solved if there was true competition in Jordan for the Islamic banking market, his only reservation being that the AIB was still not trusted by most Islamists, or Muslims in general, and thus did not represent real competition.

The Islamist view of Islamic banking in Jordan is complex. The frustrations about the mismanagement, administrative shortcomings, lack of innovation and unprofessional conduct of the JIB are deep and real but, as Jamil Abu Bakr pointed out, they are perhaps expressions of the unrealized and unrealistic expectations many Islamists had of the bank. Islamist leaders with a more acute understanding of the political realities in Jordan were quicker to find excuses for the bank than many of the grassroots Islamist cadres and Islamist businessmen whose dealings with the bank on a personal level had increased their misgivings. Ishaq Farhan said that, despite their shortcomings, the Islamic banks in Jordan continued to be appreciated by Islamists for the alternative to conventional banking practices that they were providing, and that one or two relatively small banks could not be expected to play a more political or developmental role than they already were. While Islamists in Jordan are quick to criticize some specific aspects of the JIB and the AIB, they are also quick to defend the general principles that govern how the Islamic banks undertake financial transactions and they continue to be optimistic that the banks will overcome their problems.

THE ISLAMIST ECONOMIC AGENDA

Islamists in general recognize that banking and finance is only one aspect of the larger economic questions facing Jordan. While they would prefer Islamic banks that more actively worked for larger Islamic economic principles and undertook their business in a more professional and efficient manner than is the current case with the Jordan Islamic Bank and Arab Islamic Bank, they also acknowledge that, in the absence of other conditions and policies, the banks can not be expected to fulfil the larger goal of implementing a comprehensive Islamic economic agenda. However, Jordanian Islamists also concede that they themselves have not done enough to define what exactly that agenda entails.

Jamil Abu Bakr, the official spokesman for the Jordanian Muslim Brotherhood, acknowledged that economic affairs and policies are an area in which the organization remains weak. Saud Abu Mahfudh, the editor of Jordan's main

Islamist newspaper and a leading member of the Muslim Brotherhood, recognized that the lack of a clear economic vision remains a major shortcoming of the Muslim Brotherhood in Jordan. He asserted that Islamists tended to shy away from discussions about economics, seeing economic policy-making as a 'dirty job' that bordered on Islamically-prohibited areas. Musa Hantash, a Jordanian businessman who is a member of the Muslim Brotherhood, bemoaned the fact that Islamists did not play a larger role in working to build up the Jordanian economy.[20] Hantash represented the views of many young Islamists frustrated with the leadership of the Muslim Brotherhood for not having any well-thought-out economic plans, or for using their influence in Parliament and in civil society to effect important economic change. Hantash noted that Islamists hardly ever even talked about economic issues, much less worked out plans to solve the various economic problems facing Jordan.

What the Muslim Brotherhood and other Jordanian Islamist groups have offered by way of economic policy is little more than a populist agenda. Islamist Members of Parliament and official statements from Islamist groups have opposed all IMF reforms, asserted that corruption is at the root of all the country's economic problems, called for a breaking-off of the ties of dependence with the West and all economic relations with Israel, and, occasionally, called for the Islamization of the economy without really detailing what that means.

By far the most detailed outline of an Islamist economic agenda for Jordan can be found in the political platform for candidates running for the 1997 parliamentary elections under the banner of the Islamic Action Front Party (IAF).[21] In the introduction to the platform, the IAF describes the achievements of the Islamists in the previous parliament, noting in the economic realm that the Islamists played a decisive role in the decision to form a parliamentary committee to monitor administrative and financial corruption by government officials and in the passage of a number of laws, such as one forgiving the interest on the debts of small farmers and another lowering custom duties on the cars of Jordanians returning to Jordan from the Gulf countries. The introduction also mentioned that the Islamists had taken a strong stand opposing tax increases and price-hikes on subsidized goods.

The 1997 IAF platform also included a complete section on their position towards 'Economic, Monetary, and Financial Policies'. The section called for amending financial policies 'to cleanse them from interest and other Islamically forbidden practices' while also 'providing governmental support to the existing Islamic financial institutions and working to develop their services so that they will become models for other financial institutions'. The platform also stressed working for the establishment of a pan-Arab Common Market and Arab economic integration, while calling for resistance to all economic programmes aimed at normalizing relations with Israel and monitoring all foreign investment to ensure foreigners did not gain a hold over any strategic Jordanian industries. The IAF further supported providing governmental incentives for investment in industry, agriculture and other economic sectors.

The Islamists' concern for the poor was shown in a number of points calling for better-distributed developmental programmes throughout Jordan, working to cure poverty at its roots by providing training and developmental funds to those in need, establishing a national strategy to overcome the problem of unemployment, increasing welfare funds, increasing the salaries of government workers and putting a halt to price hikes on subsidized goods. The Islamists also showed a strong concern for lowering the trade deficit, the national debt and the current-accounts deficit. The platform further called upon the government to increase its gold and foreign-currency reserves as a means of stabilizing the Jordanian dinar and lowering inflation.

There were also a number of points aimed at decreasing corruption, such as one calling for increased monitoring of how governmental ministries and agencies spent their money, another for increasing the power and scope of the governmental accounting bureau, and one for placing the budgets of all public-sector institutions under parliamentary scrutiny. Throughout the platform, the Islamists also call for policies that might provide a cultural cure to some of Jordan's economic problems. One article, for example, called for 'spreading awareness of Islamic values against excessive consumerism, for encouraging productivity, and for guiding consumption'.

In addition to the 1997 political platform, statements issued by the IAF since its founding in 1992 also provide insight into the depth of the party's understanding of economic issues and the kinds of economic policies promoted by Islamists. The relative lack of concern Islamists have shown for economic matters is underscored by the fact that, out of more than a hundred statements issued by the party since 1992, only a handful deal even remotely with economic issues.[22]

The IAF has been very critical of the peace process with Israel in both its political and economic aspects. One statement, dated 31 October 1994, condemned the Israeli participation in a Middle East Economic Conference being held in Morocco. The statement called upon the Arab nations to avoid dealing with Israel, and to work with each other in promoting Arab economic integration in a manner that would solve the economic problems of the region.

The IAF has also been extremely critical of an American–Jordanian–Israeli agreement that allows for duty-free access to the United States market for any goods manufactured in special Qualified Industrial Zones (QIZs) in Jordan, in which there are no customs duties on imported materials and at least 8 per cent of the industrial inputs come from Israel. The first of ten planned QIZs was established in the northern Jordanian city of Irbid. The IAF has also been critical of a Special Economic Zone established in Aqaba in 2000, and in a statement dated 24 July 2000 the IAF complained that Israeli and Western investors could exploit the zone. The statement attempted to refute governmental arguments that the free-trade zone would solve Jordan's economic problems and provided counter-arguments explaining how the zone would in fact exacerbate existing problems and lead to new ones.

An IAF statement dated 14 May 1996 dealt with a number of economic issues. The statement was critical of a rise in the price of water and electricity, and called for the establishment of a tangible plan to solve the problems of unemployment and poverty. A similar multifaceted statement dated 17 January 2000 was critical of governmental privatization policies, contending that only the most profitable state enterprises were being sold and that no tangible benefits were accruing from the sales, which, the statement asserted, were also allowing for Israeli and foreign penetration into important Jordanian companies, including most notably the Jordanian Water Authority. The statement was also critical of an increase in sales taxes and educational fees. A few other statements criticized the government for increasing taxes or fees. An earlier 16 June 1993 statement was very critical of price rises and an expansion of the consumption tax to cover more goods, and a 3 July 2001 statement expressed the IAF's opposition to a governmental plan to sharply increase the price of fuel in response to demands from the World Bank.

IAF officials acknowledge that the number of their statements that have dealt with economic matters are almost negligible. Ahmad Tannash, the IAF board member with the strongest economics background, recognized that during the 1990s Islamists in the Jordanian Parliament had almost no input and, more often than not, did not even take a stand on the many economic issues discussed in Parliament.[23] Jamil Abu Bakr, a member of the IAF Administrative Board, as well as the spokesman for the Muslim Brotherhood, said that Islamists felt that the real solution to the major economic problems facing Jordan lay in political rather than economic remedies.

He listed the major economic problems as corruption, poverty, unemployment, high taxes, a large income-and-wealth gap, and no consistency in government economic policies. He was especially vocal about corruption, noting that the problems of bribery, nepotism and embezzlement were rampant. The need for connections to get any matter through Jordan's bureaucracy was another major problem he addressed, as was the existence of commercial monopolies for a number of important goods. To solve those problems, Jamil Abu Bakr said the Islamists worked to expose and bring an end to all forms of corruption, allow for more democratic freedoms and demand more transparency in governmental and business dealings.

To be fair, the problems enumerated by Jamil Abu Bakr and repeated by other Islamists are real problems in Jordan and the political remedies he put forward would likely do a great deal to begin tackling them. However, as the Islamists themselves concede, they have not adequately addressed specific economic issues and their inexperience in economic affairs has been evident in their lack of action in Parliament. While more transparency in government affairs and an end to corruption would likely lead to major improvements in Jordan's overall economy, it is far too simple to assume that an increase in democratic freedoms would by itself bring about more just economic policies that could solve the problems of unemployment, poverty and the huge gap between the rich and the poor. As by far the largest political party in Jordan, the IAF has a responsibility to better study the specific economic problems facing Jordan and to begin offering detailed economic solutions to those problems. The past failure to fulfil that responsibility has already begun having a detrimental effect on their legitimacy.[24]

ISLAMIST ECONOMIC ACTIVITIES IN JORDAN

Outside the activities of the Islamic banks in Jordan, a growing number of grass-roots, usually young and well-educated Islamists are undertaking a number of their own economic activities in accordance with Islamic principles. These activities constitute an increasingly important segment of Jordanian civil society and have the potential to effect gradual but real political and social change in the country. These grassroots Islamists are distrustful of the government and its corrupt practices, are frustrated by the Islamic banks and their timidity, and are often impatient with the slow pace and seeming lack of awareness by the political leadership of the Muslim Brotherhood and other Islamist groups.

The most significant arena for such activities is in Jordan's professional associations, most notably the Jordanian Engineers Association. When Islamists decisively won the 1990 elections for the leadership position of the Engineers Association, it was already the largest of Jordan's professional groups and had assets of about $10 million.[25] In less than a decade, the Islamists had increased its assets to nearly $70 million, which was partially invested in stocks and partially used to provide financing for engineers who wanted to buy land, houses or cars. Most significant for our purposes is that all such financing, as well as the other kinds of financial transactions undertaken by the Association, is done in strict accordance with Islamic principles, though it is done almost completely outside the purview of the official Jordanian Islamic banks.[26]

The establishment of a businessman's association in 1997 that brought together seventy-nine Islamist businessmen, with the explicit goal of using their economic and organizational power to influence political, social and cultural change, marks another important kind of activity that grassroots Islamists have adopted in recent years.[27] The establishment of the *Jami'yat al-Rakha*, or Businessmen's Prosperity Association, in Jordan occurred after a visit to Jordan by members of Turkey's MÜSİAD organization.[28] The MÜSİAD is a powerful Islamist business association in Turkey whose success and economic power is believed to have played an important role in helping an Islamist political party in that country. Like the Engineers Association, many of the businessmen in *Jami'yat al-Rakha* have become disenchanted with the Islamic banks in Jordan. While members of *Jami'yat al-Rakha* are more likely to use the Islamic banks than other Jordanian businessmen, many of them privately finance their business activities without seeking bank loans and others have resorted to using conventional banks out of frustration with the shortcomings of the Islamic banks.

Ali Abu Sukur, a founding member of the *Jami'yat al-Rakha* Association, said the first goal of the group was to form an organization that could begin influencing the elections for different Chambers of Commerce in Jordan. While Islamists control nearly all the professional associations in Jordan, they have never fared well in Chamber of Commerce elections. Ali Abu Sukur noted that business in Jordan currently plays a very marginal role in influencing Jordanian politics. Most business owners, fearful of governmental retaliation, try to keep their businesses separate from politics and do not try to use their capital to influence the larger political issues facing the country.

Ali Abu Sukur, in addition to being the general secretary of the Jordanian Engineers Association, also heads the Anti-Normalization Committee that calls for exposure and boycotting of any Jordanian professional or business interest that deals with Israel. His activities with the committee have placed him in direct opposition to policies of the Jordanian king and royal family, and he has suffered because of that with imprisonment and harassment. Ali Abu Sukur is thus a living example that attempting to use one's professional or business power to influence politics can be dangerous in Jordan; but he and the other members of *Jami'yat al-Rakha* believe that business and capital have responsibilities towards their country. Ali Abu Sukur noted that all businesses have a strong interest in political stability and that such stability can best come about through a more democratic polity. *Al-Rakha* thus aimed to influence Chamber of Commerce elections in such a way that they could begin transforming them into mouthpieces for increased democratization of the country.

Musa Hantash, another founding member of *al-Rakha*, pointed out that the association has not even come close to achieving the ambitious goals it set out for itself. *Al-Rakha* remains very small because even most Islamist businessmen are scared that joining the group and becoming openly labelled as Islamist could lead to governmental harassment in a country in which governmental connections and favours are indispensable for the success of any business venture. Saud Abu Mahfudh observed that there were thousands of Islamist businessmen in Jordan, yet less than one hundred had the courage to join *al-Rakha* because of such fears. Hantash noted that a few large Islamist businessmen could have marginal influences on some minor political affairs but that such influences came about through their own personal contacts with members of the royal family or government officials, and not through the organizational activities of business associations or Chambers of Commerce. It is only such organizational power, however, that could lead business and capital to play the kind of political role in transforming the polity that Ali Abu Sukur and other Islamists feel is necessary.

Another phenomenon that perhaps more than anything else underscores the shortcomings of the Islamic banks in Jordan is the huge informal economy in Islamic finance. Networks of support exist throughout Jordan in which extended families, neighbours, friends and co-workers help each other purchase homes, jointly invest their money in various ventures, or undertake other kinds of financial transactions in strict accordance with Islamic principles. Most of those that use such networks are uncomfortable using conventional banks, but at the same time have become frustrated with the unwillingness of the Islamic banks in Jordan to provide the kind of long-term financing needed to purchase homes or to help launch new businesses, as well as the disappointing returns the banks provide on investments or deposits. While the mutual trust and close ideological ties found among Islamists encourage the formation of such networks in Islamist circles, similar networks can also be found among other Muslim Jordanians who, while not sharing Islamist ideological affinities, remain committed to abiding by the Islamic prohibition on taking or using interest.

The extensive economic activities of Islamists outside the structure of Islamic banks, whether through unofficial networks, control over the funds of professional associations, or in terms of their business and organizational strengths, in addition to their disappointment with the Islamic banks that currently exist in Jordan, has led some Islamists to consider setting up their own Islamic bank in the country. Ali Abu Sukur noted that the Engineers Association had in the past considered opening its own bank to take over and ultimately expand the extensive financial assets under its control. However, he recognized that it would be nearly impossible for the organization to obtain a licence, both because the Central Bank was convinced that there were already too many banks in Jordan and were not keen to provide new licences, and because the government would likely prohibit Islamists from having their own bank.

Jamil Abu Bakr said that the Muslim Brotherhood itself had also considered opening a bank but that the organization did not have the initial capital required. He also noted that the government often removed Islamists from local *zakat* committees, fearing that controlling *zakat* funds could give the Islamists too much power, and thus the idea of an Islamist-run Islamic bank would likely find very strong opposition in some government circles.

The widespread feeling by Islamists that they would not be allowed to establish their own bank, the fear by many Islamist businessmen to join an Islamist business association, as well as numerous cases of actual governmental harassment of those who attempt to use their economic or institutional powers to influence political change, underscore the reality that the state remains dominant over civil society in Jordan and that private-sector activities are still not powerful enough to challenge state authorities on sensitive political topics. At the same time, however, the actual formation of the businessmen's association and continued activities by professional associations indicates that there is a growing societal awareness that their activities can lead to meaningful change and that there are a growing number of people willing to sacrifice some of their own interests to help bring about such change.

ISLAMIST RELATIONS WITH THE ISLAMIC BANKS IN JORDAN

As mentioned earlier, the Muslim Brotherhood played a decisive role in providing needed support for the initial establishment of the Jordan Islamic Bank. The bank authorities, however, later took on the delicate balancing act of deliberately distancing themselves as much as possible from the Islamists, so as not to bring upon themselves governmental scrutiny, while at the same time maintaining enough legitimacy in Islamist eyes to keep their business and moral support.

The Islamic bankers were especially wary of exposing any ties whatsoever between their banks and political Islamists. Bakr Rehan, the executive manager for the Planning and Organizing Department at the Jordan Islamic Bank (JIB), discounted any ties between JIB and political Islamists and said that the bank had never requested and had received only marginal help from Islamists in Parliament, despite the bank's concern about a number of laws and regulations that had recently been debated in that body.[29] Nihad Maraqa, the manager of Planning for the Arab Islamic Bank (AIB), also asserted that AIB was a business with no political agenda.[30] While he noted that the bank played an important social role in Jordanian society, he was insistent that Islamic banks had no direct ties to Islamist political groups and certainly could not play a mediating role between governments and Islamic movements. Like Rehan, he said that the bank had never requested nor did they expect to get much assistance from Islamists in Parliament.

Despite the insistence by bank managers that there is absolutely no relationship with Islamist movements, there are some ties that the Islamists were more willing to allude to than were the bank managers. First of all, the vast majority of members of the Islamic movement who have money in a Jordanian bank have deposited it in the Islamic banks, not necessarily because of their support for the institutions themselves but for the basic reason that they believe it is the only Islamically legitimate means to deposit money. Furthermore, nearly all of the Islamist-run businesses in Jordan use only Islamic banks for all of their financial dealings. While Musa Hantash stressed that the level of influence the Islamists played over JIB policies was minimal, he noted that Islamist-run businesses provided a huge percentage of JIB's overall clientele and perhaps had the potential to begin influencing the JIB if they attempted to do so in an organized fashion.

While the Islamic banks are adamant that they have no ties to political Islamists, they do recognize the importance of Islamic movements and try not to alienate them. It was only after the establishment of the AIB in 1998 that the JIB – after 20 years of existence – set up its own marketing department. Yet even without a marketing department for most of its existence, the JIB witnessed faster growth than any other bank in the country, largely on the basis of the political Islamists' ability to popularize the idea that any kind of banking interest amounted to forbidden *riba*, an idea that government officials throughout the Arab world, sometimes with the support of Islamic scholars close to government circles, often try to debunk. Ishaq Farhan, the former leader of the Islamic Action Front Party, pointed out that Islamic scholars associated with the Muslim Brotherhood had passed clear *fatwas* asserting that it was forbidden to deal with conventional banks and they always insisted that Muslims deal only with Islamic banks.

This kind of support from the Islamic movement gives Islamic banks a degree of legitimacy and a guaranteed clientele that they could easily lose without such backing. Islamic banks recognize that the Islamists could have a profound impact on their ability to retain customers by such simple actions as harshly criticizing some aspect of the bank's activities, publicly asserting that the bank's methods were not in conformity with Islamic law, or even just ending their continued support and encouragement for the bank. Islamic banks thus recognize that their strength is in many ways affected by the strength of the Islamic movements and there are a number of indirect means the banks employ to maintain the continued support of the Islamists.

While in its early years the JIB may have gone out of its way to avoid hiring Islamists, that seems to have changed. Many young Islamists, hopeful of jobs with Islamic banks, are now studying economics and finance – once subjects that Islamists avidly avoided. Even more significantly, when the JIB expanded its *shari'a* advisor to a three-member *shari'a* board, it included two Islamists, one with ties to the Islamic Liberation Party and the second, Sheikh Ibrahim Zaid al-Kilani, one of the leading figures in the Muslim Brotherhood. Musa Hantash pointed out that being known as a committed Islamist is often seen by JIB loan officers as a sign of honesty that could help them get business loans, sometimes on easy terms.

The JIB also spends about JD 200,000 (approximately $300,000) a year on charitable contributions and donations to various Islamic causes,[31] many of which are linked to the Muslim Brotherhood. The project to which the JIB is most closely linked is the *Afaaf* Charitable Committee, which provides needy couples help in getting married. The committee is headed by the IAF Party leader Abdul Lateef Arabiyyat. Arabiyyat noted that the JIB donated JD 5,000 to the Afaaf Committee in 2000, in addition to providing every groom married with the assistance of *afaaf* with a JD 100 gift. Even more significantly, the JIB provided JD 400,000 through Afaaf as interest-free loans to grooms during the year 2000 alone.[32] The JIB provided a total of JD 4 million in interest-free loans in 2000, benefiting more than 12,000 citizens, many of whom were members of the Muslim Brotherhood. The JIB has been a frequent donor to the Muslim Brotherhood-run network of Koranic schools in Jordan, as well providing about JD 5,500 in direct contributions for Koranic memorization prizes, and easy financing arrangements for the building of new Koranic schools.[33] JIB also provided easy finance arrangements to projects of the Zarqa National University, a Muslim Brotherhood-run institution led by Ishaq Farhan.[34]

While the AIB's links to Arab Bank provide it with a cushion of support most Islamic banks do not enjoy, it also recognizes the important role Islamists can play in the success or failure of an Islamic bank. Musa Hantash noted that perhaps as many as 80 per cent of Islamists are still distrustful of the AIB because it is owned by a conventional bank. The AIB has, however, benefited greatly from the support of the Muslim Brotherhood leadership.

When debates were raging in the mainstream Jordanian press about whether the AIB could be considered a legitimate Islamic bank, the Muslim Brotherhood newspaper, *al-Sabeel*, clearly sided with the opinion that the bank was legitimate. When the AIB returned the favour by placing ads in *al-Sabeel*, the JIB broke its long-running contract with the newspaper. *Al-Sabeel* now does most of its business with the AIB.[35] It will be recalled that the two most notable Islamic scholars linked to the Muslim Brotherhood, Yusuf al Qaradawi in Qatar and Faisal Mawlawi in Lebanon, wrote the most convincing *fatwa* stating that the financial transactions undertaken by AIB were Islamically legitimate.[36] A sign of how much AIB recognizes the importance of the Muslim Brotherhood support is underscored by the fact that when the leader of the Muslim Brotherhood in Jordan, Abd al-Majeed Thuneibat, sent a letter of congratulation to the bank on its official opening, the bank had the letter enlarged, framed and placed in the lobby of its bank headquarters.

CONCLUSION

This chapter has illustrated the multifaceted relationship between Islamic banks and the Islamic movement in Jordan. It is clear that, in Jordan, Islamic banks are organizationally distinct and have very few direct ties with the Islamic movement, yet the two institutions have many interests in common and recognize that a stronger relationship could serve the needs of both. The main barrier to stronger ties are fears on the part of the banks that being too closely linked with a political opposition group could lead to governmental harassment. Thus, the state forms a barrier blocking what would be a natural tendency for the two to increase their levels of coordination and cooperation. If this barrier were removed and the political environment in Jordan opened up in the sense that the Islamists were allowed to compete against other political movements for real political power, rather than just seats in a constricted parliament, it is likely that there would be much closer ties between the Islamic banks and the Islamic movements.

The Islamic movement has acknowledged its own shortcomings in terms of providing concrete policy proposals in a number of realms, especially economics. Islamic banks, on the other hand, have been forced to deal for decades with the practical problems of implementing Islamic economic principles in the modern era. Further coordination with the Islamic banks would thus help the political Islamists better define their economic policy platform, something the Islamists would need if there were true political liberalization in Jordan.

Jordan is now facing major economic transformations, as increased globalization, the free-trade pact with the United States and entry into the World Trade Organization is forcing them to compete globally in a way they never had to in the past. Islamists have been critical of such moves toward globalization without being able to define a clear alternative. Islamic banks in Jordan and elsewhere have been forced to deal with the more globalized world in concrete terms and have often devised strategies by which they can benefit from such trends through using Islamic economic and financial principles. If Islamists want to make the transformation from being a populist organization into being a serious political party with the experience and technical skills to lead Jordan in the modern era, while at the same time maintaining their strict adherence to Islamic principles in economic affairs, they will need the technical acumen and experience of the bankers.

On the other hand, a more liberal political environment is likely to strengthen the political Islamists to the extent that they could also provide much-needed assistance to the financial Islamists, in terms of bringing about the kinds of legislative reforms that the financial Islamists need to overcome the very real problems and challenges they are currently facing. The fear of being too closely aligned with the Muslim Brotherhood has prevented Islamic banks from even seeking the support of Muslim Brotherhood parliamentarians for such simple things as changing laws that in effect tax goods purchased through Islamic banks twice,[37] or prevent Islamic banks from participating in a government-sponsored house mortgage refinancing company.[38] In a more politically liberal environment, it is likely that political Islamists would work very closely with the Islamic banks to ensure that the government provided the kind of legal and regulatory environment that would not only remove restrictions and hindrances faced by Islamic banks but also provide government sponsorship of the banks through such measures as using Islamic banks for the financial business of the state.

In addition to serving each other's needs, closer ties between Islamic banks and Islamic movements would have profound political consequences. Again, to the extent that real political liberalization comes about, a scenario could be imagined in which Islamic banks increasingly serve the role of financial and political intermediary, relating Islamic political figures to Islamist-oriented businesses and investors. Such a role would tie the banks to political patrons in ways that could substantially reduce their information costs. High information and transaction costs are, at the time of writing, one of the greatest challenges facing Islamic banks and hindering their ability to compete fairly with conventional banks. It is possible that closer ties would thus greatly reduce some of the structural disadvantages the Islamic banks have with respect to conventional banks.

It is also likely that closer ties between Islamic political and financial actors would have a significant impact on the incentive structures of the political actors, leading them to lessen their demands upon the state, become more amenable to cooperation and coexistence with opposing ideological trends, and ultimately to provide stronger support for the democratization of society.

Thus, in the case of political liberalization, Islamic banks could play an extremely important role in mediating the transition of political Islamist groups from mass-based populist organizations into conservative, religious political parties in a multi-party system, similar to the Christian Democrats in Germany. The problem is that there is not a very big likelihood of political liberalization in the near future, especially in the new international and regional order that has been established in the wake of 11 September 2001. One major problem in the post-September 11th order is the increased scrutiny and targeting of Islamic banks, often labelling them the financiers of terrorism. The attempt to escape such a label will make Islamic banks even more wary of any dealings with Islamists. If this last problem can be avoided, the ties between Islamic banks and Islamic movements are likely to increase gradually in Jordan, even in the absence of political liberalization, because of increasing competition between the AIB and JIB.

The existence of competition within the Islamic financial market will probably force Islamic banking in Jordan to become more efficient, better managed and more innovative than it has been in the past. Competition will also force the Islamic banks to compete for the large Islamist market, rather than take it for granted. As Musa Hantash pointed out, loan officers in Islamic banks are already more likely to provide business loans to committed Islamists. With increased competition between the JIB and the AIB, the banks are already becoming more innovative, and the higher level of trust the banks have in committed Islamists is likely to lead the banks to provide such clients with the more risky kinds of Islamic financial instruments. The first *istisna* contract in Jordan thus went to a committed Islamist to build an Islamic hospital. In competing for the Islamist market, banks will be likely to make more such concessions to Islamist demands in a way that, if it proves successful, will both financially empower the political Islamists while also making the Islamic banks more efficient by reducing their monitoring costs and providing them with new kinds of financial instruments.

The extent to which this takes place will depend on two factors, both relating to the Islamic movement: first, the level to which the Islamic movement can better organize itself and begin making use of its economic weight and strength in a more structured fashion; and second, the degree to which the Islamists can maintain a good enough relationship with the government and royal family to not be seen as too dangerous a political threat. If these two conditions are met, the increased coordination and cooperation between Islamic banks and Islamic movements is likely to have important political effects even in the absence of major political liberalization. In this more realistic scenario, Islamic banks can be expected to play an important role in gradually mediating the transformation of political Islamists and making them into a more effective voice for democratization through the organization and mobilization of civil-society institutions and activities.

Appendix 9.1: Table of Jordanian Islamist leaders interviewed for this chapter

Jamil Abu Bakr	Current Spokesman for the Muslim Brotherhood in Jordan.
Saud Abu Mahfudh	Editor of Jordan's Islamist newspaper, *Al-Sabeel*, and a leading member of the Muslim Brotherhood in Jordan.
Ali Abu Sukur	General Secretary of the Jordanian Engineers Association and a leading member of the Muslim Brotherhood in Jordan.
Abdul Lateef Arabiyyat	Current Leader of the Islamic Action Front Party in Jordan and the former Speaker of the Lower House of the Jordanian Parliament.
Ishaq Farhan	A prominent and long-time Islamist leader and activist in Jordan. He is currently the President of al-Zarqa University and in the past served as the founding Leader of the Islamic Action Front Party. He is a former Member of Parliament serving in both the National Consultative Council and the Upper House. He is also a former Minister of Education, Minister of Religious Affairs and President of Jordan University. He has written many books and articles.
Musa Hantash	A Jordanian businessman and member of the Muslim Brotherhood. He is also a member of an Islamist-leaning business association in Jordan (*Jami'yat al-Rakha*).
Ahmad Tannash	The member of the board of the Islamic Action Front, with the strongest background in Islamic economics. He is a professor at Yarmouk University.

NOTES

1. Hassan Al-Banna, 'Risalat al-Ta'aleem', in *Majmu'at Rasail al-Imam al-Shaheed Hassan Al-Banna* (Alexandria: Dar al-Da'wa, 1980).
2. See Ali Abdul Kazem, 'Al-Seera al-Tareekheya Li-Jama'at al-Ikhwan al-Muslimeen wa-Murji'iyyatiha al-Fikriya', in Hani Hourani (ed.), *al-Harakaat wa-Tanzhimaat al-Islamiyya fil-Urdun* (Amman: al-Urdun al-Jadid Research Center, 1997).
3. For the social and economic workings of the Mit Ghamr banks, see Ahmed El-Ashker, *The Islamic Business Enterprise* (London: Croom Helm, 1987); and Ann Elizabeth Mayer, 'Islamic Banking and Credit Policies in the Sadat Era: The Social Origins of Islamic Banking in Egypt', *Arab Law Quarterly*, 1.1, 1985, pp. 32–50 as reprinted in Tim Niblock and Rodney Wilson (eds), *The Political Economy of the Middle East* (Cheltenham: Edward Elgar, 1999), Vol. 3, pp. 389–407.
4. The reason for the liquidation of the Mit Ghamr banks is a source of controversy. The Egyptian government claimed that the banks were being mismanaged, however Mayer, as well as El-Ashker (*The Islamic Business Enterprise*, p. 158–61), argues that political reasons were behind the demise of the bank. Islamists in Egypt, Jordan and elsewhere continue to argue that the Egyptian government closed the banks because of the fear that they would strengthen Islamist sentiments.

5. Jamil Abu Bakr, spokesman for the Jordanian Muslim Brotherhood, noted in an interview on 23 July 2001 that members of the Muslim Brotherhood were the first to discuss the idea of establishing an Islamic bank in Jordan in the early 1970s. For a list of the various Islamists who were interviewed for this chapter, see Appendix 9.1.

6. For the feelings, motivations and ideas of Sami Hamoud, as well as for the historical incidents about the establishment of the Jordan Islamic Bank, see Abdullah Abd al-Majeed al-Maliki, *Al-Bank al-Islami al-Urduni* (Amma: al-Dustour al-Tijaria, 1996).

7. For a translation of Hamoud's PhD, see Sami Hamoud, *Islamic Banking* (London: Arabian Information Ltd, 1985).

8. Interview with Ishaq Farhan, 27 July 2001.

9. See interview with Hamoud as reported in al-Maliki, *Al-Bank al-Islami al-Urduni*, p. 25.

10. Mbeideen's ties to both governmental and Islamist circles is perhaps best exemplified by the fact that when he was elected as a member of the Lower House of the Jordanian Parliament in 1989 he was the only member to join both the pro-government Constitutional Bloc and the Islamic Action Front bloc, a bloc made up of Muslim Brotherhood and independent Islamist deputies. See Tim Riedel, *Who is Who in the Jordanian Parliament 1989–1993*, (Amman: Freidrich Ebert Foundation, 1993).

11. Prince Mohammad never clearly stated the reasons for his pulling out of the Jordan Islamic Bank. One controversial aspect of the 1978 Bank Law was over the Islamic legitimacy of the modern *murabaha* contract that Hamoud had developed in his book, but it is unlikely this would have led Prince Mohammad to withdraw from the bank, as these contracts were also widely used in other banks that Prince Mohammad sponsored. Another controversial part of the Bank Law was article 22, which stated that the bank would be responsible for any losses that occurred for reasons of mismanagement or corruption. Some Islamic scholars feared that mismanagement could be interpreted too broadly, thus providing a kind of deposit guarantee that goes against the very essence of Islamic banking. For a copy of the Bank Law, see al-Maliki, *Al-Bank al-Islami al-Urduni*, Appendix 1, pp. 277–93.

12. Interview with Saud Abu Mahfudh, 25 July 2001.

13. Dr Mohammed Saqr served as a discussant during a round-table discussion concluding the conference 'Investment in Jordan: Opportunities and Prospects' that was held in the Amman Chamber of Commerce on 17–18 July 2001. The conference was sponsored by the Middle East Studies Center.

14. Interview with Jamil Abu Bakr, 23 July 2001.

15. Interview with Ali Abu Sukur, 25 July 2001.

16. Interview with Saud Abu Mahfudh, 25 July 2001.

17. Since Shallah's dissertation was written, the JIB has appointed a three-member *shari'a* committee. Members of the committee can, however, still be appointed or dismissed by the bank's board of directors at any time and the board still sets their salaries.

18. Interview with Abdul Lateef Arabiyyat, 27 July 2001.

19. Interview with a small businessman who is a member of the Muslim Brotherhood but asked to remain anonymous. The interview was conducted in Amman on 4 July 2001.

20. Interview with Musa Hantash, 25 July 2001.

21. *Al-Burnamij al-Intikhabi li-Murashihee Hizb Jabhat al-Amal al-Islami li-Intikhabaat al-Majlis al-Niyabi al-Urduni*, 1997.

22. The statements were taken from the Binder of Statements and Official Correspondence of the Islamic Action Front Party that is kept at the IAF Party Headquarters in Amman.

23. Interview with Ahmad Tannash, 29 July 2001.

24. For a more in-depth analysis of the shortcomings of both the Muslim Brotherhood and the Islamic Action Front in the area of providing modern, realistic solutions to problems facing Jordan and how that has affected their legitimacy, see Hani Hourani (ed.), *al-Harakaat wa-Tandhimaat al-Islamia fi-l-Urdun* (Amman: al-Urdun al-Jadid Research Center, 1996), pp. 283–7.

25. For general information on Jordan's professional associations, see Hani Hourani (ed.), *Professional Associations and the Challenges of Democratic Transformation in Jordan* (Amman: al-Urdun al-Jadid Research Center, 2000).

26. Interview with Ali Abu Sukur.

27. See *Membership Directory* of the *Jami'yat al-Rakha*.

28. Interview with Musa Hantash, a member of the *Jami'yat al-Rakha* in Jordan.

29. Interview with Bakr Rehan, Executive Manager for the Planning and Organizing Department at the Jordan Islamic Bank, 18 June 2001 in Amman.

30. Interview with Nihad Maraqa, Manager of Planning for the Arab Islamic Bank, 19 June 2001 in Amman.

31. See Jordan Islamic Bank, *Twenty-Second Annual Report*, 2000, p. 23.

32. Interview with Abdul Lateef Arabiyyat.

33. Interview with Jamil Abu Bakr and Jordan Islamic Bank, *Twenty-Second Annual Report*, 2000.

34. Interview with Ishaq Farhan.

35. Interview with Saud Abu Mahfudh.

36. Ibid.

37. When someone wants to finance a purchase through an Islamic bank, the bank first purchases the good then resells it to a customer. At the time of writing, Jordanian laws tax both transactions.

38. This company was established in 1996 to help Jordanian banks provide long-term housing finance to banks with mostly short-term deposits by channeling long-term funds – such as pension funds or insurance companies controlled by governmental agencies – through Jordanian banks with the express purpose of providing housing finance.

10

The Political Economy of Islamic Finance in Turkey: The Role of Fethullah Gülen and Asya Finans

Filiz Baskan

The aim of this chapter is to examine the development of Asya Finans as an example of Islamic banking. Asya Finans can be regarded as an Islamic bank in two respects: first, it avoids interest-based transactions and relies instead on profit-sharing; and second, it is affiliated to the Islamic Fethullah Gülen Community. It is therefore relevant to ask: what is the difference between Asya Finans and conventional banks? What is the position of Asya Finans in comparison to other special finance houses? What are the aims of Asya Finans? Does Asya Finans benefit from its association with the Fethullah Gülen Community and does the latter gain from having its own banking affiliate? An attempt is made here to provide answers to these questions in order to obtain some indication of the interaction between political Islam and the Islamic sub-economy in Turkey. As Islam has been a sensitive political issue since the founding of the Turkish republic, it is relevant to examine first the role of Islam in politics.

ISLAM IN TURKISH POLITICS

The Turkish state has been secular since the establishment of the republic in 1923. Until 1923, the principal component in the ideology of the Ottoman Empire was Islam under the Sultan-Caliph, who represented both temporal and the spiritual power.[1] The republican elite saw secularization as the most effective way to reform the traditional state system and society. Secularization would require redefining the hold of Islam on society and removing its influence from the political, social and cultural spheres. Religion had to be confined to matters of faith and worship.[2] Therefore, the republican elite tried to create a modern, rational state with institutions and laws by means of secularization. They instigated, in effect, a cultural revolution based on a new value system expressed as a secular political ideology redefining social identity and legitimating an autonomous political authority.[3] However, this new worldview could not replace the ideology of Islam.[4] The founders of the republic did not pay attention to the necessity of a value system at the level of the individual.[5] Because of the weakness of the republican ideology, religious ideology could survive.

As a result of transition to multi-party politics in 1946, Islam has been incorporated into Turkish politics. During the 1950s, especially, the centre-right Democrat Party (DP) of Adnan Menderes was criticized on the grounds that it used religion to gain votes. As soon as the DP came to power, it lifted the ban on the recital of *ezan* (call to prayer) in Arabic, permitted the broadcasting of Koran readings over the state radio, increased the number of religious schools, and increased the government budget of the Directorate of Religious Affairs.[6] The dispute over the use of Islam for political ends continued after the establishment of the Justice Party to fill the place of the DP following the 1960 military intervention.

As a result of the liberal and pluralist atmosphere created by the 1961 Constitution, a religious political party was established for the first time in Turkish political life. Founded on 26 January 1970, the National Order Party (NOP) was then banned on 20 May 1971 by the Constitutional Court because of its support for the establishment of a theocratic order in Turkey. In 1972, a new religious party called the National Salvation Party (NSP) replaced the National Order Party. Following the military intervention of 12 September 1980, however, the NSP was banned, along with all the other political parties. In 1983, the Welfare Party (WP), a new neo-Islamic party, was founded to fill the gap left by the banning of the National Salvation Party.[7] The Welfare Party was a continuation of both the National Order Party and the National Salvation Party. On 16 January 1998, the Constitutional Court in turn banned the Welfare Party on the grounds that the party acted against the principles of the secular republic. Just before the ban on the Welfare Party, some of its members founded another party, the Virtue Party (VP), on 17 December 1997. Like the WP, the VP was then banned on 22 June 2001 by the Constitutional Court because of its action against the principles of the secular republic. However, in contrast to previous experiences, two Islamic parties were founded after dissolution of the Virtue Party. One of these is the Contentment Party (CP), which was founded by the 'traditionalist' wing of the VP under the leadership of Recai Kutan, who was the head of banned VP, on 20 July 2001. The other is the Justice and Development Party (JDP) that was set up by the 'reformist' wing of the VP on 14 August 2001.

From this brief history of political Islam in Turkey, one may argue that Islamic opposition has never been considered as legitimate by the state authorities.

Parallel to the suppression of political Islam, the Turkish state has repressed Islamic businesses, albeit not systematically. For instance, the Attorney General, who brought a lawsuit against the Virtue Party, also asked that MÜSİAD, the Independent Association of Industrialists and Businessmen, be closed down due to its close relationship with the VP.[8] At the very least, we can say that, owing to the repressive policies of the state authorities, there is an uneasy coexistence of political Islam and Islamic business in Turkey.

There is no simple relationship, either, between political Islam and the Islamic sub-economy: the relationship between political Islam and Islamic business in Turkey is multifaceted. Sometimes the Islamic capitalists are integrated with political Islam, as evidenced by the relationship between the Welfare Party and the MÜSİAD: the latter became a prominent business association in parallel with the rise of the WP to power during the second half of the 1990s.[9] Sometimes there is an uneasy coexistence, as illustrated by the relation between the VP and the MÜSİAD after the closure of the WP, which had negatively affected MÜSİAD; its members had been repressed by the secular Turkish state. Sometimes Islamic business keeps itself separated from political Islam: for instance, the Fethullah Gülen Community, which is an influential religious community in Turkish social, political and economic life, kept its distance from the WP and then the VP.

The Islamic sects gained a significant place in the economic field by using the facilities of a market-oriented economic model, which was initiated in January 1980 with the help of the World Bank and International Monetary Fund. These sects are involved in investment activity and have become one of the major actors in the economic field.[10] One of the significant examples of religious sects that entered the economic field and established holding companies is the Nakshibendi sect. For instance, Professor Esad Coşan, who is a follower of the İskenderpasa branch of the Nakshibendi sect, founded Server Holding, which includes thirty-eight companies operating in a broad spectrum ranging from the paper industry to the publishing sector, from the health sector to manufacturing industry.[11] In addition, Turgut Özal and his brother, Korkut Özal were affiliated to the İskenderpasa branch of the Nakshibendi sect. Turgut Özal founded the Motherland Party (MP) in 1983. However, his brother Korkut preferred to stay away from politics and he and the Topbas family founded several companies in sectors involved in finance, trade, construction and the petroleum industry.[12] Another significant example of religious sects that gained an enormous success in economic field during the 1980s was the Kadiri sect. The followers of this sect own a TV channel, Mesaj, three journals, Öğüt, İcmal and Mesaj, and a publishing house, as well as companies operating in the trade and manufacturing sector.[13] Enver Ören, owner of the İhlas Finance House, which will be discussed later, is affiliated with the Isıkcılar branch of the Kadiri sect.

As a result, by means of the Islamic sect networks, people from the lower socio-economic strata have gained upward social mobility. Birtek and Toprak reveal the extent of these networks as follows: 'This dimension of tarikat connections has become increasingly important in recent years for getting scholarships, establishing new businesses, holding positions of political power, and, for a few, building financial empires.'[14] Like other Muslim Brotherhood organizations, the Fethullah Gülen Community used the opportunities created by a market-oriented economic model to obtain substantial economic power. The investments of the religious Fethullah Gülen Community cover a broad spectrum of activities ranging from banking and insurance to chemicals and textiles.

However, before going into the details of Asya Finans, it is essential to examine the national and international contexts in which the special finance houses were established in Turkey and their possible relationships with political Islam.

NATIONAL AND INTERNATIONAL CONTEXT IN WHICH THE ISLAMIC ECONOMY EMERGED

Several national and international factors have contributed to the emergence of an Islamic economy as an alternative to mainstream economic activities in Turkey. One of the most important national factors was the transformation of state ideology: although the Turkish state had radical secularist policies until 1980, following the coup the military, as part of the state elite, regarded Islam as an important factor in creating social and political stability in Turkey. In this respect, the development of an Islamic economy has been encouraged, at least in part, by the state elites.

Another important factor is the globalization process. Since the early 1980s, there has been a neo-liberal restructuring process all over the world. This process means a radical transfer of the power of the state in the economic sphere to market-oriented forces. This process also has influenced Turkey. As a result of the liberalization of the Turkish economy, Islamic business has become an important sector of the economy. Examining these factors in detail helps us to understand the context in which Islamic business emerged as a significant factor in Turkish social, political and economic life.

Transformation of state ideology

Although the Turkish state has a strict secularist stance, Islam has occupied a significant place in Turkish social, political and economic life during the post-1980 period. Birtek and Toprak address this issue by asking: 'How is it in the last decade, while the reconstruction of Turkish modernization took important strides forward, the economy was radically liberalized, and a smooth transition to a post-coup democratic regime was almost thoroughly accomplished, Islam also emerged as an important political variable in Turkish politics?'[15]

Some scholars of Turkish politics argue that one of the important factors in explaining the increasing importance of Islam in Turkish politics was a major change in the Turkish state's attitudes towards Islam. For instance, Ziya Öniş suggests that following the 1980 coup, the military, as part of the republican elite, saw Islam as an important factor for social and political stability. Accordingly, they encouraged a new Constitution based on a 'Turkish–Islamic synthesis' that is a combination of nationalism and Islam, and was conceived as a restraint on the causes of political chaos: 'Hence, rather surprisingly, Islam was employed by the military as an instrument for consolidating and institutionalizing the post-1980 regime.'[16] For this purpose, first religious education in primary schools became compulsory; and second, by augmenting its financial resources, the power of the Directorate of Religious Affairs was increased.[17]

Similarly, Birtek and Toprak maintain that the reason for the increasing importance of Islam in Turkey's socio-economic life during the 1980s and 1990s lay in the transformation of state ideology. In the early republican period, a radical formulation of secularism was introduced as part of the official ideology. It was radical in so far as the policy involved state controls over religious institutions rather than a mere separation of religious institutions and the state. By exercising control, the republican elite hoped to transfer religion from the public sphere to the private sphere, and to make religion a matter of individual conscience.[18] However, republican ideology was not successful in providing an identity, hence religion has remained an important part of the identity of the Turkish people.[19]

After the transition to the multi-party period, the political elite began to utilize religion to attain their political ends. Following the 1980 military coup, the state elite also appealed to religion to put an end to the period of anarchy and chaos. The aim of the 1980 coup was to de-politicise the society so that the military elite could establish national unity, ideological conformity and political stability. These were to be achieved by 'traditionalism, religious accommodation and a sense of moral community'.[20] Hence, during the post-1980 period, Islamic elements have been incorporated into official discourse in order to tie the individual to the state and unite the different classes and strata.[21] In concrete terms, religious education in primary and secondary schools was made compulsory in the 1982 Constitution. In addition, the religious sects became very influential in all fields; 'their members have now penetrated all ranks of political society, including the parties, government, civil service, intelligentsia, and the business and the banking world'.[22]

Thus, we can draw the conclusion from the above discussion that the increasing importance of Islam in Turkish political and economic life is a result of the radical change in the policy of the Turkish state towards Islam. This change can be summarized as the incorporation of Islamic elements into official ideology as a unifying force for the Turkish nation. The meetings of Fethullah Gülen, the influential religious leader, with leading politicians during the 1990s may be considered as a good example of the change in the state's attitudes towards Islam. On 30 November 1994, Fethullah Gülen met Tansu Çiller, leader of the centre-right True Path Party and the then Prime Minister; on 20 March 1995, he met Bülent Ecevit, leader of the centre-left Democratic Left Party and a former long-serving prime minister. Other meetings took place with Hikmet Çetin, a member of parliament for the centre-left Social Democratic Populist Party, and the then Minister of State on 10 May 1995, and with Hüsamettin Cindoruk, the then speaker of Turkish Grand National Assembly on 2 August 1995. Moreover, Fethullah Gülen gets state support, especially in the field of education. He often spoke of how Turgut Özal and Süleyman Demirel during their presidencies helped his community establish schools in Central Asian countries. Another significant example that demonstrated the magnitude of the change in the Turkish state's attitudes towards religion was the encouragement it gave to the establishment of the 'special finance houses' that are considered to be 'Islamic banks'.

Globalisation and the Islamic political economy of Turkey

During the post-1980 period, international factors also influenced the development of Islamic business. Globalisation contributed to the change in the role of the state from being an instigator of economic activity to being more of a facilitator in an increasingly pluralist and market-oriented environment. As a result of this neo-liberal economic restructuring process, unemployment and inequality in income distribution has increased, and the nation-state has been incapable of providing for the needs of the people from the lower stratum. A resulting vacuum in the political arena opened the way to political movements based on extreme nationalism or religious fundamentalism.[23]

Thus, Turkey began in 1980, with the help of the World Bank and the IMF, to adopt the new market-oriented economic model. Öniş describes the success of the government's neo-liberal restructuring as follows: 'an average of 5–6 per cent real GNP growth per annum, if not outstanding, was high by international standards. The ability to shift from a highly inward-oriented economy to a significant exporter of manufactures was also quite striking. A rosy picture can thus be drawn highlighting economic dynamism, rising entrepreneurship and the growing power of private capital, as the economy became steadily integrated into international markets.'[24]

Nonetheless, as in other countries, this neo-liberal restructuring process led to rising unemployment and inequality in income distribution, accelerated by Turkey's high inflation rates. The failure of the nation-state in solving these problems led to the increase in ideological commitment to religion and ethnicity: 'In this way, the rise of the market-oriented competitive individualism contributed to the ideological appeal of Islam.'[25] As a result of the failure of both centre-right and centre-left parties to provide solutions and their consequent fragmentation, the Welfare Party, an Islamic party, gained more votes than any other party in the 1995 elections.

During the 1990s, the legitimacy crisis of the Turkish state propelled political Islam to power, and Islamic organizations also gained in importance in the economic and social spheres. For example, an Islamic association of businessman, MÜSİAD, was founded on 5 May 1990 as an alternative to the liberal TÜSİAD, the Association of Turkish Industrialists and Businessmen.[26] Pro-Islamic Hak-iş, originally founded in Ankara in 1976, finally became an influential trade union during the 1990s. In the social sphere, *tarikats* and religious communities, which had been forced underground after the formation of the Turkish republic, resurfaced during the final decade of the twentieth century. The protest movements of female university students to have the right to wear headscarves while attending classes contributed to visibility of Islamic movements in the public sphere.

Some segments of Turkish society, notably the political elite, journalists, academicians, artists and businessmen, have perceived the rise of political and cultural Islam to be a threat to the foundations of the Turkish state. Therefore, they have sought out less threatening representatives of moderate Islam to serve as safety valves against the political Islam of the Welfare Party. In this context, Fethullah Gülen, who was known until the 1990s only to a small circle of his religious followers, became an increasingly well-known person in Turkey, the focus of much public attention within a short period of time. Leading journalists interviewed him and much is known about his ideas on current issues, as well as about his private life. These interviews presented a moderate figure, who respects his 'nation' and 'state' and admires Picasso's work as well as the poems of the socialist Turkish poet, Nazim Hikmet. As a result, many secularists who had disapproved of the rise of the Islamic political party, the Welfare Party, appreciated Fethullah Gülen.[27] They saw him as a moderate person, far removed from the radical concerns of political Islam. In fact, he became popular among the liberals concerned with finding a 'broad-minded' and 'modern' figure among the Islamist leadership. Following the media campaign that made him a household name, he met with the then Prime Minister Tansu Çiller, leader of the True Path Party, thus reinforcing his image as an opinion-leader close to political decision-makers.

Fethullah Gülen's fame transcended the borders of Turkey, and he became an international figure engaging in 'a dialogue between religions'. Gülen met with the Patriarch Bartholomeos of the Orthodox Church in April 1996 and with the Pope in February 1998. Many journalists, scientists and artists supported his attempts to promote a dialogue between religions.[28] Moreover, his followers established more than 2,000 schools in 52 countries in 5 continents with his encouragement, including 125 in Turkey.[29]

Some statistics will give the reader an idea about the magnitude of Gülen's educational movement in Central Asia. For instance, the Fethullah Gülen Community established 1 university, 28 secondary schools and 1 primary school in Kazakhstan alone. These schools enrolled 4,803 students and employed 525 faculty members in 1998.[30] In Uzbekistan, 18 secondary schools were established, with 3,500 students and 200 teachers.[31] Students in these schools receive an education in English, Turkish and in their native language. In addition, they have computer-based educational facilities and modern science laboratories with up-to-date equipment. Many of them have successfully competed in the International Science Olympics.[32] Students educated in the schools established in Turkey by the Fethullah Gülen Community are also successful in national and international science competitions. Those attending schools and private courses (dershane) of the Fethullah Gülen Community usually score very highly in the national university entrance examination.[33]

Gülen claims that business enterprises provide the financial resources for these schools. In fact, commercial and educational activities go hand in hand in Central Asian countries. The host countries provide the buildings for the schools, and modest fees are collected from the students. Turkish businessmen having interests in these countries cover the rest of the costs.[34]

Fethullah Gülen and his circle chose Central Asia as the starting point for their educational movement. Gülen explained that it was necessary to fill the vacuum left by the disintegration of the Soviet Union at the end of the 1980s. Turks had to go to Central Asia to encourage the religious enlightenment of their fellow Turkic speakers, who had been dominated by atheism for seventy years.[35] Gülen asserted that if he and his followers could not support the people of Central Asia by means of education and cultural activities, these people would fall prey to others coming from other parts of the world, and would be exploited by them.[36] Hence, Fethullah Gülen had to act decisively to bring both educational facilities, and industrial and commercial activities, to Central Asia.[37]

Like other Muslim Brotherhood organizations, the Fethullah Gülen Community used the facilities of a market-oriented economic model and built a financial empire. The Fethullah Gülen Community is the richest religious community in Turkey. In addition to its schools, it owns a media empire including a television channel, Samanyolu TV, a radio channel (Burc FM), a daily, Zaman, as well as four scientific, political journals: Aksiyon, Zafer, Sızıntı, and Yeni Umut Dergisi. In addition, the Işık insurance company and Asya Finans are affiliated to the Fethullah Gülen Community, which also has a wide variety of other investments. In 1993, the Community established the Business Life Cooperation Association (İSHAD), which has 470 members. İSHAD does not cooperate with other Islamic business associations such as MÜSİAD, which is regarded as a rival; indeed, Fethullah Gülen advises members of İSHAD to avoid having business relationships with members of MÜSİAD.[38]

ISLAMIC BANKING IN TURKEY

Turgut Özal allowed Islamic banks to open in 1983, after his Motherland Party, which was established to contest elections permitted by the military, obtained the majority of seats in the Turkish National Assembly. Turgut Özal became Prime Minister on 13 December 1983. It is important to stress that the Motherland Party combined four distinct ideological strands, including religious conservatism, as well as nationalism, economic liberalism and social democracy within its ranks.[39] Just three days after Turgut Özal became Prime Minister, the governmental decree regarding the foundation of special finance houses was signed and published in the *Official Gazette* on 16 December 1983, which came into force on 19 February 1984.[40] Until 1999, the establishment and functioning of the special finance houses were regulated by this decree. On 19 December 1999, a significant amendment to the decree placed these houses under the jurisdiction of the Turkish Banking Law.

The processes whereby the special finance houses were established help to elucidate the relationships between political Islam and the Islamic economy in Turkey. In 1985, the first interest-free banks of Turkey – Faisal Finance and Al-Baraka Türk (Albaraka Turkish Finance House) – were founded by foreign capital. Al-Baraka Türk was established by Al-Baraka Investment and Development Company, owned by a Saudi Arabian national, Sheikh Saleh Kamel, and its Turkish shareholders were Korkut Özal and Eymen Topbas. Korkut Özal, the brother of the then Prime Minister Turgut Özal, had served as deputy of the religiously-oriented National Salvation Party and Minister of Agriculture in the coalition government of the Republican People's Party of Bülent Ecevit and the NSP in 1974. He subsequently served as Minister of Agriculture in the First Nationalist Front government of Süleyman Demirel's Justice Party, the NSP, the ultra-nationalist Nationalist Action Party and the Republican Reliance Party between 1975 and 1977. Eymen Topbas was the chairman of the Motherland Party's Istanbul branch until 1990.

Another indicator of the connection between political Islam and the Islamic sub-economy in Turkey was the foundation of several religious *Wakf* by economically powerful groups. Bereket Vakfi (the Al-Baraka *Wakf*) was established by Al-Baraka Türk in January 1987, with the aims of organizing meetings to celebrate religious holidays; founding mosques and organising Koran courses; supporting the publication of religious research; and giving scholarships to poor students for religious education.[41]

Another Saudi, Prince Mohammad Al-Faisal, established Faisal Finance, the Turkish shareholders being Salih Özcan and Ahmet Tevfik Paksu. Salih Özcan was a Member of Parliament for the NSP and a member of the World Muslim League. Ahmet Tevfik Paksu was Minister of Labour in the First Nationalist

Front government of the JP, the NSP, NAP and the RRP. Another shareholder of Faisal Finance was Cemal Külahlı, who was a Member of Parliament for the JP and Minister of Agriculture in its minority government between 1979 and 1980. Külahlı then became a deputy for the Welfare Party in the 1995 general elections. Similarly, M. Gündüz Sevilgen and Reşat Saruhan, who were shareholders in Faisal Finance, had also served as deputies for the NSP. Cengiz Gökçek, who was a member of parliament of the Nationalist Action Party and Minister of Health in the Second Nationalist Front government of the JP, NSP and NAP, was also a shareholder in Faisal Finance. Halil Şıvgın was another significant shareholder of Faisal Finance, being one of the vice chairman of the Motherland Party. This composition of Faisal Finance's shareholders demonstrates some of the relationships between Islamic finance and political Islam.

In 1998, Prince Mohammad Al-Faisal, the main shareholder of Faisal Finance, sold his shares to Kombassan Holding, which in turn in 2001 sold its shares to Sabri Ülker, who was among the founding shareholders of Faisal Finance. As a consequence, Sabri Ülker obtained 97 per cent of its shares, which prompted him to change the name of Faisal Finance to Family Finance.[42]

In 1989, Kuveyt Türk (Kuveyt Türk Evkaf Finance House) was established as a joint venture of the Kuwait Finance House (49.9 per cent), the Turkish Foundations General Directorate (29.9 per cent), the Kuwait State Social Security Institute (9 per cent), the Islamic Development Bank (9 per cent) and the Turkish Religious Affairs Foundation (1 per cent). A draft law providing tax exemptions for IDB activities in Turkey was passed just after Korkut Özal became director of the IDB's Islamic Research and Training Institute. Prior to Korkut Özal, the director of this Institute was Professor Nevzat Yalcintaş, who is a Member of Parliament of Recep Tayyip Erdogan's Justice and Development Party.

Originally, then, the Islamic banks became established in Turkey for several reasons. First of all, Turgut Özal may have had a personal interest. Faisal Finance and Al-Baraka Türk supposedly enriched his brother, Korkut Özal, by financing oil imported from Gulf countries in which he had a stake.[43] Second, it is claimed that the main aim of the special finance houses was to attract capital from Gulf countries to Turkey.[44] A third motive was to attract the savings of conservative people into the Turkish economy. These people had hitherto preferred to keep their savings in cash, rather than in deposits in interest-based banks because of religious concerns.[45] The question remains as to why Gulf capital wanted to open Islamic banks in Turkey. It is claimed that Saudi Arabia wanted to prevent the diffusion of secularism among Arab countries, therefore Saudi businessmen made investments in Turkey not just for economic reasons, but also for political ones.[46]

The success of the three special finance houses established by Gulf investors and Turkish shareholders during the 1980s in mobilizing conservative Turkish people's savings made Turkish Islamic businessmen aware of the financial potential of Islamic banks. Hence, during the 1990s different religious sects established three separate indigenous finance houses, Anadolu Finans, İhlas Finans and Asya Finans, in 1991, 1995 and 1996 respectively. The new founders had already accumulated substantial wealth, which constituted the equity base of these finance houses. In addition, they had captive and dependent communities who could be their customers.

İhlas Finans was a subsidiary of the Ihlas Finance House of Enver Ören, who is affiliated with the Işıkçılar religious community. Ihlas Finance House's business activities ranged from the media to the automotive industry and construction as well as finance. Enver Ören owned the daily newspaper, *Türkiye*, a television and a radio channel, TGRT, an advertising agency and a news agency. In addition, the İhlas Finance House produced electronic devices and kitchen equipment, and constructs holiday resorts. Before founding İhlas Finans, the İhlas Finance House became a shareholder of the Eurocredit Bank by buying 40 per cent of its shares and changed its name to Yurtbank. Then it acquired 31.5 per cent of Egebank.[47] However, Islamic circles heavily criticized the Ihlas Finance House on the grounds that it 'is leaving aside its Islamic characteristics and adopting the principles of an interest based banking system'.[48] As a result of the financial crisis of 2000, however, the Banking Regulating and Supervising Agency forced İhlas Finans to end its banking activities on 10 February 2001. Of the five remaining special finance houses in Turkey, only Al-Baraka Türk and Anadolu Finans are members of MÜSİAD.

The special finance houses of Turkey offer two types of account to their depositors: current accounts that do not offer a return in any form; and, more importantly, profit-sharing accounts that can be opened in US dollars, Euros or Turkish lira for a minimum of thirty days. The special finance houses do not announce a predetermined rate of return for their depositors but at the end of the investment activity, profits are shared between the finance houses and the account-holders, with the finance houses taking 20 per cent of the profit.[49]

As Table 10.1 shows, in 2000, current accounts constituted only 7 per cent of the total funds collected by the special finance houses, whereas 93 per cent of them were in profit-sharing accounts, a proportion that rose slightly by June 2001 but then subsequently fell owing to the financial crisis of Turkey and the bankruptcy of İhlas Finans.

The special finance houses use four methods for the utilisation of funds, the most popular being *murabaha*, whereby a bank will buy an asset desired by the customer and sell to the customer for a pre-agreed price.[50] The special finance houses also offer *mudaraba* to their clients, where they provide the capital while the customer provides his labour. The profit generated as a result of this investment is shared between the finance house and the customer on the basis of

Table 10.1: Funds deposited by type of account

	2000	June 2001	September 2001
Profit-sharing accounts	93%	94%	79%
Current accounts	7%	6%	13%

Sources: Banking Regulating and Supervising Agency, *Annual Report*, 2000; Banking Regulating and Supervising Agency, *Report on the Evaluation of the Banking Sector*, June and September 2001.
Note: In September 2001, 6 per cent of accounts were not designated.

Table 10.2: Financing methods

Method	2000	June 2001	September 2001
Murabaha	74%	44%	45%
Mudaraba	15%	29%	31%
Ijara	10%	25%	23%

Sources: Banking Regulating and Supervising Agency, *Annual Report*, 2000; Banking Regulating and Supervising Agency, *Report on the Evaluation of the Banking Sector*, June and September 2001.

predetermined rates. If there is any loss, the finance house loses its capital and the customer loses his labour and time.[51] A third fund-utilization mechanism used by the special finance houses is *musharaka*, a type of labour–capital partnership. At first glance it is similar to *mudaraba* but there are significant differences between these two types of financing: in the case of *musharaka* both the finance house and the customer provide labour and capital, and they share the profit in accordance with the pre-agreed ratios. When there is any loss, the finance house and the customer share the loss in proportion of the capital invested.[52] The special finance houses of Turkey also offer their clients leasing (*ijara*) where they buy an asset and rent it to the customer – so the customer does not pay the price of the item, only the rent for it. Table 10.2 shows the financing methods used by the special finance houses, with *murabaha* decreasing as imports slumped as a result of the 2001 financial crisis.

After examining how the special finance houses function, it is crucial to analyse the market share of each of the houses. During the 1980s, Al-Baraka Türk's performance was better than that of Faisal Finance's because of its government connections. The former had good relations with Turkish governments until the 1990s, since one of the shareholders, Korkut Özal, was brother of the former prime minister (and from 1989, president) Turgut Özal. As Table 10.3 illustrates, Al-Baraka Türk had the largest share in the consolidated balance sheet, with 41 per cent in 1996, but this declined with the rise of İhlas Finans. However, as mentioned above, İhlas Finans's activities ended on 10 February

Table 10.3: Share of each special finance house in the consolidated balance sheet

	1996	1997	1998	1999	2000	2001
Al-Baraka Türk	41	34	31	22	21	27
Kuveyt Türk	18	16	15	14	15	31
Faisal Finans	13	8	7	8	7	12
Anadolu Finans	8	9	8	7	8	10
İhlas Finans	–	20	27	30	40	0
Asya Finans	–	–	6	9	9	17

Sources: Central Bank *Annual Reports*, 1994, 1996, 1997, 1998; *Annual Reports* of each special finance house.

2001 because of liquidity problems. This failure resulted in increases in the market share of each special finance house, with Kuveyt Türk's share increasing sharply from 15 per cent in 2000 to 31 per cent in 2001. Similarly, the market share of Asya Finans rose from 9 per cent in 2000 to 17 per cent in 2001. Al-Baraka Türk followed with 7 per cent, Family Finance with 5 per cent, and Anadolu Finans with a 2 per cent increase in market share.

There were 142 special finance house branches all over Turkey before İhlas Finans was closed down. By May 2002, the total number was 118. Between June 2000 and November 2001, Asya Finans and Kuveyt Türk increased their number of branches from 16 to 25, and Anadolu Finans increased its number of branches from 20 to 27. By May 2002, Anadolu Finans has the greatest number of branches, 27. It was followed by Kuveyt Türk and Asya Finans with 25 branches, Al-Baraka Türk with 22 and Family Finans with 19.

It is interesting to examine the characteristics of the cities in which the special finance houses have branches, to see if they coincide with the regions in which political Islam fared well in the elections of 1995 and 1999. As Table 10.4 indicates, Adana, Ankara, Bursa, Denizli, Diyarbakir, Erzurum, Eskişehir, Gaziantep, Istanbul, Izmir, Kayseri, Kocaeli, Konya, Sakarya and Samsun are cities in which the special finance houses have branches and the Welfare Party, the Contentment Party and the Justice and Development Party have members of Parliament. When Table 10.4 is examined carefully, it can be observed that 84 of the 118 branches of the special finance houses were opened in cities where the percentage of the Welfare Party's vote in the 1995 general elections ranged from 16.56 to 41.47 per cent, and the percentage of the Virtue Party's vote in the 1999 general elections ranged from 10.03 to 30.02 per cent. Although the finance houses always try to keep their distance from religiously-oriented political parties, there is an obvious coincidence of the cities where Islamic political parties are powerful and the finance houses have branches. One exception for this generalization is Izmir, where all of the special finance houses have a branch

Table 10.4: The percentage of the votes for political Islam in cities where branches of the special finance houses are concentrated

City	Al-Bara-aka Türk	Kuveyt Türk	Anadolu Finans	Family Finans	Asya Finans	% votes for WP in 1995	No of WP deputies	% votes for the VP in 1999	No of CP and JDP deputies
Adana	x		x	x		16.56	xxxx	10.03	xx
Adıyaman						32.72	xx	27.05	xxx
Afyon		x				22.22	xx	11.04	x
Ağrı						30.06	xxx	12.08	
Aksaray		x				29.06	xx	16.08	x
Amasya						23.26	x	15.06	x
Ankara	xx	x	xxx	x	xx	20.89	xxxxxxx	16.56	xxxx
Antalya	x				x	13.22	x	6.03	x
Artvin						14.44		8.07	
Aydın					x	8.55	x	4.09	
Balıkesir	x					14.91	x	9.05	x
Batman						25.69	xx	13.09	x
Bayburt						38.51	x	26.06	x
Bingöl						51.63	xxx	24.04	xx
Bitlis						29.28	xx	20.08	x
Bolu						26.52	xx	19.05	x
Bursa	x	x	x	x	x	18.79	xxx	15.04	xxxx
Çankırı						27.13	x	19.08	x
Çorum			x			30.37	xxx	17.09	x
Denizli			x	x		10.26	x	5.08	
Diyarbakır			x		x	18.74	xxxxx	14.06	xxx
Elazığ			x			41.91	xxx	24.05	xx
Erzincan						32.37	xx	18.07	x
Erzurum			x		x	38.71	xxxxx	28.03	xxx
Eskişehir			x		x	14.04	x	9.07	
Gaziantep	x		x		x	23.08	xxx	15.09	x
Giresun						21.19	x	16.04	x
Gümüşhane						32.03	x	23.02	x
Hatay		x				18.41	xx	12.02	xx
Isparta		x				16.06	x	9.06	
İçel		x				10.58	xx	5.02	x
Istanbul	xxxxx xx	xxxxx xxxxx xxx	xxxxx xxxxx x	xxxxx xxxx	xxxxx xxxxx x	23.67	xxxxx xxxxx xxxxxx	20.73	xxxxx xxxxx xx
Izmir	x	x	x	x	x	8.34	xx	4.54	
K.maraş	x					36.08	xxxx	23.01	xxx
Karabük						21.38	x		
Karaman						33.42	xx	19.09	x
Kars						20.42	x	9.08	
Kastamonu						10.89	x	7.05	

City	Al-Bara-aka Türk	Kuveyt Türk	Anadolu Finans	Family Finans	Asya Finans	% votes for WP in 1995	No of WP deputies	% votes for the VP in 1999	No of CP and JDP deputies
Kayseri	x		x		x	33.07	xxxx	23.02	xxx
Kırıkkale						30.16	xx	15.03	x
Kırşehir						18.65	x	9.05	
Kilis						25.07	x		
Kocaeli	x	x	x		x	31.66	xxx	27.07	xxx
Konya	x	xx	x	x	x	41.77	xxxxx xxxx	30.02	xxxxx
Kütahya						24.03	xx	17.00	x
Malatya	x					37.19	xxxx	25.03	xxx
Manisa						13.05	x	8.03	xx
Mardin						19.98	xx	11.08	x
Muş						29.07	xx	10.09	x
Nevşehir						28.24	x	18.04	x
Niğde						22.52	x	14.02	
Ordu						17.84	xx	12.03	x
Osmaniye								13.03	x
Rize				x		23.08	x	20.08	x
Sakarya	x			x		28.23	xx	24.04	xx
Samsun	x				x	22.12	xxx	15.00	xx
Siirt						27.05	xx	13.04	x
Sivas		x				39.02	xxx	27.08	xxx
Şanlıurfa				x		26.08	xxxx	21.04	xxxx
Şırnak						8.26		11.01	x
Tokat						30.69	xxx	20.04	x
Trabzon				x		26.31	xxx	19.09	x
Van						29.07	xxx	18.09	xxx
Yozgat						35.94	xxx	21.01	xx
Zonguldak						14.18	x	9.07	
Total	22	25	27	19	25		158		101

Source: State Institute of Statistics, *General Election of Representatives Results by Province* 1995, 1999.

but Islamic political parties are not so powerful, having won only 8.34 per cent of the total votes in 1995 and 4.54 per cent in the 1999 general elections.

Another interesting coincidence that can be observed in Table 10.4, is that in Denizli, Gaziantep, Kayseri and Konya, the so-called 'Anatolian Tigers', the special finance houses opened branches and religious parties have members of Parliament. These cities became known during the 1990s as economic success stories,[53] and they are regarded as significant elements of Turkey's new economic scene. In these cities, small and medium-sized enterprises began to compete with large-scale companies that were the dominant actors of Turkish economic life until the 1990s.

ASYA FINANS

Asya Finans started to operate as the sixth private finance institution on 24 October 1996. It has a partnership structure that consisted by June 2002 of 249 shareholders. Their chairman is İhsan Kalkavan, who owns several companies in the shipping industry and is also on the board of directors of Işık Sigorta, an insurance company affiliated with the Fethullah Gülen Community. Asya Finans's general manager is Ünal Kabaca, who is also a member of Işık Sigorta's board of directors. One of the shareholders of Asya Finans is Osman Gürbüz Özkara, who is a businessmen from Izmir involved in exporting to Central Asian countries.[54] Tahsin Tekoğlu, who has companies in the textile industry and has a factory in Turkmenistan, is another shareholder and member of the board of directors of Asya Finans. Asya Finans provides services through 25 branches in 13 cities in Turkey, as well as its 119 correspondent banks in 62 countries abroad.

In its articles of establishment on 24 October 1996, the objectives of Asya Finans were set out as follows:[55]

- Turkish people have enormous amounts of gold and foreign currency that they hoard. Asya Finans aims at attracting these savings and injecting them into the Turkish economy.
- The share of banking without interest in the Turkish financial system is not sufficient. Therefore, the aim of Asya Finans is not to compete with the other special finance houses but to attract business from the conventional banking sector.
- Asya Finans believes that all needs of both individuals and companies can be met by interest-free banking. The objective of Asya Finans is to serve the banking needs of Turkish people who are reluctant to have a relationship with conventional banks due to interest.
- Due to improved telecommunication facilities, borders have been eliminated and the world turned into a village. For this reason, Asya Finans's goal is to operate not only in the national financial system but also in the international financial market.
- Another aim of Asya Finans is to finance the activities of Turkish industrialists abroad, especially in Central Asian countries. It hopes to attract some of the funds collected by the international interest-free banking system and to play a significant role in these countries.
- Finally, the main aim of Asya Finans is to ensure full customer satisfaction by utilizing the newest technological improvements.

One of the major aims of Asya Finans is to attract savings from conservative Turkish people who do not want to deposit with conventional banks because of

Table 10.5: Funds collected by currency

Currency (TRL million)	1999	Ratio of total (%)	2000	Ratio of total (%)
Funds in TRL	9.963.566	8.06	22.367.238	12.10
Funds USD	81.426.817	65.85	132.475.943	71.66
Funds DEM	32.217.130	26.05	29.630.917	16.03
Other	47.833	0.04	398.552	0.22
Total	123.655.346	100	184.872.650	100

Source: Asya Finans, *Annual Report*, 2000.

Table 10.6: Funds deposited by type of account, TRL million

Maturity structure	1999	%	2000	%
Current accounts	16.398.448	13.26	24.464.271	13.23
Profit-and-loss sharing accounts	107.256.898	86.74	160.408.379	86.77
30 days	66.695.930	53.94	108.551.180	58.72
60 days	32.822.563	26.54	41.445.580	22.42
180 days	5.047.883	4.08	6.588.219	3.56
360 days	2.690.522	2.18	3.823.400	2.07
Total	123.655.346	100	184.872.650	100

Source: Asya Finans, *Annual Report*, 2000.

their religious beliefs. Furthermore, Asya Finans is aware of the process of globalization. Hence, it aims to operate not only in national financial markets but also in international ones. This objective parallels the discourse of Fethullah Gülen about globalization. He expresses aspirations for dialogue with those people in the world who will share the same space by means of improved tele-communication and transportation systems. In line with his global discourse, Fethullah Gülen and his Community initiated a worldwide educational move-ment during the 1990s, as discussed earlier.

Like other special finance houses, Asya Finans offers both current and profit-sharing accounts. The latter may be subject to periods of notice of withdrawal of 30 days, 60 days, 180 days and 360 days. As Table 10.5 shows, the customers of Asya Finans prefer to have either current accounts or profit-sharing accounts in foreign currency. The ratio of accounts in foreign currency (US dollars + euro) was 91.85 per cent in 1999 and 87.69 per cent in 2000. Generally they prefer to have accounts in US dollars.

Table 10.6 indicates that Asya Finans obtains most of its funds through profit-and-loss sharing accounts, with current accounts making up only 13 per

Table 10.7: Financing methods

Method	1999	2000
Murabaha	75%	42%
Mudaraba	11%	41%
Ijara	14%	17%

Source: Asya Finans, *Annual Report*, 2000.

cent of the total funds in 1999 and 2000. For profit-sharing accounts, those for 30 days seem the most popular, as in 1999 they represented 54 per cent and in 2000 59 per cent of the total, indicating that depositors were only prepared to make limited liquidity sacrifices.

Like the other special finance houses, Asya Finans uses *murabaha, mudaraba, musharaka* and *ijara* for financing, with *murabaha* being the most popular, described as 'production support'. With this type of transaction, financing is provided to customers who need to buy investment goods. One of the managers of Asya Finans explained in an interview the mechanism of a *murabaha* transaction as follows: 'our client, who wishes to purchase equipment or goods for his business, requests us to buy this item. We buy this item and then sell it to him by adding a certain profit rate. This surplus cannot be called interest because it is not an excessive amount.' When asked what is the advantage of a *murabaha* transaction, he stated that 'in this type agreement, it is necessary to purchase and sell any good. So we are contributing to Turkish economy by financing the customers' needs that are necessary for making production. We do not earn money by selling money like conventional banks.'

Although there are four types of financing method used by Asya Finans, most funding is through *murabaha*, whereas *musharaka* is almost never used. As shown in Table 10.7, in 1999 75 per cent of the Asya Finans funds were utilized through *murabaha* transactions, 14 per cent of them were leasing, and *mudaraba* accounted for about 11 per cent of the funding. However, in 2000 there was a significant change in financing methods: *mudaraba* increased sharply to 42 per cent in 2000 at the expense of *murabaha*. This change may be due to the decline in the demand for import finance, given the difficulties facing the Turkish economy, and also to a willingness to get more closely involved in client business over the medium term in order to enhance customer loyalty in uncertain times.

One means of assessing the performance of Asya Finans is to compare the amount of net profit and loss with other special finance houses. Table 10.8 shows the relative profit positions. Between 1999 and 2000, Asya Finans's net profit increased by 147 per cent and Family Finans, the best-performing institu-

Table 10.8: Net profit (loss)

	1999	2000	2001
Al-Baraka Türk	5.907.975	6.589.126	−11.298.123
Kuveyt Türk	1.759.918	1.064.252	1.596.305
Family Finans	1.128.960	4.785.000	9.151.000
Anadolu Finans	−4.866.119	0.058.353	−11.270.848
Asya Finans	2.150.721	5.316.244	1.916.309

Sources: Annual Reports of each special finance house.

tion, increased its profit by 323 per cent in money terms. However, in 2001 the performances of all the special finance houses were poor owing to the crisis in the banking sector in November 2000, and the subsequent crisis in the Turkish economy in February 2001. These two crises affected Al-Baraka Türk and Anadolu Finans very badly. Al-Baraka Türk's profit fell from TL 6.589.126 trillion in 2000 to a loss of TL11.298.123 trillion in 2001. Family Finans was not as affected, as it increased its profit by 91 per cent in 2001. Although Asya Finans's net profit decreased from TL5.316.244 trillion in 2000 to TL1.916.309 trillion in 2001, it did not suffer a loss. The relative strength of Asya Finans could be explained by its affiliatiation with Turkey's richest religious community.

When one of the managers of Asya Finans was asked about the customers of Asya Finans, he said 'conservative Turkish people, who are reluctant to deposit their money in conventional banks because of interest, constitute our clients. Our customers who have current accounts or profit sharing accounts are generally conservative people. They prefer Asya Finans due to religious reasons.' The manager added that the employees of Asya Finans tend to be more conservative people than those of the conventional banks and consequently communicate more easily with the customers and have closer relationships with them. However, the profile of the customers who utilize the funds of Asya Finans is different: 'They are not always religious people: they can be secular. They prefer Asya Finans for financial reasons.'

When a manager was asked whether Asya Finans makes investment in every sector, he answered that 'we support investing in companies which are not contradicting Islamic norms and values. Islamic values, especially the notions of *halal* and *haram*, are very important for us. Therefore, we channelled the funds of Asya Finans into certain sectors that are compatible with Islamic values. For example, we do not have any business transaction with companies selling alcoholic drinks.'

THE FUTURE OF THE SPECIAL FINANCE HOUSES

During the banking crisis of November 2000, the Savings Deposit Insurance Fund took over five banks suffering from liquidity problems. Then, in February 2001, the Turkish economy experienced a major crisis that had serious implications for the special finance houses. According to Ünal Kabaca, general manager of Asya Finans, 'the banking crisis affected the Finance Houses severely, too. The interference of the public authority with the banks resulted in general distrust of the banking sector. Speculations about the Finance Houses influenced the clients negatively, and the interest-free banking sector had to bear the most difficult period of the last 15 years.'[56]

As stated above, İhlas Finans, which was one of the special finance houses, had liquidity problems and was taken over by the Banking Regulating and Supervising Agency in February 2001. The bankruptcy of İhlas Finans raised widespread concern about the interest-free banking sector, the total assets of which diminished by 40 per cent. When asked about the future of the special finance houses in Turkey, one of the managers of Asya Finans responded: 'the failure of the İhlas Finans created a climate of mistrust toward the Special Finance Houses. Now we are still in the process of winning back the customers' confidence.' He asserted that some of the special finance houses might merge in the future to overcome the financial difficulties. He added that as long as there are conservative people in Turkish society, the interest-free banking system would continue to keep its share of commercial banking. He believed that Asya Finans could increase its share in the sector by adopting modern technology.

The Finance Houses established the Union of the special finance houses as a requirement of the Turkish Banking Law on 26 October 2001. Its function was similar to that of the Savings Deposit Insurance Fund for conventional banks. The Union of the special finance houses provides guarantees for the deposits of the finance houses' customers in case of bankruptcy. By establishing this Union, the special finance houses are regaining the confidence of the customers. The position of the special finance houses had improved by June 2002.

CONCLUSION

The basic difference between the special finance houses and the conventional banks is that finance houses do not give credit to customers directly, but rather make payments to a third party. Thus, they try to channel their funds into commercial or productive ventures and make a contribution to the Turkish economy by supporting production. In contrast, the conventional banks do not monitor their customers' uses of credit. The Turkish state keeps the special finance houses under close scrutiny, and the Turkish Banking Law does not allow them much freedom for manoeuvre. They could not have overt relationships with political Islam, especially after the National Security Council cracked down on the Welfare Party on 28 February 1997.

Support from the state authorities had transformed the Fethullah Gülen Community into an influential social, political and economic actor, but the nature of its relationship with the Turkish state after 28 February 1997 radically changed.[57] After the National Security Council meeting, the then Prime Minister Necmettin Erbakan, the leader of the WP, was obliged to resign and the coalition government was dismantled. Parallel to the repression of political Islam, Islamic business came under close scrutiny, and the Fethullah Gülen Community suffered along with other Islamic groups.

Video cassettes of Fethullah Gülen addressing his community were leaked to TV channels in June 1999.[58] In one of them he could be heard saying 'the existing system is still in power. Our friends, who have positions in legislative and administrative bodies, should learn its details and be vigilant all the time so that they can transform it and be more fruitful on behalf of Islam in order to carry out a nationwide restoration. However, they should wait until the conditions become more favourable. In other words, they should not come out too early.'[59] According to Turkish laws, such words could be regarded as a threat to the secular Turkish republic, and in 1999 the Attorney General brought a lawsuit against Fethullah Gülen. Subsequently, the military has closely monitored the activities of the community, especially in the field of education.

Nevertheless, the Fethullah Gülen Community tries to keep its distance from any Islamic political party. Recai Kutan, the leader of the defunct Virtue Party and now leader of the Contentment Party, defended and supported Fethullah Gülen when his video cassettes were publicized. However, Fethullah Gülen did not make any comment regarding the closure of either the Welfare Party in 1998 or the Virtue Party in 2001. Although Fethullah Gülen met some politicians like Tansu Çiller and Bülent Ecevit, he carefully avoids meeting with the leaders of any Islamic political party. So it can be suggested that Asya Finans, as a special finance house operating according to Islamic norms and as an institution affiliated with the Fethullah Gülen Community, does not have an organic relationship with Islamic political parties. There is a separation rather than integration or uneasy coexistence between the Fethullah Gülen Community in general and Asya Finans in particular, and the Islamic political parties like the Welfare Party, the Virtue Party and the Contentment Party.

The 2002 general elections, however, may mark a major change in the nature of the relationship between Islamic parties and the special finance houses. The Islamic Justice and Development Party gained 34.3 per cent of the total votes and 363 seats out of 550 in the Parliament, thereby ending the long period of coalition governments (1991–2002). Following the elections, the JDP formed a majority government and obtained a vote of confidence on 18 November 2002. For the first time in Turkish politics, an Islamic party has formed a majority government. However, Recep Tayyip Erdoğan, leader of the JDP, maintains that his party is not an Islamic party but a 'conservative democratic' party. So it can be argued that, in the short run, the JDP most probably will avoid having close ties with Islamic groups. However, we will wait and see what kind of relationship between the JDP and special finance houses in general, and Asya Finans in particular, will emerge in the long run.

NOTES

1. Feroz Ahmad, 'Politics and Islam in Modern Turkey', *Middle Eastern Studies*, Vol. 27 No. 1, 1991, p. 3.
2. Ali Yasar Saribay, *Türkiye'de Modernlesme, Din ve Parti Politikasi: MSP Örnek Olayi* (Istanbul: Alan Yayincilik, 1985), pp. 72–3.
3. Ibid.
4. Ibid. p. 79.
5. Serif Mardin, 'Din Sorunu Yeni bir Duzeye Ulasirken', in Mumtazer Turkone and Tuncay Onder (eds), *Türkiye'de Din ve Siyaset* (Istanbul: Iletisim Yayinlari, 1991), p. 242.
6. Binnaz Toprak, 'The Religious Right', in Irvin C. Schick and Ertuğrul Ahmet Tonak (eds), *Turkey in Transition: New Perspectives*, (New York and Oxford: Oxford University Press, 1987), p. 226.
7. Binnaz Toprak, 'The State, Politics and Religion in Turkey', in Metin Heper and Ahmet Evin (eds), *State, Democracy and the Military: Turkey in the 1980s*, (Berlin and New York: De Gruyter, 1988), p. 128.
8. *Radikal*, 20 March 2001.
9. Ziya Öniş and Umut Türem, 'Business, Globalization and Democracy: A Comparative Analysis of Turkish Business Associations', *Turkish Studies*, Vol. 2 No. 2, Autumn 2001, p. 100.
10. Ziya Önis, 'The Political Economy of Islamic Resurgence in Turkey: the Rise of the Welfare Party in Perspective', *Third World Quarterly*, 18, 1997, p. 758.
11. Faik Bulut, *Tarikat Sermayesi 2: Yeşil Sermaye Nereye?*, 4th edition (Istanbul: Su Yayinlari, 1999), pp. 75–6.
12. Ayşe Buğra, *Islam in Economic Organizations* (Istanbul: TESEV Yayinlari, 1999), p. 17.
13. Bulut, *Tarikat Sermayesi 2*, p. 159.
14. Faruk Birtek and Binnaz Toprak, 'The Conflictual Agendas of Neo-Liberal Reconstruction and the Rise of Islamic Politics in Turkey: The Hazards of Rewriting Modernity', *Praxis International*, 13, July 1993, pp. 199–200.
15. Ibid. p. 192.
16. Öniş, 'The Political Economy', p. 750.
17. Ibid.
18. Birtek and Toprak, 'The Conflictual Agendas', p. 195.
19. Serif Mardin, *Din ve Ideoloji*, 5th edition (Istanbul: Iletisim Yayinlari, 1992), p. 149.
20. Birtek and Toprak, 'The Conflictual Agendas', pp. 195–6.
21. Ibid. p. 196.

22. Ümit Cizre Sakallioglu, 'Parameters and Strategies of Islam–State Interaction in Republican Turkey', *International Journal of Middle East Studies*, 28, 1996, p. 244.
23. Öniş, 'The Political Economy', p. 746.
24. Ibid. p. 751.
25. Haldun Gülalp, 'A Postmodern Reaction to Dependent Modernization: The Social and Historical Roots of Islamic Radicalism', *New Perspectives on Turkey*, 8, Fall 1992, p. 20.
26. For a comparison of TÜSİAD and MÜSİAD, see Ayşe Buğra, 'Class, Culture and State: An Analysis of Interest Representation by Two Turkish Business Asssociations', *International Journal of Middle East Studies*, No. 30, 1998, pp. 521–39.
27. Ömer Laçiner, 'Postmodern Bir Dini Hareket: Fethullah Hoca Cemaati', *Birikim*, 76, August 1995, p. 7.
28. For details of these meetings, see *Aksiyon*, 71, April 1996; and 167, February 1998.
29. Hulusi Turgut, 'Fethullah Gülen ve Okullari', *Yeni Yüzyil*, 15 October 1998.
30. Hulusi Turgut, 'Fethullah Gülen ve Okullari,' *Yeni Yüzyil*, 18 October 1998.
31. Hulusi Turgut, 'Fethullah Gülen ve Okullari,' *Yeni Yüzyil*, 25 October 1998.
32. See Hulusi Turgut, 'Fethullah Gülen ve Okullari,' *Yeni Yüzyil*, 31 October 1998 and 1 September 1998 for list of the awards which were obtained in International Science Olympiads.
33. Hulusi Turgut, 'Fethullah Gülen ve Okullari,' *Yeni Yüzyil*, 2 September 1998.
34. *Artihaber*, 30 May–5 June 1998, p. 24.
35. Fethullah Gülen, *Fasildan Fasila*, Vol. 3 (Izmir: Nil Yayinlari, 1997), p. 5.
36. Osman Özsoy, *Fethullah Gülen Hocaefendi ile Canli Yayinda Gündem* (Istanbul: Alfa Yayinlari, 1998), pp. 46–7.
37. Gülen, *Fasildan Fasila*, p. 5.
38. Bulut, *Tarikat Sermayesi 2*, p. 345.
39. Ersin Kalaycıoğlu, 'The Motherland Party: The Challenge of Institutionalization in a Charismatic Leader Party', *Turkish Studies*, Vol. 3 No.1, Spring 2002, p. 45.
40. They were called special finance houses instead of Islamic banks because it is constitutionally illegal to found banks named 'Islamic'.
41. Ugur Mumcu, *Rabita*, 22nd edition (Ankara: Umag Vakfi Yayinlari, 1998), p. 146.
42. From now on in this chapter, I will call it Family Finance.
43. Buğra, *Islam in Economic Organizations*, p. 29; Clement H. Moore, 'Islamic Banks and Competitive Politics in Arab World and Turkey', *Middle East Journal*, 44(2), Spring 1990, p. 248.
44. Buğra, *Islam in Economic Organizations*, p. 29.
45. Bulut, *Tarikat Sermayesi 2*, p. 73.
46. Birol Yeşilada, 'Türkiye'de Islamci Akimlar ve Suudi Bağlantisi', *Bilim ve Sanat*, No. 91, 1988, p. 23.
47. Bulut, *Tarikat Sermayesi 2*, p. 93.
48. Ibid. p. 98.
49. Ismail Özsoy, *Özel Finans Kurumlari* (Istanbul: Asya Finans Kurumu Yayini, 1997), pp. 160–1.
50. Fuad Al-Omar and Mohammed Abdel-Haq, *Islamic Banking: Theory, Practice and Challenges* (London and New Jersey: Zed Books, 1996), p. 15.
51. Philip Moore, *Islamic Finance: A Partnership for Growth* (London: Euromoney Publications, 1997), p. 240; Buğra, *Islam in Economic Organizations*, p. 30.

52. Özsoy, *Özel Finans Kurumlari*, p. 158; Moore, *Islamic Banks*, p. 235.
53. Fuat Keyman, 'Cultural Globalization and Turkey: Actors, Discourses, Strategies', Mediterranean Programme Bi-weekly Seminar, EUI, Florence, 9 March 2001.
54. Bulut, *Tarikat Sermayesi 2*, p. 234.
55. Özsoy, *Özel Finans Kurumlari*, pp. 212–15.
56. Asya Finans, *Annual Report*, 2000.
57. Owing to the policies of the Welfare Party during its stay in power as a coalition partner between June 1996 and June 1997, which were accompanied by some speeches by its deputies, the Welfare Party was regarded as being against the secular and democratic principles of the Turkish Republic. The Turkish military, which perceived itself as the guardian of the democratic and secular character of the Republic, and which tried to maintain its above-politics approach, could not remain silent. The military voiced its disturbance by the religious policies of the Welfare Party at the National Security Council meeting that was held on 27 February 1997. For details of this meeting, see Metin Heper and Aylin Güney, 'The Military and the Consolidation of Democracy: The Recent Turkish Experience', *Armed Forces and Society*, Vol. 26 No. 4, Summer 2000.
58. It was unknown who sent these cassettes but some journalists claimed that it was the military.
59. *Sabah*, 19 June 1999.

11

Aiyyu Bank Islami? The Marginalization of Tunisia's BEST Bank

Robert P. Parks

Tunisia is an unlikely case study in a volume on Islamic banking. Since its 1983 debut, the country's sole Islamic financial institution, Beit Ettamwil Saoudi Tounsi (BEST Bank) has managed to attract only a fraction more than half a percentage of all commercial banking deposits. In comparison to the development of Islamic banks in a variety of other states during the late 1970s and early 1980s, Tunisia's experience appears to be a stillborn venture condemned to languish in the financial periphery. Assuming a perfectly functioning market, BEST Bank's inability to capture a robust market share is counter-intuitive, given its nineteen-year operation and Tunisia's heritage as host to what was formerly the Arab World's most moderate, organized and vocal Islamist movement.

This chapter seeks to clarify the political barriers to the growth of Islamic banking in the Tunisian financial sector. Two factors are of particular salience: the threat posed by the continued resonance of political Islam in '*les couches populaires*', and that generated by the spectre of an autonomous private banking sector. While it is unclear which of the two is perceived as the most immediate threat, both propose alternative economic and political systems that might ultimately undermine the authority and strength of the current regime. By focusing on patterns by which the incumbent political elite has maintained its grip over the banking sector and its Islamic opposition, and the correlate effect this has had on BEST Bank, we can better underscore the political conditions that seem to play an important role in the success or failure of Islamic banking in the Muslim World.

THE POLITICS OF CONTEMPORARY BANKING: GLOBALIZATION AND ISLAMIC FINANCE VERSUS AUTARCHY AND PATRIMONIALISM

Over the last twenty years, international markets have liberalized, allowing capitalists and investors to more freely transfer their goods from one locale to another with a minimum of state intervention.[1] The currency of financial power has been upgraded, and capitalists can now pressure states to abandon parochial, introverted and byzantine systems of financial regulation or face the consequences of paltry foreign investment and reluctant currency exchanges. This has placed a premium on financial reform, and domestic capitalists, hitherto under the thumb of the state, can now join forces with globalizing interests to exert a dual interior and exterior pressure in favour of liberalization.

In tandem with a general trend toward globalization, Islamic banking, as a unique sub-set of modern finance, has gained momentum. Prior to 11 September 2001,[2] it was estimated that Islamic financial institutions held $US 200 billion in assets, with an annual growth rate of 10 to 20 per cent. Islamic finance is not unlike other forms of finance in that Islamic bankers are fundamentally interested in market power and capital. The distinguishing feature is that it rejects the notion of interest, or *riba*. As such, a number of innovative financing techniques have been developed to allow Islamic capital a role in the modern economy while avoiding risk and usury.[3] While there are four main types of financing operations, those considered the most legitimate by Islamic scholars, and perhaps the most profitable in the long-term, are the *mudaraba* or *musharaka* contracts.[4] Both rely on greater-than-average levels of transparency between the customer and bank, and so we might suppose that Islamic bankers compose the sub-set of bankers most interested in the implementation of what Henry and Springborg impishly dub 'the ten commandments of the Washington Consensus'.[5]

While authors critical of the Islamic finance project argue that, like other bankers, Islamic financiers are only interested in making a buck and will tend to keep out of politics,[6] an equally compelling argument is that, like other bankers, Islamic financiers will use their market power to change unfavourable political or economic situations. Such was the case in Latin America in the 1980s, when local financiers switched their allegiance from the ruling military regimes to the pro-democracy opposition, calculating that the opposition could better secure their financial interests in a more open and perhaps credible economic and political regime.[7]

With this in mind, we should want to determine to what degree Islamic bankers – perhaps in alliance with other pro-liberalization forces – can 'exercise influence either indirectly, reflecting structural power, or by real voice and regime change'.[8] The question is interesting and fits squarely into the emerging literature on the political economy of finance,[9] though it is not the aim of this chapter, which turns the question around. While the power of a given state to control its financial sector is variable, all states have the ability to control entry into the financial sector. If this is so, and Islamic banks pose a potential threat to the reigning political and economic order, then why allow them at all? More specifically, why would the Tunisian state allow an Islamic bank during the heyday of Islamist opposition, and subsequently, how has the state managed that sector?

There appears to be no cut-and-dry explanation. BEST's 1983 market entry was based upon relative short- and long-term political and economic utility, and a little money to grease the deal. More importantly, the case of BEST in the Tunisian financial marketplace mirrors the larger picture developed by the state's historical relationship with the private sector and with political Islam. The first part of this chapter probes the development of the private sector with a historical pointer, looking not only at the instruments the Tunisian political elite has used to maintain a strong public sector and acquiescent private capital,[10] but also the historical trends and rationales. Doing so, we see that the post-colonial order has replicated the colonial policy of a maintaining a concentrated banking sector, adding a twist of state domination.

More easily traceable, and the subject of the second part of this chapter, are the regime-imposed political constraints on BEST's marketplace development. When we transpose the political story of Tunisian government–Islamist relations onto the evolution of BEST Bank's marketshare, we see a remarkably consistent pattern: when relations are good, BEST Bank's coffers are full; when the relationship sours, BEST loses deposits. While this may be changing, as the regime becomes surer of its position and as the bank adopts a less active domestic policy, it has nevertheless been a defining feature of BEST Bank in the Tunisian financial landscape. Fitting Tunisia into the three categories presented in Clement M. Henry and Rodney Wilson's Introduction chapter, we can best approximate BEST's situation as one of 'separation and coward capital'.

DEPENDENT AND CONCENTRATED PUBLIC SECTOR FINANCING: THE COLONIAL LEGACY

Tunisia's banking system has always been concentrated. Though there is nothing inherently extraordinary about a highly concentrated public-sector-led banking system – especially in developing states[11] – what distinguishes Tunisia, and perhaps other formerly colonized polities, is the sharp continuity between the colonial and post-colonial era. Notwithstanding a 'Tunisification' of the colonial banking system in the 1960s, a few big banks with close connections to the political elite have remained the leitmotif of post-independence Tunisian banking. Just as France's Protectorate policy relied on financial power to keep local entrepreneurial politicians in check, Bourguiba and his successor have used financial ploys to pre-empt the emergence of an autonomous private sector that might be able to alter political and economic trajectories.

Pre-colonial, colonial and anti-colonial banking

The contemporary structure of the Tunisian banking sector and its political import becomes clear when we examine the impact finance had on Tunisia's early political history. During the era of Tunisia's Beys (1574–1957), capital was weak. While proto-capitalist industrial organization had begun in certain sectors,[12] insecure property rights prevented the incentives required to develop the large-scale agricultural production necessary to generate substantial capital surplus. In the absence of a capitalist class, a few families held local finance capital, hailing predominantly from the Livorno Jewish community. To pay the bills, the state was capable of levying taxes in the area immediately surrounding Tunis, but had to rely on a biannual show of force in order to get peripheral tribes to surrender part of their agricultural earnings.[13] The inability to collect stable and augmenting fiscal receipts, and the lack of a local financial market[14] that could supply state needs, would eventually entangle Tunisia in a confusing web of power, finance and interests, and played a part in the erosion of state sovereignty in the twenty years preceding the 1881 Treaty of Bardo, which formally established the Protectorate.[15]

The colonial banking system was characterized by a dearth of indigenous, much less onshore, banks. The banks that set-up shop were predominantly local branches of French institutions operating from Algiers, Marseilles or Paris.[16] Colonial Tunisian finance was governed by the Banque de l'Algérie[17] and dominated by a cartel of French bankers that quasi-exclusively financed large-scale French settler operations. Credit to small-scale French, Italian or Maltese settlers was scant, and even less was allocated to Tunisian entrepreneurs.[18] Several cooperatives[19] were created during this period to alleviate the small-credit financing problem, and though not formally limited to French nationals, little money ever went into Tunisian hands. In the absence of bank credit, Tunisian entrepreneurs were forced to rely on personal savings, familial net-works, or informal money-lenders who assigned interest rates ranging from 12 to 144 per cent per annum.[20] Attempts to set up financing for indigenous capitalist ventures were more or less discouraged by the French authorities and quickly marginalized by the bankers' cartel so as not to disrupt the colonial political economy.[21]

The 1922 incorporation of the Coopérative Tunisienne de Crédit (CTC), however, marked the beginning of a new era in Tunisian finance and politics. The CTC represented a group of Tunisois, Jerbian and Jewish capital-holders with the aim to provide credit and, by extension, market power to the nascent indigenous business class based on the model of French cooperatives. A pro-minent Tunisian businessman, M'Hamed Chenik, who was also an outspoken opponent of post-1929 Protectorate economic policy, headed it.[22] During the early 1930s, Chenik used his position as Indigenous Chamber spokesman in the Grand Conseil[23] in an attempt to extract economic guarantees that would help shelter Tunisian entrepreneurs from the deleterious effects of the Great Depression. Resident General Manceron, however, considered Chenik's growing autonomy a threat to the colonial order and, in an attempt to clip his wings, directed the Direction Générale des Finances to audit the CTC in January 1933. On 6 February, colonial journals published a series of articles alleging that the audit (which was still underway) had uncovered serious accounting irregularities and massive fraud.[24] On the same day, the colonial administration began to withdraw its deposits from the cooperative. In an effort to stem the hemorrhage of state funds, Chenik resigned the post of CTC managing director, appointing his close friend Boubaker el-Kholsi to the position.

Chenik responded politically on 13 April, when he virulently denounced the Protectorate's economic policy in the Grand Conseil. To the dismay of Resident General Manceron, the Chamber's agricultural delegate, Tahar Ben Ammar, supported Chenik. The two eventually rallied the entire Chamber to vote against French policy. Kraïem notes that: 'For the first time in the history of the Protectorate, the myth of collaboration was rejected by the Indigenous Chamber notables, so carefully chosen by the colonial administration; for the first time, the politics of the Protectorate government was systematically denounced in the Grand Conseil'.[25] Unlike the capitalists of 1980s South America, who used their portfolio assets and market power to force political change, however, the combined strength of the Chamber's capitalists did not have the structural power necessary to make the colonial regime shake and quake, and they lost the economic battle.

But while Chenik's position as spokesman for the Indigenous Chamber was subsequently revoked and he was later voted out of the Conseil, his struggle was not lost to Habib Bourguiba, then director of *l'Action Tunisienne*, a paper representing the radical wing of the Destour Party. On 8 February 1933, the opposition rag mounted a public defence of Chenik. Bourguiba's support would continue during the entire affair, marking the debut of his linkages with political finance. In repayment, Chenik funded the clandestine 2 February 1934 meeting in Ksar Hellal in which Bourguiba and the radical line split with the Destour to found the Neo-Destour.[26] Chenik continued to play an active role in the nationalist struggle, providing valuable financial assistance.[27] An ambitious Bourguiba realized, as Henry notes, that: 'However big a moral and religious explosion the charismatic leader ignited, he needed selective incentives – patronage grounded in financial obligations – in order to build an enduring organization' (Henry 1996: 168). And this political hook-up with finance played a crucial part in the transformation of the Neo-Destour from a radical wing of a moribund clique of Tunisois elites into a mass movement.

Post-colonial banking

Though known for his indifference toward economic affairs, Bourguiba was keenly aware of the powerful link between finance and politics as he consolidated his control over a newly independent Tunisia in 1956. The first strategy of the new regime would be to gain control over the central monetary authority, though Bourguiba was too politically weak in his first two years at the helm to accomplish much. Domestically, Bourguiba was tied up consolidating political control following the violent October 1955 to June 1956 inter-party conflict which sharply divided the Neo-Destour between Bourguiba's supporters and the radical Ben Youssef camp, and almost led to an all-out civil war. Internationally, events in neighbouring Algeria – where nationalists were fighting the French for their own independence – and the continued presence of French troops in the northern port of Bizerte, forced a reluctant Bourguiba to bide his time. By 1958, however, he had consolidated his domestic position enough to engage de Gaulle in a monetary battle, breaking the 1955 Franco-Tunisian convention.[28] Though certainly a dual reaction to solder the flight of nervous onshore French capital and the unilateral decision by the Banque de France to devalue the French franc, the passage of law No. 58-90 was an effort to more closely control the considerable source of power conferred by finance – a lesson taught by colonial authorities. The new law established the Banque Centrale de Tunisie (BCT), which would issue the sovereign and non-convertible Tunisian dinar according to the dictates of the Neo-Destour.

The financial strategy of the new Central Bank, governed by Bourguiba's close ally, Hedi Nouira, would be two-tiered. Because the state aimed to play a more active role in the distribution of credit (for developmental and patronage requirements), it needed a public sector avant-garde. The creation of the Société Tunisienne de Banque (STB) in 1957 and the Banque Nationale Agricole (BNA) in 1959 efficiently accomplished this. Equally important to the new strategy was 'a 'Tunisification' of the Protectorate's banking system that preserved old forms while ensuring state control'.[29] The term 'Tunisification' underscores the subtlety of the regime's strategy. Instead of full-out expropria-tion, the state gained veto-power on the boards through a series of buy-ins and buy-outs, and thus won effective control over the Union Internationale des Banques (UIB), the Banque Franco-Tunisiennne (BFT) and the Banque du Peuple (BP) by 1964. On at least one occasion, a colonial bank-owner refused to sell. As recounted to Henry by a former state inspector, the problem was solved when BFT's European owner, Monsieur Daninos, was given the choice to serve jail time for a trumped-up foreign-exchange transaction scandal or to sell his shares in exchange for safe passage out of the country.[30]

By 1963, Bourguiba and Nouira had created a banking system composed of a top-heavy public sector led by the STB and BNA – controlling a combined 45 per cent of total deposits, issuing 68 per cent of the loans (Bistolfi 1967: 241, cited in Henry 1996: 169) – and an acquiescent Tunisified private sector held on a tight leash, thus 'replicat[ing] France's colonial system of oligopolistic control'.[31] Subsequent BCT laws further strengthened the regime's regulative capacity. Noteworthy is law No. 67-51 of 7 December 1967, ceding the Central Bank autonomy over the Ministry of Finance in monetary affairs, and placing strict limitations and controls over commercial bank loans.[32] By the end of the decade, 'all banks, whether privately owned or parastatal, were so closely regulated that they effectively became state agencies'.[33]

Ostensibly, the regime's financial policy liberalized when Hedi Nouira received the Prime Minister's portfolio in 1971. A number of Tunisian-owned private sector start-ups received licences during this period. Notable was the 1976 incorporation of Banque Internationale Arabe de Tunisie (BIAT), which absorbed the ruminate holdings of Société Marseillaise de Crédit and the British Bank of the Middle East.[34] Co-founded by future Minister of Finance and party-man Mansour Moallah, Habib Bourguiba Jr, a consortium of Sfaxi businessmen, and Tunisian government participation, the bank was perceived to pose little threat to the public-sector oligopoly. The Crédit Foncier et Commercial de Tunisie (CFCT) was entirely bought-out by Rachid Ben Yedder, head of the family-owned Ben Yedder Group conglomerate, and later named AMEN Bank. Though 100 per cent privately-owned, AMEN Bank was no political liability, as the Ben Yedder Group (for a long time the bank's quasi-exclusive client)[35] had no distasteful political affinities and was in good standing with the regime. In any case, when the banks were given permission to open shop, the four public and parastatal banks – the STB, the BNA, the UIB and the Banque du Sud (BS) – controlled more than 70 per cent of commercial deposits, issued 85 per cent of all loans, and could bully their smaller private-sector competitors into submission.[36] The private sector posed no threat to the regime's financial politics.

ISLAMIC COMPETITION: THE POLITICAL ENTRY OF BEST BANK[37]

In the late 1970s, the Saudi-based Dallah al-Baraka Group (DAB) subsidiary, Al-Baraka Investment and Development Company (ABID), sought to expand its banking operations in the Middle East and North Africa. Part of the goal was to find new markets in which to sink the excess liquidity it earned from lucrative contracts during the oil bonanza. Tunisia, which by this time had shed its socialist orientation and was opening its banking sector to limited competition and Gulf money for development projects,[38] appeared a profitable venture.

While the official story is that BEST Bank entered the Tunisian market after a simple application by a pious Muslim businessman, entry was fraught with difficulties. In the years leading up to the request, the most vocal opposition had gradually shifted from 'Tissa-afril gauchistes'[39] to political Islamists[40] from the 'quartiers populaires', especially within the Bab Saadoun-Bab Souika-Halfaouine triangle.[41] This was particularly irksome to 'modernizing authoritarian'[42]

Bourguiba, who had spent a substantial part of his political career trying to sideline the '*obscurantistes*'. Though the imposition of the 1956 Civil Code Laws, the 1957 dissolution of the *Habous*,[43] and 1957 education-reform laws – which placed ez-Zitouna mosque and religious school under the tutelle of the state – moved him significantly closer to these goals, he was never successful in uprooting this element of Tunisian political society. The movement, whose organizational strength and popularity was spearheaded by the Mouvement de la Tendence Islamique (MTI) and led by the charismatically humble Rachid Ghannouchi, was beginning to pose a serious threat to the Neo-Destour/Parti Socialiste Destourien's[44] fifty-year domination of the political scene.

Given the PSD's penchant for controlled banking and a political monopoly and Bourguiba's rigidly anti-Islamist stance, one would have supposed a staunch opposition to BEST's market entry. But while the thought of a financial link between the MTI and an Islamic bank may have been threatening to the party, the real political struggle over BEST's entry was based on political positioning and economic necessity. DAB and ABID chairman Sheikh Saleh Kamel's request for a permit sparked intense debate within various factions of the ruling party, and it was not immediately obvious that he would receive his licence, as power-ful interests lined up in opposition to the idea of Islamic banking. In particular, Minister of Finance, Mansour Moallah, and the President's son and chairman of the Association Professionnelle des Banques de Tunisie (APBT), Habib Bourguiba Jr, opposed the venture.[45] Formally, the two argued that creating a new bank would undermine the concentration of the financial sector, and thus weaken the state's ability to coordinate financial investments (and perhaps to maintain the mechanisms of financial coercion).[46] As co-founders of BIAT, the two also had a personal stake in opposing the entry of BEST: the Islamic bank might siphon-off some of BIAT's steadily increasing market share, and thus erode the tax-free 2 per cent share in yearly net profits entitled to BIAT's founding members.[47]

Prime Minister Mohammed Mzali and on-and-off political ally Mohammed Sayah, then Minister of Public Works, supported the application and pushed hard to get Bourguiba's acquiescence. Both considered the controlled expansion of the banking sector a lucrative opportunity to fill state coffers and, by exten-sion, ministerial budgets. Ultimately, a scheme worked out by Sayah tipped the scale in Sheikh Saleh Kamel's favour. According to the agreement, DAB would participate in Bourguiba's pet project to clean and reclaim part of the Lac de Tunis for real-estate development.[48] In return, Salah was granted an offshore banking licence that would limit contact with the Tunisian public and, more importantly, the Islamist opposition. While it should be noted that the deal simply fit into Mzali's overall strategy to attract Gulf oil money to cover an in-creasingly populist supply-side economic policy, the Lac de Tunis Reclamation

Project also substantially increased both Sayah's ministerial budget and his standing in the aging President's eyes. In short, BEST bank provided Mzali and Sayah a substantial cash cow, all the while nurturing one of Bourguiba's long-time ambitions, and thus increasing their political leverage in the rumble-tumble succession politics of Carthage Palace.[49]

(An) institutional set-up (?)

While the political interests that transpired the deal may never be fully revealed, it is clear is that the Tunisian state planned to maintain a sure hold over the functioning of the new bank. This fitted within the state's overall strategy of maintaining a public-sector-heavy banking system. The new bank, Beit Ettamwil Saoudi Tounsi, was founded with a paid-up capital of $US 50 million: 80 per cent provided by ABID and the remaining 20 per cent evenly split between the Tunisian government and the National Social Security Office. Legally, the 20 per cent held by the state classified the new bank as a state-owned enterprise (SOE).[50] The law changed in July 1985, when the percentage was inflated to 34 per cent in an effort to lower the official number of SOEs and so as to placate international financial institutions,[51] but the effects remained basically the same,[52] at least in the executive board. According to company rules, the Tunisian government would have two seats[53] on the seven-seat board of directors, the remaining five going to the Saudis. With a voting power of 28.6 per cent, Tunisian board representation was to be greater than the state's parti-cipatory capital. This is hardly a surprise, however, as the 'set-up' merely replicated the Tunisification of foreign banks in the early 1960s, whereby the government maintained enough veto-power on the board of directors to make regular consultation a necessity in day-to-day operations.

Partial government ownership also lowered the monitoring costs of political surveillance. With managing directors nominated by the state, it was unlikely that an 'errant' loan would ever make it into political Islamist hands. Further, while ABID has a Unified Board for Sharia 'to guide all the institutions in the DBG financial services sector',[54] BEST's *shari'a* advisor was to be a government functionary from the Ministry of Religious Affairs. This would limit the ability of an upwardly-mobile *alem*[55] from Islam's private sector to engage in a costly price war that might ratchet up (or, in the Tunisian case, initiate) public debate over the role of Islamic banking in a Muslim country.[56] The Mufti of the Republic of Tunis, after all, is politically appointed.

BEST's offshore classification, as defined in law No. 76-63 of 12 July 1976, initially barred the bank from doing business in Tunisian dinars – thus denying it the right to do business with small-scale Islamically-minded investors/savers. According to the bank's statement of purpose, however, part of the aim was to provide Tunisians access to a licit form of banking. The law was amended specifically for BEST two years later (Law No. 85-51 of 6 December 1985), allowing offshore institutions the legal right to attract onshore deposits with a 1.5 per cent total deposit ceiling.[57] A slightly better deal, the 1.5 per cent pre-empted any real impact the bank might have on the financial sector, or significant relations it might establish with the popular Islamist community.

The pre-Ben Ali years: 1983–87

BEST had a rough go during its first four years, as the increasingly senile President blurred the divide between practising Muslims and the Islamist opposition, going so far as to declare: 'Eradicating the Islamist poison will be my last service to the Tunisian people'.[58] Unable to advertise for fear of being lumped into the Islamist camp, BEST instead emphasized its participatory banking techniques and project finance.[59] The fact that the regime was indiscriminately rounding up Islamist sympathizers and that BEST was once raided by security forces searching for evidence linking it with the MTI cast such a sombre shadow over the bank that any pious Tunisian considering opening a *halal* account probably thought twice.[60] Indeed, between 1985 and 1987, savings account deposits stagnated at an average $1.27 million per annum (Figure 11.1), and in 1986 the bank's onshore deposits represented a pitiful 0.2 per cent of total deposits. Although this share increased modestly over time, by 2000 it still only amounted to 0.8 per cent.

Figure 11.1: Savings account trends with BEST Bank

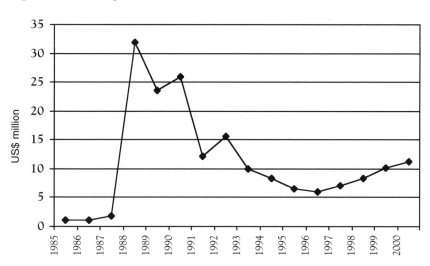

Source: BEST Bank *Annual Reports.*

Post-Bourguiba fat days

In the twilight hours of 7 November 1987, Prime Minister Zine Abdine Ben Ali convinced Bourguiba's doctor to sign an affidavit declaring the President mentally and physically incapacitated. And so the octogenarian was overthrown in what would be later dubbed the 1987 'constitutional coup'. Ben Ali announced that he intended to reconcile the people in order to forge a new and more liberal Tunisia. One of his first moves was to release the estimated three thousand Islamist political prisoners that had been arrested in Bourguiba's final days in power. He also announced the abolition of the presidency-for-life and promised free, multi-party elections to be negotiated in the context of a National Pact.

BEST appears to have profited in this liberalized environment. The percentage of total deposits in the onshore banking sector increased from 0.2 per cent in 1986 to 0.35 per cent in 1989. Using contract intensive money (CIM)[61] as an indicator of regime/financial credibility, during the same period we see an augmentation in total banking system deposits, indicating an increased confidence in the overall system. Between 1986 and 1989, CIM jumped by 2.72 per cent, the largest recorded hike since the dismantling of the cooperative experiment in 1970. It is probable that the decade of heightened religiosity through oppositional discourse, in concert with new political freedoms, impelled many Tunisians to shift their money from under the mattress and into the *halal* vaults of BEST Bank. Unfortunately, it is hard to determine how much of the increase came from money in the mattress and how much was simply a shift from *haram* to licit accounts. Dividing the difference between the 1986 and 1989 BEST onshore/total deposits ratio with the difference between the 1986 and 1989 CIM scores, it is possible to impute a *very rough* estimate of BEST's input in the growth in CIM.[62] Our 'jimmied' formula attributes 5.51 per cent of the 2.72 per cent jump to BEST. This vastly outmatches BEST's percentage of total banking sector deposits, and perhaps buttresses the claim that the 1986–89 mini-spike in both BEST's percentage of total deposits and CIM was due an infusion of 'pious' cash into the system. More telling, savings account deposits jumped from $US 1.8 million in 1987 to $31.9 million in 1988.[63]

While many observers noted that Ben Ali's National Pact appeared to mark the end of the authoritarian period,[64] the April 1989 Presidential and Legislative elections hinted that the initial post-Bourguiba exuberance might have been ill-placed. Single candidate Ben Ali won the presidency by 99.27 per cent of the popular vote. Due to a new majoritarian parliamentary electoral law, and a significant number of voting irregularities, the PSD (renamed the Rassemblement Constitutionnel Démocratique (or RCD), was able to capture all 141 National Assembly seats. Nevertheless, the Islamists did well. According to various sources, Islamists running as 'independents'[65] won between 14.5 and 24 per cent of the national vote, scoring as high as 30 per cent in the major cities.[66]

Cynical electoral engineering did not sit well with Islam's democrats, and the anticipated honeymoon between Ben Ali and the Islamists began to unravel. Tensions mounted in the days leading up the June 1990 local elections – which the opposition unilaterally boycotted. Tunisia's initial decision to support allied troops in expelling the Iraqis from Kuwait a few months later, gave the MTI/an-Nahda an excellent opportunity to mount a show of force. The mass protests, if not supporting Saddam Hussein, were against an American presence in the Gulf, and successfully pressured the regime to backtrack on its prior pro-American stance. On 17 February 1991, the Bab Souika RCD offices were raided and burned in a commando-style operation that the government attributed to an-Nahda, seriously injuring one and killing another security guard.[67] The attack provided the regime with the international and domestic cover it needed to round up, detain and try thousands from the Islamist opposition. The divorce was final.

This appears to have seriously affected BEST Bank. While claims were made in 1990 that BEST might be able attract between 3 and 4 per cent of household deposits for a market share of 7 to 8 per cent of total banking system deposits (Barbelesco 1990: 51),[68] the indicators show a decline in BEST's overall growth between 1990 and 1995. Indeed, savings deposit accounts hemorrhaged. As seen in Figure 11.1, these accounts declined in the 1990s from $US 25.9 million in 1990 to $11.24 million in 1999, or a 60.5 per cent total decrease. The sharpest year-to-year decline occurred during the peak of anti-Islamist repression, between 1990 and 1991, when accounts slipped by 53.9 per cent to $US 12.2 million. Part of this might be attributed to regional financial insecurity resulting from the Gulf War and/or mounting problems in neighbouring Algeria. Still, the depreciation also closely follows the regime's turnaround in policy towards an-Nahda, and the overall decrease in civil and political liberties. Replicating their behaviour during the Bourguiba years, pious Tunisians either preferred to put their money back in the mattress, as illustrated by a 1.83 percentage drop in CIM between 1989 and 1991, or to forego the interdiction on *riba* altogether, transferring the capital back into regular deposits.

Castrated finance: post-1991 operations

What is sure is that, by 1991, BEST gains evaporated alongside the post-1987 political and civil liberties. Since, the regime has reverted to its old tactics of repression supplemented by a healthy dose of public-sector bullying. The an-Nahda leadership has been decapitated, and many of its supporters arrested or in exile. The legal and secular opposition, while permitted, seems to have fallen into a corporatist trap, and has no more autonomy than the national professional or interest organizations.[69] In recent years, most of the important opposition-party meetings have degenerated into scraps between the pro-RCD camps and those aspiring for more autonomy.[70] Specific leaders who begin to develop autonomy have their wings clipped. Perhaps imitating French tactics in quashing M'Hamed Chenik, or Bourguiba's strategy to convince Monsieur Daninos to sell the BFT, it is striking how many aspiring opposition members cave in to economic pressure or are charged with economic crimes. Recent notable victims are Mansour Moallah[71] and the BIAT; Moncef Cheikhrouhou,[72] former BEST Bank manager (1983–93) and heir to the Es-Sabah Media Group; Ismail Sahbani[73] of the Union Générale des Travailleurs Tunisiens; Ismail Boulalyah[74] of the Mouvement Démocratique Socialiste; and Moncef Marzouki[75] of the Conféderation Nationale des Droits de l'Homme. The stories are countless, but the trend is the same and the name of the game is financial coercion and subterfuge.

To boot, the regime has tried to reinvigorate the public-sector banks. In 1986, the four public-sector banks held 63 per cent of all deposits, distributing 78 per cent of the credit.[76] Even after the 1970s decade of private-sector reforms, the state still held a 38.4 per cent stake in the banking sector.[77] But between 1986 and 1994, the public sector's hold over banking became less apparent. The combined strength of the STB and the BNA had been chiselled by 1994, perhaps due to the 1987 Banking Sector Reforms. Though still significant, their combined weight in total deposits had fallen to 34.4 per cent, dispersing but 40.5 per cent of the total credit.[78] And only half of the bank presidents, fifteen of the twenty-six, were named by the state.[79] By 2000, total deposits had fallen to 28 per cent.[80] Much of the recorded loss is due to the substantial and continued rise in AMEN Bank,[81] BIAT[82] and Union Bancaire pour le Commerce et l'Industrie (UBCI)[83] activities. To counter this trend, in late 1999 the BCT announced that it favoured the merger of the STB with public-sector Banque de Développement Économique de Tunisie (BDET) and Banque Nationale de Développement Touristique[84] (BNDT) and anxiously awaited more public-sector mergers.

BEST seems to have slowly adapted to this new environment, quietly continuing its participatory banking techniques and project finance, while downplaying its Islamic character. It is actively working to attract business investments, as well as diversifying its own operations outside of the immediate banking sector. Equity participation increased absolutely and relatively during the 1990s, as Table 11.1 shows, although the bank's total assets declined over the period when measured in terms of dollars. *Murabaha* receivables accounted for most of the assets in the early years of the bank, but by the mid- to late 1990s, receivables from instalment sales and leasing had become much more significant.

The asset composition of the bank is reflected in the figures for bank income shown in Table 11.2. Much of the bank's income derives from international trading activities, but *murabaha* income from importers, the mainstay of the

Table 11.1: Assets of BEST Bank, $ million

	1992	1995	1998	1999	2000
Murabaha	70.656	18.316	19.162	22.130	12.506
Installment sales	26.082	30.866	24.445	19.412	14.545
Leasing	24.750	34.232	37.798	16.963	13.379
Equity participations	8.942	10.128	12.353	12.191	13.786
Net fixed assets	6.025	5.483	4.513	4.439	4.147
Total assets	136.455	99.025	98.271	75.135	58.363

Source: BEST Bank *Annual Reports.*

Table 11.2: Income of BEST Bank, $ million

	1990	1995	1997	1998	1999	2000
Trade *murabaha*	20.810	1.500	1.551	2.398	2.035	1.894
Installment sales	1.415	2.192	2.086	1.691	2.201	1.630
Leasing	3.083	2.937	3.112	2.889	2.945	3.239
Investment deposits	1.173	1.766		1.342	1.342	1.342
Commodity *murabaha*	0.889		1.131	0.946	0.864	1.670
Share dividends	0.277	0.302	0.335	0.594		
Capital gains		1.071	1.228	0.274		
Total income	27.647	9.768	9.443	10.134	9.387	9.775

Source: BEST Bank *Annual Reports.*

bank in its early years, has declined dramatically in importance. Income from leasing and instalment sales has become much more significant in the mid- to late 1990s. Commodity *murabaha* largely reflects income from the purchase and sale of oil and agricultural commodities. Share dividends and capital gains are relatively unimportant, given the limited equity participation by the bank, and it is evident that the efforts in recent years to increase equity participation have not yielded the bank much income.

Demographically, the number and location of its branches and cash machines[85] do not reveal a bank actively seeking to attract simple citizen-depositors. BEST bank currently has four branch offices, two of which were opened in 1988 – the peak of post-Bourguiba liberalism. That year, the bank was given permission to open branch offices in Sfax and the Tunis medina – symbolically at the base of ez-Zitouna mosque and well within the tourist zone. Its 1989 plans to expand to Sousse and Kairouan – Islam's 'fourth' holiest city – were 'indefinitely post-poned'[86] following a change of heart in Carthage.[87] A Kairouan-location permit would simply be too politically symbolic. Much more innocuous were the 1995 requests to transfer branch office locations from downtown Sfax to the New Sfax Business District, and from the unused Le Kram location to the new Tunisois business district at al-Bouhaira[88] – built incidentally in the area of Lac de Tunis that Sheikh Saleh Kamel helped to develop. The permits were issued, if not encouraged, as both locations are in districts with limited 'popular' circulation.

In terms of advertisement, BEST is off the radar. Public advertisements similar to those vaunting the merits of the BNA on modern flat-screened TVs at the customs exit in Carthage International, or the colourful and animated billboards touting BIAT that are liberally scattered across Tunis, simply do not exist in the case of BEST. The main branch on Avenue Hedi Chaker, sandwiched between SONY and AMINA Insurance, looks like any other office building, only discreetly posting its name in Arabic cursive just above the entrance. Even its interior is harmless. Discounting an Islamic austerity and the green-and-black colouring, the main lobby has no lines or passages from the Koran or *Hadith*, as do the banks depicted in Michel Galloux's study of Egyptian Islamic Banks.[89] Finally, unlike the media productions organized by the Islamic banks of Egypt and elsewhere, BEST very discreetly donates an annual sum of illicit profit to what is oddly labelled the 'General Welfare in Tunisia', presumably the Banque Nationale de Solidarité.[90] Given its seemingly thorough efforts at self-effacement, it is little wonder that many Tunisians remain oblivious to its operations.[91]

In return for its apparent discretion and self-censorship, the state has allowed BEST to branch out of the immediate banking sector, into insurance, leasing and investment. In 1985, it got the go-ahead to create BEST Re, an affiliated insurance company. It appears profitable, and has since expanded operations to Malaysia, Lebanon and Senegal. In December 2000, it announced plans to dually float shares on the Tunisian[92] and Paris Bourse,[93] and in April 2001 was awarded the privatization tender of eighth ranked state insurance company, Lloyd Tunisien, in a TD 5 million bid.[94] The bank also received permission to create BEST Invest in 1995[95] and BEST Leasing in 1998,[96] showing that the government regards current operations favourably. These new subsidiaries have contributed greatly to BEST's recovery since *année noire* 1995, and substantially inflate its 0.77 per cent of total banking-sector deposits.

BEST AND THE HAREM

This chapter has shown that the stagnation of BEST Bank is due to political considerations. Tunisia's pre-colonial inability to cope with private finance, and the lessons pulled from colonial financial manipulation engrained a powerful template in the imaginations of its post-independence rulers. Caught between the Tunisian regime's strategy to maintain a concentrated and public-sector-dominated banking system, and its concurrent desire to crush a popular Islamist opposition, BEST simply did not have the manoeuvering room necessary to attract a large domestic clientele in the early 1990s.

The market gains scored during the 1987–90 liberal period proved to be temporary, neutering any political leverage the bank might have enjoyed in a more permissive environment. BEST currently has so camouflaged its presence from the Tunisia public that the regime seems happy to let it operate on the financial fringes. In Tunisia, the question to ask is not how BEST Bank's Islamic bankers might press for further liberalization, but rather how further liberalization might help BEST Bank out of its rut. While recent trends show it gathering some strength, and that the regime might be finally liberalizing its banking sector, the chances that BEST will rival the Islamic banks of Cairo, Kuwait City or Doha are nil in the immediate future. Until then, like the eunuch, BEST will be chained in the regime's financial system harem, bitterly realizing that it can never enjoy the sweet fruit of a substantial market share.

NOTES

1. Barbara Stallings, *Global Change, Regional Response: the New International Context of Development* (Cambridge: Cambridge University Press, 1995).
2. Ibrahim Warde discusses post-September 11th Islamic finance in detail in Chapter 2.
3. For an overview of the different Islamic financial operations, their mechanisms, and the evaluation of these different techniques by the various Islamic *ulama*, see Frank E. Vogel and L. Hayes III, *Islamic Law and Finance: Religion, risk, and return* (The Hague: Kluwer Law International, 1998).
4. A *mudaraba*, or profit-sharing contract, is formed when a bank finances a project in return for a pre-arranged share of the profit. Under this contract, the bank is responsible for all losses. *Musharaka*, or partnership contracts, are akin to equity financing. Here, the bank agrees to pre-negotiated share of the profit but shares the losses. Both require high levels of transparency between the bank and potential borrower.
5. Clement M. Henry and Robert Springborg, *Globalization and the Politics of Economic Development in the Middle East* (Cambridge: Cambridge University Press, 2001).
6. See, for example, Timur Kuran, 'The Discontents of Islamic Economic Morality', *The American Economic Review*, 86(2), 1996.
7. See Sylvia Maxfield, *Governing Capital: International Finance and Mexican Politics* (Ithaca, NY: Cornell University Press, 1990); Jeffrey A. Frieden, *Debt, Development, and Democracy: Modern Political Economy and Latin America* (Princeton, NJ: Princeton University Press, 1991).
8. Clement M. Henry, 'Islamic Financial Movements: Midwives of Political Change in the Middle East?', paper presented at the 2001 Annual Meeting of the American Political Science Association, San Francisco, 30 August–2 September 2001.
9. For more on the role of finance in politics and vice versa, see Karl Polanyi, *The Great Transformation: The Political and Economic Origins of Our Time* (Boston: Beacon

Press, 1944); Alexander Gerschenkron, *Economic Backwardness in Historical Perspective* (Cambridge, MA: Harvard University Press, 1962); Charles Kindleberger, *Power and Money* (New York: Basic Books, 1970); Chalmers Johnson, *MITI and the Japanese Miracle: The Growth of Industrial policy: 1925–1975* (Stanford, CT: Stanford University Press, 1982); and John Zysman, *Governments, Markets, and Growth: Financial Systems and the Politics of Industrial Change* (Ithaca, NY: Cornell University Press, 1983). For a more political analysis, see Maxfield, *Governing Capital*; Frieden, *Debt, Development*; Jeffrey A. Winters, 'Power and the Control of Capital', *World Politics*, 46(3), 1994; Meredith Woo-Cumings (ed.), *The Developmental State* (Ithaca, NY: Cornell University Press, 1999).

10. These elements of Tunisian financial politics are clearly elucidated in Clement M. Henry, *The Mediterranean Debt Crescent: Money and Power in Egypt, Morocco, Tunisia, and Turkey* (Gainesville, FL: University Press of Florida, 1996). For a comparison with the MENA, see Clement M. Henry, 'The Financial Arms of Industrial and Political Activity', paper presented at the international conference 'The Role of the Business Sector in Economic and Political Change', Tunis, 30 August–2 September 1998.

11. Both Gerschenkron and Zysman, for example, have commented on the potential efficacy of this sort of arrangement.

12. Chechiyya (more commonly referred to as the fez) manufacturing appears to have been one important exception. For more on this subject, see Lucette Valensi, 'Islam et capitalisme. Production et commerce des chéchias en Tunisie et en France au 18ème et 19ème siècles', *Revue d'histoire moderne et contemporaine*, 16, July–September 1969, pp. 376–400.

13. See Dalenda Larguèche, 'The *Mahalla*: The Origins of Beylical Sovereignty in Ottoman Tunisia during the Early Modern Period', *The Journal of North African Studies*, 6(1), 2001, pp. 105–116.

14. Ahmed Bey, who was in power from 1837 until 1855, attempted to create a more modern financial system by founding Tunisia's first Central Bank. The short-lived 'Ahmed Bey Bank' (1847–52) aimed to achieve monetary independence from the Ottoman Empire and insulation from shortages in northern Mediterranean currencies. Issuing paper currency with a value based on local calculations, the 'bank' tried to create a veritable capital market favouring the circulation of goods and capital. The measure was unpopular amongst both local and foreign capital-holders, who resented the 4 per cent exchange fee on metal money, and who in any case felt the bills represented a false value. (Source: Mohammed Lazhar Gharbi, *Banques et Crédit au Maghreb (1847–1914)*, Thèse d'État (Tunis: Université de Tunis I, 1998), pp. 26–36.

15. Mohammed es-Sadok Bey, who was in power from 1859 until 1882, was forced to borrow from international markets on at least two noteworthy occasions – 1863 and 1865. In both instances, then Prime Minister Khaznadar colluded with the French underwriter, Baron Erlanger, to pocket a substantial portion on the loans. Inefficiency, corruption, as well as deeper structural problems, eventually undermined the regime's financial credibility, and the Beylic fell into international receivership in 1869. With the Congress of Berlin, France was given the understanding that Tunisia belonged to its sphere of influence. Eleven years later, France invaded and in 1881 forced the Bey to sign the Treaty of Bardo, establishing the Protectorate. For a more

nuanced picture of this era, see Jean Ganiage, *Les origins du protectorate français en Tunisie: 1861–1881* (Paris: Presses Universitaires de France, 1959). For a more political approach, see Henry, *The Mediterranean Debt Crescent*.

16. These included the Banque Franco-Tunisienne (1879), the Société Marseillaise de Crédit (1879), the Banque de Tunisie (1884), the Comptoir National d'Escompte de Paris (1894), the Compagnie Algérienne de Crédit et de Banque (1900), Crédit Foncier d'Algérie et de Tunisie (1907), Crédit Lyonnais (1912), the Société Générale (1912) and the Banque Industrielle de l'Afrique du Nord (1923). The Italians tried to force entry into the market in 1924, with the dual creation of Banca Italiana de Credito and the Banque Italo-Française, but never achieved a strong foothold and were dismantled following the Second World War.

17. Original efforts to create a French-dominated Tunisian Central Bank similar to the Banque de l'Algérie were stalled in an eighteen-year battle between the owners of various French banks and their respective clienteles. The idea was shelved altogether in 1904 when the Banque de l'Algérie was designated as the Tunisian Central Bank. The bank changed its name to the Banque de l'Algérie et de la Tunisie following nationalization in 1949. For more on the battle of the banks, see Gharbi, *Banques et Crédit*, pp. 684–780.

18. Ridha Gouia, *Les investissements en Tunisie et leurs effets sur la croissance économique de 1881 à nos jours* (Thèse de l'État: Université de Paris X, 1976).

19. The Caisse Mutuelle de Crédit Agricole de Tunisie, the Banque Populaire Française de Tunisie, the Crédit Hôtelier de Tunisie and the Caisse Mutuelle de Crédit Immobilier are the most notable.

20. Islamic financing techniques, as employed in the contemporary era, appear to have been inexistent during the colonial period, and the use of interest was largely the norm. Records show that, though money-lending was dominated by ethnic, regional or religious minorities, such as the Livorno Jews or the Le Kef-based Kabyle 'colporteur credit ring', a number of Sunni religious leaders actively borrowed or loaned with interest. A prominent example is the case of marabout landowner 'Ali Ben Aïssa, who is said to have amassed his enormous estate through usurious loans on mortgaged lands. Religious figures and organizations also borrowed with interest. In the late 1890s, the Nefta-based Qadariyya (religious brotherhood) was forced to take out extensive interest-bearing loans to cover a sudden shock in its revenues. Unable to repay, it fell into financial ruin several years later. In some cases, Muslims worked with Jews to create a dense network of credit. The rural-based Bayyaa' (Muslims) worked with Jewish women (dallala) who served as female-sex intermediaries for credit operations with Muslim women in order to gain greater market penetration. For more on the Qadariyya's fall into ruin, see Tlili Ajili, 'Al wazhi'a at-toroqi bi al-Jarid fi an-nosif ath-thaani min al qarin at-taas'a 'ashar', *Revue d'histoire maghrébine*, 16, 1994, pp. 75–6. For more on the various religious and ethnic money-lenders operating in Tunisia in the colonial era, see Gharbi, *Banques et Crédit*, pp. 812–25.

21. As was the case of the Crédit Foncier de Tunisie, established in 1906 and bought up by the cartel in 1908 (Henry, *The Mediterranean Debt Crescent*, p. 168).

22. An interesting analogy might be made between M'Hamed Chenik and the Egyptian financier Tala'at Harb who founded the Bank Misr two years earlier, in 1922. For more on the subject, see Mary Jane Deeb, 'Bank Misr and the Emergence of the

Local Bourgeoisie in Egypt', in Elie Kedourie (ed.), *The Middle Eastern Economy: Studies in Economics and Economic History* (London: Frank Cass, 1976); E. Davis, *Challenging Colonialism: Bank Misr and Egyptian Industrialization, 1924–1941* (Princeton, NJ: Princeton University Press, 1983).

23. The Grand Conseil was the Protectorate's bicameral consultative organ 'representing' French settler and indigenous interests to the Resident General.
24. Abdesslem Ben Hamida, 'Les bourgeois tunisiens face à la crise économique de 1929', *Cahiers de la Méditerranée*, 45, 1992. Translated by Robert P. Parks.
25. Mustapha Kraïem, *Pouvoir colonial et mouvement national. La Tunisie des années trente* (Tunis: Éditions Alif, 1990), pp. 158–9, cited in Ben Hamida, 'Les bourgeois tunisiens', p. 134.
26. While revisionist Neo-Destourien history generally treats Chenik's role in the Ksar Hellal meeting as opportunistic, Chenik's distaste for the Destourian reformist line, and support for a more engaged nationalistic economic policy, was noted early-on in Charles-André Julien's critical essay on French North African colonialism (Charles-André Julien, *L'Afrique du Nord en Marche: Nationalisme Musulmans et Souveraineté Française* (Paris: Julliard, 1952), p. 122. Notwithstanding Julien's reference, the French-language literature has largely left this aspect of the Tunisian struggle for independence alone. Safia Mestiri-Chabbi (Chenik's granddaughter), however, has begun a more in-depth study of the role of Chenik in the struggle for independence, and is in the process of preparing a Université de Reims dissertation on the subject.
27. Perhaps more important than the finance capital to fund the Neo-Destour, Chenik's support included an extensive network of middle-class handicraftsmen and merchants that would ultimately provide Bourguiba with his mass following. Special thanks go to Safia Mestiri-Chebbi for this insight.
28. The convention stipulated that the Tunisians should continue to subscribe to the Banque de l'Algérie et de la Tunisie and its monetary policy, including that of parity between the French and Tunisian francs.
29. Henry, *The Mediterranean Debt Crescent*, p. 168.
30. Ibid. p. 169.
31. Ibid.
32. Law No. 67-51 of 7 December 1967 had a dual purpose. While it achieved Nouira's aim of consolidating the Central Bank's position in the Tunisian political economy, it also placed checks on Super Minister Ahmed Ben Salah's ambitious cooperative program, which was deemed by many of the Tunisois political elite as an increasing threat to the extant political order. Many felt Ben Salah's cooperative experiment aimed to create a 'state within a state'. Such a mechanism would too greatly empower Ben Salah in any kind of post-Bourguiba struggle for succession. By placing the Central Bank in an autonomous position, the law regulated the scope to which Ben Salah might use the Ministry of Finance to create his own political and economic clientele.
33. Henry, *The Mediterranean Debt Crescent*, p. 170.
34. Hachemi Alaya, *Monnaie et financement en Tunisie* (Tunis: CERES Éditions, 1995).
35. AMEN Bank's marriage with the Ben Yedder Group would prove to be a temporary liability when the BIAT convinced the Central Bank to modernize the banking system by forcing banks to diversify their clientele. In 1987, a BCT circular limited

loans to a single client to 10 per cent of the bank's capital. Though the level was increased to 40 per cent in 1991, it nevertheless temporarily strained AMEN Bank's growth (Henry, *The Mediterranean Debt Crescent*, p. 202).

36. Henry, *The Mediterranean Debt Crescent*, p. 177.

37. Analysis of BEST Bank is largely drawn from numerical inferences and information published in the *Annual Reports* in circulation. Repeated attempts to talk with bank officials were refused – because the direction did not feel that the author's government-issued research clearance, 'the role of private sector actors in the Tunisian political economy', included BEST's operations. Instead, the author was told to refer to recent copies of BEST's *Annual Reports* and to the Central Bank. Unfortunately the author was told that BEST did not have *Annual Reports* dating before 1997 on hand. Neither did the Central Bank library, which contained only the 1990–92 and 1998–2000 *Reports*. Of course, none of the limited quantitative information available could answer the innocuous qualitative questions the author had submitted in writing (the only way they said they would accept the questions), and bank officials knew this. Perhaps the apprehension follows confusion over the various Al Baraka groups listed in US Executive Order 13224, especially the 7 November 2001 addendum, and the author's American citizenship. Alternatively, it possibly reveals that BEST Bank is not a private-sector bank at all, but in reality a state-owned enterprise. Most plausibly, it reflects the political climate of suspicion within which BEST has had to manage its operations for the last two decades.

38. In addition to the creation of BIAT and AMEN Bank, the state issued licenses for a number of joint-venture development banks during this period. Especially note-worthy are the Société Tuniso-Saoudienne d'Investissement et de Développement (1981), the Banque Tuniso-Koweïtienne de Développement (1981), the Banque de Coopération du Maghreb Arabe (1981), the Banque Tunisio-Qatari d'Investissement (1982) and the Banque de Tunisie et des Emirats d'Investissement (1982).

39. 'Tissa Afril', or the University of Tunis located on Avenue 9 Avril, had been for a long time a hotbed of leftist criticism. Located due south of the Medina, spontaneous or organized uprisings eventually induced the regime to split up the university system into several smaller faculties located on the outskirts of the city.

40. As in other parts of the Arab World, the rise of Tunisian political Islam can be partly traced to the regime's desire to sideline radical leftists. While Bourguiba may not have actively played a role in the origins of the Mouvement de la Tendence Islmai-que, there is speculation that the Parti Socialiste Destourien did. See Mohammed Kerrou, 'Politiques de l'islam en Tunisie,» in Ahmed Benani, Moncef Djaziri and Hilary Kilpatrick (eds), *Islam et changement social* (Lausanne: Éditions Payot Lausanne, 1998).

41. These neighbourhoods are of special significance to the Neo-Destour's history as a political and social movement – so much so that Bourguiba referred to the zone as the '*souret el-bled*', or 'umbilical of the country'. The fact that these quarters had become, by the early 1980s, a hotbed of Islamist opposition provoked the ire of Bourguiba and the Neo-Destour. For more on the political and symbolic role of these neighbourhoods, see Olivier Feneyrol, 'L'État à l'épreuve du local. Le réaménage-ment du quartier «Bab Souiqa-Halfaouine» à Tunis (1983–1992)', *Monde Arabe Maghreb Machrek*, 157, July–September 1997, pp. 58–68.

42. This phrase is taken from Clement M. Henry, 'From Bourguiba to Ben Ali: the Modernization of Benevolent Development', paper presented at the Institut d'Études Politiques d'Aix-en-Provence colloquium 'Habib Bourguiba: La Trace et l'Héritage', 27–29 September 2001.

43. Also referred to as *Waqf*, *Habous* are quasi-non-transferable properties (buildings, agricultural lands, and so on) belonging to specific religious foundations. Profits generated from these properties go directly to the foundations, thus conferring them considerable autonomy from outside interference. In much of the Maghreb as well as the Mashrek, religious schools rely on *Habous* revenues to function. Bourguiba's attack on the *Habous* represented the need to create a larger property market, as well as an attack on religious instruction.

44. The Neo-Destour officially changed its name to the Parti Socialiste Destourien (PSD) following its seventh conference on 8 November 1964, in order to reflect a shift in economic orientation.

45. Henry, *The Mediterranean Debt Crescent*, p. 188.

46. Interview with a former high-ranking Tunisian official privy to the in-house debate, 10 July 2002.

47. *Maghreb Weekly Monitor*, 109, 26 June 2001, p. 17.

48. Henry, *The Mediterranean Debt Crescent*, p. 188.

49. For more on the politics of succession, see Tahar Belkhodja, *Les trois décennies Bourguiba* (Tunis: Publisud, 1999).

50. Before 1985, Tunisian law defined any company with a 10 per cent share of state capital as an SOE. The definition was altered in July 1985 to describe only those firms where the state's share of investment exceeded 34 per cent and again in February 1989 to 50 per cent.

51. See Abdelsatar Grissa, 'The Tunisia State Enterprises and Privatization Policy', in I. William Zartman (ed.), *Tunisia: the Political Economy of Reform* (Boulder, CO: Lynne Rienner, 1991). For a more up-to-date discussion on this point, see Robert King, 'Regime Type, Economic Reform, and Political Change in Tunisia', in Yahia Zoubir (ed.), *North Africa in Transition in the 1990s* (Gainesville, FL: University Press of Florida, 1999).

52. Clement M. Henry assumes, for instance, 'that a 20 per cent stake puts the state in full control' (Henry, 'Islamic Financial Movements', p. 8).

53. While Tunisian representation appears to have been based on a variety of criteria, representatives have been members of the ruling party.

54. http://www.albaraka.com/english/corporate/philosophy.html

55. *Alem* (plural: *ulama*) is a religious scholar.

56. In contrast to the Egyptian experience. See Michel Galloux, *Finance islamique et pouvoir politique: le cas de l'Égypte moderne* (Paris: Presses Universitaires de France, 1997), pp. 37–52.

57. While created specifically for BEST Bank, the passage of Law No. 85-51 was not an altogether altruistic act. In early 1985, a financial reassessment of the Lac de Tunis Development Project revealed that the original estimates could not cover the plan. Government efforts to borrow from ABID/DAB were initially refused by Sheikh Saleh Kamel. Moncef Cheikhrouhou, then Tunisian government-appointed BEST Bank director and Sheikh Saleh Kamel's intermediary, later approached high-

ranking officials and proposed a change in offshore banking regulations in return for a loan (interview with a high-ranking Tunisian official, 10 July 2002).

58. Elbaki Hermassi, 'L'État tunisienne et le mouvement islamiste', *Annuaire de l'Afrique du Nord, 1989* (Paris: Éditions du Centre National de la Recherche Scientifique, 1991). Translated by Robert P. Parks.

59. Henry, *The Mediterranean Debt Crescent*, p. 188.

60. This is amusing, considering the government essentially controls the board of directors. While the government knew that there were no connections between the heavily-monitored bank and the MTI, the raid was meant to send a clear signal to Sheikh Saleh Kamel that his increasingly frequent conversations with highly-placed government functionaries concerning the viability of an Islamic form of governance were not welcome (interview with a high-ranking Tunisian official, 10 July 2002).

61. CIM is the ratio of non-currency money (M_2 minus the money outside the official banking system) divided by the total money supply (CIM= (M_2-money held outside banks)/ M_2). It measures the amount of money in the banking system. Conversely, 1-CIM gives the amount of cash circulating in the economy, or money in the mattress. For more on CIM, see Christopher Clague, Philip Keefer, Stephen Knack and Mancur Olson, 'Contract Intensive Money: Contract Enforcement, Property Rights and Economic Performance', mimeograph (College Park, MD: Center on Institutional Reform and Informal Sector, University of Maryland at College Park, 1995); or Lewis Snider, *Growth, Debt, and Politics* (Boulder, CO: Westview Press, 1996). CIM data is from Clement M. Henry and Catherine C. Boone's banking database.

62. $Y = ([\text{BEST dinar Deposits}_{1986} / \text{Total Banking Sector dinar Deposits}_{1986}] - [\text{dinar Deposits}_{1989} / \text{Total Banking Sector dinar Deposits}_{1989}] / [\text{CIM}_{1986} - \text{CIM}_{1989}]) = ([.002 - .0035] / [.8038 - .831]) = .0551$.

63. Of course, it is possible that this hike in savings account deposits was simply a lump deposit from Sheikh Saleh Kamel in order to inflate the bank's balance sheets.

64. See, for example, Lisa Anderson, 'Political Pacts, Liberalism and Democracy: the Tunisian National Pact of 1988', *Government and Opposition*, 26(2), 1991.

65. The MTI (renamed an-Nahda in February 1989) was prohibited to present a ticket because of a Tunisian law preventing the organization of political parties based on language, race, region or religion.

66. Zakya Daoud, 'Chronique Tunisienne', *Annuaire de l'Afrique du Nord, 1989* (Paris: Éditions du Centre National des Recherches Scientifiques,1991) ; John Esposito and James Piscatori, 'Democratization and Islam', *Middle East Journal* 45(3), 1991.

67. The details of this event remain cloudy. An-Nahda attributes the attack to the government, alluding to a 'Tunisian Reichstag'. The government claims it was organized by an-Nahda. Locals in Bab Souika, however, claim that the attack was really organized by a gang of local youths outraged by the local police commissioner's heavy-handed and arbitrary behaviour. According to this story, the youth raided the centre shouting Islamist and anti-regime slogans, though were not officially linked with an-Nahda.

68. Luc Barbelesco, 'L'économie islamique dans ses rapports avec l'économie globale et en particulier avec le mouvement de liberalization', *Revue Tunisienne de Droit*, 51, 1990. The article is in the format of a conference discussion. An unnamed participant (perhaps Moncef Cheikhrouhou), citing an unreleased government banking sector report, communicated the above figures.

69. On this point, see Emma C. Murphy, *Economic and Political Change in Tunisia: From Bourguiba to Ben Ali* (New York: St Martin's Press, 1999).

70. In particular, the PSL (September 2000), PUP (March 2001) and MDS (April 2001) have had meetings marked by strife between pro-RCD and opposition camps (*Maghreb Weekly Monitor*, 91, 12 September 2000; 103, 22 March 2001; 105, 22 April 2001).

71. In 1993, Moallah half-jokingly commented that he could run for president. At the time, he was also head of BIAT, and thus stood as a credibly financed opponent. Within hours, the state began withdrawing its most lucrative public-sector accounts. According to Henry (*The Mediterranean Debt Crescent*, p. 210), BIAT lost 20 per cent of its portfolio in the following days. Historical symbolism played to the very end when Moallah, like Chenik, was forced to step down from the chairmanship to save the bank. Also similar to Chenik, Moallah was pigeon-holed in a banking sector heavily dependent on state funds, and thus unable to exercise the Latin American option. Moallah has since been bought off the board in efforts to limit future liabilities (see note 82 below).

72. Though purely rumour, some attribute Moncef Cheikhrouhou's current legal problems to his growing financial autonomy, which had soured his rapport with the Presidential Palace. He is now living abroad, perhaps not far from Monsieur Daninos' retreat in exile.

73. Ismail Sahbani was well-known for his pro-government positions during his tenure as UGTT chief. Surprisingly, in 2000 he was defeated as general secretary, and accused of stealing and destroying documents that might link him to embezzlement. In July 2001, he received a seven-year sentence (*Maghreb Weekly Monitor*, 110, 8 July 2001, p. 26). His sudden fall from power has been interpreted as a result his self-inflated perception of import in the Tunisian political arena (rumours abound that he considered himself '*présidentiable*') and his concurrent erosion of base-support within the UGTT. Thanks to Delphine Cavallo for this insight.

74. During the April 2001 meeting, MDS Secretary General Ismail Boulalyah announced that the party's financial statements were stolen from his hotel room. A Sahbani-esque warning? (*Maghreb Weekly Monitor*, 105, 22 April 2001, p. 23)

75. Moncef Marzouki, the outspoken anti-regime head of the CNLT, was sentenced to four months in January 2001 for falsely criticizing the Fonds National de Solidarité (FNS) (*Maghreb Weekly Monitor*, 99, 18 January 2001, p. 24). Ironically, the institutional operations of the FNS are so opaque that it would be difficult to say anything about it that might not be false, making state prosecutors' task of building a credible case a mind-boggling affair – assuming they are no more privy to FNS institutions than are the public. For more on the FNS, see Béatrice Hibou, 'Les marges de manoeuvre d'un 'bon élève' économique: la Tunisie de Ben Ali', *Les etudes du CERI*, (60), 1999, pp. 15–18.

76. Henry, *The Mediterranean Debt Crescent*, p. 177.

77. Ibid. p. 179.

78. Alaya, *Monnaie et financement*, p. 214.

79. Ibid. p. 212.

80. Author's database.

81. AMEN Bank has been particularly dynamic in recent years. In 1999, AMEN Bank

posted a post-tax profit of TD 16.226 million, up from 11.5 million the previous year. In February 2001, CEO Rachid Ben Yedder was named manager of the year by *l'Économiste Maghrébin*. And in June 2001, AMEN Bank introduced Tunisia's first Wire Access Protocol (WAP) Banking Service (*Maghreb Weekly Monitor*, 78, 11 March 2000; 102, 10 March 2001; 109, 26 June 2001).

82. In February 2001, HSBC (a London-based multinational) acquired a 3.4 per cent share in BIAT, announcing that it planned to play a larger role in bank management. Perhaps in order to avoid further pretext for government manipulation, in June 2001 BIAT traded 7.15 per cent of its capital (TD 15.3 million) in exchange for Moallah and Bourguiba Jr's shares in annual profits (*Maghreb Weekly Monitor*, 100, 3 February 2001; 109, 26 June 2001).

83. The UBCI was created in 1961 from a fusion of French banks. In 1979, it became a joint venture with French-owned BNP-Paribas and a Sfaxi businessman. Though more conservative than the BIAT, it is nevertheless one of Tunisia's most important private-sector banks. In May 2001, UBCI opened the BNP-Parisbas Trade Center with branches in Tunis, Sfax and Sousse, in order to provide advisory, guarantee and financial services to importers/exporters (*Maghreb Weekly Monitor*, 107, 22 May 2001).

84. The combined assets of the new company total TD 3.653 billion (*Maghreb Weekly Monitor*, 93, 13 October 2000).

85. BEST opened three cash machines in 1996 (BEST Bank, *Annual Report*, 1995).

86. Henry, *The Mediterranean Debt Crescent*, p. 189.

87. Ironically, while BEST was not given its permit, four 'secular' private-sector banks were allowed into Kairouan in 1988 (Henry, *The Mediterranean Debt Crescent*, p. 207).

88. BEST Bank, *Annual Report*, 1995.

89. Galloux, *Finance islamique*, pp. 64–5.

90. For the last decade, this has averaged approximately $US 20,000 per year, the amount being listed in the 'Ordinary General Assembly Resolutions' in each *Annual Report*.

91. The author's neighbourhood, Bab al-Akwas, is a historical stronghold of the Islamist movement. Though hardly a scientific survey, none of the locals the author talked to had ever heard of BEST Bank or had any idea that they could open *halal* accounts in Tunisia, thus the first part of this paper's title: '*Aiyyu Bank Islami?*' ('What Islamic bank?'). This further buttresses the argument that BEST has decided to eschew its onshore operations with small capital-holders in favour of large-scale onshore and offshore operations, and extra-financial-sector activities.

92. Plans to float BEST Re on the Tunisian Bourse appear to have become snagged and, as of 1 January 2003, the company remains unlisted.

93. Mahgreb Weekly Monitor, 96, 11 December 2000.

94. Mahgreb Weekly Monitor, 104, 8 April 2001.

95. BEST Bank, *Annual Report*, 1995.

96. BEST Bank, *Annual Report*, 1998.

Author's note

The author would like to thank the participants from the Third Mediterranean Social and Political Research Meeting Islamic Banking Workshop for their valuable contributions (European University Institute/Robert Schuman Centre for Advanced Studies, Montecatini Terme, 20–24 March 2002). Special thanks go to Clement M. Henry and Rodney Wilson for their insightful feedback. Research funding was generously provided by the American Institute for Maghreb Studies, and additional travel resources were provided by the European University Institute.

12

The Rise and Decline of the Islamic Banking Model in Egypt

Samer Soliman

INTRODUCTION

The experiences of two decades of Islamic banking in Egypt provide an opportunity to critically examine the results of putting Islam to work in the economy. According to the Islamist version of Islam, religion must apply to all aspects of material as well as spiritual life. Western institutions are doomed to fail in Islamic societies because they are alien to the very value-systems of these societies. As well as providing spiritual salvation to Muslims, Islamic economic institutions are supposed to be more likely to succeed in driving development because they are closer to Muslim citizens than other institutions, and because they are value-driven. Such institutions ought to be motivated towards benefiting their societies in addition to the aim of making profits, the latter being an aim that Islam acknowledges since, as a religion, it does not suppress the material aspect of human life.

To date, the most important manifestation of this idea of value-driven economic institutions has been Islamic banks, which emerged in Egypt in late 1970s. In addition to Egypt's role as the 'motherland' of Islamic fundamentalism in the 1920s – the decade which saw the foundation of the Muslim Brotherhood – it is also considered by much of the literature on Islamic banks to be the birthplace of Islamic banking. Egypt's specific case of economic Islam can give us important insights into the outcome of attempts to build modern institutions through the mobilization of religious symbols and codes.

ECONOMIC ISLAM IS ISLAMIC BANKING

One definition of economic Islam encompasses all actors who found their economic activities on the claim of conformity with the *shari'a* (Islamic law), defining themselves in opposition to all other actors. The definition does not include economic actors who simply use Islamic symbolism to attract clients. Such a definition would be too broad, including, for example, proprietors of small shops displaying verses of the Koran to prove their piety or simply to earn heavenly blessings. The narrower definition does, however, include all actors declaring their conformity with Islamic law, even if others deny this conformity. In other words, conformity with Islamic law is more a question of interpretation than of any objective criterion. Many analysts, including some Islamists, consider Islamic banks in Egypt to be no different from conventional banks, in that they are engaged in 'usury' operations.

The assumption here is that the only actors in Egypt that come under the above definition are Islamic banks, Islamic branches of conventional banks and Islamic investments companies. Since the latter disappeared a decade ago, the only remaining Islamic actors in the realm of economics are Islamic banks and Islamic branches of conventional banks. Due to a lack of hard data on the Islamic branches of conventional banks, this study is largely limited to Islamic banks, although reference will be made to the evolution of Bank Misr's Islamic deposits, which represent the major Islamic deposits in conventional banks. To put it another way, it can be said that the only form of Islamic capital in the economy today exists in the financial sector. There are certainly Islamists investing in trade and in industry, and they may even use their capital to finance Islamic groups, but in the economic field, they can hardly claim to be following an Islamic mode of functioning that differentiates them from all other actors.

Why are there Islamic capital institutions – Islamic banks, Islamic investment companies – but no Islamic industry, Islamic agriculture or Islamic trade? Why do advocates of the Islamic economy show such great interest in the field of finance, a field that is, in any case, suspicious from an Islamist standpoint? Why have Islamists not directed their investments towards fields such as industry, where there is less risk of committing the 'sin' of dealing with interest? In fact, the very reason that Islamic actors are attracted to the financial sector is to do with its suspicious nature. Because of the Islamic prohibition on *riba* (usury), new actors can penetrate the financial sector and carve out a niche in the market by simply convincing a section of the population that the interest given and taken by banks is to be considered as *riba* and that only Islamic banks are respecting the prohibition of *riba* in Islam. They cannot apply the same strategy in the industrial sector, in which they would have to compete on purely economic grounds by convincing their customers that they were providing the best product at the lowest price. In the financial sector, however, they can compete without economic efficiency. Islamic banks have simply to convince the public that their competitors – that is, the conventional banks – are illicit and so anyone who deals with them is destined to go directly to hell. Who could dream of a better marketing tactic, one so potent that it not only sends competitors out of the market, but also to hell?

In 1997, the semi-official newspaper *Akhbar Al-Youm* launched a campaign against Islamic banks. The campaign was prompted by an Egyptian television commercial for an Islamic bank, in which a pious-looking man claimed that only the bank in question could guarantee to Muslims that their money was being invested in conformity with Islamic law.[1] It was a clear message to readers that conventional banks were to be considered illicit. *Akhbar Al-Youm* initiated its campaign against Islamic banks on the grounds that these banks were not, in fact, Islamic in nature. The newspaper seized the opportunity to uncover several scandalous episodes involving the banks. The semi-Nasserist, semi-Islamist and pro-government weekly *Al-Osbou* took up the defense of Islamic banks, maintaining that Swiss banks were behind the campaign against Islamic banks because they were increasingly anxious about the rise of Islamic banks in the Gulf. Loyal to its tradition of finding some Jewish conspiracy or other in every matter, the newspaper discovered a Jewish man named Tosson Halton implicated in this campaign.[2] *Al-Shaab*, mouthpiece of the Islamist Labour Party, went so far as to charge the World Trade Organization (WTO) with masterminding the campaign. According to the newspaper, the organization was seeking to buy up Egypt's public banks, and it knew that the most important obstacle would be Islamic banks. The newspaper concluded that attacking Islamic Banks was an offence to be considered nothing short of national treason.[3]

Both publications failed to consider the possibility that the discourse of Islamic banks could itself provoke non-Islamic banks and some of their clients, leading to a reaction on their part or from 'secular' journalists such as the editor-in-chief of *Akhbar Al-Youm*. But such provocation is an inherent feature of Islamic banking. These institutions are built on the basis of negation – negating the 'sin' of other banks in dealing with interest. The more they affirm the contrast between themselves and conventional banks, the more they can mobilize customers.

IDENTIFYING THE ORIGIN OF ISLAMIC BANKS IN EGYPT

Much of the literature on Islamic banks identifies Mit Ghamr, founded by Ahmed al Najjar in 1963, as the first Islamic bank in Egypt and the world. Al Najjar earned his PhD in Germany in the field of social economics, then returned to Egypt in the early 1960s with the idea of founding a bank based on the German savings bank model, which he had become familiar with during his stay. He contacted the Germans, who agreed to support his project, and then contacted the Egyptian authorities. Using family contacts, he managed to elicit the support of the director of the State Intelligence Agency (al Mokhabarat), who introduced him to high-ranking officials in the Ministry of Economy. After a long and drawn-out process, he managed to get the official stamp of approval. The bank was established as a public entity by a German grant of DM 780,000 and an Egyptian government contribution of LE 60,000. Nevertheless, as he himself has maintained, al Najjar never made any reference to Islam in the process of founding the bank for fear that his project would be rejected. He qualifies the experience as 'being covered by the mask of a savings bank and by the name of a European country in order to find a place among usury banks, in an era when hostility to the Islamic tendency was at its peak'.[4] From al Najjar's statement, we can conclude that the only person who believed in the Islamic nature of the bank was al Najjar himself. Neither the state nor the public was informed that the motive behind the creation of the bank was an Islamic one. Given this, it is legitimate to cast doubts on the contention that Mit Ghamr was the first Islamic bank.

Just as there is no Islamic movement without reference to Islam, there can be no Islamic bank without an Islamic reference and discourse. Hostility to usury is not specific to Islam. Christian theology also maintained a long tradition of hostility to usury. While Judaism forbade interest in dealings between Jews and permitted it in dealings with foreigners, the medieval Christian church placed usurers in the same moral category as prostitutes, for their overt greed and lack of charity.[5] Interest has also been attacked on secular grounds. Some socialist ideas ascribe the existence of interest rates to some form of exploitation or maldistribution of wealth. The socialist categorization of interest, along with rent and profits, as surplus value extracted from labour, condemns it by association. The ideas of theorists Proudhon, Gesell and Douglas belong to the same school of thought, since they believe that interest is the artificial shortage of capital produced by a defective monetary system.[6] What makes a bank Islamic is therefore not avoidance of interest alone but the location of this avoidance in an Islamic framework and discourse that prohibits *riba*. This did not happen in the case of Mit Ghamr. Al Najjar's account is teleological: it was only after Islamic banking became legally possible in the late 1970s that al Najjar baptized his bank as the first Islamic bank in history. Unfortunately, we have only one version of the story of Mit Ghamr, and that is al Najjar's. The story has not been told from the point of view of the economic authorities. Thus, we are forced to ignore the manner in which economic authorities approved the bank. If we are to believe al Najjar, however, the logic of their approval was socio-economic – that is, to encourage the rural population to save money, and to mobilize resources. Al Najjar mentions that a leftist thinker, who thought that a banking system not based on interest could destabilize the very logic of the capitalist system, supported the bank's creation.[7] This fact confirms that nobody else knew that the model al Najjar had in mind was Islamic. It is also not clear if it was President Nasser who approved the bank, or whether it was merely a decision taken by the Minister of Economy. In any case, the bank was unsuccessful and was liquidated in 1973.

By the same token, the Nasser Social Bank created in 1971 can hardly be regarded as an Islamic bank. As in the case of Mit Ghamr, this bank was created as an interest-free bank. The law creating the bank, however, did not explain its interest-free nature through any religious reference:

> Due to the social responsibility of the bank, its operations are not to be based on interest rates in the giving and receiving of money. It is acknowledged that capital has first of all a social function. In a society based on justice and sufficiency, in contrast to capitalist societies, capital has to be subjected to the service of citizens without exploitation and injustice. It has thus been decided that the principle of participation substitutes fixed interest rate.[8]

It is clear that the law was using the jargon of Arab socialism. As we said before, Islamism is not the only ideology hostile to interest. A version of socialism can also take the same position. Neither does the fact that the bank distributed *zakat* (alms) support the case for considering it an Islamic bank. It is also worth noting that the Nasser Social Bank is managed under the authority of the Ministry of Social Affairs, which does not have any religious competence.

Why is it important to distinguish between Mit Ghamr and the Nasser Social Bank on the one hand and Islamic banks on the other? The reason is that the very logic of the two types of bank is different. The first type is intended to fill a gap in social and economic life, to support the poor by increasing the population's awareness of saving and by mobilizing their resources. This type of institution is conceived of as working side by side with other banks. But the second type is based, both in its foundation and its development, on the idea that all other banks are illicit and that Islamic banks should replace them. The logic of the two types is different, which makes it more analytically useful to classify them into two different categories.

THE EMERGENCE OF ISLAMIC BANKS

According to our definition of Islamic capital, the first Islamic bank to appear in Egypt was the Faisal Islamic Bank of Egypt in 1979. The contention that the introduction of Islamic banking took place in the 1970s should not, however, obscure the fact that suspicion about conventional banks has been in evidence since the late nineteenth century. While there were some *fatwas* (religious rulings given by a scholar) legitimizing the idea of interest rates – such as the *fatwas* of reformer Mohammed Abduh and those of his disciple Rashid Rida – there were also other *fatwas* which prohibited dealing with banks. Good examples are the 1907 *fatwa* of Sheikh Bakri Al-Sadafi, then Mufti of Egypt, and the several *fatwas* of Sheikh Abdel Megid Selim, who was Mufti of Egypt during the 1930s and 1940s.[9] The appeal of these ideas seems to have lost ground with the rise of the nationalist movement under the leadership of the Wafd Party, however. During the nationalist era, the dominant problematic in Egyptian politics was of national liberation from British colonization. The materialization of this on the economic level was the foundation of Bank Misr by Talaat Harb, with the intention of creating an 'independent' economy. The main question raised concerning banks was not of licit *versus* illicit but, rather, of national *versus* foreign. Talaat Harb has thus been constructed as one of Egyptian history's champions of national liberation.

In other words, condemnation of banks as usury institutions has been around since the country first knew banks. But it seems that it was confined to limited circles. This is manifest in the development of the Egyptian banking system in the twentieth century. It was only in the 1970s that the prohibition of interest was actually given material form with the creation of Islamic banks. The reason the development came when it did was that those who opposed usury were given a golden opportunity to impose their hegemony on society with the direct support of the state. The roles the state played in the 1970s in empowering the Islamic movement to counterbalance the Nasserites and the Marxists are now well-known. One of the fields in which the state empowered the Islamic movement was the field of economics. For evidence of this process, we need look no further than the creation of Faisal Islamic Bank.

This bank was created by a special law, 48 of 1977, which accorded many advantages to the new institution. To mention just some of these: Article 10 of the law stipulated that the bank and its assets could not be nationalized or confiscated; the bank was not made subject to laws controlling foreign currencies; the bank was exempted from many taxes for a fifteen-year period; the bank's accounts enjoyed complete secrecy except in case of final juridical decision; Article 16 give the bank an exemption on customs duties and taxes imposed on import equipment; Article 3 gave the bank the right to include the *zakat* paid by the bank in its costs.[10]

It is clear from the above that the law gave Faisal Islamic Bank advantages over other banks. True, the *infita* laws accorded some advantages to joint-venture banks, but at least Faisal Bank had an outstanding symbolic advantage: the Islamic nature of the bank which the state accepted to meet Prince Moham-mad Al-Faisal's wishes. It is worth noting that in the parliamentary discussions that preceded the passing of the law, some opposition members objected to these advantages. They also objected to the fact that it was Sheikh Al-Shaarâwi – a celebrated Islamic figure and Minister of *Awqâf* at the time – who submitted and defended the law before parliament, rather than the Minister of Economy. The government's response was that the advantages given to the bank were due to its special nature, and that it was the Minister of *Awqâf* who was responsible for the promulgation of the new law because the bank was meant to work in conformity with Islamic law. In any case, the Minister of Economy appeared before Parliament in another session and announced his acceptance of the law. The big surprise, however, was that in voting the law gained the support of all parliamentarians. Even the leftists, who had entertained many reservations when the law was first proposed, ended up voting for it. Members of Parliament, it seems, considered voting against the law as akin to voting against Allah. It should be noted that some of Faisal Islamic Bank's law was amended by the state in 1981. This fact does not, however, affect our contention that the 'visible hand' of the state was behind the foundation and the promotion of Islamic banking in the 1970s.

ISLAMIC BANKING: A PUBLIC AS WELL AS PRIVATE PHENOMENON

The three Islamic banks operating in Egypt at the time of writing are Faisal Islamic Bank (FIB), the Islamic International Bank for Investment and Development (IIBID) and the Egyptian-Saudi Investment Bank (ESIB). They are often labelled as the 'private Islamic banks',[11] which is not precise. In fact, the state has been equally present with the private sector in Egypt's Islamic banking. The state (represented by the Ministry of Awqâf and by public banks) holds 20 per cent of the capital of FIB, 40.8 per cent of ESIB and 80 per cent of IIBID. If the state-held share in Islamic branches of conventional banks is also taken into account, we can conclude that Islamic banking in Egypt is as much a public sphere of operation as a private one.

It has also been argued that conventional banks rushed to create Islamic branches after they were impressed by Islamic banks' ability to mobilize savings by appealing to religious legitimacy. A simple chronological note reveals that this contention is not precise, however. The first Islamic branch of the conventional, publicly-owned Bank Misr – the Al-Hussein branch – was registered in January 1979. This occurred before Faisal Islamic Bank's main branch opened its doors in June 1979. It can be plausibly argued that Egypt's economic authorities, predicting the success of FIB, decided to carve out their share of the pie of Islamic deposits ahead of time. Equally, it is possible that the state wanted to promote Islamic banking by converting some public banking activities to Islamic finance. Even though the creation of the Al-Hussein Islamic branch preceded the operation of dedicated Islamic banks, it can still be maintained that the proliferation of these branches during the 1980s – to reach seventy-five branches by 1995[12] – was due to the success of Islamic banks in attracting savings.

The state's contribution to Islamic banking has not been confined to the capital of these banks, however. It has also extended to ideology. Al Azhar University, for example – a public institution whose head is appointed by the Egyptian president – operates the Saleh Kamel Center for Islamic Economic Studies. As its name suggests, the centre was founded with funding from Sheikh Saleh Kamel, the owner of Al-Baraka Group and the main shareholder in the Egyptian-Saudi Investment Bank. Al Azhar has been the site of many conferences on Islamic banking and Islamic economics. Moreover, the creation of Islamic banks has led to the appointment of al Azhar scholars in several posts as members of religious boards of supervision. These boards are appointed by Islamic banks and charged with deciding whether banking operations are in conformity with Islamic law.

In dealing with the state–Islamic banks relationship, then, it must be noted that the state not only played an important role in the creation and promotion of Islamic banking but that it has also been present in the operation of these banks. In order to better understand the attitude of the state towards Islamic banks, a deconstruction of the state into its various apparatuses and functions should be included in the analysis. The three types of state institution concerned with Islamic banks are financial authorities (the Ministry of Economy and the Central Bank), religious authorities (the Ministry of Awqâf, al Azhar and the Mufti of Egypt) and security authorities (State Security Office).

The Central Bank's preoccupation has been to ensure that Islamic banks should be subjected to its supervision just as other banks are. This has, in fact, been the case since 1981, when the law of Faisal Islamic Bank was amended to permit the Central Bank to supervise it. The amendment coincided with a decision by the state to cease the promulgation of special laws to create Islamic banks. The Central Bank's discourse on Islamic banks is always economic in tone. It maintains that Islamic banks are similar to other banks and should be subject to the same rules. As mentioned above, the religious authorities, represented by the Ministry of Awqâf and al Azhar, have been very supportive of Islamic banking. The head of al Azhar, who is also a former Mufti, is an exception in this regard. In 1989, during his tenure as mufti, he issued a *fatwa* conferring religious legitimacy on interest taken and dispensed by conventional banks. Furthermore, during the last public debate on Islamic banking in 1997 – by which time he was already head of al Azhar – he publicly stated that, in his opinion, conventional banks were closer to Islam than Islamic banks.[13] As for the State Security Office, its main concern with Islamic banks is that they could be a potential threat to security, since they are susceptible to being used as a vector of political Islam. According to Fouâd Allâm, ex-director of the State Security Office, the state security apparatus intervened in Islamic banking during the early 1980s. The state managed to 'convince' Prince Mohammad Al-Faisal, head of the administration board of Faisal Islamic Bank, to expel some members of the Muslim Brotherhood who had managed to 'infiltrate' the administration board of the bank.[14]

To summarize, dealing with the state–Islamic banks relationship necessitates taking into consideration the different, and sometimes contradictory, policies of the state. The differing policies for dealing with Islamic banks account for the many apparent contradictions in how the state deals with these banks. The state's decision to permit the emergence of Islamic banking as part of its policy of encouraging the Islamic movement can be seen as nothing less than casting doubts on basic legitimacy of the entire banking system, which is based on interest rates. To give some banks the right to use the label 'Islamic' is to automatically strip other banks of any Islamic value. As a result, the state itself is rendered as sinful because it permits conventional banks to exist and to function on the basis of interest rates. This is the paradox of state policy towards Islamism: the state creates and empowers its own gladiator. Just as Sadat encouraged the Islamic movement in the 1970s and ended up being assassinated by some of its members, the regime itself encouraged Islamic banks and ended up being dis-credited on the grounds that it still permitted 'usury' institutions. This paradox cannot be explained except by the different and contradictory logics that prevail in the state position vis-à-vis Islamic capital.

ISLAMIC BANKING AND ISLAMIC MOVEMENTS

Hardline opponents of Egyptian Islamism tend to label Islamic banks as the economic branch of the Islamic movement. This is a simplification of the com-plex relationship between the two parties, however. In reality, Islamic banks are not monolithic actors. If we conceive Islamic banks as a 'champ' (field) in the sense of Pierre Bourdieu, we find that there are in fact many actors playing in this field, each with its own agenda.

It is evident that the 'reformist' wing of the Islamic movement, principally embodied by the Muslim Brotherhood, is implicated in the propagation of an Islamic economy and in the foundation of Islamic banks. After its return to the political scene in the 1970s and acting in accordance with its bottom-up strategy of Islamizing Egypt, the Muslim Brotherhood tended to become parti-cularly active in the economic field. Certain members of the Muslim Brother-hood were involved in the creation of Faisal Islamic Bank and the movement managed to install some of its members and sympathizers (such as Youssef Nada, Yusuf al Qaradawi and Abdel Latif Al-Sherif) onto the board of directors. Furthermore, Ahmed Adel Kamal was installed as vice-president of the board of directors. With the deterioration in relations between the regime and Islamic movement after 1985, however, these members were expelled from the board by Prince Mohammad Al-Faisal at the request of the State Security Office.[15] The Islamic International Bank for Investment and Development (IIBID) provides a similar example. At least one member of the Muslim Brotherhood, Abdel Hamid Al-Ghazali, was involved in founding the bank in 1980. He was, however, later marginalized. By 1988, the bank faced near financial collapse and the state was obliged to intervene by raising the bank's capital via the 'big four' public banks. Since that time, the IIBID has become a predominantly publicly-owned bank, the state holding an 80 per cent stake. In other words, then, it can be argued that the strong involvement of fundamentalist activists in Islamic banks in the 1970s reflected a honeymoon period between the state and the Islamic movement. This came to an end in the 1980s, when the activists were marginalized in these banks.

Despite the involvement of activists in early Islamic banking, however, it should be noted that most of the founders of the Islamic banks were not engaged in politics, even if some held sympathies with the Islamic movement. Instead, most of the actors working in this field seem to have been driven by financial motives. As stated above, the 'Islamic' status enjoyed by these banks gave them the ability to penetrate the financial market and rapidly carve out a significant niche. The story of Islamic banking, therefore, bears some similarity to the story of the veil.

The dramatic spread of the veil in the 1970s and 1980s was one of the main symbols and indicators of the rise of political Islam. For the Islamic movement, this was a major success, in so far as the movement had succeeded in imposing its preferred lifestyle on a large section of Egyptian society. In contemporary Egypt, however, the veil has broken away from Islamic movements and established a logic of its own. Nowadays, the veil in Egypt is not necessarily a sign of religiousness and rarely a sign of sympathy with Islamist organizations. Its functions today extend to its being sometimes used by women moving in conservative milieus to gain free access to outdoor activities, since the veil serves to appease their families' fears about the external activities of their daughters. Furthermore, the veil confers a sort of social respectability in some milieus. To the great displeasure of fundamentalist groups, the prevalent type of veil in Egypt is in fact not the *chador*, as stipulated by them. Instead, a less restrictive headscarf is more popular. This can even be limited to a simple foulard that does not fully cover the hair and can be worn along with blue jeans. Why is this the case? The reason is that the veil has been appropriated by actors with motives that are significantly different from those of Islamic activists. By the same token, Islamic banking has not in practice been the monopoly of the Islamic movement, nor the monopoly of its founders. For many of those involved with it, Islamic banking has lost a great deal of its messianic nature. Indeed, most of the legions of day-to-day workers in the Islamic banking business are apolitical and some of them move back and forth between Islamic banks and conventional banks.

THE EVOLUTION OF ISLAMIC BANKING

Islamic banking has gone through three phases: impressive growth, deep crisis and finally a relative recovery followed by stagnation. The figures here do not include Islamic branches of conventional banks.

Impressive growth

Immediately after they first appeared, Islamic banks witnessed an impressive growth in their deposits, which carried on unabated throughout the first half of the 1980s. During this period, the annual average rate of growth of their deposits (of Islamic banks only and excluding Islamic deposits in conventional banks) was 88.2 per cent, which increased their share of the total savings in the banking system to 9.8 per cent by 1986, as shown in Figure 12.1.[16] This rapid growth can be explained by a widespread religious revival during the period, which held that any deposits made in conventional banks were not in accordance with Islamic law. That is not the whole story, however; there was also an element of rational choice operating amongst customers. At the time, Islamic banks yielded greater returns on deposits than did conventional banks. While conventional banks offered an interest rate of 8 per cent on the Egyptian pound in 1980, Faysal Islamic Bank was offering a return equivalent to a 12.03 per cent rate.[17]

To all intents and purposes, it seems that Faisal Bank sought to give itself a head start in the market by attracting custom using not only religious criteria but also economic criteria. The impressive early growth rates of Islamic banks can also be explained by their foreign-currency accounts. Islamic banks kept a high proportion of their deposits in foreign currency. They then distributed a return on these deposits quoted in the respective foreign currencies – a practice that attracted many depositors in a time when the local currency's interest rate was low and the Egyptian pound was facing a gradual devaluation. The massive devaluation of the Egyptian pound during the period 1980–90 (by approximately 350 per cent) contributed to the growth rate shown in deposits denominated in foreign currencies when they were accounted using the Egyptian

Figure 12.1: The evolution of Islamic banks' share in total deposits

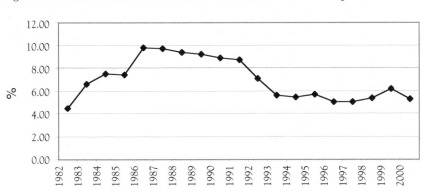

Source: Islamic Banks and Central Bank of Egypt, *Annual Reports.*

pound. The proportion of Islamic banks' total deposits kept in foreign currency accounts was more than 70 per cent in the 1980s.[18]

Deep crisis

By the second half of the 1980s and up until 1993, however, the growth rate of Islamic bank deposits began to decline and negative growth values were recorded in some years, such as 1989 (–0.03 per cent), 1992 (–4.9 per cent) and 1993 (–6.8 per cent). The deterioration was reflected in the shrinking proportion of total Egyptian savings being kept in Islamic banks – from 9.8 per cent in 1986 to 4.8 per cent in 1994.[19] The real rate of decline was even greater, however. As mentioned above, successive devaluation of the Egyptian pound artificially inflated the deposits of Islamic banks. If the same deposits were to be accounted in US dollars instead of Egyptian pounds, the positive growth rates recorded by Faisal Bank in this period in fact turn out to be negative: –32 per cent in 1986 and –23.9 per cent in 1987. This decline can be explained by factors relating to the functioning of Islamic banks and by transformations in the banking market.

First, this decline was due to fierce competition in terms of using religious legitimacy to attract savers during the 1980s. When Islamic banks first emerged, they enjoyed an almost complete monopoly on the claim that their deposits were in conformity with the Islamic law. The increasing number of Islamic branches of some conventional banks began to attract potential clients of Islamic banks. The most important of these conventional banks was Bank Misr, which had thirty Islamic branches by 1996. According to some estimates, Islamic deposits as a percentage of total conventional bank deposits reached 3.1 per cent in 1988.[20]

A few years after the first Islamic banks were created, Islamic investment companies also appeared on the scene. These companies were able to make the same claim as Islamic banks of functioning in conformity with the shari'a. Tacked on to this religious legitimacy, however, was a second attraction that many customers could not resist: the fund management companies offered a 26 per cent return at a time when the return offered by banks, including Islamic banks, did not exceed 11 per cent. Islamic investment companies therefore had a negative effect on the growth of Islamic banks during their rise; but they also had a second negative effect when they crashed in the late 1980s. The fall of the companies had the side-effect of discrediting all economic projects working under the banner of Islam, and raising fears about the safety of such operations. After the crash of Islamic investment companies, long queues of account-holders were to be seen in front of Islamic banks to withdraw their money. It was rumoured that Prince Mohammad Al-Faisal loaded planes with billions of US dollars, with orders that they be sent directly from Cairo airport to Faisal Bank branches in order to meet the withdrawal demands of depositors. Equally, however, most of these people re-deposited their money at Faisal Bank when it appeared that the government would not shut down Islamic banks as it did had done with Islamic investment companies.[21]

A further decisive factor in the fall in the Islamic banks' share of total deposits was a decline in the rate of return on their deposits, which nosedived until they were below the interest rates offered by conventional banks. Of course, Islamic banks retained a core of pious customers who kept their money there regardless of the rate of return. Other customers, however, may have only accepted a return below standard interest rates for some time, and then only as long as they were told that the rate of return ought to change soon and would not remain fixed in order to conform with Islamic law. When the gap between the Islamic banks' rate of return and the conventional interest rate persisted for several years, however, the price of conformity with Islamic law become very high and the temptation towards the 'sin' of receiving interest become stronger. Another major factor which contributed to the heavy withdrawal of deposits from the IIBID in 1989 – about 54 per cent of the bank's total deposits – was its delay in distributing returns to its customers in that year and the preceding year. At that moment, the bank seemed to be facing very serious problems indeed. The bank's board of directors was torn by internal conflicts and on the verge of bankruptcy when the Central Bank intervened. The board of directors was dissolved and the bank recapitalized by the 'big four' public-sector banks.

The reason for the decrease in the rate of return offered by Islamic banks was mismanagement – something that was reflected in the high rate of bad loans given by these banks. The percentage of debts in which Islamic banks' debtors were late in reimbursing reached about 70 per cent of total credit. Furthermore, Islamic banks had to go before the courts in order to try to recover half of these debts. The crisis of bad loans led Islamic banks to try to impose fines on debtors in delay. This raised a debate amongst Islamic scholars, many of whom forbade the fines on the basis that they were a form of interest. Ultimately, however, the religious supervisory boards accepted that the fines were in conformity with Islamic law. The crisis faced by Islamic banks can also be explained by the way these banks engaged in some risky investment activities. These included speculating in metals and depositing large sums of money in banks that appeared to be very risky – such as the Bank of Credit and Commerce International (BCCI), which crashed with the money of Faisal Islamic Bank.

In 1989, Sheikh Mohammed Sayed Tantâwi, the Mufti of the Republic, issued a *fatwa* that ruled that the type of interest charged and received by conventional banks was in fact lawful from a religious standpoint. The *fatwa* raised both debate and opposition. Some commentators believe that the *fatwa* affected the number of deposits made in Islamic banks, which showed a negative growth rate in deposits that year. As mentioned earlier, however, 1989 was a year of several different obstacles for the IIBID and Faisal Bank. It is, therefore, difficult to know quite how much the *fatwa* was responsible for withdrawal by depositors.

Relative recovery

The third and final phase extends from 1994 to 2000. During this period, Islamic banks regained their positive growth rates and even saw their share of total savings increase in some years. This recovery is reflected by the growth of total savings held by Islamic banks. Within this total, however, it should be noted that Faisal Islamic Bank in particular saw its share of Islamic bank deposits tumble from 91.1 per cent in 1991 to 60.5 per cent in 2000. This can be seen as a normal development, since Faisal Bank offered lower returns than those offered by both conventional banks and other Islamic banks over this period. While the return offered on the Egyptian pound by Faisal Bank in 2001 was 8.1 per cent, the interest rate offered by conventional banks in the same year exceeded 9 per cent.[22] Upward and downward movements in the Islamic banks' deposits serve to demonstrate that economic rationality could not have been absent from the motivations of depositors. Some officials at Islamic banks, such as Ahmed Al-Bashâri, have even confirmed this.[23] There remained, however, a 'core' of depositors who insist on depositing their money in Islamic banks, even if those banks offered fewer returns, and even if they offered no returns at all. This constitutes a particular sub-set of depositors, however, and not the entirety of the market.

THE EVOLUTION OF BANK MISR'S ISLAMIC DEPOSITS

There are, unfortunately, no exhaustive figures on the deposits held by Islamic branches of conventional banks. Here Bank Misr's Islamic deposits are used as an approximate measure of total Islamic deposits held by conventional banks, as Bank Misr has the bulk of these deposits. As indicated already, Bank Misr registered it first Islamic branch in January 1979, before Faisal Islamic Bank opened its doors in July 1979. By 2003, Bank Misr had thirty-three Islamic branches. As shown in Figure 12.2, the share of Islamic branches' share of Bank Misr's total deposits was growing impressively during the 1980s, and reached its peak in 1990 when it amounted to 12.5 per cent. During the second half of the 1980s, Islamic banks (especially Faisal) were in a deep crisis and saw their share of total deposits in the banking system fall. It is almost certain that Bank Misr's Islamic branches profited from the crisis of Islamic banks. In addition to the internal malfunctioning of Islamic banks, which caused them big losses, the state was launching an assault on Islamic investment companies that created fears about the future of Islamic economic institutions. It was very natural that a portion of the Islamic banks' clientele shifted their deposits from Islamic banks

Figure 12.2: Share of Islamic deposits to total deposits in Bank Misr

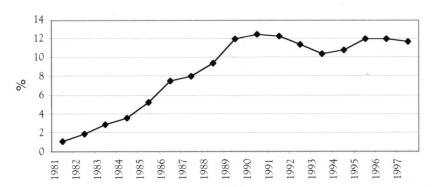

Sources: Michel Galoux, 'The State's Responses to Private Islamic Finance Experiments in Egypt', *Thunderbird International Business Review*, Vol. 41, July–October 1999, pp. 481–500.

to Islamic branches owned by a public bank. They can therefore enjoy two things: avoid committing the sin of taking interest and guarantee the safety of their deposits by putting them in the hands of a public bank.

This growth, however, did not last for a long time. As shown in Figure 12.2, the share of Islamic deposits of Bank Misr to total deposits of the bank started to fall in 1991, then stagnated for the rest of the decade. The stagnation of these deposits is probably due to the decline of Islamic economic institutions in Egypt, with the collapse of Islamic investments companies and the crisis of Islamic banks. True, Islamic branches of Bank Misr gained at the beginning of this fall when depositors shifted from Islamic investment companies and Islamic banks to Islamic branches of Bank Misr. Yet the assault on Islamic economic institutions in general touched them finally. It is worth noting that the Mufti of Egypt at that time, Sheikh Mohammed Sayed Tantâwi, did not exclude Islamic branches from his attacks on what he thought was the myth of Islamic banking. Islamic branches were also discredited on the ground that conventional banks do not separate Islamic deposits from other deposits in their business. At any rate, the stagnation of Islamic deposits in Bank Misr supports the same conclusion as in the case of Islamic banks: at the time of writing, Islamic banking is no longer rising in Egypt.

THE FALL OF THE ISLAMIC BANKING MODEL

After two decades of Islamic banking in practice, it seems that the model has lost much of its appeal. The practical application of economic Islam has brought the concept down to earth, and has provided an opportunity to test its claims against its achievements. A similar argument can be made about political Islam.

Table 12.1: Share of financing by Islamic and conventional banks in Egypt in 1996 (%)

Sector	Islamic banks	Conventional banks
Agriculture	4.2	3.0
Industry	11.9	32.0
Trade	23.5	21.9
Services	60.4	44.6

Source: Faisal Islamic Bank and Central Bank of Egypt, *Annual Reports.*

Putting Islamism to work in societies as diverse as Iran, Sudan and Afghanistan has demystified large sections of the populations of those countries about what can be achieved under Islamist rule. As far as economic Islam is concerned, the degree of demystification may be even greater than with political Islam, since many economic variables are quantifiable. Beautiful words are a poor substitute for a negative balance sheet.

The major problem with Islamic banks is that they did not merely limit themselves to their original proposal of sparing Muslims the 'sin' of paying and receiving interest. They claimed, furthermore, to offer a developmentally-oriented banking model. Much of the early literature of Islamic banking suggested that, because of their religious nature, Islamic Banks were better disposed to contribute to the development of Muslim societies than were conventional banks. It was claimed that Islamic Banks would direct more resources to productive activities such industry – a supposition that, in practice, proved to be unfounded. As Table 12.1 shows, the share of industrial investment as a proportion of total investment made by Islamic banks is less than that made by conventional banks, which in any case do not make developmental claims. Worse, the proportion of industrial investment made by Islamic banks actually declined, dropping from 16.9 per cent in 1987 to 11.9 per cent in 1996.[24]

The past decade has seen a large number of advocates of Islamic banking switch camps and become critical of the Islamic banking experience. The extensive list includes such significant figures as Ahmed al Najjar, considered to be the godfather of Islamic banking; Ahmed Zendo, former governor of Faisal Bank; Abdel Sabour Marzouk, a well-known religious scholar; and Fouâd Riyâd, an ex-manager of an Islamic branch of a conventional bank. One of the harsher critiques to date, however, has come from Ahmed Kamâl Abou El-Magd, a prominent Islamic thinker, who said 'the managers of these banks are neither honest nor efficient; that is why I transferred my money to conventional banks. I got the opportunity to see the contracts signed between an Islamic bank and the Bank of Credit and Commerce, and I discovered then that the managers of these banks lacked even the capacity to administer a financial institution.'[25] But certainly the most severe critique (to the extent that it may be considered an insult) came from Sheikh Al-Azhar, who abandoned all diplomacy when he branded Islamic banks as nothing more than a band of thieves![26]

One of the principal criticisms revolves around the practice of *murabaha*, which has been attacked on both religious and economic grounds. In a *murabaha* contract, the provider of capital buys, for example, a car for LE 50,000. The borrower later buys it back from the bank for LE 60,000. According to the *murabaha* rules, the LE 10,000 represents a 'mark-up'; in practice, it works in the same manner as interest in everything but name. Some scholars have criticized *murabaha* on the basis that it is actually a disguised form of interest. Ahmed al Najjar has added a further critique – *murabaha*, he claims, has very limited utility in terms of development. According to him, Islamic banks overuse the method at the expense of other Islamic methods, such as *mudaraba* and *musharaka*. He adds that Islamic banks disguise many *murabaha* operations under the guise of *mudaraba* and *musharaka*.[27] Furthermore, Ahmed Zendo, ex-governor of Faisal Bank, has revealed that under his presidency the bank both invested in bonds and received interest payments. These kinds of operation were often disguised in the budget of the bank under the title 'religiously legal operations'.

This kind of debate and discourse on Islamic banks is radically different from that which existed at the beginning of the Islamic banking experience. In the last parliamentary debate on Islamic banking in 1997, a member asked the Minister of Economy to prohibit Islamic banks from using the label 'Islamic', since, according to him, Sheikh Mohammed Sayed Tantâwi had issued a *fatwa* which stated that conventional banks were closer to Islam than Islamic banks. The Minister refused the request. What is interesting, however, is the logic upon which the refusal was based: she said that there was not justification in shutting down Islamic banks because the banking system comprises many types of banks that are diversified in their mode of functioning. The Minister also confirmed to parliamentary members that these banks were subject to the control of the Central Bank.[28] In other words, the Minister's answer was based on nothing more than the contention that Islamic banks should not be shut down because they cater to a specific demand in the financial market. There was no place in her defence of Islamic banks for the argument that these banks belong to Islam. To demonstrate the extent to which this differs from the prevailing discourse on Islamic banking when the experience began, it is useful to briefly paint a picture of the parliamentary discussion that preceded the passing of the Faisal Bank law in 1979.

As mentioned above, it was the well-known Sheikh Al-Shaarâwi who defended the law before Parliament. The Minister of *Awqâf* – an Islamic scholar – was presenting an economic law! It is worth noting that Sheikh Al-Shaarâwi's speech was interrupted many times by members yelling 'Allahu Akbar' ('Allah is great'), as if the Sheikh had declared holy war against the enemies of Islam. One member commenting about the law said: 'this is the greatest and the most eternal day in our lives'. Such glowing praise was not confined to members of the majority government. One opposition member, Olwi Hâfez, said: 'Sheikh Al-Shaarâwi is a divine source in this place. I hope that he will agree to present all future laws formulated by the government, so that we can ensure the religious legitimacy of those laws.' The most interesting comments, however, came when the Minister of Economy defended the presentation of a banking law by Sheikh Al-Shaarâwi, although such laws were supposed to be under the Minister's supervision. The Minister defended Al-Shaarâwi's actions on the ground that the new bank would be in conformity with the *shari'a*, unlike other 'usury banks'. It is noteworthy that here we have a Minister of Economy describing conventional banks, most of which are public and under his control, as being 'usury'. One leftist tried to oppose the fact that the law exempted the new bank from the supervision of the Central Bank, but another member replied that the most important control on the new bank would be the Islamic conscience of its founders. Another member objected to the article that exempted the bank from respecting the labour code of Egypt, which ensures certain workers' rights. Another member told him that Faisal Bank had an equivalent in Saudi Arabia, in which no worker had been unfairly dismissed. As mentioned above, when it came to voting, no one dared to oppose the law.

The above description demonstrates the extent to which perception and discourse vis-à-vis Islamic banking in Egypt had changed by the 1990s. At the time of writing, Islamic banking is no longer perceived to be a complete substitute for conventional banking, apart from by some (and by no means all) advocates of Islamic banking. The Sheikh of Al-Azhar himself has said that Islamic banks should be shut down, since by using the label 'Islamic' they create suspicions about all other banks. This argument has not gained widespread support. The dominant logic today is that Islamic banks respond to a particular demand in the market and that they thereby receive savings that would otherwise remain outside the banking system. Islamic banks are thus perceived as a form of product diversification. They can coexist with other conventional banks, each having its own market and its own customers, in a similar manner to the veil that today coexists with Western dress. In contemporary Egypt, it is not uncommon to see a veiled mother walking side-by-side with her non-veiled daughter. Furthermore, the kind of polarization around the issue of Islamic *versus* conventional banks that prevailed in the 1970s and 1980s all but disappeared in the 1990s, as public debate about Islamic banking dwindled. In many ways, Islamic banks are becoming more and more banal.

Since the late 1990s, discourse about Islamic banks is often less coherent than one might imagine. In October 2001, the governorship of the Central Bank was offered to the governor of Faisal Bank, who had worked at the Central Bank before joining the Islamic banking business. He did not accept the post. Nevertheless, the very fact that the state proposed such a position to an Islamic banker who considers all other banks to be 'usury' is an apt demonstration of the extent to which Islamic banks have become 'banal'. After all, the state permits Islamic scholars to preach the use of the veil on its television channels despite the fact that none its presenters is veiled.

CONCLUSION

In this chapter, Islamic banking was treated as a facet of the Islamization of Egyptian society. In reality, however, despite the Islamic movement's success in imposing its symbols and institutions on certain sections of Egyptian society, these symbols and institutions later gained lives of their own and were subject to further social transformations. The development of Islamic banking would not have come about without the direct and indirect contributions of the state. In other words, we can refute the argument[29] that Islamic banking is an inherent or embedded characteristic of Muslim societies that was simply waiting to be discovered or revealed. Rather, the emergence of Islamic banking in Egypt should be firmly located in the rise of Islamic fundamentalism and the state's investment in this movement. Far from being a latent element of Islamic culture, Islamic banking is instead a creation of the state and of a coincidence of social and political forces.

Furthermore, the trend amongst some sections of the population to avoid dealing with conventional banks altogether is more an outcome than a cause of the emergence of Islamic banks. The economic law proposed by the French economist Jean-Baptiste Say, which states 'supply creates its own demand', can be directly applied in this case. The contention by advocates of Islamic banking that these banks attract savings that would otherwise remain outside the banking system cannot be empirically verified. Egypt's economy has an underdeveloped banking sector. The ratio of total bank deposits to GDP was 78 per cent in 1997. This is not specific to Egypt, or to Islamic societies; rather, it is characteristic of many developing countries. By contrast, the equivalent ratio in Jordan is 172 per cent, and in Lebanon it is 204 per cent. Can the marked difference between Egypt and these countries be explained by cultural factors? A better explanation is that in Egypt the dominant public-sector banks do not market their services aggressively, whereas in Jordan and Lebanon the predominately private banks compete vigorously for business. There is a bank counter for every 5,730 citizens in Lebanon, 10,045 citizens in Jordan and 45,429 citizens in Egypt.[30] Per capita income – which is the lowest in Egypt and the highest in Lebanon – may also explain the underdevelopment of banking in Egypt.

To explain away the problems of the banking system in Egypt by reference to the Islamic 'factor' and by cultural hostility to 'usury institutions' is, therefore, to overestimate the role of culture in Muslim societies. It will be recalled that hostility to interest was common in Europe in the Middle Ages, but the sentiment did not result in blocking the development of interest-based institutions. The hostility was, rather, overcome either by religious reform or by the force of economic development – or indeed by the interaction of these two variables. That is to say, the banking sector in Egypt could very well have developed without Islamic banks. Nevertheless, the very emergence of these banks along with other factors has created an entire segment of society that has ceased to have any relationship with conventional banks. Given this, it remains very probable that the disappearance of these banks would result in a certain number of people who currently deposit with Islamic banks withdrawing their money from the modern banking system altogether. For this reason, the dominant logic concerning these banks in Egypt today is 'live and let live'.

NOTES

1. *Al-Ahram Weekly*, 26 February 1997.
2. *Al Osbou*, 10 March 1997.
3. *Al-Shaab*, 7 February 1997.
4. Ahmed al Najjar, *Islamic Banks: the Truth of Origin and the Myth of Image* (Cairo: Sprint, 1993). (Arabic)
5. Paul Mills and John Presley, *Islamic Finance: Theory and Practice* (London: Macmillan Press, 1999), p. 106.
6. Ibid. p. 118.
7. al Najjar, *Islamic Banks*.
8. See an earlier study by the author: Samer Soliman, 'Islamic Banks', in *The State of Religion in Egypt in 1997* (Cairo: Al-Ahram Center for Political and Strategic Studies, 1998). (Arabic)
9. The Center for Islamic Economy, *The Guide to Fatwas in Banking Affairs: The Most Important Fatwas on Usury, Interests, Modarabat, Mosharakat and Murabahat* (Cairo: The Islamic International Bank for Investment and Development, 1986).
10. Tawfiq Al-Shâwi, *The Story of Islamic Banks* (Cairo: Sprint, 1996). (Arabic)
11. See Michel Galloux, *Finance Islamique et Pouvoir Politique: le Cas de l'Egypte Moderne* (Paris: Presse Universitaire de France, 1997); Mahmoud Mohieildin, *On Formal and Informal Islamic Finance in Egypt*, The Middle East Studies Association Twenty-Ninth Annual Conference, December 1995.
12. Fayad Abdel Moheim, *An Economic Evaluation of Islamic Banks: The Egyptian Case*, PhD dissertation, Al-Azhar University, 1999. (Arabic)
13. *Al-Alam Al-Youm*, 5 January 1997.
14. Fouâd Alâm, ex-director of State Security Office, interviewed on 13 December 2001.
15. Ibid.
16. Calculated by the author from the data of *Annual Reports* of Islamic Banks.

17. Calculated by the author.
18. Mohieildin, *On Formal and Informal Islamic Finance*, pp. 17, 18.
19. Calculated by the author from the data of *Annual Reports* of Islamic Banks.
20. Michel Galloux, 'Finance islamique privée en Eqypt: performances et contraintes étatiques, le cas de la Banque Faysal', in Gian Maria Piccinelli, *Banche Islamiche in Contesto Non Islamico* (Rome: Instituto Per L'Oriente, 1994), pp. 207–48.
21. Mohammed Adel, manager at Faisal Islamic Bank, interviewed on 24 December 2001.
22. Calculated by the author from the data in *Annual Reports* of the Central Bank of Egypt and of Islamic banks in Egypt.
23. Ahmed Al-Bashâri, manager at IIBID, interviewed on 7 December 2001.
24. Even researchers sympathetic to Islamic banks have noted the failure of their developmental function, which was supposed to be one of the pillars of economic Islam. See Moheim, *An Economic Evaluation*.
25. *Al-Akhbâr*, 8 March 1997.
26. *Al-Alam Al-Youm*, 5 January 1997.
27. *Al-Akhbâr*, 3 August 1993.
28. Ibid.
29. Elias Abou Haidar, *Libéralisme et Capitalisme d'État en Egypte* (Paris: Harmattan, 2000), p. 40.
30. Ibid. p. 41.

Conclusion

Clement M. Henry and Rodney Wilson

World politics, notably the United States' policies concerning Palestine and Iraq, have mobilized many Muslims, albeit ineffectively, against American imperialism and against the governments in the Muslim World which are allied with the United States. Despite the success of the United States in ending the regime of Saddam Hussein in Iraq, America's 'war against terrorism' may in fact become a self-fulfilling prophecy, as the various, supposedly related efforts, notably the attempt to ensure that the clergy play a minimal role in Iraqi politics, produce a counter-reaction and increase support for the transnational terrorist networks associated with Osama Bin Laden.

Islam in the modern world, however, presents a complex of personal and social as well as political meanings, and they are undergoing constant change. Islam may, in theory, be a unified body of thought but political Islam should not be conflated with Islam's other economic and societal dimensions. Even governments in the Muslim World that wage war against political Islamists and do not readily distinguish moderate partisans from terrorists recognize the distinction between Islam's political and economic practitioners. Yet the distinction should not be cast in stone. Any rigid analytic separation of the economic from the political aspects of Islamic revival may obscure some of the rich potential for political development implied by a steady accumulation of Islamic capital.

This book has examined a force for change that is far less powerful, at least in the short term, than American imperialism; indeed, as Ibrahim Warde has documented, Islamic banks remain highly vulnerable to external forces emanating from New York and Washington, DC, since the bombings of the World Trade Center and the Pentagon. In most of the Muslim World they remain marginal to national commercial banking systems, and globalization is meanwhile eroding protective national barriers – especially in the areas of trade and finance.

As Monzer Kahf implies, however, Islamic finance allied with local leaders of religious opinion – the *ulama* – may exercise an influence in the Muslim World at least as profound as the Bush Administration's hopefully short-lived adventures in imperialism. Political Islam in the modern world is suspended between radical and moderate poles, and the gradual emergence of a distinctively Islamic form of capitalism – exemplified by the alliance between the *ulama*, bankers and entrepreneurs – could tip the balance and effect a deep structural transformation in much of the Muslim World. In fact, United States policy-makers concerned with the lack of democracy in the Arab World and the need for 'regime change' might well ponder the implications of Kahf's argument. US and international programmes designed ultimately to build democratic institutions often focus for a start on civil society, so as to avoid upsetting incumbent dictators. But instead of supporting bunches of upper-middle-class NGOs – a cottage industry in the developing countries that are endowed with international aid programmes – they might assist Islamic institutions that promote the spirit of capitalism and free enterprise. Any stable democracy presupposes an indigenous capitalist class that animates vibrant middle and working classes.

Unfortunately the events of 11 September 2001 triggered the 'clash of civilizations' that most American foreign-policy strategists had previously dismissed as an imaginative but tendentious neo-conservative mapping of the post-cold war world – an American equivalent of Muslim fundamentalist views that many Islamists appreciated. Ibrahim Warde shows how the paradigm 'went mainstream' when President Bush 'foreclosed any discussion of US foreign policy' and asserted 'if you're not with us, you're with the terrorists'. A Manichean neo-conservative ideology currently guides the American 'war against terrorism', with very adverse consequences for Islamic finance and the development of any sort of capitalism or democracy in the Middle East. Indeed, the American Secretary of Defence targets 'bankers' pinstripes' as much as the actual terrorists. They are easier prey. Apparently, Islamic banks are suspected of money-laundering for transnational networks of terrorists and judged guilty unless they can prove their innocence. The Saudis, in particular, are the 'kernel of evil', and the Saudi leaders of both Islamic banking transnationals, Faisal and Al-Baraka, were among those accused of 'racketeering, wrongful death, negligence and conspiracy' in a lawsuit raised by families of victims of the September 11th attacks. Though the case was subsequently dismissed, all Middle Eastern banks, and Islamic ones in particular, are subject to pressures that may deter potential Muslim investors and depositors. The growth rates of Islamic deposits diminished during the year following September 11th.

The logic of Islamic finance remains intact, however: driven by the demand of pious investors, investments in Islamic banks and in the Islamic instruments engineered by international banks will probably continue to grow faster in most MENA countries than will conventional bank deposits. This book has examined the competitive advantages and disadvantages of the Islamic banks. We conclude that, in much of the MENA, the Islamic banks still enjoy a prime advantage of being able to reach significant market segments that distrust conventional banks. They are not usually able, however, to generate as much profit from their investments as the latter, at least not without incurring significantly greater risk. Most commentators agree that they are in need of a broader portfolio of religiously-acceptable financial instruments. Acceptable markets in options to buy and sell commodities on forward markets would be particularly useful.

Ellis Goldberg concluded on the basis of Egypt's experience with cotton options that powerful economic interests can, if necessary, override any legal obstacles to innovative financial engineering. Tarik M. Yousef indicated, however, that the MENA, like other developing regions of the world, requires substantial political reform as well as structural adjustment if Islamic finance is to transcend its 'murabaha syndrome'. For reasons that are extrinsic to Islamic finance, it cannot yet fulfil its potential to finance development in its true spirit of venture capitalism, but it may still sensitize traditional Muslims to new arts of economic management. Parallel to Yousef's macroeconomic analysis, Clement M. Henry's micro-analysis of financial performances also suggested that Islamic finance is most likely to prosper in domestic environments that are politically as well as economically liberalized. Otherwise, Islamic finance tends merely to siphon-off Muslim deposits into overseas investment, as Rodney Wilson demonstrated to be the case in the GCC countries. Much of it is funnelled into a variety of mutual funds and other investment vehicles that follow Islamic conventions. Much of the vaunted growth in Islamic financial instruments may thus simply constitute new forms of capital flight. Passive rentiers, not dynamic bourgeoisie, may be their principal beneficiaries (along with the Western or Asian recipients of their investments). In Jordan, too, substantial investment revenues of the Islamic banks come from foreign trade finance and commodity markets rather than Islamic investments inside the country or region. Greater domestic investment evidently requires both political and economic reform.

But our case studies suggest that a relatively liberal climate may be a necessary prerequisite if Islamic finance and commerce are to animate a new form of capitalism. Indeed, more political liberalization may be needed even to achieve the benefits that Montesquieu ascribed to 'gentle commerce' before the rise of capitalism. Le doux commerce was supposed to polish tyrants' political manners by making them realize that their Machiavellian tactics were counter-productive and politically irrational – but perhaps the polishing already required a smooth surface. Let us here recall the three scenarios that the case studies were supposed to illustrate – the possibility of integration, separation, and uneasy coexistence between Islamic capital and political Islamists.

The first scenario only concerned relatively liberal political climates, where Islamic banks could work comfortably with political Islamists. Whether or not they did so was an empirical question that the case studies of Jordan, Kuwait, Turkey and the Sudan addressed. In theory, the political movement could help monitor the uses to which Islamic finance is put and extend the ability of the banks to engage in profitable *musharaka* and *mudaraba* operations. By reducing the banks' monitoring costs, they would render them more profitable. Bankers and politicians would share an interest in the success of the Islamic financial experiment, and the politicians, enjoying financial support, would presumably strengthen the political movement's business interests and further moderate opposition to the incumbent regime. This ground-up approach suggests a gradual increase in the power of political and business Islam, operating in a relatively stable pluralistic political environment. It assumes that political liberalization is a gradual process and that money can soften up the opposition by bringing it into the moneyed establishment. But it runs against the grain of recent political development in the MENA. Since the early 1990s, the political trend has been one of de-liberalization and reinforced authoritarianism. Politics remain too turbulent and frightening to business and banking interests in much of the region, and the new American war against terrorism and aftermath of the Iraqi conflict, even when not targeting Islamic banks, is bound to further authoritarian trends, just as the Desert Storm and Desert Shield were partly responsible for the hardening of opposition between regimes and Islamist parties in the 1990s.

In framing this first scenario, we originally thought that Jordan and Turkey could exemplify synergies between Islamic financial networks and the members and sympathizers of Islamist political parties as much as could Kuwait and the Sudan. Mohammed Malley and Filiz Baskan discovered some affinities between Islam's financial and political forces, but they concluded, even in these relatively liberal climates, that Islamic financiers and businesspeople had to keep their distances from their respective country's Islamist politicians, lest they antagonize their governments. Only in Kuwait, it seems, could the politicians and financiers mutually benefit each other, advancing the bank and encouraging moderate tendencies within the Islamist political movement, as Kristin Smith demonstrates. In the Sudan, by contrast, Turabi's political Islamists co-existed uneasily with the military, but Turabi, who in association with the Faisal Islamic Bank of Sudan had originally achieved power with the help of the Islamic banks and their new business constitutencies, lost them when General Beshir removed him from power in 1999.

For Jordan, however, Malley still sees interesting prospects, albeit only if the regime first engages in real political liberalization, whereby the elected elements of the Jordanian Parliament actually exercise some power. In the regional and international climate at the time of writing, such liberalization seems extremely unlikely; but in the longer run, Malley envisions a pivotal role for the country's two Islamic banks. They could serve as intermediaries between the government and the political Islamists, and help transform the latter from a populist mass party into a conservative party, like the Christian Democrats in Germany, that would coexist more easily with other parties in a constitutional democracy.

Filiz Baskan is less sanguine about Turkey, but the victory of the moderate successor to Turkey's series of Islamist parties in the November 2002 elections may augur closer relations between Islam's political and financial wings. The Justice and Development Party has apparently occupied the political spaces of Turkey's centre-right, suggesting that the political Islamists have already effected the sort of transformation that Malley envisions for the Jordanian Muslim Brotherhood. The special finance houses may have played some part in this major change. Baskan's research before the elections already indicated that these banks tended to concentrate in the Turkish cities that had registered the most votes for the Islamists in previous elections; in the previous Parliament, moreover, the deputies who joined the more moderate and progressive of the two Islamist parties that succeeded the banned Virtue Party tended to be more closely associated with those cities than were their colleagues who opted for the more conservative successor party. Of course, it is too early to say whether the Islamic banks, businessmen, *ulama* and religious orders may overtly support the new ruling party, much less whether the banks, now integrated into the Turkish commercial banking system, will ever wield market power commensurate with the Justice and Development Party's electoral power.

Our second and third scenarios, by contrast, suggest a top-down development of Islamic finance in alliance with incumbent regimes. In politically repressive settings, there may be few real affinities between timid Islamic business and banking interests on the one hand, and radicalized Islamist oppositions on the other. Alliances with economic reformers within the government, however, may enable the Islamic banks gradually to gain market share. Protected by their governments, they may offer modest 'profits' to their depositors and lure more of them away from non-interest bearing accounts in conventional banks. The financial returns of these Islamic banks under these scenarios were expected to remain modest, however, because the banks are at a disadvantage in generating revenues, even if they can gain more deposits. But no matter: they are protected. The major competitive threat then comes from conventional banks that open Islamic windows to prevent the hemorrhaging of their non-interest bearing deposits. They, too, may then acquire a greater interest in structural adjustment, market reforms, better accounting procedures and the like. Under this top-down approach, the Islamic banks may offer cover to the government for further engagements with international financial institutions and the Washington Consensus. Even where, as in Algeria, their market share is miniscule, their approval can contribute to the (sorely deficient) legitimacy of a government embarked on structural reforms. However, the public-sector banks of countries like Egypt and Tunisia may oppose any globalizing alliance that takes deposits away from their weak balance sheets and endangers their state patronage machines.

Egypt did not, in fact, fulfil the heady expectations of Islamic finance in the mid-1980s. While losing market share, however, the Islamic banks nonetheless managed to survive the country's political de-liberalization in the 1990s. After veering between our second and third scenarios, Egypt settled down to into a revised third scenario of easy coexistence between government, Islamic banks and Islamist parties. This pattern of coexistence illustrates the survival capacity of Islamic financial institutions in authoritarian settings. Although the Mubarak regime hardened up and de-liberalized during his second decade of power, it still permitted enough space for Monzer Kahf's alliance between the financiers and some of the *ulama*; for the regime lacked the will as well as the capacity to subordinate the latter to any single line of religious interpretation, however much it pre-empted political space and denied any voice to Islamist political oppositions. Samer Soliman concluded by observing that Islam's financial banners wave freely in the air like women's headscarves, unfolding a harmless variety of meanings.

Authoritarian rule in Tunisia has yet to develop the depth and sophistication of its Egyptian counterpart. Consequently, as Robert P. Parks observed, its sole Islamic bank is strictly confined, for the most part offshore, to the margins of the Tunisian commercial banking system. For fear of being associated with Tunisia's outlawed Islamist opposition, BEST Bank dared not even advertise itself as an Islamic bank. Tunisia is, in fact, the only case among the countries studied in this volume that exemplifies our second scenario, a sharp separation between financial and political expressions of Islam in this 'republic of fear'. Even in neighbouring Algeria, where the government was at war with sub-sets of self-proclaimed Islamist *mujahidin*, Islamic financial institutions enjoyed more opportunities for growth and development.

Indeed, the most interesting experiments in Islamic finance may be occurring in relatively underbanked countries, such as Algeria and Yemen, which were not among our case studies. Here, the heavy hand of state banking institutions discouraged people away from banks altogether, as evidenced by the relatively high proportion of the money supply held in cash outside their respective commercial banking systems, so that they offer their newly established Islamic banks virtually untapped markets. Syria and Iraq may also offer fertile fields for Islamic finance when they eventually permit it, like most other Arab states.

At the time of writing, the future governance of Iraq remains uncertain, as does the possible shape of its financial sector. Nevertheless, the demise of the Saddam Hussein regime opens up new possibilities for Islamic finance. The Islamic Development Bank, although wary of post-Taliban developments in Afghanistan, was disappointed not to be involved in the reconstruction of that country's economy. It is likely to push for a greater role in Iraq, a much more significant economy. If foreign banks are allowed to operate in Iraq, then the Islamic banks from the Gulf, such as the Dubai Islamic Bank, are likely to want to open branches, not least because the significant amount of trade between Dubai and Iraq brings financing opportunities. In 2002, the Dubai Islamic Bank opened a branch in Tehran, the first Arab Islamic bank to do so, largely in response to increasing UAE–Iranian trade.

The other major state in the Arab world that does not yet permit Islamic banking is Morocco, whose King and Commander of the Faithful has understandably hesitated to risk his religious authority being contested by any alliance of capitalists and *ulama*. Morocco's relatively liberal political system, however, could perhaps tame some of the political Islamists in a ground-up alliance with the financiers.

In the Gulf countries, where Islamic banking is developing substantial market shares, the impetus seems to come from wealthy individuals who refuse interest as a matter of principle and who seek substitutes for conventional banks where their funds may lie idle. At the time of writing, Saudi Arabia is likely to be the major battleground for Islamic finance in the coming five years. Substantial non-interest bearing deposits seem ripe for redeployment to Islamic financial institutions and markets. Al-Rajhi Banking and Investment Corporation, an exclusively Islamic bank, has the largest branch network in the Kingdom and almost 5,800 employees, the majority of whom are Saudi citizens. Customer deposits are increasing by 10 per cent annually, well above the average for all banks, and the bank has become the third largest in the Kingdom after the National Commercial Bank and the Saudi American Bank. This has occurred despite minimal profit pay-outs to depositors, partly a consequence of the bank's exposure to the failed US energy trading company, Enron.

In response to the success of Al-Rajhi, the other Saudi conventional banks have opened Islamic deposit facilities, notably the National Commercial Bank that has almost 20 per cent of its network of 258 branches providing dedicated Islamic financial services. Some *ulama* and Islamic bankers argue that this provision cannot really work in accordance with the *shari'a* because their funds cannot be separated from the others based on *riba*. They appear to be losing the argument in Saudi Arabia, however, although one of the smaller Saudi institutions, Bank Aljazira, is converting all its operations to comply with the *shari'a*, ending Al-Rajhi's monopoly as the only wholly Islamic bank.

In Jordan, the Arab Bank was required to build up an entirely new bank for its Islamic operations. Were such a ruling to take effect in Saudi Arabia, there could be a major shake-up in the commercial banking system. An influx of Islamic banking might then tip the scales within the government in favour of its economic reformers. Paradoxically, however, the risk of rapid economic change in Saudi Arabia is that its principal beneficiaries might be members of the royal family, like Prince Walid al-Talal and other less professional uncles and cousins, the Saudi equivalents of the nomenclatura in single-party regimes.

The potential political fallout from Islamic banking differs widely from state to state in the MENA. The ground-up view of synergies between political and financial Islam seems less likely today, however, in this era of de-liberalization, than the top-down approach. Whether further structural adjustment will lead to greater political liberalization in the long run is yet to be seen, but so far, in the MENA at least, neither process has been linear and uni-directional. Meanwhile, Islamic finance, with its small shares of the market to date, may incrementally acquire larger shares of many MENA markets. Self-consciously Islamic financiers seem bound to prosper, irrespective of the regime's treatment of political Islamists.

Paradoxically, the end of the Saddam Hussein regime, far from impeding Islamist influence, may have actually strengthened it by eliminating one of the most secularist governments in the region. The position of other authoritarian regimes in the MENA countries, notably in Syria, has been seriously weakened, and the radical Islamist opposition emboldened by the power vacuum. Rather than the United States embarking on further confrontational policies, and intensifying a clash of civilizations, it is surely in the Western world's interest to encourage a more benign sort of globalization whereby Islamic financial instruments are integrated into international finance. Islamic capitalism is not a threat to Western capitalism in the way that Soviet Communism was. Respect for property rights and the defence of trade and commerce is a feature of all forms of capitalism, Western and oriental. Both systems can coexist, and gain from cooperation.

To some extent, such cooperation is already evident as the International Monetary Fund and the World Bank encouraged the establishment of the Islamic Financial Services Board that will advise central banks on the regulation of Islamic banks, and facilitate much needed standardization. Although based in Kuala Lumpur, Dr Rifaat Karim, formerly head of the Bahrain-based Accounting and Auditing Organization for Islamic Financial Institutions, has been appointed as secretary-general, and the Saudi Arabian Monetary Agency and the Malaysian Central Bank are cooperating closely over technical matters concerning the Board's remit and operational procedures.

Although the scope of this book is confined to the MENA countries, Islamic finance is a worldwide phenomenon, and developments in Malaysia – a country that has a more liberal interpretation of *shari'a* law – are starting to have a major impact on the more conservative MENA states. Ibrahim Warde pointed to the increasing influences from Malaysia, and indeed Muslims in the West and Western universities with specialists in Islamic economics, on the Islamic finance movement.

One example of this has been the development of new Islamic financial instruments, notably Islamic bonds. Conventional bonds, as fixed-interest debt instruments were, of course, prohibited under *shari'a* law; but the Malaysian government in the 1980s saw the value of bonds as a means of raising government finance, and raising funding for semi-state enterprises. They invented Islamic bonds that had exactly the same properties as their conventional equivalents, but were backed by real assets and yielded a fixed return that was comparable to, but not solely determined by, market rates of interest. *Shari'a* scholars in Malaysia, but not initially in the Gulf, accepted these Islamic bonds as legitimate. By 2000, however, seeing the success of the Malaysian Islamic bonds, there was a change of mind amongst at least some of the *shari'a* scholars in the Gulf, which was justified in terms of *ijtihad*, the reinterpretation of Islamic law. As a consequence, in 2001 the Bahrain Monetary Agency issued its first *sukuk* securities in the form of Islamic bonds and bills, an exercise that has been repeated every three months since. By 2002, the government of Malaysia felt confident enough to launch a *sukuk* bond issue for $600 million targeted at Gulf Islamic banks and businessmen that was oversubscribed. The Islamic Development ment Bank is now planning to raise capital through similar issues, demonstrating just how far thinking has moved. It seems only a matter of time before the Saudi Arabian government does likewise, given its need to diversify its sources of financing.

A younger, much better qualified and financially aware generation of *shari'a* scholars in the Gulf is approving radically innovative Islamic financial products. These include the National Commercial Bank's *tayseer* financing that has provided cash advances to its Saudi Arabian clients since 2001, and the Shamil Bank of Bahrain's *tamweel* scheme that has provided consumer finance in Bahrain since 2002. The Shamil Bank has developed Islamic credit cards that involve repayment by instalment, but no interest, the product being called the Shamil Al-Ruban Mastercard. In contrast, the Visa cards offered by other Islamic banks are really debit rather than credit cards, with the whole amount deducted from the client's account at the time of the transaction.

The new generation of *shari'a* scholars is typified by Dr Mohamed Elgari, the former director of the Centre for Research in Islamic Economics at King Abdul Aziz University, but now *shari'a* advisor to numerous banks, including the National Commercial Bank. He has now established his own *shari'a* consultancy at the Arabian Business Centre in Jeddah. Issues such as accreditation of *shari'a* advisors and professional standards are now being openly discussed for the first time, indicating just how far the Islamic finance movement has advanced. There is a desire to be treated seriously and respected internationally, as well as within the confines of the MENA region.

This book has drawn attention to the conditions that may facilitate the growth of what appears to be a distinctively Islamic variety of capitalist development. We have identified self-consciously Islamist financiers and tried to discover the conditions under which they best thrive. Distinctive financial practices seem to be mobilizing capital that would otherwise stay hidden in mattresses in much of the MENA region. The processes of economic globalization, coupled with the steady accumulation of Islamic capital, may eventually overcome the present barriers to integration and promote more political pluralism in the region. The studies in this book have identified Islamic capitalism as a natural evolution of gentle commerce. If big international business can polish the manners of the Bush Administration sufficiently to avert a clash of globalizations, it may also help Islamic finance promote the steady structural transformation of the region that our essays have envisioned.

Notes on the Contributors

FILIZ BASKAN, Faculty of Cosmmunications, Baskent University, Turkey

ELLIS GOLDBERG, Department of Political Science, University of Washington, Seattle, USA

CLEMENT M. HENRY, Department of Government, University of Texas at Austin, USA

MONZER KAHF, formerly Islamic Development Bank, Jeddah, Saudi Arabia

MOHAMMED MALLEY, Department of Government, University of Texas at Austin, USA

ROBERT P. PARKS, Department of Government, University of Texas at Austin, USA

KRISTIN SMITH, Department of Government, Harvard University, USA

SAMER SOLIMAN, Department of Social and Political Science, University of Lausanne, Switzerland

ENDRE STIANSEN, Centre for Development and the Environment, University of Oslo, Norway

IBRAHIM WARDE, Center for Middle Eastern Studies, Harvard University, USA

RODNEY WILSON, Institute for Middle Eastern and Islamic Studies, University of Durham, UK

TARIK M. YOUSEF, Center for Contemporary Arab Studies, Georgetown University, USA

Index

AAOIFI (Accounting and Auditing Organization for Islamic Financial Institutions), 5
Abacha, Sani, 55
Abadan refinery, Iran, 96
Abd al-Majeed Shoman, 193
Abd al-Majeed Thuneibat, 196, 209
Abd Hameed Al-Saih, Sheikh, 195
Abdu, Shaykh Muhammad, 92
ABID *see* Al-Baraka Investment and Development Company
ABM Amro, 136
Abou El-Magd, Ahmed Kamâl, 280
Abu Bakr, Jamil, 197, 198, 199, 200, 203, 206, 213
Abu Dhabi Islamic Bank, 144
accountability, 10, 71
accounting standards, 5
advance purchase financing *(istisna)*, 134, 212
Afaaf Charitable Committee, 209
Afghanistan, 43–4, 150, 179, 291
agency
    contracts, 171
    problem, 68, 69, 70
    rights, 130
AGPA (Alexandria General Produce Association), 91
Agricultural Bank of Sudan, 160
agricultural finance
    Egypt, 88–90
    Saudi Arabia, 134
    Sudan, 156, 160–1, 163, 164
agriculture, Islamic, 266
Ahli Bank, Jordan, 116–18
AIB (Arab Islamic Bank), 191, 193, 196–7, 199–200, 207, 209, 212
Akhbar Al-Youm (Egyptian newspaper), 266–7
Al-Ahli
    Arab Equity Fund, 144
    Asia Pacific and European Equity Funds, 143
    Asia Pacific Trading Equity Fund, 145
    Global Trading Equity Fund, 140–1, 142, 146–7
    International Trade Fund, 146, 147
    Saudi Riyal Murababaha Trading Fund, 145
    Saudi Trading Equity Fund, 145, 147–8
    Secured Funds, 143
    Short Term Dollar Fund, 145
    South East Asia Fund, 145
al Aqsa mosque fire (1969), 38
Al Arabi Saudi Company Shares, 145
Al Azhar University, Cairo, 135, 271–2
Al-Bait Global Equity, 141
Al-Baraka Global Equity, 141
Al-Baraka Investment and Development Company (ABID), 157, 224, 246, 247, 248
Al-Baraka Türk (special finance house), 134, 224, 225, 227, 228, 234
Al-Baraka Group, 1, 5, 8, 24, 108, 119, 125, 271
Al-Dar World Equities, 141
Al-Enma'a company, 181
Al Hilal Fund, 144
Al Kawthar Fund, 142
al Khatmiyyah Sufi order, 157
Al-Noor (KFH monthy magazine), 181–2
Al Qaeda (Al-Qaida), 55, 179
Al-Rajhi
    Balanced Funds, 143
    Banking and Investment Corporation, 56, 108, 145, 292
    Egyptian Fund, 144
    Global Equity, 141
    Local Share Fund, 145
    Middle Eastern Fund, 144
Al-Sabah family, 170, 171, 172
Al-Wafa, 54
Alexandria, 84, 86
Alfanar Funds, 143
Alfanar Investment, 141
Algeria, 7, 8, 9, 10, 20, 21, 28, 51, 57, 245, 251, 290
    credit to private sector, 108
    economic freedom in, 107
    Islamic banking, 105, 106
Allâm, Fouâd, 272
alms-giving *see* *zakat* funds
Amanah Saham Bank Islam Fund, 148
AMEN Bank, 246, 252
Amman Stock Exchange, 115
Anadolu Finans (special finance house), 119, 125, 226, 228, 234
Ansar movement, 23, 158
anti-communism, 43

Arab Bank, 114, 193, 196, 209, 292
Arab Islamic Bank, 8
Arab League, 132
Arab-Malaysian Unit Trust, 145
Arab National Bank, 145
Arabi, Mohammad Abdullah al, 19
ARABIC (Al Rajhi Banking and Investment
    Corporation), 8, 108, 109, 110, 113, 114
Arabism, 38
Arabiyyat, Abdul Lateef, 198, 209, 213
Aramco (US oil company), 42, 43, 98–9, 100
Ashmuni contracts, 90
Asian financial crisis (1997), 6, 131, 148
asset ownership, 65, 70
Asya Finans (special finance house), 119, 216,
    223, 226, 228, 231–5, 236, 237
Azhar, Sheikh Al-, 281

backwardation, 90
Bahrain, 7, 57, 74, 144
    credit to private sector, 108
    economic freedom in, 106, 107
    Islamic banking in, 114
bai al dawn (sale of debt), 148
balanced funds, 137, 143
Bangladesh, 22, 28, 39, 74
Bank al Taqwa, 25, 54
Bank Aljazira, 292
Bank Bumiputra, 6
Bank Islam Malaysia Berhad (BIMB), 6, 148
Bank Misr (Egypt), 8, 106, 197, 270, 271, 276,
    278–9
Bank Muamalet, 7
Bank of Commerce (Malaysia), 6
Bank of Pakistan, 31
Bank of Sudan, 159, 161–2, 164
Bankers Trust, 45
banking see conventional banking; Islamic
    banking; private banking; special finance
    houses
bankruptcy, 226, 235
Banna, Hassan Al-, 191
Banque de France, 245
Banque de l'Algérie, 243
Banque Nationale de Paris, 6
Basel capital adequacy accords, 113
Bashâri, Ahmed Al-, 278
Bashir, Omar Hassan al-, 30, 161
Basle Committee on Banking Supervision of the
    Bank of International Settlements, 50
BAT (Banks Association of Turkey), 120
BCCI (Bank of Credit and Commerce
    International), 48, 51, 118, 277
BCT (Banque Centrale de Tunisie), 245, 246, 252
BDDA (Banking Regulation and Supervision
    Agency), 120
BDET (Banque de Développement Économique
    de Tunisie), 252
Bedouins, 171–2, 175, 177
Ben Ali, Zine Abdine, 250, 251

Ben Ammar, Tahar, 244
Ben Yedder, Rachid, 246
Ben Youssef, Salah, 245
Bereket Vakfi, 224
Berger, Sandy, 54
BEST (Beit Ettamwil Saoudi Tounsi) Bank, 247–
    55, 291
BFT (Banque Franco-Tunisienne), 245, 252
Bhutto, Zulficar Ali, 39
BIAT (Banque Internationale Arabe de Tunisie),
    246, 252
BIB (Bahrain Islamic Bank), 114
Bin Laden, Osama, 41, 44, 54, 56, 143, 286
Bin Mahfouz, Khalid, 143
Bin Mahfouz, Mohammad, 143
Birtek, Faruk and Toprak, Binnaz, 218, 219, 220
BNA (Banque Nationale Agricole), 245, 246, 252
BNDT (Banque Nationale de Développement
    Touristique), 252
bonded warehouses, 4, 5
bonds, 137, 140, 148, 293–4
Boulalyah, Ismail, 252
Bourdieu, Pierre, 273
Bourguiba, Habib, 242, 244–5, 247, 249, 250
Bourguiba Jr, Habib, 246, 247
BP (Banque du Peuple), 245
BP (British Petroleum), 96–7
Brent crude, 99
Bresciani-Turroni, Constantino, 91
British Bank of the Middle East, 246
British Virgin Islands, 143
Brunei, 141
Brzezinski, Zbigniew, 43–4
BS (Banque du Sud), 246
bureaucratic quality, 73, 74, 75, 77
Bush, George Herbert Walker, 44
Bush, President George W., 52, 53
business associations, 23, 31, 204–7, 217–18, 222,
    223

Cairo-Amman Bank, Jordan, 116–18
capital flight, 125, 129, 131, 135–6, 137–40, 140–
    4
Caravan Fund, 142
Central Bank of Egypt, 118, 272, 283
Central Bank of Jordan, 116, 195, 206
Central Bank of Kuwait, 182, 183–4
Central Bank of Malaysia, 7
Central Bank of Pakistan, 31
Central Bank of Tunisia, 245
Central Bank of Turkey, 119, 120
central banks, 25, 50
central planning, 45
Çetin, Hikmet, 221
CFCT (Crédit Foncier et Commercial de Tunisie),
    246
charity, 179, 209; see also zakat funds
Cheikhrouhou, Moncef, 252
Chenik, M'Hamed, 243–4, 252
Choudhury, Alam, 132

Christianity, 268
Çiller, Tansu, 221, 222, 236
CIM (contract intensive money), 250
Cindoruk, Hüsamettin, 221
Citi Global Portfolio, 141
Citibank, 4, 6, 49, 109, 136
civil law, 69, 70, 71, 73
civil society, 46–7, 204, 287
Civil Transaction Act (Sudan), 155, 156
Cohen, David, 55
Commercial Bank of Qatar, 142
Commercial Companies Law (Kuwait 1960), 171
commodities markets, 81–100
common law, 69, 70, 71, 74, 76
communications, 134
Communism, 43, 44–5, 51, 158
compensatory rates, 161–2
consumer finance, 175–6, 180–1, 182
Contentment Party (Turkey) see CP
        (Contentment Party)
contract intensive money (CIM), 250
contracts, 156, 159–61, 162, 171; see also mudaraba
        contracts; murabaha contracts
conventional banking
    compared with Islamic finance, 104–26, 266–7
    compared with special finance houses, 123
    deregulation of, 4, 45
    Islamic windows, 49, 109, 136, 271, 290; see
        also Bank Misr
    losing clients to Islamic banking, 25
    progress of Islamic banking share of, 6–7
    hare of debt in external finance, 67
    standard debt contracts, 64
    stocks in, 149
    Turkey, 121
corporate bonds, 136
corporate governance, 68, 69–70
correspondent banking, 55
corruption, 71, 74, 75, 77, 202, 203
Coşan, Professor Esad, 218
cotton, 134
cotton futures markets, 85, 86–93, 288
Council on Foreign Relations, 51–2, 55
CP (Contentment Party), 119, 217, 228, 236
credit, 66, 77, 84, 107–8
credit cards, 294
credit protection, 69
creditors, 70
CTC (Coopérative Tunisienne de Crédit), 243–4

Dallah al-Baraka Group (DAB), 41, 50, 56, 246, 247
Daninos, Monsieur, 245, 252
Dar al-Maal al-Islami Group, 158
Darif, Muhammad, 57
Darir, Muhammad al Siddiq al, 24
debt
    consumer, 176
    financing, 64, 65–7, 70
    management, 148, 277
    national, 138

debt-to-equity ratios, 67, 70, 71–5
Demirel, Süleyman, 221
Democratic Left Party (Turkey), 221
Democratic Party (Turkey) see DP (Democratic
        Party)
democratization, 69–70, 71, 74, 75, 76, 78, 287
deregulation, 45, 47
Destour Party (Tunisia), 244
Deutsche Asset Management, 142, 143
Deutsche Bank, 136
devaluation, 275, 276
development assistance, 133–4
Din, Sa'd al-, 194
DMI (Dar al-Maal al-Islami) Group, 5, 41, 50, 56
Dow Jones Islamic Index, 141, 149
DP (Democratic Party), 217
dress code, 2, 222, 274, 282, 283
drugs, 53
Dubai, 21, 99
Dubai Islamic Bank, 6, 8, 20, 21–2, 39, 113–14, 292
DUP (Democratic Unionist Party) (Sudan), 157,
        158

East Asia, 73, 74, 75; see also individual countries
Eastern Europe, 44–5
Ecevit, Bülent, 221, 224, 236
economic cooperation, 132
economic liberalization, 106–7, 221–2, 240–1, 250
education, 222–3, 236
Egebank, 226
EGF Hermes, Cairo, 144
Egypt, 2, 7, 9, 10, 18, 21, 29, 74, 265
    Bank Misr in, 8, 106, 197, 270, 271, 276, 278–
        9
    credit to private sector, 108
    economic freedom in, 107
    economic indicators for, 138
    futures markets, 81–2, 84, 86–92, 288
    government banking control, 105, 106
    IMMCs, 8, 48
    Islamic banking in, 19–20, 22–3, 49, 118, 269–
        84, 291
    Mit Ghamr experiment, 19, 20, 29, 192, 267–9
    newspaper campaign against Islamic banks,
        266–7
    and oil price increases, 133
    portfolio investment from the Gulf into, 144–5
    and Soviet Union, 37, 39
    S&P/IFCI price indices for, 149–50
    veiling in, 274, 282, 283
Egyptian-Saudi Investment Bank (ESIB), 271
Eizenstat, Stuart E., 56
Elgari, Dr Mohammed, 294
embezzlement, 114
Emerson, Steven, 52
Engineers Association, 204, 206
Enron, 292
entrepreneurs, 47
    debt contracts and, 68, 70
    in Egypt, 19, 20

and futures markets, 85
  in Islamic finance, 28, 172, 180
  in Islamic investment, 168
  and partnership finance, 40
  in Saudi Arabia, 130
  in Tunisia, 243
equity funds, 65–71, 76, 136, 137, 138–9, 141,
    143, 147, 156, 175
Erbakan, Necmettin, 23, 30, 31, 119, 120, 236
Erdoğan, Recep Tayyip, 237
ethical finance industry, 131, 136
Eurocredit Bank, 226
executive constraints, 74, 78
exports, 45, 86, 135, 163, 170
expropriation risk, 71, 74–5, 77, 138

Faisal, King, 38, 39, 42–3
Faisal, Prince Mohammad Al-, 5, 22–3, 40, 50, 54,
    56, 119, 158
  and Faisal Islamic Bank of Egypt, 272, 276
  and Jordan Islamic Bank, 194, 195
  and special finance houses in Turkey, 224, 225
Faisal Bank (Turkey), 23, 125
Faisal Finance House, 134, 224, 225, 228
Faisal Group, 5, 8, 108
Faisal Islamic Bank of Egypt (FIB), 22, 66, 106,
    118, 269, 270–1, 272, 275, 276–7, 278
Faisal Islamic Bank of Turkey, 134
Family Finans, 233–4
Farhan, Ishaq, 193, 195, 208, 209, 213
fatwas (religious rulings), 21, 269
  on Arab Islamic Bank, 196, 209
  on conventional bank interest rates, 272, 277–
    8, 281
  to curb abuses of murabaha contracts, 162
  from Muslim Brotherhood, 208
  from the OIC Fiqh Academy, 135
  on postal savings accounts, 82, 92
  on salam contracts, 160
  on Western-style banks, 18
Faysal Shield Fund, 144
fertilisers, 134
Fethullah Gülen Community, 216, 218, 219, 223,
    231, 236
FIB see Faisal Islamic Bank of Egypt
fibres trade, 82
FIBS (Faisal Islamic Bank of Sudan), 22, 41, 52,
    156–7, 158–9
filières, 87
financial compensation, 56
financial seminars, 24, 26
financial services, 45–6
financial structure data, 71–5
fines, 277
fiqh, 24, 26–7
First Islamic Investment Bank of Bahrain, 114
FIS (Algerian Islamic Salvation Front), 51, 57
fixed-return payments, 3, 64
Flood Enquiry, 143
food cooperatives, Kuwait, 177–8

Foreign Affairs (journal of Council on Foreign
    Relations), 51–2
foreign direct investment, 130
foreign exchange hedging, 27
Forward Contract Exchange Company,
    Amsterdam, 95
forward markets, 84; see also salam contracts
France, 6, 83, 88, 243, 245
free enterprise, 47
Friedman, Milton, 47
FTSE index, 149
fund management, 142, 148, 151, 276
fundamentalist Islam, 52, 265, 274
fuqaha, 24, 27
futures markets
  criticism of, 82–3
  Egypt, 86–93
  oil, 93–100
  politics and, 84–5

GCC (Gulf Cooperation Council) countries, 2, 8
  banking comparison of, 109–10, 111, 114
  Islamic share of commercial bank deposits per
    GDP, 9–10; see also individual countries
gender segregation, 180–1
General Motors, 89
Germany, 83, 88
Ghannouchi, Rachid, 247
gharar (futures), 82
Ghazali, Abdel Hamid Al-, 273
Glass-Steagall legislation, 45
Global Equity 2000 Sub Fund, 141
globalization, 44, 129, 210, 293, 295
  and Asya Finans, 232
  futures markets, 83
  and Islamic banking, 241
  oil industry, 93–100
  and Turkey, 219, 221
Gökçek, Cengiz, 225
government bonds, 136, 193–4
government policy
  agricultural price support, 89–90
  banking regulation, 8, 22, 105–6, 111–13, 113,
    125
  BEST Bank, 248, 254
  on capital control, 132, 135, 144
  on corporate governance, 69–70
  Egyptian Islamic banking, 270–3
  and foreign direct investment, 130
  Islamic banking relationship with, 28–9
  and musharaka finance, 160
  special assistance for Islamic finance, 108, 125,
    169
  Sudan, 156, 161
  towards Islamism, 273
grains futures markets, 85
grains trade, 82
Greenberg, Maurice R., 55
Gülen, Fethullah, 220–1, 222–3, 236
Gulf International Bank, 142, 143, 145

Gulf states, 38–9, 135, 137, 168, 292; *see also* individual countries
Gulf War (1991), 51, 183, 251

Hadar, Leon, 51
Hâfez, Olwi, 282
hajj, 18, 38
Halim Isma'il, Abd al, 22
Hamas, 46
Hamoud, Sami, 22, 23, 192–4
Handbook of Islamic Banking, 41
Hantash, Musa, 201, 205–6, 208, 209, 212, 213
haram, 151, 250
Harb, Talaat, 196, 270
hard currency earnings, 135
Hassan, Hussain Hamed, 24
Hassan, King, 107–8, 194
Haughey, Charles, 143
hedging, 97, 99
Hegira Global Equity Fund, 142
Heritage Foundation, 106
Hezbollah, 43, 46
HIFIP (Harvard Islamic Finance Information Program), 5, 49
Horsnell, Paul and Mabro, Robert, 95
HSBC, 4, 6, 49, 136
Huntington, Samuel, 51–2

IAF (Islamic Action Front Party), 198, 201–3, 208
Ibrahim, Issa Abdu, 22
Ibrahim, Saad Eddin, 130
IDB (Islamic Development Bank), 5, 6, 19, 20–2, 39, 41, 129, 133, 192, 225, 291, 294
İhlas Finance House (Turkey), 8–9, 119, 120, 122, 218, 226, 227–8, 235
IIBID (Islamic International Bank for Investment and Development), 271, 273–4, 277
ijara (leasing), 33n, 134, 159, 227, 233
ijtihad, 49
Illinois, 88
IMF (International Monetary Fund), 8, 41, 45, 47, 50, 164, 201, 218, 221, 293
IMMCs (Islamic Money Management Companies), 48
imports, and Kuwait Finance House, 175, 178
Index of Economic Freedom (Heritage Foundation/ *Wall Street Journal*), 106–7
India, 50
Indonesia, 74, 132, 141, 145
    economic indicators for, 138
    Islamic solidarity, 38
    mutual funds, 137
    S&P/IFCI price indices for, 149–50
industrial intermediate goods, 134
industry, 134, 266, 280
infita laws, 270
inflation
    Sudan, 162–3
    Turkey, 221

institutional quality, and Islamic finance, 73, 75, 76, 77
insurance, 50, 81
interest *see riba*
International Association of Islamic Banks, 5, 40
International Cotton Federation, 88, 90, 92
International Financial Corporation (World Bank), 6
International Investor of Kuwait, 114
International Turnkey Systems (ITS), 178
inventory maintenance, 98, 99
investment funds, 24, 45, 109
    management, 27, 137, 276
    rates of return, 111
    special finance houses, 123–4
investments, 129–51, 131–2, 145–8, 160, 225; *see also* property investments
investor protection, 69
IPE (International Petroleum Exchange), 97
Iqbal, Munawar, 132
Iran, Islamic Republic of, 6, 7, 8, 50, 74, 292
    capital flight, 131
    economic indicators for, 138
    hawkish member of OPEC, 42
    and Islamic Development Bank, 134
    Islamization of banking sector, 29, 31, 39, 76
    oil industry, 96, 99
    private sector banking, 105
Iran, Shah of, 38, 42
Iran-Contra affair, 43
Iranian Islamic Revolution (1978–79), 43
Iraq, 8, 150, 291–2, 293
    government banking monopoly, 105
    invasion of Kuwait, 44
Iraq War (2003), 289
İŞHAD (Business Life Cooperation Association), 223
ISI (Inter-Services Intelligence), 43
Işik Sigorta (insurance company), 231
Islam
    Islamist version of, 265
    perceived as new global enemy, 51–3
    in Turkish politics, 216–20, 222
Islamic Action Front party *see* IAF (Islamic Action Front Party)
Islamic Al-Shamal Bank, 41
Islamic Bank of Jordan, 23
Islamic Bank of Malaysia, 19
Islamic Bank of Sudan-West, 28
Islamic banking/finance, 2–6, 266
    apostates of, 280–1
    capital flight funds, 129–51
    during cold war, 41
    compared with conventional banking, 104–26
    entrepreneurial financing, 28
    first aggiornamento of, 39–41
    'integration' scenario, 12, 288–90
    and Islamist politics, 41–4, 118, 191, 207–9, 273–4
    modes of financing in, 65–6

murabaha syndrome in, 63–78
perceived as funding terrorism, 52
relationship with government, 28–9
religious boards of, 3–4, 5, 22, 24, 25, 108, 160, 161, 162, 208, 272
second aggiornamento of, 48–51
'separation and coward capital' scenario, 12, 242, 288, 290
and *ulama*, 23, 25–6
West's suspicion of, 54, 56, 287; *see also* individual countries and banks; special finance houses
Islamic Development Bank *see* IDB (Islamic Development Bank)
Islamic Financial Services Board, 5, 293
Islamic International Bank for Investment and Development *see* IIBID (Islamic International Bank for Investment and Development)
Islamist Constitutional Movement, 183
Islamist politics, 2, 10
during the cold war years, 37–9
demystification and, 280
and end of Saddam Hussein regime, 293
and investment, 131–2
Islamic banks relationship with moderate, 29
and Islamic finance, 41–4, 118, 191, 207–9, 273–4
in Jordan, 191–6, 207–9, 210–12
and Kuwait Finance House, 172, 173, 176, 178, 179, 183, 184
and non-allied *ulama*, 28
post-September 11th, 57
professional associations and, 204–7
revivalism, 46
state policy towards, 273
in Sudan, 157, 158
in Tunisia, 250–2
in Turkey, 119–20, 124, 221–3, 224–37
veiling, 222, 274, 282
view of Islamic banking in Jordan, 196–200
Islamization, 180–2
Israel, 39, 42, 202, 205
istisna (advance purchase financing) contracts, 134, 212

Jamaat Tabligh, 46
Jami'yat al-Rakha Association (Businessmen's Prosperity Association), 204–7
Japanese cotton industry, 91
JDP (Justice and Development Party), 119, 217, 224, 228, 236–7, 290
JIB (Jordan Islamic Bank), 22, 28, 114–18, 191–200, 207–9, 212
Jihad, 52, 198
joint ventures, 119, 270; *see also musharaka* contracts
Jordan, 7, 8, 9, 10, 28, 29, 74, 105, 109, 133, 144
banking competition, 283
credit to private sector, 108

economic freedom in, 107
economic indicators for, 138
Islamic banking in, 191–200, 288, 289, 292
Islamic *versus* conventional banking, 110, 114–19
Islamist economic agenda in, 200–12
professional associations, 204–7; *see also* JIB (Jordan Islamic Bank)
Jordan Islamic Bank for Finance and Investment, 4
Jordan Islamic Bank *see* JIB (Jordan Islamic Bank)
Jordanian National Bank, 110, 192, 193
J. P. Morgan, 45
Judaism, 268
jurisprudence, Islamic *see* OIC *Fiqh* Academy, Jeddah
jurists, 3–4, 5
Justice and Development Party (Turkey) *see* JDP (Justice and Development Party)

Kabaca, Ünal, 231, 235
Kadiri sect, 218
Kahf, Monzer, 286–7, 291
Kalkavan, _hsan, 231
Kamal, Ahmed Adel, 273
Kamel, Sheikh Saleh, 22, 23, 24, 41, 50, 54, 56, 119, 271
and Jordan Islamic Bank, 194, 195, 199
and special finance houses, 224
and Tunisia, 247, 254
Karim, Dr Rifaat, 293
Kazakhstan, 223
Kelani, Ijaz, 20
Kemalism, 23, 30, 31
Keppel Insurance, 141, 142
KFH (Kuwait Finance House), 8, 22, 111–13, 125, 168–9, 171, 172, 173–6
and Islamization of Kuwaiti society, 180–2
politics in, 176–82
regulation of, 182–5
Kilani, Ibrahim Zaid al-, 194
Kitchener, Lord, 88
Klat, Jules, 92
Knox Smith, Herbert, 85
Kombassan Holding, 225
Koran
on private property rights, 47
on profits from commerce, 40
Koranic schools, 209
Kuala Lumpur, 145
Kuala Lumpur Stock Exchange, 148
Külahi Cemal, 225
Kutan, Recai, 217, 236
Kuveyt Türk (special finance house), 225, 228, 234
Kuwait, 7, 9, 10, 74, 168
credit to private sector, 108
economic freedom in, 107
effect of increased oil revenues, 175
Iraqi invasion of, 44
Islamic *versus* conventional banking in, 110–14

Islamization of, 180–2
merchant families in, 170–1
National Assembly of, 177, 178, 179, 183–5
oil industry, 100; *see also* KFH (Kuwait
    Finance House); NBK (National Bank of
    Kuwait)
Kuwait Turkish Evkaf, 119

La Porta, R., Lopez-de-Silanes, F., Shleifer, A. and
    Vishny, R. W., 68, 69
La Porta, Rafael, 106
Lac de Tunis Reclamation Project, 247–8, 254
Land Acquisition Program (Kuwait), 170
Latin America, 74, 241
law
    banking regulation, 184–5
    Egyptian banking, 281–2
    and financial structure, 68–71, 72–3
    futures markets, 83, 92–3, 100
    Jordanian banking, 195, 196
    special financial, 23, 270
    Turkish banking, 119; *see also shari'a*
law and order tradition, 69, 74
leasing (*ijara*), 33n, 134, 159, 227, 233
Lebanon, 7, 8, 106, 144
    banking competition, 283
    credit to private sector, 108
    economic freedom in, 107
legal origin hypothesis, 71, 72–3, 77
Leigh-Pemberton, Robin, 51
Lenczowski, George, 42
lending transactions, 50
Lewis, Bernard, 52, 53, 57
Libya, 8, 10, 105, 106
loan recovery, 277
Lutah, Sa'id, 22

macroeconomics, 120, 138
Mahdi, Sadiqh al-, 23, 157, 161
Maher, Mustafa, 90
Malaysia, 6–7, 9, 10, 21, 46, 74, 76, 132, 133, 141,
    145
    bond funds, 137, 140, 148, 293–4
    economic indicators for, 138
    fund management, 142
    hajj funding, 18–19
    Islamic solidarity, 38
    local investment in, 148
    second aggiornamento of Islamic finance, 49
    S&P/IFCI price indices for, 149–50
managed funds, 129, 136, 140–4, 146, 147–8, 148
Manceron, Resident General, 243–4
Mani', Abdullah Bin, 24
Maraqa, Nihad, 207
Marcos, Ferdinand, 55
mark-up contracts *see* debt contracts
Marzouk, Abdel Sabour, 280
Marzouki, Moncef, 252
Mastercard, 294
Mawdudi, Abu'l-A'la, 192

Mawlawi, Faisal, 196, 209
Mbeideen, Yousef al-, 194
media, 223, 226
Meeker, J. Edward, 84
MENA (Middle East and North Africa) states, 1,
    2, 4, 9, 78, 109
    economic freedom within, 106
    Islamic banking in, 6–7, 9, 114, 287, 293
    murabaha syndrome in, 74, 288
    Western multinationals in, 5–6; *see also*
        individual countries
Menderes, Adnan, 217
merchant banking, 48
Merrill Lynch, 136
Mexico, 44, 96, 99
micro-finance programmes, 28
middle class, 27, 46, 173
Middle East Economic Conference, 202
Middle East Economic Digest reports (2001/2), 110–
    11, 112, 113
Middle East *see under* individual countries
migrant workers, 135, 158, 172
militant Islam, 179, 251
Miller, Judith, 51
Mirghani, Muhammad Uthman al-, 157
Mirghani, Sayyid Ali al-, 23, 157
Mit Afifi, 87
Mit Ghamr experiment (in Egypt), 19, 20, 29,
    192, 267–9
Moallah, Mansour, 246, 252
Mobutu, Joseph, 55
money-laundering, 1, 53, 108, 287
money market funds, 147
Moriarty Tribunal, 143
Morocco, 8, 9, 57, 74, 106, 107, 108, 138, 144,
    149–50, 292
Mortimer, Edward, 39
Mosseri, Victor, 90–1
MP (Motherland Party), 218, 224
MTI (Mouvement de la Tendence Islamique), 247
mu'ajjal contracts, 84
Mubarak, President, 291
mudaraba contracts, 3, 4, 40, 104, 145, 173, 227,
    233, 241, 281
mullas, 31
muqawala (contract finance), 161
murabaha contracts, 3–4, 5, 21, 40, 64, 73, 104
    BEST Bank, 252–3
    criticism of, 281
    and Islamic Development Bank, 134
    in Islamic finance, 63–78
    Kuwait Finance House use of, 174–5, 177
    in Muslim and non-Muslim countries, 74
    in Saudi Arabia, 147
    share of total Islamic financing, 65–6
    special finance houses, 226, 233
    in Sudan, 159–60, 161, 162, 163
Murawiec, Laurent, 55
musharaka (joint venture) contracts, 3, 4, 40, 104,
    159–60, 227, 233, 241, 281

MÜSİAD (Independent Association of Industrialists and Businessmen), 23, 31, 205, 217–18, 222, 223
Muslim Brotherhood, 19, 22, 37, 172
  and AIB, 199–200
  basic principles of, 191
  control of Islamic finance, 41
  in Egypt, 192
  and Faisal Islamic Bank, 272, 273
  in Jordan, 191, 193, 194, 195–6, 197, 199, 201, 207–9, 211
  in Sudan, 157–9; *see also* Fethullah Gülen Community
Mutawwa, Abdel Aziz al-, 172
mutual funds, 50, 111, 136, 137, 145–6, 149–50, 288
Mzali, Mohammed, 247–8

Nabulsi, Mohammed Saeed al-, 193
Nahas, Yusuf, 88, 90, 91, 92
Najjar, Dr Ahmed al, 3, 19, 22, 192, 267–8, 280, 281
Nakshibendi sect, 218
NASDEQ index, 137, 139
Nasr, Hamdi Sayf al-, 90
Nasser, Gamal Abd al-, 37, 38, 132, 268
Nasser Social Bank *see* NSB (Nasser Social Bank)
National Assembly of Kuwait, 177, 178, 179, 183–5
National Bank of Kuwait *see* NBK (National Bank of Kuwait)
National Commercial Bank of Saudi Arabia, 25, 108, 140–1, 143, 144–7, 292, 294
National Islamic Front, 161
National Order Party (Turkey) *see* NOP (National Order Party)
National Pact (Tunisia), 250
National Reconciliation, 158
National Salvation Coup (1989), 28, 161
National Salvation Party (Turkey) *see* NSP (National Salvation Party)
National Welfare Party, 119
nationalism
  Egyptian, 269–70
  Tunisian, 244
  Turkish, 219–20
Nationalist Action Party (Turkey), 224, 225
nationalization
  of foreign-owned banks in Sudan, 156, 158
  of oil production, 95–7, 99
Nazir, Hisham, 98
NBK (National Bank of Kuwait), 110, 112–13, 142, 169, 174, 180, 183, 185
Neo-Destour, 244–5, 247
New World Order (1990–2001), 39, 44–52
New York Stock Exchange, 137, 139
Niger, 74
Nigeria, 74
Nilein Bank, 161
Nimairi, President, 23, 157, 158
Nixon, Richard, 42

non-interest bearing deposits, 110–11
NOP (National Order Party), 217
Norbec, 99
North, Douglass, 100–1
Nouira, Hedi, 245, 246
NSB (Nasser Social Bank), 19–20, 268–9
NSP (National Salvation Party), 217, 224, 225
NYMEX (New York Metal Exchange), 97–8

October War (1973), 20, 38
OECD countries, *murabaha* syndrome in, 74
OIC *Fiqh* Academy, Jeddah, 4, 5, 24, 26, 83, 134–5
OIC (Organization of the Islamic Conference), 20, 38, 39, 132, 192
oil industry, 82
  embargoes, 39, 42, 95
  futures market, 81–2
  globalization, 93–100
  Kuwait, 170, 171
  price fall, 46
  price increases, 9, 20, 41, 42, 132–3, 156, 168
Oman, 8, 9, 106, 107
on-call sales, 87–8
O'Neill, Paul, 53, 54
Öniş, Ziya, 219–20, 221
OPEC (Organization of Petroleum Exporting Countries), 42, 96, 99
Ören, Enver, 218, 226
Ottoman Empire, 216
overseas investment *see* capital flight
Özal, Korkut, 22, 218, 224
Özal, Turgut, 23, 119, 218, 221, 224, 225, 227
Özcan, Salih, 224
Özkara, Osman Gürbüz, 231

Pakistan, 6, 22, 43, 57, 74, 133, 179
  anti-Soviet resistance in Afghanistan, 43
  economic indicators for, 138
  Islamic solidarity, 38–9
  Islamization of banking sector, 29, 31, 39, 49, 76
  subject to sanctions, 50
Paksu, Ahmet Tevfik, 224–5
Palestine, 132, 151
Palestinian migrant workers, 172
pan-Arabism, 38, 132, 172, 201
pan-Islamism, 37–8, 134, 135
patronage, 10, 171, 173, 179, 291
Pemex, 96
Perle, Richard, 55
Permal Asset Management of London, 141, 142, 143
petrodollars, 41, 44, 168
Petroleum Exchange, 95
petroleum industry *see* oil industry
phosphoric acid, 134
Pictet & Cie, 141, 142
pietism, 46, 48, 114, 168
Pipes, Daniel, 52, 56
PLO (Palestine Liberation Organization), 195, 199

PLS (profit-and-loss-sharing) contracts, 40, 48, 49, 64, 232–3
politics
    and finance view of corporate governance, 69–71
    and futures markets, 84–5, 89–90
    and Islamic finance, 241
    in Kuwait, 171–2, 176–82
    liberalization, 211, 212
    in Sudan, 157–8
    in Tunisia, 244–5, 246–7, 250
    in Turkey, 216–22, 236–7; see also Islamic politics
portfolio investments, 124, 137, 144–5
Post Office Savings Bank (Sudan), 155
potash, 134
Powell, Colin, 53
private banking, 67, 77, 105, 107–8, 121, 122, 136, 151
private charities, 179
privatization, 45, 47, 203
professional associations, 23, 31, 204–7, 217–18, 222, 223
project finance, 134
property investments, 136, 144, 175, 181, 247
property rights, 47, 71, 72–3, 74, 77, 97, 156, 293
PSD (Parti Socialiste Destourien), 247
public opinion, 17
public utilities, 134

Qaradaghi, Muhammad ali al, 24
Qaradawi, Yusuf al, 24, 196, 209
Qatar, 7, 9
    credit to private sector, 108
    economic freedom in, 107
    Islamic banking in, 114
QIZs (Qualified Industrial Zones), 202

rates of return, 111, 277, 278
Reagan, Ronald, 43
real estate see property
refined petroleum products, 134
regulation, 50–1
    Egyptian futures market for cotton, 86–93
    financial, 68–9
    I'hlas Finans, 226, 235
    Islamic banking, 293
    of Kuwait Finance House, 182–5
    Sudanese banking, 164
    Tunisian banking, 246
Rehan, Bakr, 207
religion
    dialogue between, 222
    and investment, 131–2
    and state politics, 220
    and usury, 268
religious observance, 46
religious sect networks in Turkey, 218–19
rental income, 144
Republican Reliance Party (Turkey), 224

republicanism, 220
research, 26, 63, 65, 68
research institutes, 39
RHB (Rashid Hussain Berhad), 142, 148
riba (usury), 2–3, 18, 20, 21, 24, 27, 40, 49, 81, 155, 241, 266, 270
    Muslim view of, 104–5
    on postal savings accounts, 82
    purifying, 136, 140
    religion and, 268
ribha (profits), 2
rice, 134
risk-management techniques, 45, 49
risky assets, 117–18, 122–3
Riyâd, Fouâd, 280
Riyadh Bank, 110, 145
Riyadh Equity Fund, 145
Rule of Law, 69, 70, 71, 73, 77
Rumsfeld, Donald, 53

Sadafi, Sheikh Bakri Al-, 269
Sadat, President Anwar, 23, 39, 42, 43, 273
Saddam Hussein, 251, 286, 291, 293
Sahbani, Ismail, 252
Sakel contracts, 87, 90, 92
salam (forward) contracts, 82, 84, 147, 160–1, 164
Saleh Kamel Center for Islamic Economic Studies, 271
SAMBA Global Equity, 141
SAMBA (Saudi American Bank), 109, 110, 292
sanctions, 50
Saqr, Dr Mohammad, 194, 197
Saruhan, R., 225
Saud Abu Mahfudh, 197, 199, 200–1, 205, 213
Saud Nasser Al-Sabah, Sheikh, 179–80
Saudi Arabia, 7–8, 9, 20, 76, 144
    capital flight, 135–6, 139–40
    during the cold war, 37–8
    conventional versus Islamic banking, 105, 147
    credit to private sector, 108–9
    economic freedom in, 107
    economic indicators for, 138
    entrepreneurs in, 130
    and first Gulf War, 51
    foreign portfolio investment in, 149–50
    investment in Turkey, 225
    Islamic banking, 292
    and Islamic Development Bank, 132–3, 134
    Islamic versus conventional banking, 109–11
    Islamist opposition in, 10
    local investment in, 145–8
    oil production in, 96, 98–9, 100
    promotion of Islamic finance, 40–1, 49
    relations with the United States, 42–3, 55–6
Savings Deposit Insurance Fund, 235
Say, Jean-Baptiste, 283
Sayah, Mohammed, 247–8
Sayyid Qutb, 29
Schumer, Charles, 56
Schwartz, Stephen, 52

secularism, 216, 220
SEDCO (Saudi Economic and Development
    Company), 141, 142, 143
Selim, Sheikh Abdel Megid, 269
Senegal, 74
September 11th terrorist attacks (2001), 52, 53,
    56, 139, 144, 151, 179, 185, 286, 287
Server Holding, 218
'Seven Sisters' firms, 94
Sevilgen, M. Gündüz, 225
Shaarâwi, Sheikh Al-, 270, 281–2
Shallah, Ramadan, 198
Shamil Bank of Bahrain, 144, 294
Shareef, Kamil al-, 193–4, 195
shari'a, 294
    capital flight and, 130–1
    on futures markets, 82
    Islamic banks, 3
    Islamic bonds, 294
    and Islamic Development Bank, 134
    and murabaha contracts, 162, 163
    and private Islam finance alliance, 17–21, 23–9
    in relation to state laws, 135; see also fatwas
Shatti, Ismail Al-, 183
shayl (forward-purchase contracts), 156, 160
Shiism, 43, 44
Şivgin, Halil, 225
Six-day war (June 1967), 38
Sloan, Alfred P., 89
Social Democratic Populist Party, 221
social projects, 134
Social Reform Society, 172
socialism, 46, 268, 269
Société Marseillaise de Crédit, 246
socio-economics, and effect of ulama alliance, 27, 28
Soliman, Samer, 118
Somalia, 20
South Asia, murabaha syndrome in, 74
Soviet Union, 37, 39, 43–4, 45
S&P/IFCI (Standard and Poors International
    Finance Corporation), 149–50
special finance houses, 221
    Kuwait Finance House, 8, 22, 111–13, 125
    Mit Ghamr experiment, 19, 20, 29
    Turkey, 119–25, 134, 216–37, 290
speculation, 92, 97
spot markets, 83, 84, 85, 86–7, 88, 89, 90, 91, 92,
    95
spreads, 123–4
Standard Oil, 94
statism, 44–5, 47
STB (Société Tunisienne de Banque), 245, 246,
    252
stock prices, 138–40, 149–50
structural adjustment policies, 45
Sudan, 6, 7, 9, 23, 50, 74, 133
    case study of Islamic finance, 155–65, 289
    free-market reforms in, 47
    Islamization of banking sector, 29, 30, 39, 41,
        52, 76, 156

micro-finance programmes, 28
Sudan Communist Party, 158
Sudanese Faisal Islamic Bank, 28
Sudanese Islamic Bank, 157
sukuk securities, 294
Sukur, Ali Abu, 197, 200, 205, 213
Sunni Wahhabism, 44
Suq al-Manakh crisis (1982), 113, 173, 183
Switzerland, 6
syndicated finance, 27
Syria, 8, 74, 291, 293
    economic indicators for, 138
    Islamic banking, 105, 106
system tenure, 74, 75, 78

Tabung Hajji (Pilgrims' Administration and
    Fund), 18, 20
Tabung Ittikal Arab-Malaysian Fund, 145
Tadamon Islamic Bank (Sudan), 157
Tadawul, 150
Takaful Global Fund, 141
Taliban, 44, 46
tamweel scheme, 294
Tannash, Ahmad, 203, 213
Tantâwi, Sheikh Mohammed Sayed, 277, 279, 281
Tanzania, 74
Tarki, Abdullah, 96
taweed, 132
tayseer financing, 294
technology stock, 137, 139, 148, 149
Tekoğlu, Tahsin, 231
Telekom Malaysia, 148
terrorism, 1, 50, 52, 53, 56, 179, 185, 211, 286, 287
time-sharing, 27
Topbas, Eymen, 224
tourism, 144
trade, 266
    financing arrangements, 133–4
    Jordan, 202–3
    Kuwait Finance House, 175–6
trade unions (Turkey), 222
transfer prices, 94
transport, 86, 134
True Path Party (Turkey), 221, 222
trust, 104
Truth in Lending Act (US), 50
Tunisia, 7, 8, 10, 28, 74, 105, 106
    BEST Bank, 247–55, 291
    colonial banking in, 242–4
    credit to private sector, 107, 108
    economic freedom in, 107
    post-colonial banking, 244–7
Turabi, Hassan al-, 23, 30, 41, 52, 157, 161, 289
Turkey, 1, 6, 7, 10, 22, 28, 57, 74, 144
    credit to private sector, 108
    economic freedom in, 107
    economic indicators for, 138
    Islamic banking in, 29, 30–1, 109, 290
    Islamic solidarity, 38
    Islamic versus conventional banking, 119–25

Islamist prime minister, 51
political Islam in, 221–3
private Islamic banks in, 8–9
religious sect network in, 218–19
S&P/IFCI price indices for, 149–50
special finance houses in, 119–25, 134, 216–37, 224–37
transformation of state ideology, 219–21
Türkiye Vakiflar Bankası, 119
TÜSIAD (Association of Turkish Industrialists and Businessmen), 222

UAE (United Arab Emirates), 7, 9
credit to private sector, 108
economic freedom in, 107; see also Dubai Islamic Bank
UBCI (Union Bancaire pour le Commerce et l'Industrie), 252
UBS, 6, 49
Islamic Fund-Global Equities, 141
UIB (Union Internationale des Banques), 245, 246
ulama, 23–9, 25–9, 27–8, 30–1
Ülker, Sabri, 225
umma, 21
Umma Party (Sudan), 157
unemployment
in Jordan, 203
in Kuwait, 178–9
in Turkey, 221
Unit Trust Managers, 142
United Kingdom, economic indicators for, 138
United States
aid for Afghanistan, 43
anti-communist alliances, 43
anti-Saudi constituency within, 55–6
cotton, 89
economic indicators for, 138–9
financial deregulation, 45
free-trade pact with Jordan, 210
Islamic financial institutions in, 50
Islamic fund management, 137–8, 141, 142, 147
oil markets, 97, 98
relations with Saudi Arabia, 42–3
Saudi Arabian students in, 151
September 11th terrorist attacks, 52–6
war against terrorism, 52–6, 179, 185, 211, 286–7, 289
universities, 209, 222
Usmani, Shaikh Muhammad Taqi, 24
usury see riba
Uzbekistan, 223

vegetable oil, 134
veiling, 2, 222, 274, 282, 283, 291
Venezuela, 42
venture capitalism, 3, 40, 48
vertical integration, in oil industry, 94
Virtue Party (Turkey) see VP (Virtue Party)
Visa cards, 294
VP (Virtue Party), 119, 124, 217–18, 228, 236, 290

Wafd Party (Egypt), 89, 90, 269
Wahhab, Ahmad Abdel, 89, 90, 91
Walid al-Talal, Prince, 108–9, 292
war against terrorism, 52–6, 179, 185, 211, 286–7, 289
Warde, Ibrahim, 3, 5
Washington Consensus, 10, 45, 47, 241, 290
Webster, William H., 55
Wechsler, William F., 55–6
welfare, 47, 202
Welfare Party (Turkey) see WP (Welfare Party)
Wellington Management, 142
West Texas crude, 99
wheat, 134
Williams, Jeffrey, 84
'with profits' bonds, 144
women
consumer finance, 180–1
wearing the veil, 222, 274, 282
World Bank, 6, 45, 50, 134, 218, 221, 293
WP (Welfare Party), 121, 124, 125, 217, 218, 222, 228, 236
WTI (West Texas Intermediate), 95
WTO (World Trade Organization), 50, 210, 267

Yakan, Adli, 90
Yaqubi, Nizam, 24
Yasin, Ahmed al, 22
Yemen, 7, 9, 10, 27, 105, 107
Yom Kippur war (October 1973), 20, 38
Yurtbank, 226

Zaid al-Kilani, Sheikh Ibrahim, 193, 195, 208
zakat (alms) funds, 19–20, 27, 40, 41, 47, 54
and Faisal Islamic Bank of Egypt, 270
and Faisal Islamic Bank of Sudan, 157
and Islamists, 206
in Kuwait, 179
Zakat House, 54
Zarka, Sheikh Mustafa al, 26
Zarqa National University, Jordan, 209
Zendo, Ahmed, 280, 281
Ziwar, Ahmad, 89
Zumeili, Misbah al-, 194, 195

Islamic Finance in the Global Economy

Ibrahim Warde

Lecturer at the University of California, Berkeley

February 2000 256pp Hb 0 7486 1216 5 £70.00

'..the author provides a profound analysis of the connection between Islamic finance and politics.'
Seif I. Tag El-Din, *The Muslim World Book Review*

'a well-researched and concise book on a fluid, complex, and sometimes misjudged concept.'
MESA Bulletin 36

'A forthright and scholarly survey of a subject that deserves the attention of both international bankers and area specialists who are interested in Islamic culture of political economy... It offers a much-needed introduction to a highly complex set of economic, cultural, and political phenomena.'
Middle East Journal

In the past decade, Islamic finance has grown at rates exceeding 20% a year. Islamic finance is now a $200 billion industry, with operations in over 70 countries. This book explains the paradox of a system rooted in the medieval era thriving in the global economy. It traces the evolution of Islamic finance, explores its significance from a historical and comparative perspective, and considers the strategic, marketing, managerial, political, economic, regulatory and cultural challenges faced by Islamic institutions. Based on rigorous academic research as well as considerable empirical work, this authoritative book is set to become an invaluable reference work for all those with an interest in Islamic and Middle Eastern economics, business and finance.

"A good political economy account of Islamic finance. Its general viewpoint is well-informed but sensibly critical; this is rare in writings on this topic. It contains a wide range of material in one place in a way that is probably unique."
David Cobham, University of St Andrews

Order from
Marston Book Services, PO Box 269, Abingdon, Oxon OX14 4YN
Tel 01235 465500 • Fax 01235 465555
Email: direct.order@marston.co.uk

Visit our website www.eup.ed.ac.uk

All details correct at time of printing but subject to change without notice

Medieval Islamic Political Thought

Patricia Crone

Mellon Professor of Islamic History at the Institute for Advanced Study, Princeton

January 2004   Hb   0 7486 1870 8   £25.00

'The book combines erudition with analytical brilliance. The author knows how to make sense of things, highlight them, and put them in perspective. Readers should come away with a satisfying depth of understanding of the full range of medieval Islamic political thought.'
Professor Michael Cook, Princeton University

This book aims to present general readers and specialists alike with a broad survey of Islamic political thought in the six centuries from the rise of Islam to the Mongol invasions. Based on a wide variety of sources, some of a type not previously considered in works on political thought, it seeks to bring out the enormous scope and high level of historical (and, in some cases, contemporary) interest of medieval Muslim thinking on this subject.

The author aims to make Islamic political thought easier for modern readers to understand by relating it to the contexts in which it was formulated, analysing it in terms familiar to the reader, and, where possible, comparing it with medieval European and modern thought.

Guiding the reader through this complex history on a tour of one of the great civilizations of the pre-modern world, the book brings out the fascinating nature of medieval Islamic political thought, both in its own right and as the background to political thinking in the Muslim world today.

Features

- Written by one of the most renowned scholars in the field
- All concepts have been glossed and all persons, events and historical developments have been identified or summarised, both on first encounter and in the index (where the number of the page containing the gloss is emboldened)
- Specialists are addressed in the footnotes; non-specialists are free to skip these and read an uncluttered text.

Order from
Marston Book Services, PO Box 269, Abingdon, Oxon OX14 4YN
Tel 01235 465500 • Fax 01235 465555
Email: direct.order@marston.co.uk

Visit our website www.eup.ed.ac.uk

All details correct at time of printing but subject to change without notice

Rethinking Islam in the Contemporary World

Carl W. Ernst

February 2004 Pb 0 7486 1959 3 £15.99

'A major contribution to explaining the faith of Muslims to people in the West.'
Professor Francis Robinson, Royal Holloway, University of London

'It works splendidly as an introduction that can be used both in the classroom and for the general public.'
Professor Michael Sells, Haverford College, PA

An introduction to Islam, today the faith of more than a billion people, set in the context of world history and of religious studies.

Carl Ernst brings together Islamic religious thought and lived experience to examine traditional spirituality and the contentious issues confronting Muslims today. His approach is balanced – both sympathetic and critical.

Besides providing a guide to the fundamental aspects of Islam – its sacred sources, ethical systems and spiritual practices – the author encourages the reader to reflect on these topics. This compact introduction will appeal to all those who want to understand both the historical aspects of Islam as well as the place of Islam in the contemporary world.

Features
- A critical perspective on Western attitudes toward Islam
- A clarification of the contemporary importance of Islam both in Euro-American and in Afro-Asiatic countries and a context for understanding extremist movements like fundamentalism
- Access to the voice of Muslims, through translations of texts into English
- An overview of the critical debates on such important contemporary issues as gender and veiling, state politics, and science and ethics

Order from
Marston Book Services, PO Box 269, Abingdon, Oxon OX14 4YN
Tel 01235 465500 • Fax 01235 465555
Email: direct.order@marston.co.uk

Visit our website www.eup.ed.ac.uk

Islamic Aesthetics
An Introduction

Oliver Leaman

Professor of Philosophy at the University of Kentucky

March 2004   Hb   0 7486 1734 5   £55.00   Pb   0 7486 1735 3   £16.99

'This is a useful and imaginative project and clearly fills a need... Leaman is an accomplished and productive author and the book will be of genuine and considerable interest.'
Professor Lenn E. Goodman, Vanderbilt University, Nashville

'Oliver Leaman is a very distinguished, internationally regarded scholar of philosophy... his profound philosophical knowledge enables him to apply and analyse concepts of aesthetics to a multitude of art forms.'
Professor Ian R. Netton, University of Leeds

Is there something unique about Islamic art? This book argues that there is not – that Islam does not play an leading role in the aesthetic judgements that we should make about objects created in the Islamic world.

It is often argued that a very special sort of consciousness went into creating Islamic art, that it is very different from other forms of art, that Muslims are not allowed to portray human beings in their art, and that calligraphy is the supreme Islamic art form. Oliver Leaman challenges all these ideas, showing them to be misguided. Instead he suggests that the sort of criteria we should apply to Islamic art are identical to the criteria applicable to art in general, and that the attempt to put Islamic art into a special category is a result of orientalism

Key Features
- Criticises the influence of Sufism on Islamic aesthetics
- Deals with issues arising in painting, calligraphy, architecture, gardens, literature, films, and music
- Pays close attention to the Qur'an
- Argument includes examples from history, art, philosophy, theology and the artefacts of the Islamic world

Order from
Marston Book Services, PO Box 269, Abingdon, Oxon OX14 4YN
Tel 01235 465500 • Fax 01235 465555
Email: direct.order@marston.co.uk

Visit our website www.eup.ed.ac.uk

All details correct at time of printing but subject to change without notice

Related Reading from Edinburgh University Press

Published for The Centre of Islamic Studies at SOAS

Journal of
Qur'anic Studies

The *Journal of Qur'anic Studies* is a biannual, bilingual, peer-reviewed journal, published by Edinburgh University Press.

The *Journal of Qur'anic Studies* aims to encourage and promote the study of the Qur'an from a wide range of scholarly perspectives, reflecting the diversity of approaches characteristic of this field of scholarship. In addition, *JQS* publishes articles both in English and Arabic, to encourage the bridging of the gap between the two traditions of Muslim and Western scholarship.

The journal is principally dedicated to the publication of original papers, with a book review section including reviews of new works on the Qur'an in the various languages of the Muslim world, as well as the output of the western academic presses. In addition, *JQS* includes a 'Notes and Correspondence' section, which is intended as a space for members of the Qur'anic studies community to contribute news and information on current research, projects and developments in the field, including new courses, conferences, Qur'an-related activities on the Internet, CD-Rom releases, and other items of interest.

Contact Details

To subscribe or order a back issue:
Contact Edinburgh University Press, 22 George Square, Edinburgh EH8 9LF, UK
Tel. 0131 650 6207
Fax 0131 662 0053
Email: journals@eup.ed.ac.uk

For editorial queries:
Centre of Islamic Studies,
SOAS, University of London,
Thornhaugh Street, Russell Square,
London, WC1H 0XG
Tel: 020 7898 4393/4380
Email: jqs@soas.ac.uk

JAIS Monographs

Al-Daylami's Treatise on Mystical Love

Ali b. Muhammad al-Daylami
Edited by Joseph Norment Bell
Translated with an introduction and annotations by Joseph Norment Bell and Hassan
Mahmoud Abdel-Latif el-Shafei

June 2004   Pb   0 7486 1915 1   £30.00

'An important work and really marvellous to have it available.'
Professor Francis Robinson, Royal Holloway, University of London

The earliest major Islamic treatise on mystical love, this work reflects a moderate version
of the ecstatic mysticism of the Sufi martyr al-Hallaj. Writing around 1000 C.E., the
author summarizes the views of lexicographers, belletrists, philosophers, physicians,
theologians, and mystics on love, providing much information that would otherwise have
been lost. In setting forth his own opinions he relies heavily on erotic poetry with
accompanying frame stories from the Umayyad and early Abbasid periods, Sufi biography,
the lives of the prophets, and personal information.

JAIS Monographs

The Qur'anic Term *Kalala*

Notes on the Origins of Islamic Law

Agostino Cilardo
Professor at the Instituto Universitario Orientale, Naples

June 2004   Pb   0 7486 1916 X   £19.99

This work discusses the origins of diverging Islamic views regarding collateral inheritance.
Drawing on early poetry, the works of lexicographers and grammarians, hadith, Qur'anic
commentary, and numerous works of jurisprudence, it demonstrates how the particular
interpretation by the law schools of the term *kalala* (roughly: leaving no parents or
children; collateral relationship) enabled jurists to create new rules in areas of inheritance
law that were not covered by Qur'anic provisions.

A History of Christian-Muslim Relations

Hugh Goddard, *Senior Lecturer in Islamic Theology at the*
University of Nottingham

April 2000   256pp   Pb   0 7486 1009 X   £18.00

The relationship between the Christian and Muslim worlds has been a long and tortuous one. Over the course of the centuries the balance of power has swung in a pendulum motion – at times the initiative seems to have lain with the Muslim community, while at other points the opposite has been true and Muslims have found themselves having to respond to Christian challenges in different forms. This book investigates the history of the relationships between Christians and Muslims over the centuries, from their initial encounters in the Medieval period when the Muslims were the dominant group, through to the modern period when the balance of power seems to have been reversed.

'Well-written, densely-packed, comprehensively documented and skilfully analysed' *Journal of Qur'anic Studies*

Persian Historiography

Julie Scott Meisami, *Lecturer in Persian at The Oriental Institute, Oxford*

July 1999   336pp
Hb   0 7486 0743 9   £56.00   •   Pb   0 7486 1276 9   £20.00

Persian historical writing has received little attention as compared with Arabic. Within the larger context of the development of Islamic historiography from the tenth through the twelfth centuries, the case of Persian historical writing demands special attention. Discussions tend to concentrate on its sources in pre-Islamic Persian and in Arabic works, while the reasons for its emergence, its connections with Iranian and Arabic models, its political and cultural functions, and its reception, have been virtually ignored. This study answers these questions and addresses issues relating to the motivation for writing the works in question; its purpose; the role of the author, patrons and audiences; the choice of language and the reasons for that choice; the place of historical writing in the broader debate over the suitability of Persian for scholarly writing.

'Meisami is out to set the record straight, and the result is the most original and scholarly contribution to our knowledge of the formative years of this rich and vibrant field of Persian literature.' *Journal of the Royal Asiatic Society*

> **Winner of the 1999 British-Kuwait Friendship Society Prize in Middle Eastern Studies.**

Order from
Marston Book Services, PO Box 269, Abingdon, Oxon OX14 4YN
Tel 01235 465500   •   Fax 01235 465555
Email: direct.order@marston.co.uk

All details correct at time of printing but subject to change without notice